# Praise and Controversy

"You should buy John Hoberman's *Darwin's Athletes*. It's provocative, disturbing, important, and particularly relevant ... Hoberman may be the first to carefully expose the turgid history, both in America and Europe, of the 'tabloid science' of racial biology as it applies to athletics ... This is serious reading. It's also a valuable defense against the pornography of the Bell Curvers." — **Robert Lipsyte,** *New York Times*

"Few other writers have seen fit to tackle a sensitive subject whose importance transcends the games-world on which it's based."
— *Wall Street Journal*

"Painfully important." — *Modern Maturity*

"Hoberman has written with courage and wisdom. Readers will either love him or hate him. But no one can peruse his pages without being disabused of many illusions about sports and their effects on black America."
— *Newsday*

"*Darwin's Athletes* is an intelligent addition to the discussion of racial concerns in the United States." — **Gerald Early,** *Chicago Tribune*

"Hoberman challenges established beliefs in a thought-provoking, albeit disturbing, manner, offering arguments that are convincing, controversial, and guaranteed to spark debate." — *Library Journal*

"You may never look at Michael Jordan the same way again." — *San Diego Union-Tribune*

"*Darwin's Athletes* is meticulously researched with fascinating material on changing white and black views of race-based athletics over generations."
— *Detroit News*

"Excellently researched." — *Washington Times*

"A strongly argued book." — *Newsweek*

"Author Hoberman's thesis is a damning one: sports fosters an image of black intellectual inferiority and other stereotypes while providing the false appearance of integration. Taking issue with other black writers as well as long-held establishment views, this controversial book is certain to invite heated debate." — *USA Today*

"Hoberman takes dead aim at our society's fixation on black athletes."
— *Denver Post*

"Hoberman has brilliantly synthesized racial arguments swirling around us today." — *Houston Chronicle*

"The nature-versus-nurture boat is about to be rocked in 1997 with the publication of *Darwin's Athletes*." — *Globe and Mail*

"This book will shock some people. Americans cherish a progessive myth about sports, a notion that sports provide an escape from the ghetto for poor minorities and, in the Jackie Robinson model, a blow against racial stereotypes. John Hoberman blows large holes in that myth. He identifies a continuing American tragedy in sports that pereptuates stereotypes and subjugation instead of liberating Americans from them. Whether you agree with his ideas or argue with them, Hoberman will make you think."
— **Clarence Page, author of *Showing My Color:
Impolite Essays on Race and Identity***

"Hoberman treads with intelligence, skepticm, and courage through the thickets of race, atheletics, and 'scientific' racial study and comes out standing tall. His research is remarkable, and the myths he destroys and the questions he ultimately raises will have readers doubting everything they once knew about race and racial stereotypes."
— **Rick Telender, special contributor to *Sports Illustrated*
and lead sports columnist, *Chicago Sun-Times***

"*Darwin's Athletes* fearlessly skewers white and black America's sacred-cow hope that in celebrating the black athlete, America celebrates equality. John Hoberman's book will profoundly change the way you think about race and sports, and the role of the black athlete in our culture."
— **Steve James, director of *Hoop Dreams***

# Darwin's Athletes

Books by John Hoberman

John Hoberman

# Darwin's Athletes

HOW SPORT HAS DAMAGED

## Black America

AND PRESERVED THE

## Myth of Race

*A Mariner Book*

HOUGHTON MIFFLIN COMPANY

BOSTON · NEW YORK

For information about permission to reproduce selections
from this book, write to Permissions,
Houghton Mifflin Company, 215 Park Avenue South,
New York, New York 10003.

*Library of Congress Cataloging-in-Publication Data*
Hoberman, John M. (John Milton).
Darwin's athletes : how sport has damaged black America and
preserved the myth of race / John Hoberman.
p.    cm.
Includes bibliographical references (p.    ).
ISBN 0-395-82291-2
ISBN 0-395-82292-0 (pbk.)
1. Afro-American athletes — Public opinion. 2. Public
opinion — United States. 3. Stereotype (Psychology) in sports.
4. Afro-Americans — Attitudes. 5. United States —
Race relations. I. Title.
GV583.H6   1997
796'.089'96073 — dc20   96-36170 CIP

Printed in the United States of America

Book design by Robert Overholtzer

QUM 10 9 8 7 6 5 4 3 2

*This book is*
*dedicated to the memory*
*of*
RALPH ELLISON

# Acknowledgments

Many people have contributed to the making of this book. I would like to thank Lincoln Allison, Katie Arens, Cara Averhart, John Bale, Bjørn Barland, David Black, Claud Bramblett, David Broad, Lindsey Carter, Mike Fish, Alan Goodman, Edmund T. Gordon, Allen Guttmann, David Hoberman, Henry Hoberman, M.D., Craig Hodges, Richard Holt, Philip Houghton, Tim Hutton, Grant Jarvie, Andrew Jennings, Bruce Kidd, Tim King, William Kraemer, Sigmund Loland, John Loy, Robert Malina, Jonathan Marks, Charles Martin, Dennis McFadden, Patrick Miller, Lesley Nye, Robert Nye, Jeffrey Sammons, Clark T. Sawin, M.D., Lawrence Schell, Yevonne Smith, Waneen Spirduso, Melbourne Tapper, Rick Telander, John Valentine, David Wiggins, John Williams, Bruce Wilson, and Charles Yesalis.

Among this group, I am particularly grateful to those colleagues who read, assessed, and criticized portions of the manuscript. It goes without saying that I bear full responsibility for the text, which benefited so much from their efforts. Special thanks go to my research assistant, Laura Issen, whose hard work and initiative made a real difference to this book.

I would also like to thank the many students who took my course "Race and Sport in African-American Life" at the University of Texas, and in particular those who shared with me their personal knowledge and experiences regarding race relations and racialistic thinking.

To my editor, Steve Fraser, I convey my deepest thanks for his unwavering commitment to a project whose potential value he saw from the very beginning. Steve's enthusiasm and intellectual companionship are what made this book possible.

And once again I thank my wife, Louisa, for the patience and generosity she has shown in the course of a long project.

I PROPOSE THAT WE VIEW
THE WHOLE OF AMERICAN LIFE
AS A DRAMA
ACTED OUT UPON THE BODY
OF A NEGRO GIANT.

■

Ralph Ellison, *Shadow and Act*

# Contents

## III. Dissecting John Henry
### The Search for Racial Athletic Aptitude

■ ■ ■ ■

# Preface to the Mariner Edition

The publication of *Darwin's Athletes* in early 1997 set off a national debate that lasted for months and has now begun to reverberate in the pages of academic journals. Widespread media interest in the book led to dozens of radio, television, and newspaper interviews that provided millions of people in the United States and Canada with a rare opportunity to ask themselves some basic questions about the racial dimensions of the modern sports world: What accounts for "black dominance" in so many popular sports? Have we overestimated the value of racially integrated sport? What price have African Americans paid for their image as "natural" athletes? Why does the racial division of labor in the world of sport continue to concentrate power in white hands?

The publicity surrounding this book was intensified by two virtually simultaneous events that focused public attention on the role of the black athletic hero in American life: the fiftieth anniversary of Jackie Robinson's breakthrough into major-league baseball and Tiger Woods's dramatic victory at the Masters golf tournament. The celebration of one legendary figure appeared to prefigure the birth of another, as Americans indulged once again in the time-honored fantasy that black athletic heroism can inspire the racial healing that has eluded generations of dedicated reformers. The origins and consequences of this popular fantasy (as well as other seductive illusions about the social value of integrated sport) are discussed at length in this book. Indeed, the book's reception owes much to this skeptical appraisal of the black athlete's role as a promoter and beneficiary of social healing — a skepticism that blacks and whites are likely to find equally distressing from their respective positions within our society's uneasy racial truce.

It is hardly surprising, then, that responses to the book reflected this distinction between "black" and "white" perspectives. At a time when black and white New Yorkers, for example, cannot agree on any major issue whatsoever, including the quality of the city's drinking water, it should come as no surprise that responses to *Darwin's Athletes* divided in significant ways along racial lines. It would be fair to say that the white reviewers who appreciated this book evinced an excitement, and at times an exuberance, about its contents that their black colleagues have not and probably could not share. I can only thank (among others) the journalist who found the book both riveting and full of moral energy, its "biting gladiator's prose relentlessly cutting racists down to size." I am similarly grateful to reviewers who called the book "provocative, disturbing, important," and "brutally honest." For these readers, at least, the book provided the exhilarating (and at times dismaying) ride its author had intended for a general audience unaccustomed to heretical ideas about the racial dimensions of sport.

At the same time, *Darwin's Athletes* may disappoint white (and black) readers bent on confirming the existence of alleged racial differences which have excited the popular imagination for centuries. Two such reviewers felt positively betrayed by a book that perversely refuses to announce the long-awaited scientific confirmation of black athletic superiority. Alas, as the third section of the book amply demonstrates, such evidence does not yet exist, even if lopsided disparities in certain athletic performances suggest this.

Black reviewers have not responded to the often disturbing contents of this book with the sort of emotional freedom that encourages intellectual exuberance or racial fantasy. It is an understatement to say that black commentators have generally adopted a cautious approach. Even the few black journalists who offered *Darwin's Athletes* unstinting praise did so in a somber tone befitting the African-American predicament the book describes. This white author, they wrote, has produced an accurate diagnosis of our condition. Now it is up to us to take action. Suffice it to say that such commentaries are the ones I most hoped for. Other black reviewers, however, found the book valuable in some ways but with reservations that deserve our careful attention.

There is no question that *Darwin's Athletes* became a hotly contested book in part because its author is white. For many African Americans, this raised once again the specter of intellectual imperialism, of white incursions into black cultural space, and of the grotesque difference between the numbers of white and black scholars who are willing and able to write about racial issues and the African-American experience. Yet the fact remains that no black commentator flatly disqualified me on the basis of color. The closest anyone came to such an argument occurred when a highly qualified black academic told a national television audience that "one thing the world needs is fewer white men telling black folks what to do." I might add that this blunt statement did not put an end to the electronic correspondence this scholar and I have about the issues we have both studied from our different perspectives, since we both recognize that interracial (and thus intercultural) dialogue that transcends the anodyne will often involve emotional discomfort on both sides.

Other black commentators found me to be relatively ignorant about African-American life in general. "Hoberman," one reviewer wrote, "draws conclusions based on assumptions about black people's beliefs and fears, demonstrating little knowledge of the historical or contemporary black engagement with their reality." Another academic critic found my "discussion of black intellectuals and sports to be oversimplified and incomplete because [the author does] not seem to know a great deal about black cultural life in its broader reaches."

It would be impossible and foolhardy for me to try to refute such criticism in its entirety. The fact that I cannot draw on a lifetime of experience as an African American in unquestionably one of the limitations of the book. At the same time, I do not fully accept this argument, for two reasons. First, the research for *Darwin's Athletes* included interviews with many African Americans and voluminous reading of African-American sources. If I am somehow estranged from "black reality" (even in its diversity), then there are a lot of black people out there who share this condition with me to one degree or another. My second, and less diplomatic, point is the following: even though I am not black, it is also true that none of the African-American lives lived by black scholars in this country has resulted in a book remotely similar to this one. Outsider status, in short, can confer unique advantages on the observer who is willing to stop, look, and listen to people whose experiences are often very different from his own.

Interestingly, my claim that much of the black male intelligentsia is generally unprepared to think critically about the role of sport in black life has evoked little published response. (The few protests I did receive, all of them signed and all of them civil, arrived in the mail.) The reviewer who argued most effectively on this and other points was Gerald Early, director of African and Afro-American Studies at Washington University and an accomplished essayist on matters pertaining to race and sport. In several published commentaries, Early suggested that my portrait of black anti-intellectualism had overlooked a number of important factors, such as "the fact that America is generally anti-intellectual, that it is largely a culture that prizes engineers and businessmen — people who do things rather than people who merely think." In addition, I had not reflected on "the fact that . . . blacks have never understood as a group how to make use of their intellectuals. They could never properly reward them and so always felt a bit skeptical of their intellectuals, more so than the average American." And it was Early who found me inadequately prepared to deal with "black cultural life in its broader reaches." While I cannot fully subscribe to this assessment, I do accept Early's other points as telling ones that complement, rather than contradict, my own interpretation — and herein lies the point, not only of this preface but of the book itself as an exercise in racial dialogue.

Other black reviewers published remarks that strike me as plainly mistaken. One writer claimed that the recent ascension of Tiger Woods invalidates my point about the damaging effects of less dignified images of black athletes — as if the aura of this self-possessed prodigy had suddenly undone the deeply rooted stereotypes about black physicality that have formed over centuries. Another reviewer made the remarkable claim that today "sports offer the best chance for a show of black intelligence coupled with a chance for a better life" — a statement that only confirms how easy it can be for some people (including academics) to confuse athletic skill with professional training and thereby discourage young blacks from entering the learned professions. Most serious, however, is this critic's dismissive approach to "the presumed anti-intellectualism among black youth," which has been confirmed by black scholars and others. Whether this remark expresses real ignorance or a peeved disingenuousness, I cannot say. What we do know is that the widespread persecution of academically healthy black children by frustrated and angry black children is a social disaster that few public figures have even bothered to address. If such destructive peer pressure is not an urgent issue for black intellectuals, then who will find the time to deal with it?

Having spoken of this African-American "disaster," I will conclude by addressing a sore point that virtually all reviewers of *Darwin's Athletes* have avoided, namely, the role of white observers in formulating ideas about "damaged" black people. Many readers will have noted that the subtitle I chose for this book appears to situate it in the tradition of the Moynihan Report of 1965 and its controversial reference to the "tangle of pathology" that had supposedly damaged countless African-American lives. My own position is that it is intellectually dishonest and self-defeating not to acknowledge and analyze the damage that racism has done to both blacks and whites. Nor does it dishonor the former to accord them more attention in this regard than whites, whose status and power have protected them from certain kinds or degrees of psychological harm. It is only natural that our sympathetic attention should go first and foremost to those who have been harmed by others, whose destructive behavior deserves clinical study rather than sympathy. And acknowledging that a group of people has been harmed does not mean "pathologizing" them as inherently deviant or irreparably damaged.

Our understanding of the "pathologizing" of black people has been greatly enhanced by the publication of Daryl Michael Scott's *Contempt and Pity: Social Policy and the Image of the Damaged Black Psyche, 1880–1996* (1997). This book, the author states, originated in his "opposition to the use of damage imagery in the process of making and justifying social policy. I believe that depicting black folk as pathological has not served the community's best interest." The problem with this position is that it appears to rule out public discussion of the effects of racism on African Americans. Indeed, a remarkable aspect of this book is the author's provocative refusal to acknowledge that black people in the United States have been psychologically damaged at all, an act of denial that signals the victory of black pride over the black realism of W.E.B. Du Bois, Martin Luther King, Malcolm X, and many other African-American luminaries cited in Scott's book.

Scott's rhetoric concerns me because his feelings about black privacy have profound implications for interracial dialogue bearing on African-American problems. Social analysts, in his opinion, "should place the inner lives of people off limits," because knowledge of these inner lives can be misused to the great disadvantage of those studied. He even goes so far as to fault the countless black people who in one way or another have failed to keep "an inner sanctum hidden from whites."

My response to Scott's emphasis on the emotional privacy of the oppressed is *Darwin's Athletes,* which spends more time illuminating the inner lives of whites and their racial complexes than it devotes to plumbing the thoughts and emotions of the black people who have had to cope with white racism. This emphasis on white pathology is due not to any reluctance to violate a black "inner sanctum" but to my incomplete knowledge about the inner lives of black people. Had I known more, it would have appeared in the book.

I oppose the idea of emotional separatism, because black privacy is indistinguishable from the black anonymity that has facilitated American apartheid. For a long time, as Scott himself points out, "most whites,

including many experts, treated blacks as if they lacked an inner world."
Indeed, the fundamental axiom of Western racism has always been that
the black psyche is less complex than its white counterpart. For that
reason, attempts to render the inner lives of black people invisible to
whites can only delay the destruction of a literally dehumanizing stereotype. Similarly, white scholars who submit to the notion that the African-American experience is somehow too complex for them to grasp
will eventually find that they have forfeited their chances to promote an
interracial agenda that can move us beyond the unhappy stalemate that
now prevails.

# Preface

I will begin this book with the story of a white man who did the right thing. Back in the late 1960s, the young scholar Thomas Kochman was asked by the director of Chicago's Center for Inner City Studies to teach a graduate course on black language. He carried out this assignment with exemplary care, acknowledging how little he knew about this topic and appealing to his black students to teach him all they could. This arrangement continued until he began to understand that he was no longer wanted in the classroom. "I was never asked outright to step aside," he wrote, "but the signs coming from black students and colleagues were clear and compelling. Therefore I asked to step down, having overcome my initial reluctance to give up a course that I had come to be identified with and so thoroughly enjoyed." With a grace not all instructors could have mustered, the young white teacher saw this sacrificial act as a contribution to black self-determination and as one more phase of his political education. His years of fieldwork and teaching eventually led to the publication of *Black and White Styles in Conflict,* an interesting book that at times takes interracial empathy perilously close to caricaturing the black people whose cultural traits the author seeks to explain.

Kochman's story interests me because I have a comparable story of my own. Like Kochman, I have sought out black students to create an interracial classroom. Of the nearly one hundred students who have taken my course "Race and Sport in African-American Life" over the past few years, half have been black. Like Kochman, I have made a point of learning what all my students have to teach me about the racializing of American life, and some of their stories appear in the larger story I have to tell. And like any white instructor who has chosen this role, I have seen my share of angry, suspicious, or transfixed faces as

I have scraped the bottom of the racist barrel to show where ethnic folklore comes from.

Yet even though I identify with Kochman's integrationist goals and good intentions, his 1982 memoir of white self-abnegation has the almost fairytale quality of a remote and exotic era. A generation after his interracial adventure, the fantasy of black power that animated his black separatist colleagues stands in stark contrast to the multiple disasters that have since befallen great numbers of African Americans. One of these disasters is playing itself out in the academic world, where twice as many black women as black men are pursuing degrees and the number of black men receiving Ph.D.'s is actually falling. Those who feel that a black scholar should have written a book like *Darwin's Athletes* should keep these trends in mind. What is more, and for reasons this book explains, it is unlikely that any black intellectual would choose to write so critically about the impact of athletic achievement on African-American life.

I embarked on this project for several reasons. First of all, I was fascinated by the cultural complexities of race inside the sports world, which I have studied for twenty-five years, a racialized universe that is seldom brought to life by the sportswriters who cover it. A second stimulus was the taboo that has wrapped the issue of racial athletic aptitude in a shroud of fear; I resolved to follow the evidence wherever it led, and I have done so. A third motive was to produce a socially useful analysis of black subjugation to white institutions and the racial folklore that sustains it; this meant following the black athlete around the postcolonial world and connecting his status to that of his ancestors, who once dealt with colonial masters whose interest in sport was both passionate and political in nature. I understand, of course, that this account of my purposes will not satisfy everyone. As one black professor of history put it last year, "Caucasian researchers who study African-American history only exploit African Americans to benefit their careers." In a similar vein, a prominent black writer has insinuated that any white observer who analyzes black problems is a "professional critic of black character." I hope that at least some readers will find that I have done better than these commentators might expect.

Resentments of this kind concern me because *Darwin's Athletes* discusses aspects of the black experience that are seldom addressed because they point to the terrible damage that racism has done. The delicate status of these "family secrets" has produced two contrary approaches to public discussion of such traumas. For some critics, white research on black predicaments is just more evidence of "the growing

black-pathology business," a separatist view I find profoundly self-defeating. Many ethnic outsiders, after all, have offered useful observations to groups to which they do not belong. Yet some people seem to
believe that cross-cultural perspectives on black life have to be perversely motivated. An alternative to the intellectually truncated world
of the racial separatist is understanding that the most delicate secrets
must be studied to bring about the healing process made possible by
knowledge, and that outsiders have a role to play in explaining the
travails of people whose experience they have not shared.

Of the major questions this book attempts to answer, the most urgent
are the following: Why are many African Americans' feelings about
athletic achievement so intense that they amount to a fixation that
almost precludes criticism of its effects? How do white-controlled institutions profit from the perpetuation of the sports fixation? Finally, how
has the cult of the black athlete exacerbated the disastrous spread of
anti-intellectual attitudes among African-American youth facing life in
a knowledge-based society? That the black intelligentsia has had so
little to say about the ruinous consequences of making athletic achievement the prime symbol of black creativity is in itself a cause for concern.
This book should give those who want to confront such issues a place
to begin.

# Flying Air Jordan

## The Power of Racial Images

THE MODERN WORLD is awash in images of black athletes. The airborne black body, its sinewy arms clutching a basketball as it soars high above the arena floor, has become the paramount symbol of athletic dynamism in the media age.[1] Stereotypes of black athletic superiority are now firmly established as the most recent version of a racial folklore that has spread across the face of the earth over the past two centuries, and a corresponding belief in white athletic inferiority pervades popular thinking about racial difference. Such ideas about the "natural" physical talents of dark-skinned peoples, and the media-generated images that sustain them, probably do more than anything else in our public life to encourage the idea that blacks and whites are biologically different in a meaningful way. Prominent racial theorists of the 1990s such as Charles Murray and Dinesh D'Souza have declared that black athletic superiority is evidence of more profound differences. The world of sport has thus become an image factory that disseminates and even intensifies our racial preoccupations.[2] Centuries of racial classification have made exceptional athletes into ethnic specimens. "Are you a nigger or an Eskimo?" one racist sports fan asked the finest high school basketball player in Alaskan history, displaying a curiosity about human biology that is always latent in multiracial athletic encounters.[3] Interracial sport has thus breathed new life into our racial folklore, reviving nineteenth-century ideas about the racial division of labor that then recur in a trend-setting book like *The Bell Curve*.[4]

Ideas about racial athletic aptitude reign virtually uncontested outside the small number of classrooms in which they are examined. The

idea that African Americans are the robust issue of slave-era breeding experiments has served the fantasy needs of blacks and whites
alike.[5] ("I propose," Ralph Ellison once wrote, "that we view the whole
of American life as a drama acted out upon the body of a Negro
giant.")[6] "We were simply bred for physical qualities," the Olympic
champion sprinter Lee Evans said in 1971, and better-educated black
men have embraced the same eugenic fantasy.[7] Decades of popular scientific speculation about the special endowments of black athletes have
shaped the thinking of entire populations. White television sportscasters have long employed a special vocabulary to distinguish "natural"
black athletes from "thinking" whites and have referred to black athletes as "monkeys" on more than one occasion.[8] African-American college students who suddenly discover that their assumptions about
"natural" black athleticism are illusory can feel as though they are
waking from a dream. For their white counterparts too, critical scrutiny
of racial stereotypes can take on the power of revelation, because it
challenges conventional assumptions about the natural distribution of
human abilities. The study of racialistic thinking changes people by
exposing unconscious mental habits that permeate everyday life and
shape our identities. Conversations with young blacks and whites reveal
an unpublicized but thoroughly racialized social universe in which sport
functions as a principal medium in which racial folklore flourishes. Here
we find the schoolchild who cannot believe that the black college student who is his mentor is not a football player, since television has
persuaded him that every black male student is an athlete; here too is
the academically precocious child whose athletic skills save him from
harassment by his black peers, whose hostility to intellectual development (and even "whitey's" habit of using seatbelts) only intensifies as
they enter adolescence. Some black children still face overt hostility in
interracial games. In east Texas in the 1990s, black junior high school
boys sometimes play football against whites whose parents shout "Niggers!" from the stands as they watch their sons lose.

This racialized universe of everyday encounters receives far less attention than the highly public and officially deracialized theater of professional and collegiate sport, which white administrators present as an
oasis of racial harmony. The sports media do not identify or investigate
conflicts between blacks and whites, or they portray them as idiosyn-
cratic episodes; young black athletes are immature rather than angry,
while older white coaches are curmudgeons whose decency (if not always their authority) remains firmly intact. The realities of race are
more evident in the unvarnished world of high school athletics, where

far greater numbers of people engage in race relations, absorb ideas about racially specific traits and abilities, and grapple with their own racial dramas in athletic terms. Here, for example, we find a black nerd, the bookish son of a physician, whose conflicts about blackness prompt him to find his athletic identity in ice hockey and other "white" activities. A more common character is the young black athlete who is persuaded, at times by a black coach, that he or she enjoys a physical advantage over whites.

Such black self-confidence has contributed to self-doubts on the other side of the racial divide. A gifted white high school athlete told me that he found himself wondering why the muscles of some black teammates seem to be better defined than his own, and some white professionals are simply fatalistic about their ability to match up against blacks. "You have to be a realist," says Scott Brooks, a guard on the Dallas Mavericks basketball team. "White people can't jump as high." "There aren't many white guys who can jump the way they can," says Pete Chilcutt, white player for the Houston Rockets.[9] White spectators at an interracial high school basketball game may find themselves expecting their team to fail and hearing racial taunts from the other side. White high school players may also perceive a bias in calling fouls that favors black players, as if prevailing stereotypes had persuaded referees that whites are simply incapable of making extraordinary moves while obeying the rules of the game.

Yet it is also possible to face and conquer self-defeating mental habits. A white basketball team in Texas openly confronted the internalized stereotype of black superiority that had ruined one season and proceeded to finish third in the state the following year. This true story of white demoralization and subsequent self-assertion represents a variation on the storyline of the popular film *Hoosiers,* in which a tiny white Indiana high school wins a state championship over a predominantly black city team whose leaping ability is emphasized by the camera. In fact, this storyline has known many variations over the past century of interracial athletic competition, as racial dominance in sport has changed color from white to black.

Racial folklore can also provide modern whites with various compensations for their lost preeminence and the feelings of physical inferiority that are now immortalized in the popular slogan "white men can't jump." A young woman who played high school basketball told me of her coach's habit of giving white players custodial control of presumably less disciplined black teammates. Naive biological racism can also play a compensatory role in the minds of anxious whites. A black teenager who worked as a lifeguard in the Dallas area in 1990 was told by his white counterparts that the peculiar capacity of black skin to absorb water reduced buoyancy and that this explained the scarcity of good black swimmers. When the golfer Jack Nicklaus told an interviewer in 1994 that blacks were anatomically unsuited to play golf ("Blacks have different muscles that react in different ways"), he too was employing an eccentric racial biology to rationalize the absence of black athletes in a segregated country club sport.[10] Such are the culturally acquired mental habits that can preserve the racial balance of power more efficiently than any policies enacted by legislatures and public officials.

While the racial stereotypes that flourish in the sports world can impair white performance, they are capable of damaging African Americans in much more serious ways. The images of black athletes that fill television screens and the pages of newspapers and magazines only sustain the traditional view of blacks as essentially physical and thus primitive people, and variations on this theme are absorbed by blacks as well as whites. In this category we find the young black man who told a Hispanic friend that it was harder for blacks to master the art of pitching a baseball because blacks are not as "in control" as whites. Here too is the black football player who grew up believing that blacks were "genetically superior" athletes while "white men can't jump, but they are hell in the classroom." Another young black athlete adopted the habit of calling a white teammate "nigger" in recognition of his superior skills, an awkward variation on the popular idea that athleticism is literally a black trait. Nor are such ideas about the inherent limitations of robust black males expressed only by athletes. A young black woman told me that she had thought of her football-playing cousin as an insensate "buck" until she learned something about the travails of black college athletes, at which point she was able to empathize with him as a person who had feelings of his own. Confinement within the athletic syndrome is maintained by powerful peer-group pressures which ridicule academic achievement while stigmatizing blacks who do not beat "whitey" at whichever game is at stake. In these and many other ways the sports fixation permeates the lives of countless people whose ideas about their own developmental possibilities are tightly bound to the world of physical self-expression.[11]

The interracial sport of earlier decades offered profound emotional gratifications and a measure of hope to most African Americans, and the integration of college and professional sports played a dramatic (if also overrated) role in the civil rights movement. Today, however, the sports world is a battleground on which the symbolic integration that reigns on television confronts a black male stereotype that feeds on media images of black athletes and other black male action figures. "It is no exaggeration to say," Glenn Loury has written, "that black, male youngsters in the central cities have been demonized in the popular mind as have no other group in recent American history."[12] This aggressive stereotype flourishes in the minds of everyone who is constantly exposed to images of black athletes who can appear to be threatening or dangerous. The sports world they inhabit is, after all, an extraordinary social space in which black men are expected to act out their aggressions, so the "violent black male" becomes the dangerous twin of the spectacular black athlete.

While it is assumed that sport has made an important contribution to racial integration, this has been counterbalanced by the merger of the athlete, the gangster rapper, and the criminal into a single black male persona that the sports industry, the music industry, and the advertising industry have made into the predominant image of black masculinity in the United States and around the world.[13] Convinced that black athleticism alone cannot sustain market appeal, these commercial interests dramatize and embellish the physical and psychological traits of athletes whose public personalities come to embody the full spectrum of male pathology. From the National Basketball Association comes Charles Barkley, "the frowning clown" whose deodorant advertisements play cleverly on tacit racist ideas about the black man's inherent lack of refinement.[14] Here too is the self-mutilating eccentric Dennis Rodman, whose hair dyes and tattoos have turned his entire body into a kaleidoscopic demonstration of how black self-hatred can be marketed as spectacle to white America, which has always embraced variations of the ridiculous black jester. Here is the young star Alonzo Mourning wearing "a scowling mask of rage" that could be depthless black anger or just the personality quirk of an "intense competitor." Some magazine advertisements confront whites with hard black faces in a safe setting, counterfeit versions of the "bad nigger" of black lore and white nightmares. "You got something to say?" asks a belligerent Shawn Kemp in a Foot Locker ad, presumably thrilling and intimidating insecure white men with his disdain. The broad, sullen face of the football player Greg Lloyd covers two full-color pages of *Sports Illustrated,* every pore visible and glistening to produce the effect of personal confrontation within the safe confines of a photograph, exemplifying the "male restrictions on emotional expression" that reign in the ghetto.[15]

Yet the appeal of such images has less to do with athleticism per se than with a black male style that counts as one of the major cultural myths of our era, for while it is true that black men fill sports teams, hip-hop groups, and prisons in disproportionate numbers, these numbers alone cannot account for the manner in which this notably powerless group of people is presented by various media to the American public.

The black male style has become incarnated in the fusion of black athletes, rappers, and criminals into a single menacing figure who disgusts and offends many blacks as well as whites. The constant, haunting presence of this composite masculine type is maintained by news coverage and advertising strategies that exploit the suggestive mixture of black anger and physical prowess that suffuses each of these roles. Rap music, as the black feminist Trisha Rose once pointed out, "is basically the locker room with a beat" — a perfect fusion of the rhythm and athleticism that are found in so many folkloric images of blackness.[16] In fact, the athlete and the rapper have a relationship that is more reciprocal than popular images might suggest. Shaquille O'Neal serves as a primary symbol of black physical domination in the NBA and is also a highly publicized rap singer. The most aggressive or radical rappers brag about their pugilistic as well as sexual prowess: "I'm like [Mike] Tyson!" crows the rapper L.L. Cool J.[17] The conversation of the rapper Run (Joseph Simmons) of Run-D.M.C. is strewn with sports metaphors, since rappers as well as athletes express "the style and attitude and identity of the street,"[18] while many black youths idolize rap artists, just as they do athletic heroes.[19] "I'm a hip-hop man," says the football star Natrone Means, summing up the effect of his baggy jeans, baseball cap, and diamond earrings.[20] Numerous rappers return the compliment by pursuing physical training regimens to build muscle and endurance for their stage routines. "A lot of us have been in and out of jail," says Tom Guest of Young Gunz. "Once you develop a body in the penitentiary, you want to keep it."[21] The hip-hop dancer who calls himself "Incredible" describes his troupe's production as "the most physically demanding show on or off Broadway" and refers to break-dancing competitions as "musical football without teams," thereby extending the range of black athleticism as an idiom that can encompass black creativity in general.[22]

Criminality, real or imagined, is an essential ingredient of this charismatic black persona. One major producer of "gangsta rap" is a former football star who thrives in the music business by projecting an aura of incipient criminality, thereby combining all three roles into a thuggish identity presented to the world by an awestruck white journalist in the pages of the *New York Times Magazine*.[23] Numerous rappers, including such celebrities as Tupac Shakur and Snoop Doggy Dogg, have been arrested for serious crimes, thereby achieving the "ghetto authenticity" that is glamorized by white-owned corporations and the advertising experts who adapt the black "homeboy" style for consumption by affluent white wannabes. The police blotter also includes many black athletes, some of whom (like O. J. Simpson) have battered wives or girlfriends.

The thoughtful black athlete recognizes the commercial value of violence and understands that he has been cast in two grotesquely incongruous roles, impersonating the traditional sportsman, who honors fair play, while being paid to behave like a predator, a role to which the black athlete brings a special resonance. When the Pittsburgh Steelers linebacker Greg Lloyd blindsided a quarterback who suffered a concussion, he was fined $12,000. "Come to a game early and watch the Jumbotron scoreboard," he objected, pointing out the hypocrisy of the penalty. "You'll see 'NFL's Greatest Hits,' with guys getting their helmets ripped off . . . They're marketing that."[24]

Finally, just as the black athlete may radiate an aura of criminality, so the black criminal can radiate a threatening aura of athleticism. Several states have enacted vindictive anticrime laws that have deprived predominantly black prison populations of weightlifting facilities, on the grounds that more muscular convicts are more dangerous when released — as if muscles were more influential than minds in determining the behavior of black men.[25] But the modern archetype of the black criminal-as-superathlete is now Rodney King, whose beating by a crowd of Los Angeles police officers is best understood as a kind of perverse athletic event that matched a team of unathletic white policemen against a black behemoth descended from the mythical John Henry. "It will be very interesting," an attorney for one of the indicted officers said before the trial, "to see him standing next to these officers, because it will be like a giant standing next to pygmies."[26] Officer Stacy Koon, who was eventually convicted and imprisoned for his role in the attack, stated that Rodney King possessed a "hulk-like super strength" and arms that were like unbendable "steel posts."[27] Related imagery also appeared in the "liberal" media. The same artist who produced the notorious darkened *Time* magazine cover of O. J. Simpson in late June 1994, Matt Mahurin, contributed a strikingly apelike depiction of Rodney King's cranium to the same publication a few weeks earlier. Indeed, it would be interesting to know to what extent folkloric ideas about black primitiveness and physical prowess have shaped police behavior toward black men throughout the twentieth century.

The dissemination of aggressive black male images by corporations and their advertising media threatens to alienate the white public if displays of black assertiveness are not rationed and counterbalanced by others that domesticate and gentrify virile black men. The National Basketball Association, for example, must somehow defuse the "undertone of violence" that surrounds its dynamic but sometimes unstable black players, and it does so with the cooperation of the sporting press.[28] Black as well as white sportswriters have warned black players not to act out degenerate roles that threaten the league's profitability by creating an image of chaos and incipient revolt.[29] The besieged white NBA coach who simply cannot grasp "the bewildering mentality of today's [black] players" has become an emblematic martyr of white failure inside the sports world.[30] The domestication of the black male in our mass media also occurs outside the sports world.[31] Perhaps the most striking images occur in advertisements for fashionable men's clothing, in which a handsome and well-built black man can be racially neutralized as he is absorbed into a white cultural context. Here, for example, we find a statuesque and impeccably groomed black male model posing in a full-page advertisement for the polo sports tie from Ralph Lauren. He is paired with a white counterpart who combines rugged outdoorsiness with evident good breeding. This is one of many men's fashion ads that symbolically induct the stylishly athleticized black male into the squeaky-clean prep school world of inherited money and the symbolic racial vigor of demanding physical exercise. Fitted out in a dark blazer with insignia, this man wears a tie that shows two white polo players in action on their charging horses. Ethnic blackness is dissolved in a sporting world that is exclusively and impeccably white: golfing, fishing, tennis, rowing, sailing, and polo — the sports of dynamic imperial males unwinding from the rigors of colonial administration. Here in its purest form is the dream of the black athlete as a natural gentleman, a cherished white fantasy that culminated in the lionization of a deracialized O. J. Simpson and then met a grotesque end in his fall from grace.

The sports world and the advertising industry that feeds on its celebrities pursue the domesticating strategy on a continual basis. Every black man who smiles for the camera, whether he has scored a touchdown or endorsed a product in a commercial, is participating in the detoxification of his own image in the eyes of a white audience that seldom perceives the redemptive function of these images.[32] This process is one example of what may be called "virtual integration," an effortless commingling of the races (almost always in the service of corporate profits) that offers the illusion of progress to a public that wants both good news about race and the preservation of a racial status quo that seldom forces whites to examine their own racial attitudes. (The aftermath of the O. J. Simpson verdict was one of these rare occasions.) The same passive longing for racial peace once prompted the veteran sportswriter Dan Shaughnessy to beg his readers to believe that the white arm of a Boston Celtics player draped around the shoulder of a black teammate was a sign of hope for race relations in the United States. A standard technique for delivering this message is to place big black athletes in the company of small white children; such juxtapositions appear frequently, for example, on the cover of *Sports Illustrated for Kids,* thereby reassuring the many whites who believe that black men are by nature physically dangerous.[33] The Boston Red Sox slugger Mo Vaughn, who has become a rare black symbol of reconciliation in a racially troubled city, appeared on the cover of *Sports Illustrated* in the company of a small and adoring white boy.[34]

Ralph Ellison pointed out many years ago that such idealized versions of the gentle black man are rooted in white fears of black retribution for the humiliations of slavery.[35] Such symbolic figures also represent an unconscious attempt to resurrect the docile black male of southern racial lore.[36] They are of doubtful social value if only because they cannot resolve the white psyche's anxious oscillation between idealized and demonized images of blacks, who are always denied normal human status. A similar gentling technique appears in a Nike-sponsored, pseudo public-service ad that features the meditative face of Michael Jordan as he contemplates a world without his own celebrity ("Would I still be your hero?"). The cynicism of such corporate advertising is rooted both in its commercial motives and in its entrapment of the black athlete in the vicious cycle of demonization and domestication.

Another domesticating strategy uses the black man's body to accentuate his vulnerability. American publications have a conspicuous tendency to publish naked black male torsos more often than white ones, a practice that expresses the same racial mentality that has long permitted the undressing of racial exotics in *National Geographic* and that plays on the tantalizing themes of miscegenation and human bondage.[37] Yet another pictorial device is the comic-racist celebration of the obese black athlete, who is symbolically neutered the moment he becomes the jolly fat man. The media celebrity once accorded to William (The Refrigerator) Perry of the Chicago Bears is the best-known example of a racist fixation on the black body that becomes acceptable as harmless burlesque. *Sports Illustrated,* the most widely circulated and Middle American sports publication of them all, has published an entire series of such entertainments in recent years, oblivious to the fact that the gratification experienced by its white readers is rooted in an elaborate racist folklore about blacks and their appetites.[38] Here is Nate (The Kitchen) Newton, a Dallas Cowboys guard, surrounded by a dozen bags of fattening snacks and a watermelon, his eager lips pursed for a potato chip. There is Dwayne (Road Grader) White of the St. Louis Cardinals, his dark face averted from the camera as his belly bulges obscenely over an invisible belt. In another photograph Dan (Big Daddy) Wilkinson sits before a heaping plate of food, his large fists grasping an enormous wooden fork and matching spoon, which he holds erect like an African chief posing for *National Geographic.* Nate Newton reveals that he is paid personal appearance fees "so they can see how fat I am" — the bloated black athlete as commercialized human specimen and Garfield-like house creature. "Across the country," *Sports Illustrated* reports, "he is perceived as some kind of enormous, lovable Chia Pet, a big huggy-bear of a man in the NFL's cast of cartoon characters."[39] Yet even this saccharine nonsense has its social significance, in that these relentlessly upbeat makeovers of black giants for white audiences express a racist wish to find comfort in the domestication of big black men.

The virtual integration of interracial sport is only one aspect of a larger racial coping strategy described by the cultural critic Benjamin DeMott. American mass media, he argues, have been engaged in the relentless promotion of "feel-good images" of black-white sameness that systematically evade all of the deep conflicts between blacks and whites: "Round the clock, ceaselessly, the elements of this orthodoxy of sameness are grouped and regrouped, helping to root an unspoken but felt understanding throughout white America: race problems belong to the passing moment. Race problems do not involve group interests and conflicts developed over centuries. Race problems are being smoothed into nothingness, gradually, inexorably, by good will, affection, points of light." This propaganda of racial bonhomie is also a de facto policy of the American sports industry and is elaborated most effectively and ingeniously in advertisements. The athleticizing of the black male image is thus an integral part of corporate enterprises worth billions of dollars a year. This contributes in turn to the perpetual underdevelopment of people to whom athleticism seems to offer both personal fulfillment and social liberation. At the same time, it is only fair to ask whether these "friendship dogmas" might also serve a useful purpose. As DeMott points out, "friendship ideas do, after all, represent a step forward from yesterday's race-viciousness. Combined with an intelligent address to the problems of non-middle-class blacks, the friendship faith could move us toward a positive interracial future. Some sameness themes radiate real moral energy and carry an inspiring, even lyric charge."[40]

The problem is that "feel-good" initiatives do not seem to transform racial attitudes in socially effective ways. The fifty years of integrated sport that produced a miraculously deracialized O. J. Simpson could not obscure, let alone prevent, the bitter racial antagonisms revealed by his acquittal. Indeed, friendship dogmas may be worse than useless if they are offered as a substitute for social policies that redistribute power toward the powerless, because they help whites avoid "the hard truth that a caste society attempting erratically to dismantle its caste structures can't expect to get the job done without making commitments to developmental assistance on a scale this country has never imagined."[41]

Black athleticism has complicated the identity problems of black Americans by making athletes the most prominent symbols of African-American achievement. This has done much to perpetuate the invisibility of the black middle class, by making black professional achievement a seldom-noted sideshow to more dramatic media coverage of celebrities and deviants. As the critic Walter Goodman once said of local television news in New York City, "If a rule went out excluding entertainers, athletes, and criminals from a night's report, the only black faces you could be sure of seeing would be those of the anchors." The "tabloid style" of such programming virtually prescribes a demoralizing image of blacks as a group: "The opening headlines are about mayhem, not classes for the gifted. The accomplishments come across as flowers in a world of weeds; on local television, social aberration is the norm."[42]

Responses to this process of continuous defamation are strikingly selective, in that members of the black middle class who rightly resent the notoriety of black criminals appear to be unembarrassed by the omnipresence of black athletes, who serve as the reigning symbol of black "genius" for a majority of blacks and whites.[43] "For many years," a black sociologist once noted, "blacks were politically powerless to affect the imagery and metaphor of popular media expression."[44] Yet even after they acquired some influence over their media images, if only the right to censor the worst of them, their lobbying efforts have rarely targeted disproportionate emphasis on athleticism as an obstacle to

progress. A black middle class (and its intelligentsia) that remains in-
fatuated with sports cannot campaign effectively against racial stereotyping that preserves the black man's physicality as a sign of his inherent
limitations.[45]

This appearance of passivity is, however, misleading, for there are
both working-class and middle-class African Americans who do resist
the sports propaganda by encouraging their children to pursue more
productive cultural and intellectual interests.[46] At this point we do not
know how many people offer this sort of guidance to black children.
What is more, their voices are unlikely to be heard above the din of a
sports industry that profits from the athleticizing of young blacks. Another obstacle is the athleticizing of black life itself, a sense that giving
expression to the ordeal of black survival has long required the visceral
power of athletic metaphors — or as one black patient told his psychiatrist: "The black man in this country fights the main event in Madison
Square Garden every day."[47]

*Darwin's Athletes* is a racial history of modern sport that explores our
racial predicament in its broadest dimensions. The first section of the
book describes the origins of the African-American preoccupation with
athletic achievement and shows how this cultural syndrome has subverted more productive developmental strategies founded on academic
and professional achievement. It argues that Western racism inflicted on
African Americans a physicalized (and eventually athleticized) identity
from which they have yet to escape. The cult of black athleticism continues a racist tradition that has long emphasized the motor skills and
manual training of African Americans. While the idea of black athletic
superiority serves the fantasy needs of blacks as well as whites, providing symbolic victories and a renewal of survivalist thinking about black
toughness, the sports fixation is also emblematic of an entire complex of
black problems, which includes the adolescent violence and academic
failure that have come to symbolize the black male for most Americans.

The second section of the book presents the past century of sport as
an arena of racial competition. The ascendancy of the black athlete and
the growing belief in his biological superiority represent a historic reversal of roles in the encounter between Africans and the West. The
Anglo-Saxon racial self-confidence of the nineteenth century prided
itself on an athleticism of both physique and temperament, and the
conquered racial inferior played a role in confirming the masculinity of
the explorer or colonist. Sport in the colonial context was both an
instrument of domination and a field of conflict. The European coloni-

alist's emotional stake in his own sense of physical vitality made the issue of racial athletic competition a sensitive one. The decline of the European empires has been accompanied by the decline of the athletic white male as well, and the world of sport is still adjusting to the psychological dislocations brought on by this loss of prestige.

The third section of the book shows how ideas about black athletic superiority belong to a more comprehensive racial folklore that has long imagined black people to be a hardier, physically stronger, and biologically more robust human subspecies than other races. Nineteenth-century racial science took an intimate interest in the black body and intensified a fixation on black physicality from which there appears to be no escape. The rise of the black athlete during this century has thus given the biological racism of the last century a new lease on life. The emergence of African and African-American athletes as the most spectacular stars of the summer Olympic Games has also led to white fatalism and fears that the twilight of the Caucasian athlete has at last arrived. Images of superior black athleticism have also taken on a special power in the context of a resurgent neo-Darwinian interpretation of the black male and his allegedly criminal propensities. Persistent racial stereotyping has thus made racial athletic aptitude a controversial and even disreputable topic that some would ban from the scientific agenda. The concluding section of this book opposes such censorship and proposes a "postliberal" approach to biomedical racial differences, since a fear of racial biology can only encourage racist interpretations of the genetic research of the future.

PART I

# Shooting Hoops Under the Bell Curve

# 1

## The African-American
## Sports Fixation

I N  A N  E S S A Y that accompanied the publication of their controversial bestseller *The Bell Curve,* Charles Murray and Richard J.
Herrnstein offered a measure of solace to an African-American
population doomed, according to their theory, to irremediable intellectual inferiority. The healthy response to permanent residence at the
bottom of the mental ability scale, they advised, would be to cultivate
a "clannish self-esteem" based on the demonstrated aptitudes of the
group. "Given a chance, each clan will add up its accomplishments using
its own weighting system, will encounter the world with confidence in its
own worth," the authors enthused on behalf of their model of "wise
ethnocentrism." And what would African Americans bring to America's multicultural carnival? The only claim to preeminence they could
think of was "the dominance of many black athletes." If blacks could
build their clan pride on superior athleticism and perhaps some other
signature achievements, then it would be "possible to look ahead to a
world in which the glorious hodgepodge of inequalities of ethnic groups
— genetic and environmental, permanent and temporary — can be not
only accepted but celebrated."[1]

The celebration of black athleticism as a source of clan pride does not
need to be predicted, because it already exists on a scale most people do
not comprehend. What is more, this pride is damaging black America
in ways that African Americans in particular find hard to acknowledge.
As one critic of *The Bell Curve* has noted, the "wise ethnocentrism" of
Murray and Herrnstein "is a perfectly destructive recommendation"
precisely because "a clan pride based on revering Michael Jordan —
and rejecting intellectual role models — would only increase the envi-
ronment-based black-white differential."[2]

Here too there is no point in speaking hypothetically, since African Americans' attachment to sport has been diverting interest away from the life of the mind for most of this century. The rejection of academic achievement as a source of "clan pride" is already rampant among black boys, whose preferred models are rappers and athletes.[3] Sports themes and styles have soaked into the fabric of African-American life, as black identity is athleticized through ubiquitous role models who stimulate wildly unrealistic ambitions in black children (an improbable number of black boys expect to become professional athletes) and initiate athletic fashion trends and hairstyles. In short, it has become all too easy for many blacks and whites to assume that the horizons of black life are coterminous with the achievements of athletes, and one of the most damaging and least publicized corollaries of the sports obsession has been a pronounced rejection of intellectual ambition. As the black Harvard psychiatrist Alvin Poussaint noted many years ago, one of the consequences of identification with physical prowess "has been the contempt in which many young blacks hold their peers who have opted for success in more sedate activities."

While the disastrous effects of the sports fixation have drawn only sporadic and ineffectual attention in a society that regards black athleticism as a natural phenomenon, a few observers have pointed out what is at stake. The black activist and sports sociologist Harry Edwards has been the only consistent critic of this syndrome, calling black society "a co-conspirator" in the exploitation of its own children by a white-dominated sports establishment.[4] The black economist Glenn Loury has pointed out that it is a "pernicious chauvinism that leads a black to feel himself superior in view of the demographic composition of the NBA."[5] The worst aspect of this particular chauvinism, however, is not that it is arrogant but that it plays a role in maintaining large numbers of African Americans in a premodern condition which is promoted by the same college and professional sports industries that many blacks regard as places of opportunity for social and economic advancement.

The entrapment of African Americans in the world of athleticism is the result of a long collaboration between blacks seeking respect and expanded opportunity and whites seeking entertainment, profit, and forms of racial reconciliation that do not challenge fundamental assumptions about racial difference. The power of these white interests notwithstanding, the most important factor in the development of the sports fixation is that athletic achievement has served the clan pride of African Americans in an absolutely unique way, to the point where it is embraced as a foundation of black identity. As Rudy Washington, executive director of the Black Coaches Association, said in 1991, "The fundamental problem is the home life, the black community, because in no other race is sport such a dominant factor every day as it is in the black community."[6]

This attachment to physical prowess should be understood as a cultural syndrome that affects the lives of black people both inside and outside the United States. When the sociologist Ellis Cashmore argued in *Black Sportsmen* that blacks in Britain had embraced a self-destructive belief in their own athletic superiority, "the response from some areas of the black community in Britain was that the book destroyed vestiges of pride. 'Sport is one of the few areas where blacks can feel superior and gifted; now the book has taken even that away from us', was how one sprinter put it."[7] There is no reason to believe that African Americans as a group would react differently. "The apathy out there is phenomenal," a young black educator in Chicago told me when I asked him whether blacks were concerned about children's infatuation with sports stars. Protests against the black sports fixation, he said, would in all likelihood be both futile and resented.[8] A black high school teacher in Houston told me that most black people would regard such dissent as "radical" and disruptive. When I asked a socially conscious black man who had played in the National Basketball Association (NBA) whether there were interest groups in the black community that might be mobilized against the sports fixation, his look of bitter amusement told me all I needed to know.

The sports fixation lives on in stereotypes about black physical superiority that have become nothing less than a global racial folklore. The effects of these ideas on blacks have been little noted, but they are profound. Black soldiers have been told by white drill instructors that they can endure physical stress, such as grueling marches, better than whites because they are the toughened progeny of slaves — a eugenic fantasy shared by both whites and blacks. At the same time, countless blacks believe in their own athletic superiority. The social process that imposes an athleticized identity on blacks takes various forms. Many black children grow up assuming that they were simply born with athletic ability, and some coaches encourage them in this belief. Some black boys are told by black coaches that they have no future if they do not develop their athletic talent.

The idea of black athletic superiority can also produce racial arrogance. A high school sprinter in Houston told me he has challenged white distance runners to compete and called them "punks," "fags," and "cowards" when they have refused. A prominent track-and-field coach told me that a few black runners will play the race card as a psychological ploy at the starting line, murmuring to certain competitors, "You're in trouble now, white boy." He has also coached white sprinters whose development was stunted by a racial inferiority complex. When one African-American woman lost a race to a white Briton at the 1993 World Track and Field Championships in Stuttgart, some black athletes said to her, "How could you lose to that white girl?" My African-American informant took a different view: the winner had earned her gold medal through hard work, he said, and her victory was good for track and field, because it promoted racial integration in an increasingly black-dominated sport.

Sport has become an arena in which the athletic version of black male style is enacted for a mass audience whose ideas about racial identity have been shaped by years of emphasis on black physicality and its special qualities. Black athletes and intellectuals alike insist that the "black athletic aesthetic" is an important element of black culture. The social critic Nelson George speaks of an "aggressive" African-American aesthetic and the African deity Oshoosi, who represents a "prideful assertion of mind and muscle." Analogies between black athletes and jazz musicians have become a convention among the black intelligentsia. Sport is quite simply more important to most black men, including the highly educated, than to their white counterparts. But the sports fixation is not mere spectatorship; it is also the virtual compulsion to demonstrate athletic ability that has been felt by so many black men, and basketball, of course, is the black sport par excellence. "You had to have your shot," one man told me of his days growing up in a Chicago housing project in the early 1960s. Not everyone could play basketball well, but every boy had to have his signature move to establish his identity as a male. In a similar vein, a world-class black runner told me he would look down on any black man who could not play basketball. Even for many black professionals, the ability to play basketball at a respectable level is a matter of self-respect.

The sports fixation is a direct result of the exclusion of blacks from every cognitive elite of the past century and the resulting starvation for "race heroes"; it has always been a defensive response to the assault on black intelligence, which continues to this day. That is why the sports syndrome has made athleticism the signature achievement of black America, the reigning symbol of black "genius." Attachment to athletics has been a coping strategy for dealing with "the Negro 'inferiority complex'" identified by Gunnar Myrdal in *An American Dilemma* in 1944. This syndrome "cannot be admitted publicly," he said then, and it remains difficult to talk about and for that reason has received little systematic study.[9]

The sports fixation has also fed on the productive yet overestimated alliance between the civil rights movement and the integration of college and professional sport, which contributed to the athleticizing of the black image.[10] It has been reinforced by a selective and sentimental approach to African-American history, which has converted athletes such as Joe Louis and Jackie Robinson into messiahs and avoided awkward questions about the unintended effects of integrating the American sports world. The sheer volume of sentimental and intellectual energy that has been invested in the mythic saga of Jackie Robinson has discouraged further thinking about what his career did and did not accomplish. The point is not to deny the importance of this African-American hero but to recognize that black America has paid a high and largely unacknowledged price for the extraordinary prominence given the black athlete rather than other black men of action (such as military pilots and astronauts), who represent modern aptitudes in ways that athletes cannot.[11]

The sports fixation has been made possible in part by the black middle class, which appears to have accepted athletes as the most prominent symbols of black achievement. Indeed, the media invisibility of the black middle class and its successes is one of the social costs associated with the athleticizing of black life. A "tabloid style" that is "made to order for racial provocateurs" seizes naturally upon the flamboyant black athlete (and his misbehaviors) while ignoring the careers of doctors, lawyers, and business people.[12] Rather than resisting this process, a consummately middle-class publication such as *Ebony* fawns over a galaxy of celebrities, including athletes, whose prominence obscures more important stories of black professional achievement, which receive only token coverage.

When E. Franklin Frazier described this form of status-worship in his 1957 book *Black Bourgeoisie,* the athlete was only one celebrity among others. Today he enjoys unprecedented commercial exposure but has lost the moral stature that once made him a middle-class icon. Apart from maintaining their prosperity and emotional health, the most important problem affecting middle-class blacks today is what to do about the influence of rappers and athletes who teach their children not to "act white." "Too many affluent black youths," the black psychiatrist James Comer said in 1978, "mistakenly associate black identity with admiration of what is most self-destructive about the behavior of blacks with lower income."[13] A generation ago some black professionals were campaigning against "blaxploitation" films.[14] Today the black middle class confronts a sports world in which some of the most celebrated black representatives no longer present a clear alternative to the violent, narcissistic, and antisocial norms glamorized in *Superfly* and other black action films of the 1970s.

The sports fixation damages black children by discouraging academic achievement in favor of physical self-expression, which is widely considered a racial trait. Some educators understand that the self-absorbed style promoted by glamorous black athletes subverts intellectual development. A school for black boys in Chicago has therefore adopted a policy of stylistic abstinence: "No gum-chewing is allowed. No sagging pants. No sunglasses, biker pants or tank tops. No earrings worn by boys. No designs carved in the hair" — in short, a complete repudiation of the showy male style flaunted by many black stars.[15] Such policies confront an intense peer pressure that equates academic excellence with effeminacy and racial disloyalty and identifies "blackness" with physical prowess.

Educators who think about solutions to this crisis see themselves in direct competition with the sports world, and some try to harness its appeal on behalf of learning. "While negative peer pressure tends to diminish African American males' propensity to succeed academically," writes one author, "that influence can be reduced, if not entirely eliminated, by verbally and materially rewarding academic achievement in the same way that society acknowledges and even extols athletic performance."[16] John Ogbu, a Berkeley sociologist who has done pioneering work on the academic self-destruction of black children, takes the same approach even as he warns that "the black community must reexamine its own perceptions and interpretations of school learning. Apparently, black children's general perception that academic pursuit is 'acting white' is learned in the black community." So what is to be done? "Cultural or public recognition of those who are academically successful should be made a frequent event, as is generally done in the case of those who succeed in the fields of sports and entertainment."[17] Once again the proposed strategy is to imitate the practices of the athletic culture. What Ogbu does not do is to confront the black community directly with its anti-intellectual dynamic and demand a new attitude toward athletic prestige.

In fact, this demand is seldom made by anyone, both because it is politically incorrect and because cultural habit seems to legitimate itself. "How do you end some of the traditions that have become dysfunctional for the black male, like the idea that he has to behave in certain unacceptable ways to be 'cool' or 'hip'?" asks Alvin Poussaint, especially when "in nearly every other way but sex and physical brawn, the black male is impotent institutionally in our society."[18] Cornel West, who understands all too well the African-American intellectual's marginal status among his fellow blacks, has called for "new stylistic options for black men caught in the deadly endeavor of rejecting black machismo identities."[19] Yet his analysis of this predicament never identifies athleticism as a major obstacle to socializing young black men into less macho roles.

Black intellectuals have shown little interest in pursuing Ogbu's criticism of black attitudes toward "school learning" or in confronting the sports fixation. In 1979, for example, a contributor to the *Journal of Negro Education* argued that the urgent need "to dispel anachronistic and stereotypical notions regarding the cognitive and psycho-motor abilities of Black students" would be achieved not by reducing their attachment to athletics but by promoting diversification of their sports interests in order to demonstrate that blacks are as heterogeneous as whites, and he opposed reducing the "role basketball may play in Black Culture."[20] As of 1987, the sociologist Robert Staples regarded "black male dominance in sports" as "a bright spot in an otherwise bleak picture."[21] Even Harry Edwards, who has spoken out against the sports fixation for many years, has declared that the highest form of human genius is athleticism: "If I were charged with introducing an alien life form to the epitome of human potential, creativity, perseverance and spirit, I would introduce that alien life form to Michael Jordan."[22]

Black athleticism has also been rationalized as an economic and social policy. Jesse Jackson, breathing new life into the industrial education movement of Booker T. Washington, has declared that young black athletes "create a tremendous industrial base for black America. We cannot just settle for the pleasure of watching them perform."[23] As his colleague Charles S. Farrell, national director of the Rainbow Coalition for Fairness in Athletics, put it, "Athletics is to the Black community what technology is to the Japanese and what oil is to the Arabs. We're allowing that commodity to be exploited." If sports cannot bring freedom, then at least they can produce revenue. "We want more African-Americans in sports," says Rudy Washington, "not just in coaching, we want them to work for Champion, Nike, Adidas, Russell Athletics. We want them to work for people who make money on sports, because sports is a billion-dollar business and African-Americans make up a great portion of that business and that image. Why shouldn't we be a part of that?"[24]

But the sports fixation can also be dressed up in a grander purpose. "We believe," Jackson wrote in 1993, "that sports can help change the despair in our communities into hope, replace low esteem with confidence and rebuild a true sense of community that transcends neighbor-

hood and racial boundaries."[25] For all of its noble intentions, this declaration revealed a stunning lack of historical perspective. Could Jesse
Jackson not have known that he was invoking the millennial hopes for
sport that the NAACP had proclaimed back in the 1920s and 1930s?[26]
Had the passage of most of a century taught him nothing about what the
African-American engagement with sports could and could not do for
his people? The recycling of noble rhetoric is, in fact, a constant bypro-
duct of the black sports fixation precisely because it has produced so
little of permanent value for most black Americans.

The social costs associated with the athleticizing of black life remain
unaddressed because sober and unsentimental analysis of black cultural
preferences will inevitably appear as racist denigration to some people.
"The profitable literary scam nowadays," according to the novelist Ishmael Reed, "is to pose as someone who airs unpleasant and frank facts
about the black community, only to be condemned by the black community for doing so."[27] The critique of acquired cultural habits is not the
same thing as denigration, but many people find it difficult to make this
distinction when dysfunctional habits are ascribed to African Americans. Those who resent the cultural history presented here as an alien
intrusion into black life should think about why the authors of *The Bell
Curve* also oppose cross-cultural criticism of this kind. No one, they
write, "needs to tell any clan how to come up with a way of seeing itself
that is satisfactory; it is one of those things that human communities
know how to do quite well when left alone to do it." This is a specious
formulation, because it provides for no way to assess the beliefs or the
behaviors of the clan in relation to other norms, which might find them
deficient or even dangerous. In the context of *The Bell Curve,* which
postulates a lamentable and irreparable deficiency in blacks, this version of cultural laissez faire is less an appreciation of cultural difference
than a formula for benign neglect. The cynical nadir of the Murray-
Herrnstein "celebration" of African-American uniqueness is the claim
that blacks are defining themselves "in the streets. The process is not
only normal and healthy; it is essential."[28] While it is hard to imagine a
more mindless description of what is happening on the streets of America's black ghettos, it is not so hard to characterize this sort of romanticism, which combines the pleasure of the cross-cultural voyeur with the
detachment of the spectator. It is the conservative policymaker's saccharine version of *Hoop Dreams.*

The special preoccupation with athletics that characterizes African-
American life today did not exist a century ago. At a time when the

black mathematician Kelly Miller found it necessary to refute the widespread idea that the black race was physically deteriorating and headed for extinction, the black athlete was an unusual figure, even if we seem to remember otherwise. The modern need to find historical significance in the black fighters of this period — the apolitical Jack Johnson foremost among them — can create the false memory of a race of black athletes who supposedly flourished in an era when interest in the black body generally meant alarm over the state of Negro health.[29] Today, awash in modern images of superlative black athletes and *Mandingo*-style stereotypes of robust slaves, we find it hard to imagine that an apparent surplus of healthy black bodies has not always been a part of the American racial landscape. When W.E.B. Du Bois addressed the issue of sports in 1897, it was not to warn of black athleticism but to deplore the poor physical fitness of Negro youth: "Here again athletic sports must in the future play a larger part in the normal and mission schools of the South, and we must rapidly come to the place where the man all brain and no muscle is looked upon as almost as big a fool as the man all muscle and no brain; and when the young woman who cannot walk a couple of good country miles will have few proposals of marriage."[30]

This version of the well-balanced man *(mens sana in corpore sano)* found wide resonance among educated blacks during the early period of black interest in athleticism, and there were practical as well as idealistic reasons to encourage physical fitness. A black teacher of "physical culture" told the *Indianapolis Freeman* in 1901 that he was running "the only colored school of this kind in [New York; I] receive doctors, lawyers and businessmen daily at my gymnasium for exercise, and I think there should be more bright, young colored fellows take up the art of self defense and learn how to defend themselves."[31] A reflective article on "Art and Intellect" in the *Chicago Defender* in 1915 invoked an evolutionary interpretation of brain and brawn in order to defend the importance of the latter: "The physical power of man has always played a prominent part in his affairs. In the primitive stages of development it was the most important factor in the struggle for existence, and though the process of evolution has reached that point where the development of the mind is most essential to success, the physique still has a conspicuous place in all that concerns men."[32] Later that year the *Defender* published a huge drawing of Howard P. Drew, the "World's Greatest Sprinter," engaged in studying as well as running — the classically developed Negro par excellence.[33]

The fateful question was whether the development of the black mind would be able to keep pace with the development of the black body. Anticipating the outcome of this contest, the author of "Art and Intellect," having conceded that "the development of the mind is most essential to success," goes on to glorify athletic achievement with a passion neither art nor intellect could inspire. "All nations and races are proud of their athletic heroes and their skill," he writes. "We have had and have ours and are exceedingly proud of them." By winning a gold medal for the University of Chicago, he says, the premedical student Binga Dismond had inspired in black Americans "the incomparable thrill of race patriotism." The fact that Dismond was "a serious-minded young man, with well developed tastes and ambitions to succeed in a profession," somehow prompted less excitement. Still, this early booster of black athleticism clearly enunciates at the end of his essay the fundamental thesis of what Patrick Miller has called the "muscular assimilationism" strategy of twentieth-century African Americans: "Men like Mr. Dismond and his fellow athletes are of infinite value to us as a race, as they do much to eliminate prejudice and gain new respect for us, especially when possessing that valuable combination of physical and intellectual development."[34]

Often invoked but seldom examined, this faith in the black athlete as a politically invaluable role model became one of the ruling dogmas of American thinking about race and was eventually incarnated in the person of Jackie Robinson. The fields of sport appeared as a utopia of equal opportunity where blacks could demonstrate their long-denied "manhood" and "fitness" for full citizenship. Athletic competition was also an extraordinary opportunity to deal out some licks to members of the "superior" race, both in the arena and on the sports page. "Walcott was in fine shape," the *Freeman* wrote in 1899 of a black fighter, "his black skin shining like polished mahogany and standing out in strong contrast to the sickly white of Johnson's complexion."[35] "We are truly sorry," a *Defender* editorial lamented in 1915, "that we cannot offer anything more substantial than advice to the white sporting world as to the best way to whip the [black] champions." Blindfolding Jack Johnson or tying one of his hands behind him, this editorial proposed through its crocodile tears, might do the trick.[36] "The white boys," the *Crusader Magazine* reported of one interracial basketball game in 1919, "were disposed of to the tune of 21 to 10."[37] The gratifications offered by such remarks were inadequate compensation for the daily indignities served up by a Jim Crow society, but they were real enough. Today it is clear that they were only the embryonic stage of an attachment to black athletic achievement that, along with musical performance, has come to overwhelm all other forms of black talent in the public mind. This triumph of the dynamic black body eventually achieved its apotheosis in the corporate-sponsored, media-driven, pan-racial cult of Michael Jordan.

A century after these stirrings of athletic chauvinism, it is important to realize that black thinking about the value of athletics during the early 1900s was more divided than these quotations suggest. Today, when black criticism of the fixation on athletics is alive but almost inaudible, it is instructive to know that some African Americans were experiencing second thoughts about sports even before athletes became the principal standard-bearers of black achievement. William Pickens, a professor at Talladega College, warned in 1905 that the benefits of athletic victories would be sharply circumscribed by reigning assumptions about black potential. Whites, he predicted, "would accept from a Negro physical and athletic superiority but . . . stand aloof when one approaches with moral or intellectual superiority."[38] And some criticized the black triumphalism evidenced in the mockery of failed "white hopes." In the same year that Professor Pickens spoke out in the *Voice of the Negro,* the "ex-colored pugilist" Allen Johnson told the *Freeman* what one great black fighter had felt about racial chauvinism in sports: "Peter Jackson, with whom I had a speaking acquaintance, never did anything to lower the fighting game. If he ever heard any of the so-called riff-raff of his own race gloating over the fact that he was better than some white fighters he would walk away from them."[39]

Ten years later the *Defender* published some unusually enlightened remarks by the white heavyweight Jess Willard, which clearly had a sobering effect on the black sportswriter who reported them. "A championship fight between a black man and a white man," Willard asserted,

makes bad blood between the races. Jack Johnson did more to hurt his people than Booker Washington did to help them. I am not saying this in a mean way. I'm not excusing white men for feeling that way. I think it shows ignorance. But lots of white men did feel that way. Who doesn't remember all the sickening "white hope" business? And just as ignorant white men thought their race disgraced, so did a lot of ignorant colored men think that their race had been proved the better by Johnson's victory. That's why I'm going to draw the color line. I say this because I don't want anybody to think that I'm doing it from any mean, petty little prejudice.

Willard's declaration was welcomed by the *Defender*'s man, who joined in lamenting the damage that boxing had done to race relations.

This "honest, frank statement," he said, would "take a little of the rough edges off" Willard's decision to "draw the color line" against black fighters, a position normally associated with racial prejudice. What was more, "the thinking element in our race agree in the main with what he says. The public have taken prize fighting too seriously; they have let the winning or losing of a fight sway their prejudices; they have taken prize fighters out of the class where they belong and have made idols of them. The erroneous opinion gained currency that our race held up our champion as a little god. We did, only in the same degree that the white race held up their would-be champions."[40] This long-forgotten exchange shows that it was perfectly possible at the time for both blacks and whites to see through "the sickening 'white hope' business" as well as the emotional needs that made idols out of athletes.

Blacks could also reject conspicuous displays of black athleticism out of racial and class self-consciousness. Jack Johnson, the first black heavyweight champion, provoked mixed feelings among his fellow blacks. For many people he was a source of racial pride; the *Defender,* for example, noted with satisfaction that the heavyweight championship had been "transferred from the brow of Caucasia to the brow of Ethiopia" by "the pugilistic sensation of the modern world."[41] But to others Johnson "was a source of embarrassment and resentment. Many middle-class, upwardly mobile blacks tended to accuse their less-refined, less-reserved, and less-cultured brethren" of reflecting badly on the race as a whole.[42] Black middle-class reactions to Joe Louis in the 1930s were equally ambivalent.

Across the Atlantic, a similar reaction against athleticism had occurred during the 1880s and 1890s among the educated Euro-Africans of the Gold Coast (now Ghana), who rightly feared that imported British-style athleticism might subvert the educational aspirations and behavioral standards of the younger generation. Their Euro-African "anti-sporting ideology" held that community standards were to be derived from "the chapel, the marketplace and the classroom" rather than the fields of sport. The wisdom of this policy, as Ray Jenkins notes, was evident: "The struggle for the salvation of Euro-Africans, in their unequal imperial contest with the British, required weapons of survival which were to be found in the classroom rather than on the playing fields."[43]

Part of the African-American tragedy of this century is that the black middle class at this time was too small and too impoverished to promulgate and enforce such standards, so the vacuum was filled first by Booker T. Washington and his truncated version of Negro education and then by the puritanical administrators of struggling Negro colleges, who waged war on amusements like dancing and card-playing while building athletic programs meant to forge the character of black youth.[44] In the meantime, "the thinking element" among African Americans relinquished most of its doubts about the benefits of sports and focused instead on achieving athletic equality as one part of the educational enterprise.

The deficiencies of Negro education in the decades following the Civil War are a major theme in W.E.B. Du Bois's eloquent and poignant memoir, *The Souls of Black Folk,* which both documents and mourns the devastating effects of slavery and Reconstruction on attempts to create not just black literacy but "the ideal of 'book-learning'; the curiosity, born of compulsory ignorance, to know and test the power of the cabalistic letters of the white man, the longing to know." Du Bois's compassion enabled him to record with painful honesty the underdevelopment of the man who "felt the weight of his ignorance, — not simply of letters, but of life, of business, of the humanities; the accumulated sloth and shirking and awkwardness of decades and centuries." Du Bois also knew that perhaps the greatest obstacle to progress was a stubborn conviction about the black organism itself, "the sincere and passionate belief that somewhere between men and cattle, God created a *tertium quid,* and called it a Negro, — a clownish, simple creature, at times even lovable within its limitations, but straitly foreordained to walk within the Veil [of Race]."[45]

The agonizing progress of these "misty minds" toward literacy conferred unusual status on an entire range of physical accomplishments, which represented achievement even in the absence of book learning and professional training. The legendary figures of the mighty laborer John Henry and other black men endowed with heroic physical abilities like speed and strength are the late-nineteenth-century forerunners of the black athlete who embodies the hopes and talents of his people.[46] Indeed, "John Henryism" has entered the medical literature as a synonym for a self-imposed work regimen that imperils health.[47]

Yet the vast majority of African Americans have always had to be satisfied with less conspicuous achievements than those of John Henry or Jack Johnson. Showing respect for the mastery of more modest physical skills thus served the needs of many people by making these abilities respectable and even worthy of special recognition. A striking example of the symbolic importance of manual labor appeared in the January 1923 issue of *Opportunity,* the magazine published by the Urban League. "The World's Fastest Mail Sorter" celebrates "the phenomenal accomplishment of Miss Lulu Cargill, a young colored woman who sorted 30,215 pieces of mail in the allotted hours — a margin of superiority equivalent to an ordinary day's work." While it is tempting to compare Miss Cargill with the Stakhanovite superworkers of the Stalinist 1930s, her record-breaking performance must instead be understood in the context of the American racism of the 1920s. A few months before her feat, a group of federal "efficiency experts" had visited the New York and Philadelphia post offices and "arrived at a most peculiar division of skill and aptitude along racial lines. The 'average' black employee of the system was declared inferior to the 'average' white employee." On the basis of this statistical competition, the efficiency experts recommended that black workers be fired and replaced by whites. The contest won by Miss Cargill thus amounted to an inadvertent test of the ability of black clerks to demonstrate "efficiency on processes requiring rapid mental coordination and dexterity"; that the black Miss Cargill had shattered the record previously held by the white Miss Holmes by almost 10,000 letters suggested that they could.[48]

This ostensibly trivial contest was only one small part of an ongoing assessment of black potential that could mean a decent life or poverty for many vulnerable people. At a time when the results of the army intelligence tests administered during World War I — which implied lower intelligence among blacks — were common knowledge among the general public,[49] even mail sorting could be turned into a test of the black person's ability to demonstrate the "rapid mental coordination" required by modern employers.[50] The example of mail sorting thus showed how physical and mental dexterity could be different aspects of a single useful aptitude, thereby giving "manual" labor a new respectability in the eyes of blacks who depended on it. The fact that no one appears to have studied black attitudes toward the meaning of manual work in this sense makes it that much more difficult for us to understand how black attitudes toward a wide variety of physical performances have served to compensate for the deficiencies of Negro education.

Educational deficiencies among African Americans resulted from the assault on black intelligence, which had been a constant of the African-American experience since the arrival of the first slaves in 1619. Now, trapped in their own colonial predicament, those blacks who became involved in education faced a profound dilemma as they attempted to create an economically viable workforce while repairing centuries of damage to the intellectual reputation of their people. Should blacks adopt the intellectually stultifying vocational training devised by European colonialists to control them, or should they aim at developing an independent class of thinkers who could challenge white domination of the intellectual life of the nation? For many years during the late nineteenth and early twentieth century, "the quarrel as to whether the Negro should be given a classical or a practical education was the dominant topic in Negro schools and churches throughout the United States."[51]

In *The Souls of Black Folk,* Du Bois both acknowledges and deplores the success of Booker T. Washington, whose educational philosophy stressed "industrial education" over independent thinking. "Among his own people," Du Bois writes, "Mr. Washington has encountered the strongest and most lasting opposition, amounting at times to bitterness, and even today continuing strong and insistent even though largely silenced in outward expression by the public opinion of the nation . . . There is among educated and thoughtful colored men in all parts of the land a feeling of deep regret, sorrow, and apprehension at the wide currency and ascendancy which some of Mr. Washington's theories have gained." For Du Bois it was a choice between "self-assertion" and "submission," and he asserts that "Mr. Washington's programme practically accepted the alleged inferiority of the Negro races."[52] Thirty years later, Carter G. Woodson's stimulating, if sometimes bilious, polemic *The Mis-Education of the Negro* argued that Washington had been right, that higher education had made malcontents of the blacks who had received it, and that the practical-minded black businessman was the key to progress.[53] Although neither *The Souls of Black Folk* nor *The Mis-Education of the Negro* contains a word about sports, both address with disarming candor the demoralizing educational predicament that encouraged a growing adulation of Negro athletes during the 1920s and 1930s.[54] The black athletes who today refine their athletic skills and little else at American universities are thus the damaged inheritors of an educational philosophy that once promoted manual training as the highest cultural achievement to which black youngsters should aspire.

Woodson's endorsement of Booker T. Washington–style practicality did not concede the intellectual inferiority of the African American. When Woodson wrote that "the Negro lacks mental power," he was describing not an inherent deficiency but the accumulated effects of centuries of subjugation and forced inactivity. He saw the blacks of his own era as pathetically dependent on white standards and, for that reason, "mis-educated," intellectually lazy, and complacent about their helpless state. Among the many useful insights that appear throughout his book, one in particular resonates through contemporary black commentaries on intellectual development: "Negroes, then, learned from their oppressors to say to their children that there were certain spheres into which they should not go because they would have no chance therein for development."[55] Intellectual curiosity itself was being strangled at birth. Woodson's angry demand that blacks learn to *think* was thus directed against a whole complex of self-limiting and self-inhibiting attitudes and behaviors that are constantly referred to in the black publications of the period between 1920 and 1940.

In his 1925 manifesto "The New Negro," the writer Alain Locke took the bold position of announcing the end of a long night of psychological bondage. The mind of the Negro was now shedding the "protective social mimicry forced upon him by the adverse circumstances of dependence"; he was "shaking off the psychology of imitation and implied inferiority" and making a "gradual recovery from hyper-sensitiveness and 'touchy' nerves." As for education, "in the intellectual realm a renewed and keen curiosity is replacing the recent apathy; the Negro is being carefully studied, not just talked about and discussed."[56]

Reading other assessments of black intellectual life published not long before and after Locke's commentary makes it difficult to understand why he announced this bright new dawn at all. In 1920 the NAACP's magazine *The Crisis* had deplored the "religious dogmatism" and "mediaeval tendencies" of the typical Negro college, which remained "apparently deaf to the newer demands of the age."[57] In 1923 *Opportunity* described "the environment of the average Negro child" as steeped in "religious beliefs that are but one step removed from crass superstition, beliefs shot through with the otherworldliness of the Middle Ages," constituting "a very potent reason why the army scores for Negroes were not high and could not in the nature of things have been otherwise."[58] For years after Locke's announcement of "a fundamentally changed Negro," a chorus of more skeptical and sometimes scathing black observers continued to paint a dismal picture of the dysfunctional syndromes that were condemning black minds to endless stagnation.

One measure of the retrograde state of Negro education was the continued influence of Booker T. Washington's doctrine of limited black potential. "The Negro student," Professor Arthur P. Davis of Virginia Union University wrote in *The Crisis* in 1930, "is at heart a utilitarian. His mind is circumscribed by the shibboleth of practicality." A year later, responding to the indignant protests provoked by this depiction of "exceedingly lazy" students, Davis denounced the newly fashionable and "pragmatic" field of educational psychology, which was spreading through "all our liberal arts colleges," as a pseudo-discipline that would inevitably lead to a dogma "as vicious, as pernicious as the old 'trade-school' conception of Negro education."[59]

In 1934 the poet Langston Hughes, having completed a lecture tour of more than fifty Negro schools and colleges, reported that he had found "some of the most amazingly old-fashioned moral and pedagogical concepts surviving on this continent." The custodians of these institutions, he said, were "doing their best to produce spineless Uncle Toms, uninformed, and full of mental and moral evasions." Hughes even got a taste of the political passivity of the black athlete before it became institutionalized. Why, he asked, "did a whole Lincoln University basketball team and their coach walk docilely out of a cafe in Philadelphia that refused to serve them because of color?"[60] Pursuing this theme two years later, Karl E. Downs criticized "the deplorable timidity" of the Negro college student, while Arthur P. Davis was back writing about "the 'goose-step' Negro schools," which were imposing on their students "a regimentation so stringent that only the utterly spineless can teach in them."[61] In 1938 the writer George S. Schuyler still saw "the gropings of the Aframerican mind: fearful, uncertain, ignorant," while in 1940 T. S. Jackson described the Negro child's sense of his own intellectual limitations as "a pathological condition."[62]

The darkest and most penetrating analysis of the strangulation of intellectual curiosity in black children appears in Ralph Ellison's 1945 essay "Richard Wright's Blues." It is especially interesting that Ellison ties the theme of limited intellectual horizons to the experience of the black body in two ways. First, he argues that the migration of the southern Negro to the North had affected "his entire psychosomatic structure" by casting him into a new environment characterized by an unprecedented emotional and intellectual complexity: "In the North energies are released and given *intellectual* channelization — energies which in most Negroes in the South have been forced to take a *physical* form or, as with potentially intellectual types like Wright, to be expressed as nervous tension, anxiety and hysteria. Which is nothing mysterious. The human organism responds to environmental stimuli by converting them into either physical and/or intellectual energy." The southern Negro, says Ellison, had always been condemned to live through the ostensibly inarticulate substance of his body: "The 'physical' character of their expression makes for much of the difficulty in understanding American Negroes. Negro music and dances are frenziedly erotic; Negro religious ceremonies violently ecstatic; Negro speech strongly rhythmical and weighted with image and gesture." The conspicuous physicality of the southern black laborer had contributed to the racist misunderstanding that he was a simpleton, when in fact "the 'physical' quality offered as evidence of his primitive simplicity is actually the form of his complexity." Always the genuine integrationist, Ellison insisted that this corporealized black experience was also a genuinely American one: "The American Negro is a Western type whose social condition creates a state which is almost the reverse of the cataleptic trance: Instead of his consciousness being lucid to the reality around it while the body is rigid, here it is the body which is alert, reacting to pressures which the constricting forces of Jim Crow block off from the transforming, concept-creating activity of the brain."[63]

The originality of Ellison's theory is that it makes the sense of black physicality that permeates our racial folklore an acquired rather than an essential trait. Unlike later black commentators, who have responded to the intelligence issue by interpreting "superior" black physicality (including athleticism) as a form of intelligence, Ellison saw the physicality of black self-expression as an unsatisfactory substitute for unhampered intellectual development. Here, as elsewhere, he opposed a notion of racial essence that is conducive to both black and white separatism.

Ellison's first theory is that the body of the oppressed black man stifles his intellectual potential by absorbing energy that should have reached the brain. His second reiterates the critique of black passivity: "The pre-individualistic black community discourages individuality out of self-defense. Having learned through experience that the whole group is punished for the actions of the single member, it has worked out efficient techniques of behavior control." The heartbreaking aspect of this behavior modification was that fear had prompted black parents to choke off the intellectual energy of their own children: "Within the ambit of the black family this takes the form of training the child away from curiosity and adventure, against reaching out for those activities lying beyond the borders of the black community." And the deterrent of last resort was severe physical punishment: "The extent of beatings and psychological maimings meted out by Southern Negro parents rivals those described by the nineteenth-century Russian writers as characteristic of peasant life under the czars. The horrible thing is that the cruelty is also an expression of concern, of love."[64] Perhaps it was an awareness of this kind of repression that prompted one black editor to idealize the superliterate black child. "The gifted child," *The Crisis* told its black readers in 1936, "is almost always a voracious reader, exhibiting an intellectual curiosity which is seemingly insatiable." One can only wonder how the black inhabitants of "peasant homes where the stimulus and leisure for academic scholarship are lacking" reacted to this counsel.[65]

The idea that the pursuit of knowledge presented a danger to blacks could also take the form of a practical argument about avoiding trouble. In 1905, for example, a contributor to the *The Freeman* argued Booker T. Washington's line, insisting that "the false idea that an industrial education would only fit the race for continued servitude, and thus become a bar to higher education, is simply absurd. There is no possible danger of too much industrial education while a general higher education would possibly cause too much professionalism, which would produce race enmity."[66] It is reasonable to assume that, as Ellison asserts, the fear of entering into conflict with whites produced countless examples of such risk-aversive behavior, which stifled intellectual development.

That Ellison's grim analysis has apparently found no subsequent interpretors demonstrates the traumatized state of scholarship on this aspect of the black experience. It is probable that the compelling authority of the civil rights and black studies movements, which emphasized white misbehavior and black self-assertion, discouraged scrutiny of dysfunctional syndromes that developed as defensive responses to white racist terror. But for Ellison the physical punishments that black parents inflicted on their male children to increase their chances for survival in the hostile world of the South were a crucial technique for "training the child away from curiosity and adventure, against reaching out for those activities lying beyond the borders of the black community." "One of the Southern Negro family's methods of protecting the child," he wrote, "is the severe beating — a homeopathic dose of the violence generated by black and white relationships."[67]

Several years before Ellison published his meditation on the difficult childhood Richard Wright describes in *Black Boy,* the anthropologist Melville Herskovits had observed that "the importance of whipping among American Negroes as a technique of training the young has been frequently remarked." Yet the cultural origins of this practice were not clear. Herskovits rejected the view that blacks had adopted whipping in imitation of the slavemasters, arguing that this claim "completely disregards the fact that the outstanding method of correction in Africa itself and elsewhere among New World Negroes, whether of children or adults, is whipping . . . Whipping is considered an integral part of West African pedagogical method."[68] Bertram Wyatt-Brown has also linked the slaves' capacity to endure punishment to African ordeals. The slaves, he says, "exercised remarkable control" when subjected to whippings by slavemasters. "Their fortitude certainly had African roots. In some tribes, thrashing ceremonies, called in northern Nigeria *sheriya,* tested stoic manhood."[69]

Whatever the origins of this behavior, it appears to have persisted in African-American life in more than one form. The psychiatrist authors of the 1968 book *Black Rage* follow Ellison in connecting both corporal punishment and intellectual underdevelopment with a brutal past.[70] "We must conclude," they write, "that much of the pathology we see in black people had its genesis in slavery. The culture that was born in that experience of bondage has been passed from generation to generation. Constricting adaptations developed during some long-ago time continue as contemporary character traits." One of these adaptations was physical punishment: "Beating in child-rearing actually has its psychological roots in slavery and even yet black parents will feel that, just as they have suffered beatings as children, so it is right that their children be so treated. This kind of physical subjugation of the weak forges early in the mind of the child a link with the past and, as he learns the details of history, with slavery per se." Given this indoctrination and the "constricting adaptations" it produces, "eagerness for learning on the part of black people becomes a curiosity worthy of study" rather than the natural curiosity about the world that we expect to find in children everywhere.[71]

The idea that there is a special affinity among some African Americans for physical punishment appears again in a more recent and systematic study of family life: "Comparing the rate of violence used by black parents to violence used by white parents, we find that black parents are more likely to report throwing things at their children and hitting or trying to hit with an object. This is consistent with other studies of disciplinary techniques in black families that report black parents using belts, cords, switches, sticks, and straps to discipline their children."[72]

The ethnologist Carl Husemoller Nightingale has pointed out that sensitivity about race has inhibited public discussion of black family violence:

> Experts on inner-city family life have sometimes been tempted to understate the importance of corporal punishment in poor African-American families, often for understandable reasons. Too often, evidence of beatings and child abuse in poor African-American families has been used to support theories that "bad parents" are to blame for the inner-city crisis or, worse, that some kind of racial proclivity toward violence is at work. But keeping the subject under wraps or romanticizing inner-city family

life only undermines efforts to find alternative explanations and under-standings of inner-city violence that help to fight insensitive or racist thinking.[73]

One might add that the experts' failure to address this damaging tradi-tion is not the only obstacle to putting such knowledge to constructive use, for it is also clear that virtually all observers have lost sight of (or have refused to examine) the causal relationship Ellison saw between family violence and the suffocation of intellectual curiosity. As Ameri-can society wrestles ineffectually with the crucial issue of black aca-demic achievement, such evasive stratagems can only postpone a more adequate understanding of the cultural dynamics that have estranged so many black children from the educational process.

Hazing rituals in black fraternities represent another enactment of this violent tradition. Like black family violence, the "issue of hazing in black fraternities and sororities has either been avoided or benignly neglected" by those concerned with black student life.[74] The man who wrote this, who was himself pushed out of a second-story window dur-ing a hazing incident, has interpreted these ordeals as a legacy of slav-ery, in that modern rituals of suffering that dramatize the ability to withstand physical abuse may well reënact the primal victimized state, in which the slave's survival is assumed to have depended on physical strength and toughness.[75] As a member of a black fraternity at the University of Texas pointed out to me, this subculture makes a point of preserving racial types and acting out in symbolic form the ordeals of the African-American past. Members of Omega Psi Phi and Phi Beta Sigma tend to be dark-skinned and athletic, and most are actually branded on the shoulder, calf, or chest.[76] Pledges about to submit to hazing may be given numbers in a line — "as in slave days," as my informant put it. Less athletic types gravitate to Alpha Phi Alpha (pro-spective clergymen, engineers, lawyers) and Kappa Alpha Psi ("the pretty boys," who may become professors).

Black fraternity abuses differ from the equally sadistic (and some-times fatal) excesses of their white counterparts precisely because they are symbolic practices that are meant to evoke (and perhaps exorcise) a terrible past. These rituals and the corporal punishment tradition are additional evidence that African-American experience has been "physicalized" in intense and varied ways that make this experience qualitatively different from that of other ethnic groups. "Why is sport so important to Black males?" asks a contributor to the *Journal of Negro Education*.[77] One answer is that athletic achievement both expresses the "physicalization" of black identity and is itself a ritual of survival, quite apart from its role in achieving upward social mobility for a small number of people. This physicalized sense of self is powerful precisely because it grows out of the mandate to survive at any cost, and a part of that cost has been the widely noted lack of intellectual ambition among young black males.[78]

Demoralization about the results of education has also played a role in making athleticism a basis of self-respect. The intimate tie between anger about black passivity and a compensatory physical narcissism had already been displayed in one militant black periodical in 1919. "The Negro and His Instinct" offers a scathing portrait of black mental subjugation to white aesthetic standards. Decades before Kenneth Clark observed the reactions of black children to brown and white dolls, the author of this article was excoriating the practice of giving white dolls to black children, whose inevitable response was "to worship and envy the physical characteristics of the whites." Unless this self-destructive behavior stopped, he warned, blacks would have trouble "forcing the other races to recognize us as rational, intelligent human beings." Anticipating the emotional desperation and racial vanity of many black nationalists, this black supremacist pointed to the fact that "the Negro population are better looking than the whites. Take the colored women for instance; they are much more beautiful, judging them by every physical measure that might be applied." In this physical superiority, he suggested, was the key to black self-respect.[79] It is a short step from this kind of racial aesthetics to the now widespread idea that athletic success is a significant foundation of black self-respect.

In 1940 *The Crisis* paraphrased white thinking about black intelligence as follows: "Negroes possess some sort of biological equipment which limits their psychological development. This handicap prevents the Negro from making responses to stimulus objects of a 'higher' order."[80] Black awareness of this racist image has prompted many efforts to dignify the fact or even the appearance of black achievements of various kinds. Various examples of these exercises in public relations are subjected to scathing analysis in *Black Bourgeoisie,* where E. Franklin Frazier cites one popular myth about "a Negro who knows so much about his subject that no university in the world has a faculty with sufficient knowledge to award him a doctorate."[81] Such popular fables serve to compensate for alleged black deficiencies and thus resemble the legends of John Henry and other mythical strongmen; the difference is that they emphasize the "finer" qualities of character and intellect rather than brute strength.

Black athleticism too could gentrify the Negro image by demonstrating good taste and intelligent behavior. The black publications of the prewar period make it clear that the increasing involvement with sport was seen as conducive more to refinement than to a coarsening of African-American life. One proponent of this view was Edwin Bancroft Henderson, physical director of the Colored High Schools of Washington, D.C., and later an influential sportswriter. "Within a decade," he wrote in 1915, "we have witnessed progressive stages of football, from the oft-times rowdy demonstrations by players and spectators of the past to the sportsmanly conduct of gentlemen on the field, and orderly gatherings of onlookers."[82] The young men of the Hampton Institute, Henderson wrote a year later, "have applied brains to brawn in so telling a fashion that the city and college teams with whom they played could at no time quell the Hampton spirit, nor outwit the athletes on the court. To Coach Charles Williams must go the credit for the victory, for his quiet, gentlemanly, masterful methods of coaching having produced good results."[83]

Sport could also be presented as a path toward a kind of intellectual development that might do something to repair the race's reputation for mental indolence. In 1934 *The Crisis* reported that Negro college and university administrators had come to view competitive sports as "an inherent and permanent part of the educational scheme." Their athletic personnel responded to this increased support by embarking on "such scientific study of the game of football as is necessary to produce good teams" and enrolling in courses that would give them an even better command of the game. At Hampton Institute's first annual school for coaches, held in the fall of 1934, the white coach imported from Colgate University as a lecturer "expressed surprise at finding so many colored coaches who not only were interested in learning more about football, but who had already such a vast amount of information and experience regarding the teaching of the game. Colored coaches, he found, were not necessarily infants in the fine points of football."[84] Small wonder that thirty years earlier even a sympathetic white observer had asserted that blacks had "no natural aptitude" for the study of military tactics.[85] Shut out of leadership positions in the segregated armed services, blacks could now rehearse their roles as "field generals" in command of football players.

Of primary importance, however, was the fact that most blacks believed that their athletic achievement could improve race relations. "Athletics is the universal language," the Howard University newspaper declared in 1924. "By and through it we hope to foster a better and more fraternal spirit between the races in America and so to destroy prejudices; to learn and to be taught; to facilitate a universal brotherhood."[86] Writing in *Opportunity* in 1933, its editor, Elmer A. Carter, explained the appeal of the dynamic athlete as a response to the classic white male stereotype of American character:

> It is natural perhaps that a young and vigorous nation of pioneers should develop great respect and regard for physical prowess, for stamina and for that courage which finds expression in the heat of athletic competition. That the Negro was deficient in the qualities of which athletic champions are made was long one of the accepted shibboleths of the American people. That rare combination — stamina, skill and courage — it was commonly believed were seldom found under a black skin. Like many other myths concerning the Negro, this myth is being exploded. Not by theory, nor argument, but by performance.[87]

The implicit anti-intellectualism of this argument, which ranks physical performance above mere theory or argument, assumed more overt forms in other writings of this period, which pointed out how much more popular athletes were than thinkers. Edwin Bancroft Henderson argued that the white press had "referred to Negro athletic achievement more than to any other artistic, political or educational phase of Negro life."[88] In 1945 a columnist for the (black-edited) *Pittsburgh Courier* commented, "None of our scholars, scientists, artists or writers has received the popular acclaim" accorded to Joe Louis.[89]

Henderson went so far as to propose a psychosocial theory of athleticism's appeal that further devalued the role of thinking in human affairs. Black athletes like Joe Louis, he said in 1936, "have helped to increase tolerance and respect for Negro peoples by the great mass of Americans whose social behavior is modified more through their feelings and the thrills they experience than by recourse to principles of reasoning with regard to race," and he offered a physiological explanation of this effect: "Our keenest pleasures and most poignant pains are born of feelings rather than intellect. The whole biological history of man is recorded somewhere in these histological structures of the human glands and behavior patterns are recalled when the secretions of these glands seep into the blood." Only by undergoing a manipulation of their most deeply rooted emotions could whites overcome their racist feelings. Even if Negro "artisans and intellectuals" could impress some people of other races through "values that transcend the physical," it was "education through the physical" that was now pointing the way to racial understanding.[90]

In 1917 Henderson had coauthored an article on "Debating and Athletics in Colored Colleges," which saluted a more balanced approach to the development of black youth: "Debating is fast assuming a place of primary importance in the student activities of the colored schools. More than any physical exercise, it is an activity directly in line with the training of the class room. The development of the 'debating mind' is the result of a discipline severer and more concentrated than any class room exercise."[91] Whatever interest there may have been in developing the minds of black debaters, it does not figure in the major commentaries on African-American education that appeared for many years after this hopeful prediction. (In 1988 the New Orleans Public School Study on Black Males recommended "debate teams . . . and not just athletics" to redirect the energies and interests of black boys, but this idea does not seem to have spread.)[92] On the contrary, the new prestige of athletic achievement was becoming increasingly evident.

Following Joe Louis's victory over Primo Carnera in 1935, *The Crisis* offered its own assessment of which black aptitudes served the best interests of the race. Having confessed that they had gone "into something like ecstasy" when Louis won, the editors added a note of caution: "We do not advise our race to hitch its wagon to a boxer, or base its judgments of achievement on the size of a black man's biceps or the speed and power of his left hook." The problem was that even if blacks had the good sense not to overestimate the importance of biceps, whites (as Henderson argued) were not that rational. "Those who maintain that a Negro historian or editor or philosopher or scientist or composer or singer or poet or painter is more important than a great athlete are on sound ground, but they would be foolish to maintain that these worthy individuals have more power for influence than the athletes. After all, it is not the infinitesimal intellectual America which needs conversion on the race problem; it is the rank and file," who would never read or hear the works of black writers and artists.[93]

Such pessimism about the power of the rational faculties expressed a kind of pragmatism rather than anti-intellectualism. The real failure of vision inherent in this strategy was rooted in the improbable assumption that blacks were somehow less vulnerable to seduction by athleticism than their white fellow citizens. The evidence suggests instead that African Americans were exceptionally vulnerable to displays of black physical prowess because of their desperate need for "race heroes" of any kind.

# 2

# Jackie Robinson's Sad Song

## The Resegregation of American Sport

THE ARGUMENT for integrated sport has always been that inter-racial teams and events promote better race relations. There is undoubtedly some truth to this claim, even if these social benefits can be transitory and difficult to confirm. Indeed, the primary social value of integrated sport and its prominent role in the public sphere may well be to keep alive the idea that racial integration can actually work. If integrated sport boosts the morale of a multiracial society in this way, then it may buy time for more significant bridge-building measures to take effect. Yet even this commonsensical argument is vulnerable, because it may not anticipate certain unintended effects. The desegregation of American high schools, for example, was a historic and progressive social event, yet it also made possible the era of black dominance in high-profile sport and a new intensification of the African-American sports fixation. It marked the beginning of the end of the white sprinter in the United States and thereby breathed new life into traditional ideas about racial differences.

Acknowledging that the integration of sport is a complex social process was long unfashionable, because traditional ideas about the innocence and simplicity of the sports world placed it beyond the realm of social and political conflict. Today it is widely recognized that the sports world absorbs and displays the human flaws that afflict society as a whole: egotism, greed, drug abuse, hypocrisy about values, and all of our discomfort with the subject of race. There is, however, a conspicuous lack of interest in examining the racial dynamics of integrated sport. The presence of large numbers of black athletes in the major sports appears to have persuaded almost everyone that the process of integration has been a success. This sense of closure is an illusion that is rooted not in the fact of racial equality but in a combination of black apathy and white public relations efforts.

The integration of American sport has been accorded an almost millennial significance that has escaped serious scrutiny. "The integration of baseball," Jules Tygiel has written,

> represented both a symbol of imminent racial challenge and a direct agent of social change. Jackie Robinson's campaign against the color line in 1946–47 captured the imagination of millions of Americans who had previously ignored the nation's racial dilemma. For civil rights advocates the baseball experience offered a model of peaceful transition through militant confrontation, economic pressure, and moral suasion . . . Baseball was one of the first institutions in modern society to accept blacks on a relatively equal basis. The "noble experiment" thus reflects more than a saga of sport. It offers an opportunity to analyze the integration process in American life.[1]

While the personal heroism of Robinson and the social significance of this American drama are not in doubt, the legacy of this integrationist campaign has been a great deal of sentimentalism and a willed evasion of issues that are more complicated than the ideal of integration. Indeed, the enormous amount of attention that blacks and their liberal white sympathizers have paid to the Robinson saga and to Negro League baseball has long served as a distraction that has obscured racial struggles directly affecting the rights and dignity of far larger numbers of black Americans.

Influenced by his interest in promoting the baseball story, Tygiel makes contradictory claims about its importance. While he maintains that white Americans' reaction to the "Negro problem" in baseball "laid the foundations for the postwar onslaught against the color barrier," he concedes several pages later that it was "World War II, more than any other event, [that] caused Americans to re-evaluate their racial attitudes." This is an instructive lapse, in that it demonstrates the author's inclination to inflate the social significance of the black athlete in relation to his black male contemporaries. Of almost a million black servicemen drafted for World War II, thousands experienced far more dramatic ordeals during and after the conflict, but these experiences could not be presented as entertainment and have therefore disappeared from public consciousness. The overestimation of the black athlete's status in American society is also promoted by Tygiel's claim that Robinson represented "a type of black man far removed from prevailing stereotypes," an assessment that overlooks the dominant and demeaning stereotype of black physicality, which limits the stature of any black athlete in the white imagination.[2] The fact that Robinson's paramount biographer did not even see his protagonist in this context shows how easy it has been to equate black athletic self-assertion with racial progress without further reflection on how black athleticism can reinforce stereotypes instead of counteracting them.

Optimistic and unexamined assumptions about the effects of integrated sport have always encouraged the idea that the sports world is a kind of racial utopia. Here, as in few other social venues, wishful thinking has shaped assumptions about the usefulness of promoting integration as a form of social engineering. In fact, the social and political importance of pursuing integration within the sports world varies by historical period, but the wish to believe in its transforming power has persisted and is constantly assuming new and sometimes extravagant forms.

In 1948 the *Cleveland Plain Dealer* declared that white acceptance of black athletes was "more spectacular and noble than all the [Fair Employment Practices Commission] laws ever devised . . . Talents and skills are above city ordinances and they don't need their specious support."[3] Appearing only a year after Jackie Robinson's breakthrough into the major leagues, this editorial addressed a real turning point in American race relations. Yet we should recognize the hyperbole of this broadside for what it is — a white auto-intoxication that is fed by the impossible dream of being rid of racial conflict as a factor in everyday life. Twenty years after this editorial asserted that the goodwill inspired by black athletic talent vitiated the need for fair employment laws, *Sports Illustrated*'s justly famous series on the black athlete concluded that the social utility of integrated sport had proven to be largely fraudulent. "The cliché that sports has been good to the Negro," Jack Olsen wrote, "has been accepted by black and white, liberal and conservative, intellectual and red-neck." A retired basketball coach at the University of Kansas "says that the concept of sports as an integrating force is a myth in the first place, a legend nurtured by people who should know better." Most college coaches "go about in a dream world of race, imagining that they are assisting in the slow evolutionary process of integration" while remaining unaware of their own racist behavior.[4]

While neither the optimism of 1948 nor the disillusion of 1968 had any basis in formal social science research, Olsen's many interviews rendered him immune to the romantic view of the benevolent white coach and the contented black athlete as symbols of progress in race relations, and this independence made him a more reliable judge of events. Olsen argued that belief in the social efficacy of interracial sport rested on a false assumption about white racial psychology. What blacks did not realize, he said, "was that the white American was able to compartmentalize his attitude toward the Negro, to admire his exploits on the field but put him in the back of the bus on the way home" — the very point that William Pickens, of Talladega College, had made back in 1905. Tygiel too points to the psychological adjustment that at least partly neutralized the impact of integration on the white sensibility: "Confronted by the influx of black athletes, whom they widely regarded as 'entertainers,' southern whites seemed wary, but unthreatened. To most, racial traditions did not hinge upon occurrences on a baseball diamond."[5]

While this white perception of the black athlete as politically unthreatening made it possible to integrate baseball, it also preserved the black athlete's subordinate racial status, and this is the dirty little secret of the integrationist romance with sport. Even the self-styled and self-assertive black athlete of today, who would have been unthinkable in the days of Jackie Robinson, may have little or no positive impact on race relations.[6] More than a decade ago the critic Martha Bayles pointed out "the simple fact that whites can genuinely appreciate black cultural styles without necessarily acquiring new sympathy or liking for their black fellow citizens." This is an arresting thought precisely because we find it difficult to see black performances as unrelated to the forward or backward progress of race relations. "It is a powerful myth," Bayles notes, "shared by many performers, which decrees that widespread white acceptance of a black act can mean only one of two things: either the act is a coon show, or another breakthrough has occurred in American race relations."[7] The preintegration "coon show" phase of American sport insisted that the appeal of black athletic talent be subverted by mocking the Negro athlete as a clown, hence the popularity (and notoriety) of the Harlem Globetrotters. Reacting to the indignity of the "coon show," the "breakthrough" model imposed its own progressive interpretation on the integration of athletics, resulting in the hopeful and hortatory liberal historiography represented by Tygiel and many others.

One response to the forced choice between progressive and regressive interpretations of the black athlete is to make the more compelling case that the black athletic star exists for most whites primarily as a vehicle for advertising that exploits crossover appeal, even if this does not resolve all our questions about his social status. Arthur Ashe answered one such question by correctly asserting that "advertisers want somebody who's politically neutered."[8] That black athletes have been willing to conform to this standard is borne out by their conspicuous political quiescence; almost all African-American athletes have refused to constitute themselves as an interest group since the dramatic (and abortive) Black Power demonstration at the 1968 Mexico City Olympic Games. The only exceptional figure after 1968 was Muhammad Ali, a consummate one-man show for whom political action meant self-display rather than political organization. For this reason Ali's political career expired when he lost his championship and his health. His television advertisements for an insect-killing product late in his career were pathetic precisely because his audience understood that they were witnessing the political emasculation of a singularly rebellious black athlete. The hiatus in racial politics that has persisted in the American sports world since his demise as a militant testifies to the skill with which the college and professional sports establishments have colonized our most celebrated form of racial theater.

The illusory (or "virtual") integration of American sports serves commercial empires that could not survive without black athletes: the National Collegiate Athletic Association (NCAA), the professional football, basketball, and baseball leagues, and the United States Olympic Committee, whose success has been largely underwritten by black sprinters, jumpers, and basketball players since the 1960s. The racial equilibrium that prevails within these fiefdoms is the product of a genuinely colonial arrangement that has preserved traditional white hierarchies in an era of so-called black dominance. When the imperialist Henry Morton Stanley looked at black Africans in 1885 and announced that "the force of those masses of muscle had become marketable and valuable," he was anticipating the athletic market to come as well as more conventional uses of black labor.[9] The essence of Western colonialism has always been the monopolizing of authority and prerogatives by men of European origin, and these prerogatives have always included the mastery of administration and technology, which keeps the "natives" in a premodern state.

Resistance to a colonial interpretation of race relations in the American sports world is rooted in an uncritical faith in the model of equal opportunity, which envisions a linear expansion of minority participation and power over time. Within the sports world, however, the expansion predicted by this model has been very limited, and there is no reason to believe it will increase substantially in the foreseeable future. At a time when black political power is actually shrinking, there is no political mandate to enhance black representation in any social sector. The sports media, which serve predominantly white audiences, see no advantage in ceding a share of their power to blacks; the black media (and the black middle class they serve) have embraced the abundance of black athletic celebrities as emblems of racial achievement. There is not enough black wealth to purchase controlling ownership in professional teams or major media, and black athletes, like the vast majority of elite athletes around the world, possess neither the interest nor the political sophistication to mount a campaign against the prevailing order of things.

This imbalance of power has made integrated sport an arrangement of convenience, a mutually profitable racial truce, rather than a partnership in a more meaningful sense. The real symbiotic alliance is between the white administrators and owners of college and professional teams and the white-dominated media, which employ very few blacks to write about sports or broadcast the games. What is more, black access to the media seldom translates into distinctively black or antiestablishmentarian viewpoints. Only a few black sportswriters show any interest in social issues, and racial militancy on the air is virtually unthinkable for the black sportscaster who wants to keep his job.[10] Both he and his white counterpart are expected to provide relief from societal complications, not to exacerbate them by making discomfiting observations about racial politics. (The on-the-air deference routinely shown to team owners by sportscasters is only the most blatant sign of fealty to the powers that be.) These limitations, whether voluntary or involuntary, are inherent in sports journalism, which routinely combines factual reporting and promotional work on behalf of the industry it serves. Investigative reporting is a rarity on the sports page, not to mention in televised sportscasts, because there is little incentive to criticize the industries that help to support newspapers and networks. More sophisticated media such as the *New York Times* and *Sports Illustrated* exercise their social consciences infrequently while functioning primarily as pillars of the status quo, creating a general perception among their readers that illicit drug use, self-serving sports bureaucrats, and racial tensions are exceptional conditions rather than the institutionalized phenomena they are. Lacking intellectual curiosity, reformist zeal, and the professional aggressiveness that is characteristic of investigative reporters, most people working in the sports media do their part to present the American sports world as a theater of reconciliation that is largely untroubled by the racial tensions in other sectors of American society.

The National Basketball Association has for many years offered the most interesting interracial theater in the sports world, combining white managerial control, black athletic domination (now more than 80 percent of the players and virtually all of the superstars), and a crossover appeal that has combined the efforts of league executives, major advertisers (like Nike and Gatorade), and "creative" advertising personnel, who are assisted on occasion by the "black nationalist" film director Spike Lee.[11] The result is what might be called "virtual integration," the illusion of a genuinely collaborative biracial community that has resolved the conflicts the rest of society cannot.[12] Charles Grantham, the black executive director of the NBA Players Association, offered this assessment in 1991: "A few years ago the NBA was perceived on Madison Avenue as being too black and too drug-infested. Once that was turned around, the league was able to promote its new personalities as exciting stars who were caring and concerned about their communities."[13]

In addition to creating the illusion of substantial player involvement in the black community, this theater of pseudo-reconciliation also serves to mitigate the pathos of American segregation, as Peter de Jonge has pointed out, by creating one-sided relationships between white fans and the black athletes they admire from afar: "In the last decade, the N.B.A., long considered too black to attract a mainstream audience, has prospered by giving middle-class whites, desperate for some semblance of a connection to black America, a series of unthreatening yet bigger-than-life cartoon superheroes called Magic, Michael, Charles and Shaquille."[14] Far from concealing this manipulative campaign, the president of the NBA, David Stern, has boasted of the league's image-based strategy to gentrify its black giants and in the process create crossover market appeal in the manner of the Disney entertainment empire: "They have theme parks, and we have theme parks. Only we call them arenas. They have characters: Mickey and Goofy. Our characters are named Magic and Michael [Jordan]. Disney sells apparel; we sell apparel. They make home videos; we make home videos."[15] This mythifying, deracializing strategy transforms black athletic superiority into "magical" entertainment — the fabled leaping ability of the black player is incorporated into playfully surreal television and magazine ads for athletic shoes and energizing drinks.

The more cynical purpose of the crossover marketing strategy is to encourage affluent young whites to adopt the athletic clothing and speech styles of black "homeboys" while learning nothing else about black life. The barren emotional landscape of the ghetto is converted into pure style, so that a white male audience can take a vicarious walk on the wild side. As one black NBA player put it, "They want to dress like them, talk like them, everything except live in the same neighborhood."[16] The postmodern rationalization for this kind of cultural borrowing conforms perfectly to the operative conceit of the NBA — that race has ceased to be a societal issue and is now a style issue. Race is seen here as "freed from genes and made available to the will, as the rootedness of racial style evanesces in absurdity" and racial identity goes onto the market as a commodity available to any purchaser of rap music or athletic apparel or a black hairstyle.[17]

The white managerial monopoly is only slightly less complete in the NBA than in the other major professional sports or the Division I universities regulated by the NCAA. While the league's official position on race is that it is "colorblind," its real position is one of avoiding the issue. "The N.B.A. doesn't want you to think or read about its racial issues," as one journalist aptly put it in 1995.[18] Reinforcing the image of colonial hierarchy are countless television images of well-groomed white coaches who look like business executives, dressed in jackets and ties and appearing to be clearly in charge of their sweating, half-dressed black players. Here the integrated sports world functions symbolically as a modernizing school of discipline in which the wilder impulses of the black male are domesticated by putting him in a uniform and making his athleticism the product of an organization with white corporate values and organizational strategies. This arrangement is well suited to satisfy audience expectations, judging from a 1991 poll about race and sport, which showed that "whites tend to endorse a social order that keeps whites in the leadership positions and thinking positions."[19] The white corporate style has also been adopted by certain hard-driving high school coaches. As one disciplinarian put it, "I demand uniformity from my [white] players. I always felt the most successful companies are very uniform."[20]

This view is shared by the NBA commissioner, David Stern, who is more interested in acquiring compelling images of white authority than in finding blacks to integrate the head coaching ranks. At the end of the 1993–94 season, *Sports Illustrated* reported that Stern wanted to bring Duke University head coach Mike Krzyzewski into the NBA as a model leader to dampen the growing disorder: "The commissioner worries privately about the league's growing problem with trash talking and violence, and a hire like Krzyzewski — intelligent, disciplined, respected — would be a public relations coup."[21] White managerial authority is often reinforced by a coach's emphasis on systematic planning and the use of up-to-date technology. A 1993 profile of John Lucas, the newly hired (and instantly successful) black head coach of the San Antonio Spurs, drew a sharp distinction between his style of leadership as a sympathetic mentor to black players and the white "fast-talking tough guys who 'get the most' out of" their young blacks. The modern white stereotype is that of the "strategy guru," the "Telestrator type" who is attached to his electronic drawing board and puts in endless hours studying game films like a military planner. During the 1980s, Harvey Araton writes, "many N.B.A. coaches became as cloistered as their football counterparts, who often imagine themselves protecting great Pentagon secrets." Stan Albeck, the white coach whom Lucas replaced, reacted to his dismissal by implying that Lucas was not cerebral enough to be a tactician in the white mold: "He's a master psychologist, but does that override your inability to draw up a play? I don't know."[22]

In the early 1990s NBA teams became interested in mobile computing devices; by 1993 all twenty-seven were equipped with IBM Thinkpad notebooks loaded with specialized basketball software that coaches and scouts could use to diagram and store up to ninety-nine plays per team.[23] The racial meaning of these technological innovations derives from traditional ideas about the inability of blacks to master military tactics or machinery. "African cultures," Michael Adas has noted, "were considered by almost all nineteenth-century European observers to be devoid of scientific thinking and all but the most primitive technology," and the legacy of this mindset has persisted throughout the twentieth century.[24] In the 1930s half of all Americans agreed that "members of the Negro race are ill-adapted for work with machines."[25] The reluctance of American authorities to employ blacks in weapons factories or let them fly military aircraft during World War II was rooted in the same lack of confidence in their technological aptitude that continues to play a role in severely restricting their access to head coaching positions in college and professional sports, which retain a symbolic military ambiance (police escorts are still mandated for the more prominent southern football coaches). "All-white units compose the most effective fighting teams," said General Mark Clark, the former commander of United Nations forces in Korea, in 1956, fully eight years after the integration of the U.S. armed services.[26]

White supremacism, which denigrates the black man's capacity to lead, is part of a long racist tradition that survives within the officially biracial world of the NBA as a determination to reserve almost all leadership positions for whites. This monopoly on managerial and technological competence is the essence of any colonial arrangement, and it is instructive to see how effectively the managers of the most "integrated" sports industry have been able to preserve it a full generation after the breakthroughs of the civil rights movement. The de facto invisibility of this colonial order is made possible by the reluctance of the sports media to interpret conflicts between white management and black athletes as symptoms of racial tension.

White managerial control of the NBA favors the orchestration rather than the full domestication of its black athletes. The racial paradox of the NBA and some other sectors of the sports world is that they both exploit and control black violence like a commodity. The "Bad Boys" video marketed in 1988 by N.B.A. Properties, featuring "a montage of elbows, body slams and assorted flagrant fouls" committed by the Detroit Pistons during their successful 1987–88 season, markets what is perceived as black criminality in a sublimated form.[27] At the same time, the NBA-media partnership must enforce minimum standards of civility to preserve the relationship, such as it is, between the athletes and their public; when, for example, Shaquille O'Neal and other members of the Orlando Magic refused to talk to the media during the 1995 playoffs, the NBA's vice president of communications told the press, "I'm sure you'll see an increased spirit of cooperation after the next game," and the NBA commissioner threatened to fine teams if players did not behave in a media-friendly fashion.[28]

Such incidents only confirm that racial cohabitation as it is practiced in the NBA is a less amicable and less stable arrangement than it appears to be on television or on the typical sports page. This fraying at the edges of the truce is important both as a symptom of disordered race relations in the larger society and as a potential instigator of defiant behavior among black youths who imitate highly publicized athletes. It is also a test of the media's ability to deracialize conflicts in order to retain their white audience and preserve the crossover appeal of major stars who endorse products for advertisers. As the financial power of the prominent black players grows, the sports media feel constrained to extinguish a constant stream of brushfires that may signal racial discontent.

The "inexplicable" anger of Alonzo Mourning illustrates this constant uncertainty, or what has been called the "latent crisis" of colonial rule.[29] "The media think I'm an angry person," Mourning told an interviewer, "an out-of-control player. But I think my game thrives off intensity."[30] There was even a time when Michael Jordan criticized management "with an angry edge to his voice and a hard stare," the precise meaning of which was open to interpretation.[31] The essence of such performances is the ambiguous status of publicly expressed black anger: is the "mask of rage" or "hard stare" the result of black outrage, or is it simply the idiosyncracy of a particular player? ("It's my intensity level on the floor," says Mourning.) A similar ambiguity attaches to the assurance that the black athlete offers the white sportswriter and his public — that there is nothing racially specific (or threatening) about his behavior or facial expression. There are probably black NBA players who could make such a statement and mean it, but is the moody Mourning one of them? Was he speaking sincerely, or did he tell his white fans what he knew they wanted to hear? The clear purpose of the sportswriter who interviewed him was to soften the angry image; in the course of doing so, he described the difficult life of a onetime foster child who now did volunteer work but was still angry enough to want to "strangle" any child abuser he might encounter. Having been introduced as a potential threat, Mourning was now redeemed as a citizen.

The black athlete who makes a boorish statement about race is likely to get a less sympathetic journalistic reception, especially if he has already established himself as a notorious character. When the *Chicago Tribune* sports columnist Bernie Lincicome reported that Charles Barkley had said he hated whites, he protested the double standard that applies to race talk by playing a racial card of his own. While whites in the sports world who publicly express disdain for blacks are often punished, Lincicome correctly noted, blacks are not penalized for comparable offenses. For this white sportswriter, however, the argument for evenhandedness was not enough, and he proceeded to cut Barkley down to size, insisting with cold irony that the offense was in fact moot, because "the point is, nothing Charles Barkley has to say about anything is important. Nothing any jock who is not Bill Bradley has to say about anything is important."[32] Brandishing this evenhanded disdain, the writer proclaimed every professional athlete — with the exception of the white Rhodes Scholar turned U.S. senator — an intellectual and political nullity, thereby implying that not a black man in the NBA had an opinion worth hearing.

Increasing defiance of white managerial control in recent years has made it more difficult to conceal racial tensions from the public. Sportswriters and sportscasters, who are the primary interpreters of race relations within the NBA, are also protagonists in these conflicts. Of these two intermediaries, the live sportscaster is the more important representative of managerial power, because he has the power to frame issues and interpret behavior instantly to enormous audiences. This custodial role became evident in March 1995 during an on-the-air tantrum by a white television announcer over the perceived insubordination of a black player, Latrell Sprewell of the Golden State Warriors, who had written the uniform numbers of two departed teammates on the backs of his sneakers. Sprewell, the announcer warned, had better learn what the "nature of this business" was, and this did not include symbolic protests against trading players.[33]

Other, more cryptic behaviors seem to invite psychiatric interpretation, raising the uncomfortable possibility that a mostly white audience is watching the disintegration of a black personality that has been overwhelmed by the pressures of race. In 1994 Kevin Johnson of the Phoenix Suns told a columnist for the *Arizona Republic* that he had once invented an evil alter ego for himself, a fast-talking bad guy named Mevin Johnson: "I put these dark glasses on and start talking slang, like a hip-hop guy," he said. After two violent incidents during games, the columnist started to wonder if Kevin had begun to assume the personality of Mevin on the court. "KJ doesn't have a split personality," the columnist assured his readers, dismissing the possibility that black athletes might be acting out the social schizophrenia that is an integral part of the African-American experience.[34]

The most bizarre personality currently on display in the NBA is that of Dennis Rodman, once of the Detroit Pistons and the San Antonio Spurs and then a starting player for the Chicago Bulls. With his brightly tinted hair and clearly displayed tattoos, Rodman is the defiant self-mutilator of the NBA, a public-relations nightmare who is impossible to diagnose and hard to expel from the kinky world of American entertainment on the basis of eccentricity alone. Despite Rodman's obvious wish to depart from the black phenotype — a self-transformational urge that has brought notoriety to Michael Jackson — even his black interpreters have treated him as an isolated case rather than as the exemplar of a black malaise engendered by a racist environment. "Don't let him back on a basketball court," wrote the black sports columnist Bryan Burwell, "until all those mysterious demons that are buzzing around in his head are eliminated."[35] But how are we to disentangle Rodman's personal demons from the more general problem of being black in a society that regards most black males as dangerous or superfluous? White spectators might see Dennis Rodman as the latest black clown act. But how many African Americans look past his antics and find themselves engaged in the spectacle of his loneliness and psychic pain?

The slow unraveling of white authority in the NBA has thus been occurring in the public arena rather than in the boardrooms where policy is made. This erosion has been made possible by the power vested in celebrated black athletes by major sponsors, who are less interested in preserving league discipline than in promoting the images of their spokesmen. Because the endorsement fees paid to major stars often exceed their NBA salaries, those stars' primary loyalty is to the corporations that fund them and the advertising experts who create their public images. ("What I really want is that commercial to establish me as a unique person" is how one NBA head coach paraphrases this mindset.)[36] The intensified commercialism of the game has now subverted the traditional chain of command on the court to the point where the authority of white managerial types is being frequently challenged. When Scottie Pippen of the Chicago Bulls said in December 1994 that the team was collapsing and the general manager, Jerry Krause, was a liar, he was not even disciplined.[37] A white columnist for the *Chicago Tribune* came to Krause's defense by cleverly playing on the physical contrast between the sleek black athlete and the aging, physically unkempt white bureaucrat, whose untended body — "fat" and "rumpled" — was presented as a sign of integrity, with no apologies made: "In an age of cosmetic surgery, when style matters more than substance, Krause can't or won't go with the photogenic flow."[38] Rearguard actions like this have become common as whites respond defensively to conflicts in an increasingly black sports world whose racial dimension is seldom discussed in the press.

The most evident symptom of racial confrontation in the NBA (and to a lesser degree in college basketball) has been the "burned-out" white coach who finally succumbs to the alleged intransigence and churlish behavior of his black athletes. These confrontations, which are almost always narrated by white sportswriters, are interesting because they express both modern and archaic aspects of the power balance between the races. They are modern events in that blacks sometimes prevail and may even be conceded a modicum of good judgment, as when Ira Berkow of the *New York Times* argued that the young Earvin (Magic) Johnson of the Los Angeles Lakers showed a better understanding of basketball strategy than the head coach he managed to evict.[39] These confrontations are archaic in that their dramatic suspense hinges on whether the wisdom and authority of the older white man will prevail over the emotional instability of the young black.

In January 1995 there was suddenly a great deal of coverage of this culture war. "In a lot of ways, the stuff we put up with as coaches is insane," said George Karl, the head coach of the Seattle Supersonics. It is no longer possible for an NBA coach to play the raging white autocrat in the style of the racist football coaches of the Old South, and it has become increasingly difficult in college basketball as well; the intemperate and foul-mouthed Bob Knight of Indiana University, who brandished a whip over a black player in 1992, is the last surviving practitioner of white rage among coaches, and his symbolic value to the old guard will persist as white power in the sports world slowly recedes. This loss of stature has at times compelled white sportswriters to find sympathetic images for beleaguered coaches who can no longer be presented as hard-jawed authoritarians still in control of their blacks. Battered by public criticism from two of his black stars, the "congenial" head coach of the Denver Nuggets, Dan Issel ("a very sensitive human being"), resigned that January in a state of emotional exhaustion.[40] Sam Smith of the *Chicago Tribune* was also beating the drums that hectic month for Don Nelson, head coach of the Golden State Warriors, who found himself bewildered by and estranged from the young star Chris Webber. "Root for him not to fall to the monsters of greed, immaturity and selfishness," wrote Smith, "root for Don Nelson for the sake of seeing someone who does a job well remain . . . as a symbol of resistance in the fight to retain discipline in the NBA."[41] In February Nelson resigned. "Once a revered leader of men," said the *New York Times,* "Nelson is the latest coach unable to master Generation X." Even the liberal *Times* called his young black antagonist "an oversensitive manchild" who had never been taught discipline in college.[42]

Nor was this conflict a strictly black-versus-white affair. Black sportswriters also criticized the behavior of the most controversial players.[43] Phil Taylor's cover story in *Sports Illustrated* was more alarmist in tone than any of Sam Smith's pointed commentaries:

> A form of insanity is spreading through the NBA like a virus, threatening to infect every team in the league. Alarmingly, its carriers, pouting prima donnas who commit the most outrageous acts of rebellion, include some of the league's younger stars. There is a new outbreak nearly every week, with yet another player skipping practice, refusing his coach's orders to go into a game, demanding a trade or finding some new and creative way to act unprofessionally. Fines are levied, suspensions imposed, but such measures are nothing in the face of the epidemic. The lunacy is contagious. Madness reigns.[44]

(Taylor's hyperbolic emphasis on mental pathology is striking. "The nigger's crazy," says a character in *Huckleberry Finn,* evoking a long and ignoble racist tradition.) In March 1995 the black icon Michael Jordan,

who had once employed his own "hard stare" when confronting management, returned to the NBA and was immediately hailed by the press
as a disciplinarian who would set an example for the unstable young
vandals who were ruining the game.[45]

The most popular explanation of these confrontations is that they
express tensions between generations possessing different standards of
behavior, hence the reference to Generation X and the publicly expressed wish that the messianic "elder statesman" Michael Jordan
might inaugurate a new era of improved deportment. The appeal of the
generational interpretation is that it offers an alternative to the more
discomfiting possibility that problems inside the NBA are symptomatic
of the racial imbalance of power within the league, or even of the racial
hostilities that afflict American society as a whole. While this is surely
the case to some degree, there is no question but that the generational
argument is partially valid. The revered college coach John Wooden,
who had good relations with his black players at UCLA in the 1960s and
1970s, has lamented the physicality, showmanship, and taunting that
typify the modern game, in contrast to the self-effacing team play he
taught during his long career, and there are doubtless many older blacks
who would agree with him.[46] There is, as Alvin Poussaint said in 1987,
"a lot of anger within the black community toward the young black
man," and it is logical to assume that some of this is directed at conspicuous young malefactors who do their acting-out as highly publicized
athletes.[47] Behind this conflict is the largely unremarked contrast between the behavioral norms of the quasi-invisible African-American
middle class and the highly publicized underclass behaviors that are
constantly being presented as characteristic of blacks as a racial group.
This is an important topic, yet I have never seen a study of the defense
mechanisms employed by middle-class blacks to cope with a constant
barrage of pathological images, including the drug addictions, sexual
assaults, and other crimes of famous black athletes.

The generational hypothesis cannot account, however, for the deepest tensions between blacks and whites in the NBA and elsewhere in the
sports world. The fundamental schisms result from the colonial imbalance of power as well as contrasting cultural styles and the divergent
value systems they represent. While any theory of black and white
cultural styles invites a degree of oversimplification, there is a broad
transracial consensus that some cultural differences, pertaining especially to music, language, and sport, are real and important elements of
racial identity, for blacks in particular.

In *Black and White Styles in Conflict,* Thomas Kochman points out that establishing "an underlying structure to black behavior" has served to refute the once influential view that an autonomous black culture did not even exist. "The Negro is only an American and nothing else," the sociologist Nathan Glazer wrote in 1963. "He has no values and culture to guard and protect."[48] While it is hard today to imagine a comparable degree of educated ignorance about black culture, there is also a greater awareness of black urban disorder. Kochman's impeccably liberal analysis accents the positive aspects of black style to the point of romantic indulgence, emphasizing black vitality and improvisation in contrast to white sobriety and rationality, which come off as lifeless by comparison. The "black argumentative mode" does not aim at achieving "totally neutral objectivity"; whereas whites "debate an issue as impersonally as possible," blacks reject the white norm that one should "behave calmly, rationally, unemotionally and logically when negotiating," which makes possible the "greater capacity of blacks to express themselves forcefully." The "animation and vitality of black expressive behavior" require "a mind/body involvement of considerable depth," which is uncharacteristic of whites. Not surprisingly, then, "there is a difference between the way blacks and whites walk," reflecting the role of the body in the expression of cultural style. While blacks supposedly do not inhibit their emotions in unhealthy ways — a particularly unfortunate generalization — "white culture compels individuals to internalize and repress anger."[49]

Such exercises in empathetic cross-cultural understanding are particularly vulnerable to an overcredulous reliance on how the Other represents himself. Half a century ago Gunnar Myrdal commented, "This trait of singing and dancing is so deep in the American Negro's culture that he sometimes falls into the white man's error of talking of it as a racial trait: 'white people have no rhythm'; 'they can't dance with feeling'; 'whites are naturally cold.'"[50] The black psychiatrists William Grier and Price Cobbs, by contrast, argue that these internalized stereotypes serve the purpose of creating a distinctive black identity: "By appearing to accept the ethnic stereotypes that are intended to depreciate them, they turn these stereotypes to their own group purpose." This legitimacy is also accorded to racial athletic aptitude: "The stereotype that Negroes have some kind of animal-like capacity to excel in athletic events is embraced by blacks who say: 'Yes, we are stronger, swifter, and more beautifully coordinated than the whites.'" This stereotype "and other demeaning attributes are turned to a positive and elevating use, and continue to bind black people together with a sense of identity and group solidarity."[51] The fact that these sophisticated men are willing to incorporate an "animal-like" athletic ability into black identity is more evidence of the "physicalizing" of the African-American self-image even among black professionals.

Sport and music are the two great theaters of black style, which Kochman characterizes as "more self-conscious, more expressive, more expansive, more colorful, more intense, more assertive, more aggressive, and more focused on the individual than is the style of the larger society of which blacks are a part." Today Kochman's analysis of race-specific sport styles has become part of American folk wisdom about racial difference. Differences in basketball style reflect "the more animated and energetic black style" of the athlete as well as conflicts regarding the meaning of team play. "The black athlete . . . adds elements of performance style — vitality and individuality — to the team's shared goal of winning the game." White hostility to black style is due in part to the fact that "whites view many of the moves that blacks make for style to be irrelevant to the concepts of 'team' and 'winning.' They are considered extraneous to the concept of efficiency, which requires that only simple, straightforward, and necessary moves be made." Consequently, it is accurate to describe "the coach-dominated white style of play as machine-like, characterized by mechanical repetition and interchangeable parts, although it is definitely also warlike in its exclusive focus on winning." Responding to this surfeit of bureaucratic rationality, the black athlete cultivates an improvisational style that suggests "he is no longer properly subordinating himself to the complete authority of the coach."[52]

Precisely because of his excellent intentions, Kochman's portrait of conflicting racial styles walks a fine line between descriptive analysis and caricature, between sympathetic understanding and apologetic rationalization of behaviors that are disadvantageous in ways the author does not seem to understand. At the same time, Kochman could not anticipate fifteen years ago the degree to which high-profile sports would magnify for public consumption the foibles and crimes of black athletes, which can only reinforce traditional ideas about the dangerous and unstable black male. Defining "black style" is thus inseparable from making judgments about its wholesome or unwholesome effects and the values they represent.

In addition, the cultural significance of black style has changed over time. "From the beginning," *Ebony* told its readers in 1995, "Negro Leagues baseball distinguished itself from that in the Major Leagues with a more daring, exciting and aggressive style of game that utilized speed."[53] Today, however, black style has lost the novelty and the innocence of the Jackie Robinson era and is often associated with the ritual-ized taunting known as "trash talking" and with what some whites regard as exhibitionistic displays after dunks are made or touchdowns are scored. What is more, these displays have created a considerable amount of tension along racial lines within the NBA and the National Football League (NFL). "How long is it going to be," asks Scott Skiles, one of the NBA's more outspoken white players, "before every single play needs some kind of trash talking or celebration?"[54] The president of the Utah Jazz, Frank Layden, has said he would like to root out the exhibitionistic style — "the trash talking, the sloppy uniforms, all that in-your-face stuff" that has "influenced an entire generation of play-ers."[55] The racial irony of this "excessive" black behavior is that it appears to please white audiences even as it tests the patience of many white coaches.

The popular success of such showboating behavior raises an interest-ing point about the relationship between uninhibited black performers and the whites who watch them. Today's overwhelmingly white NBA audiences seem to be less interested in watching a white coach disci-pline an unruly black player than in watching black athletes act out the "dangerous" stereotypes of black masculinity in a safe setting. This balance between estrangement and attraction, between the urge to dis-cipline and the desire to enjoy the racially exotic performer, is inher-ently unstable, and its role in shaping race relations in the United States remains unclear.

The artificiality of the social bond between white spectators and black athletes was dramatically demonstrated at a Rutgers University basketball game in February 1995 in the wake of a controversial remark made by the university's president, Francis L. Lawrence. Speaking to faculty members in a closed meeting shortly after the publication of *The Bell Curve,* he referred to "a disadvantaged population that doesn't have that genetic hereditary background" for high-level academic per-formance. When this remark was made public, a scandal ensued, and on the evening of February 7 black student protestors interrupted a basket-ball game between Rutgers and the University of Massachusetts. Mem-bers of the audience demanded that the (mostly black) teams play for them, and demonstrators reported that white spectators shouted epi-thets like "Niggers and spics . . . Go back to Africa" and threw paper at them.[56] Few incidents could better illustrate the double consciousness of whites who can accept blacks as performers but not as citizens with real grievances.

While many whites have hostile or ambivalent feelings about black athletic style, many blacks embrace this expressiveness as an authentic form of Afrocentric self-assertion. Even Arthur Ashe, the most "integrated" of black athletes, said that he took pride in this kind of cultural difference. The writer who extols "the Black game's verticality, intensity, and panache" signals his belief in separate racial worlds even if he does not mean to do so. Small wonder that some militant Afrocentrists see the athletic arena as a theater of racial defiance and adopt black athletes as symbols of racial style. The physically imposing Afrocentrist can even adopt the athletic style as his own, as when the demagogic Professor Leonard Jeffries "moves across the [City College] campus like a heavyweight champion, trailed by an entourage that often includes bodyguards."[57] Professor Kariamu Asante, a member of the large Afrocentric establishment at Temple University, has invoked the supreme athletic icon on behalf of African-American cultural distinctiveness: "When you see Michael Jordan going to the hoop . . . you're seeing the African-American approach to things. Some may call it a 'natural' phenomenon. It's really a cultural phenomenon, based in rhythm. It's what these athletes grow up with. From the moment they're carried into the room as babies, they're immersed in an environment of rhythm that's rooted in traditional African culture."[58] As we shall see, it is a small step from talk about African rhythms to the Afrocentric lunatic fringe and its biological theory of black athletic supremacy.

Many blacks embrace with relish the idea of their own physical superiority; prominent athletes such as O. J. Simpson, Joe Morgan, Carl Lewis, and Barry Bonds have made public statements to the effect that black success in sports is due to the fact that blacks are physically superior to whites. While this view challenges current norms of political correctness, black violations are seldom publicized, even though whites are pilloried for expressing the same ideas. When a candidate for the presidency of Michigan State University was rejected in 1993 because of statements he had once made about the anatomical superiority of black athletes, a black columnist for the University of Michigan newspaper reported that what this white academic had said was no different from "what I've heard numerous black people say in private conversations."[59]

Finally, there are the melanin theorists, a motley collection of pseudoscientific cranks and better-known members of the black academic demimonde who attended the Fourth Annual World Melanin Conference in Dallas in April 1989 — Leonard Jeffries, John Henrik Clarke, Ivan Van Sertima, and others. For these racial biologists, the pigment that makes skin dark is "the Chemical Key to Black Greatness" and accounts for an entire range of superior black aptitudes: "The reason why Black athletes do so well and have these 'natural moves' is these melanic tracks in the brainstem tie into the cerebellum . . . a part of us that controls motor movement" (Dr. Richard King).[60] The real significance of melanin theory is that it is the *reductio ad absurdum* of black racial separatism, putting its adherents in a de facto alliance with white racists, who have their own reasons to establish separate racial physiologies. Afrocentric science curricula that promote melanin theory have been introduced in a number of urban school districts in the United States, thereby doing educational damage to those children who can least afford it.[61] Blacks who claim a racial advantage in "motor movement" ought to be aware that the racist (White) Citizens Council has made a point of publicizing research reporting precocious motor development in black infants.[62]

Similarly, the claim that blacks have a rhythmic gift is a deeply rooted racial stereotype that many blacks as well as whites have accepted.[63] "Today," a black physical educator wrote in 1939, the Negro "is looked upon as being exceptionally rhythmical, expressing himself in a way that is peculiar to his race."[64] More recently, one black author has noted the "strong rhythmic mode of walking" of his people, and the choreographer Alvin Ailey referred to "the rubato [rhythmic flexibility] of the black body."[65] But the black sense of rhythm has the same ambiguous status as other allegedly racial traits. One noted academic proponent of black intellectual inferiority, the racial psychologist Michael Levin, has called the sense of rhythm "perhaps the most tabooed" of the "noncognitive race differences" and proposed that "the evolutionary origin of this aspect of Negroid culture and its connection to personality may well repay investigation."[66] The authors of *The Bell Curve* gladly endorse the view of one Wade Boykin, "one of the most prominent academic advocates of a distinctive black culture," that movement, rhythm, music, and dance belong to "that mix of qualities that makes the American black clan unique and (appropriately in the eyes of the clan) superior."[67] In short, blacks who flirt with the often hazy boundary between culture and biology should not be surprised when their findings are endorsed by white supremacists.

Sportive Afrocentrism is one symptom of the larger cultural estrangement that separates blacks and whites in American society. Within the sports world this estrangement is the product of the conflict between cultural temperaments described above: "classroom" (white) basketball versus "schoolyard" (black) ball, "the straight way" versus "the black way." Although this conflict represents a fateful divergence rather than the result of a perverse wish to alienate the racial adversary, arguments over style eventually turn into disagreements about cultural (meaning racial) values and character. This clash of styles is frequently commented on by white sportswriters, whose traditional distinction between the "natural" black athlete and his more industrious, more cerebral white counterpart has been the target of much black resentment. When Isiah Thomas, the Detroit Pistons star, caused a scandal in 1987 by claiming that the celebrated Larry Bird was overrated because he was white, he argued that his real concern "was not so much Larry Bird but the perpetuation of stereotypes about blacks. When Bird makes a great play, it's due to his thinking, and his work habits. It's all planned out by him. It's not the case for blacks. All we do is run and jump. We never practice or give a thought to how we play. It's like I came dribbling out of my mother's womb."[68]

Despite this and subsequent media scandals about the stereotyping of African-American athletes, sportswriters and the whites they quote continue to employ a racial characterology that sometimes draws on traditional white male archetypes, such as that of the military man. Thus Phil Jackson, head coach of the Chicago Bulls and once a fabled liberal free spirit of the NBA, contrasts today's "bad boys," meaning blacks such as Charles Barkley and Dennis Rodman, with Mickey Mantle and Stan Musial, the white "warriors" of yesteryear.[69] Rich Kotite, former head coach of the Philadelphia Eagles, once characterized his black quarterback Randall Cunningham as deficient in a vaguely military sense: "He's not a Phil Simms or Joe Montana type that teammates seem ready to go to war for."[70] A white college basketball star from a working-class background is depicted as "a blue-collar warrior."[71] Chuck Cecil, an otherwise obscure white free safety for the Phoenix Cardinals, appears on the cover of *Sports Illustrated* ("Is Chuck Cecil Too Vicious for the NFL?") simply because he has become known as an unusually violent, out-of-control hitter. "He's a hero to every small, slow kid in the secondary," says his former coach, employing coded language that refers to whites.[72] Underlying such positive characterizations of white athletes is a touchy defensiveness in response to black dominance that draws on the traditional denigration of black military aptitude and recalls similar white reactions during the colonial encounters of the British Empire.

The racial characterology that has developed in American sport since integration has grown out of what were perceived to be different attitudes toward the meaning of the sports experience. Jack Olsen's pioneering study of the black college athlete concluded in 1968 that even black dominance in a sport did not change the fact that "the essential character of the game, the ethics and folkways, remain white." The difference between the white ethos and "the black or 'soul' way," he says, "shows up most clearly before a game. For as long as sports historians can remember, the white way to prepare for a game has been to sit around looking somber, serious, almost funereal. Too much is at stake out there today for any joking around." In contrast, black athletes "look on it as a game," a college football player told Olsen. "We're relaxed. But the coaches will look at you and frown if you're not getting yourself all psyched up like the white athletes do."[73] This emphasis on mobilizing body and soul for the struggle ahead clearly imitates a kind of military preparedness, which blacks may feel is a vestige of the militant white supremacy of the Old South. Indeed, the sheer force of white willpower, contrasted with black passivity, is an important theme in the proslavery literature of the 1850s. Bertram Wyatt-Brown has pointed out that the white southerner "insisted that the white naturally assumed command in play and sport owing to superior genetic endowment, and the black naturally learned the proper role of subordinate."[74]

While black dominance has done much to challenge this racial hierarchy, the unofficial white supremacist ethos of the modern American sports world is still evident in its colonial power structure, the paucity of black coaches and quarterbacks, and racial typologies that usually imply difference by accentuating "white" virtues such as attachment to tradition, mental acuity, and true grit. Gary Williams, the white basketball coach at the University of Maryland, is thus described as "one of those classic guys who succeeded through diligent labor"; now he sees a generation of black players who build up their bodies to play an essentially physical game and neglect the "lost art" of basketball strategy built on "fundamental" skills.[75] Mark Price of the Cleveland Cavaliers is "a walking basketball textbook."[76] John Stockton of the Utah Jazz is the perfect antitype of the trash-talking black exhibitionist: "One could no more imagine John Stockton dying his hair green, for example, or throwing a tantrum at a coach's decision, or beating his chest and howling after committing a good play than seeing him do something dumb on the court."[77]

It is hardly surprising that physically outclassed white athletes have identified with this idealized image of self-discipline and mental acuity. "I'm a smart player," says Pete Chilcutt of the Houston Rockets, one of the virtually unknown white players in the NBA.[78] "I know that, in terms of running and jumping, I'm sometimes the worst athlete on the floor," says the DePaul University basketball star Tom Kleinschmidt, a borderline candidate for the NBA, "but I'll say this: I think, a lot of times, I'm the smartest player on the floor."[79] The towering Oklahoma State center Bryant (Big Country) Reeves, too modest to sing his own praises, is presented to white fans as a wholesome throwback to the (segregated) 1950s who possesses "a tireless work ethic" and employs a "fundamentals-first approach as his textbook."[80] "He should have been born 100 years ago with Daniel Boone [sic]," says his coach, Eddie Sutton, thereby inducting this countrified giant into the pantheon of legendary white male heroes.[81]

A particularly emblematic white athlete in the NBA is Scott Skiles of the Washington Bullets, hailed for his "bulldog leadership and fiery determination," who "watches game tapes at home every day" — a perhaps unintended allusion to the traditional idea that blacks are either unable or unwilling to study strategy on the battlefield or on the playing field.[82] Skiles is among the few white players who have criticized black showmanship on ideological grounds: "In my opinion, all it is is a bunch of immature guys showing off . . . So many of the guys now are built up beyond belief in high school. Then they get to college and their coaches don't have the nerve to say anything to them, and then they come into our league. I'm from the old school. I think you should go out, play hard and keep your mouth shut." Appropriately enough, it was the short and earthbound Skiles who served as the model for the basketball-hustling hero of the hit film *White Men Can't Jump.*[83] Commenting on a campaign to name the flamboyant Dennis Rodman to the U.S. Olympic team, *Sports Illustrated* noted acerbically that if a devotion to the work ethic meant anything, then it was the marginal white NBA player Scott Brooks who should be dressed in "a red, white, and blue uniform."[84]

These images are released continuously into our public discourse on sport and gradually acquire racial meaning even if blacks are not mentioned at all. The routine association of white athletes with attributes such as mental dexterity, integrity, tenacity, and willpower establishes an effective sense of difference, even in the absence of their black counterparts, because this distribution of virtues is only one recent version of a racial taxonomy that has soaked into the Western sensibility over centuries. Idealizing the white athlete also responds to anxieties that are now a part of white male identity. Half of the respondents to a poll in 1991 agreed that "blacks have more natural athletic ability."[85] "I can assure you," a nationally known sportswriter wrote to me in 1990, "that white athletes are aware of what they feel is black athletic superiority and that steroid-taking is just one of their attempts to 'catch up.'" On basketball courts across America, young whites have been succumbing to internalized stereotypes of their own athletic inferiority while their black opponents laugh at the paralyzing syndrome whites have inflicted on themselves.

At the same time, it is difficult to address these differences in public without giving offense, thereby fueling latent white anger at the politically correct suppression of the "truth" about racial difference. "Isn't Matt Williams boring?" asked Mark Fainaru of the *Boston Globe,* referring to the San Francisco Giants' stolid white home-run hitter. "No earrings, no backward caps, no untucked jerseys, no haughty stares or trashy taunts."[86] As of early 1996 a site on the World Wide Web was serving up the arrest records of NBA players as a form of racist entertainment.

The sarcasm and contempt that prompt these behaviors point to the prospect of even greater racial separation and sociocultural apartheid than already exist, for an "integrated" sports world that promotes the idea of racially distinct athletic styles can only help to "strengthen notions about a separate black reality, unknowable to whites and subversive of the fragile bases for interracial dialogue."[87]

# 3

# Joe Louis Meets Albert Einstein

## The Athleticizing of the Black Mind

WE HAVE SEEN that athleticism carries a special authority inside the "separate reality" of African Americans because it can express black suffering and style in uniquely dramatic ways. More surprising is the fact that for some people, athleticism has come to mean nothing less than black intelligence itself, which gives athletic champions a significance beyond the familiar themes of courage and force of character. Joe Louis has served as a paradigmatic representative of black potential in this sense. The sheer longevity and adaptability of his symbolic persona became evident, for example, in 1994, when O. J. Simpson's black trial attorney, Johnnie Cochran, emerged as "our new Joe Louis," as the publisher of *Black Enterprise* magazine phrased it. An announcer on a black talk radio program in Chicago reported that after Cochran made his opening statement, the station was inundated with callers "hollering and clapping and laughing, saying that Cochran had spoken so well, he put the white prosecutor in the hospital,"[1] as though he and his adversary had been in a boxing ring. It would be interesting to know how many of these callers were older people who had once listened to Joe Louis fights on the radio, and how many were younger people whose cultural legacy includes Joe Louis as the preeminent exemplar of black achievement. Such demographic questions are in the end less important than the question of why verbal skills were converted into physical ones in some of the minds that made up this black audience.

My answer to this question is one of the major arguments of this book, namely, that traumatic aspects of the African-American experience have prompted black people to regard athletic proficiency as a comprehensive representation of all proficiencies, including intellectual skills. This is one of the deeper connections between black athleticism and the unresolved (and destructive) public debate about black intelligence, which has frequently used uneducated and inarticulate black athletes as symbols of racial intellectual deficiency, thereby combining the race-neutral image of the "dumb jock" and the special burden of being black. An understanding of the culturally acquired habits that imagine black potential in physical terms, that convert intellectual performances into physical ones and vice versa, offers an alternative to a resurgent biological theory of racial intelligence. The fact that this cultural syndrome has never been studied in a systematic way suggests that belief in the essential physicality of black people is an unspoken premise of modern thinking about race. This is why confronting black athleticism as a form of entrapment is of potential social value. At a time when the leaders of American society are doing little or nothing to reverse the decline of the black male, a reckoning with this legacy of slavery belongs on our social agenda.

The "athleticizing" of their potential by African Americans is a cultural process that can be traced back for more than a century. In retrospect, it is clear that the primary role of this process has been to compensate for alleged racial differences in intelligence. We can learn more about this tradition by examining how the use of Joe Louis as a symbol of black potential established a model that is continually being adapted to changing circumstances.

Our point of departure is a characterization of Louis that appeared in a 1936 article titled "The Negro Athlete and Race Prejudice," by the black sportswriter Edwin Bancroft Henderson. The great boxer, he wrote, was "a human replica of Rodin's 'Thinker.' In the ring he associates ideas and responds with lightning-like rapier thrusts about as rapidly through the medium of mind and muscle as an Einstein calculates cause and effect in cosmic theory."[2] A year earlier, the *New York Daily Mirror*, echoing the black-edited *Chicago Defender*, cast the value of Joe Louis's victories in a very different light. "Some suggest," this editorial read, "that it would have been better for the colored race had it shown excellence in something more important and noble than fist-fighting." The problem with this important (if mildly sardonic) argument was that it did not address the historical forces that had largely confined conspicuous black achievement to professional boxing and Olympic track-and-field events. Channeling effort into athletics was a natural consequence of the intellectual starvation of black Americans during and after slavery and the resulting intellectual deficit that most whites had long regarded as a fact of nature. In addition, U.S. Army intelligence tests carried out during World War I had produced "scientific" confirmation of popular stereotypes. "So popular are mental tests today," a black observer wrote in 1923, "that even the man in the street knows of them and has his prejudices."[3]

This climate of opinion is the context in which the symbolic inflation of the black athlete must be understood. Henderson's equating of Louis and Einstein, as hyperbolic as it may seem today, was in fact a serious attempt to find intellectual dignity in black athleticism by fusing physical and cerebral stereotypes of human greatness, and there is every reason to believe that this approach to the problem of racial intelligence was acceptable to many African Americans at this time and for years to come. But while some blacks engaged in this sort of thinking, others regarded intellectual achievement as ineffective in promoting the welfare of black Americans. By 1935 this group included Jack Johnson, the former (and first black) heavyweight champion of the world. "If Joe Louis beat Professor Einstein at his own game, whatever that is," he told the *Daily Mirror,* "white men would pay no attention," whereas knocking him on his back was sure to make a lasting impression.[4]

An equally serious intellectualized version of Joe Louis appeared many years later, in 1962, as an editorial in the black-edited *Journal of the National Medical Association.* "Joe Louis — Model for the Physician" starts off by pointing to Louis's undisputed middle-class virtues: his modesty, his stature as a "gentleman," and his brevity, which contrasted favorably with "the confused and excessive verbosity of certain prominent athletes with college educations" — an early swipe by the black bourgeoisie at the new assertiveness of the black athlete. Louis's famous rejoinder — "I do all my talking with my two fists" — would seem to be unstable ground on which to build an argument for the fighter's high intelligence, yet the editorialist cites it and refers approvingly to a white journalist's view that another of Louis's one-liners outdid Shakespeare. Louis's taciturnity is presented as a "gift for cryptic, incisive comment [which] approached the amazing." "Let no man presume," the writer concludes, "that with proper training Louis could not have made a good Medical College Admissions Test score."[5]

Muhammad Ali, the exemplar of black athletes' verbosity, has offered much greater opportunities for construing pugilistic skills as brain power. In 1975 a contributor to *Black World* praised Ali's "originality of thought" and "the positive creative powers of his imagination."[6] As we will see, a white scientist sympathetic to African-American causes would make his own, more highbrow contribution to the conversion of black athleticism into "cognitive ability."

The question of whether Ali's athletic genius was an expression of cerebral intelligence was debated by two academic psychologists who have played major roles in the bitter debate about black and white IQ scores. The publication in 1969 of Arthur R. Jensen's controversial essay "How Much Can We Boost IQ and Scholastic Achievement?" breathed new life into the racial intelligence issue at the end of a decade of civil rights activism. Over the next twenty-five years, Jensen became a hero to genetics-oriented psychologists and to an international hodge-podge of racists. Departing from his hotly disputed work on the heritability of IQ scores, he set out to demonstrate that blacks and whites process information at different rates of speed. His procedure was to measure the "reaction times" (RT) of his subjects, meaning the brief period that elapses between the presentation of a stimulus, such as a light or a sound, and the subject's response, which often takes the form of pressing a button. Jensen assumed that the greater intelligence of the white subjects would be reflected in faster reaction times, and he attempted to bolster this claim by offering the following observation: "It is taken for granted even by many psychologists, for example, that highly skilled athletes should outperform, say, university students in all RT tasks. Yet Muhammad Ali, perhaps the greatest boxer of all time in his prime, was found to show a very average RT."[7]

Jensen was soon challenged by Leon Kamin, a Princeton University psychologist well known as a critic of work purporting to demonstrate the heritability of IQ. Kamin demonstrated that the researcher Jensen cited had misunderstood the *Sports Illustrated* account of the unorthodox procedure that had supposedly measured Ali's RT. Kamin had no difficulty in showing that if this experiment had demonstrated anything, it was that Ali's reaction time approached the recognized limits of the human organism.[8]

This debate about the speed of Muhammad Ali's physiological reflexes, which took place in professional journals far removed from the public eye, is a textbook example of how black athleticism has been a factor in the larger ideological conflict over race, which has been exacerbated by *The Bell Curve* and its gloomy assessment of black potential. Perhaps the most important aspects of this debate were that both academicians took seriously the idea that at least one type of physical aptitude is a reliable index of mental ability and that the black athlete was appropriated as a relevant exhibit in this context. The fundamental point is thus not that their interpretations of a black man's neural processes differed, but that both were willing to treat physiology and intelligence as linked variables to advance their respective arguments regarding racial intelligence.

Of the two protagonists, it was Kamin, not surprisingly, who revived the Joe Louis strategy on behalf of black intelligence. The "brain activity" represented by reaction time, he asserts, "must have been extraordinarily rapid inside Ali's skull," and there is no mistaking the flattering conclusion we are meant to draw from the great boxer's astonishing performance. Kamin's elliptical rhetoric is a scientist's tempered version of the hyperbolic inflation of black athleticism we have seen in testimonials to the latent intellect of Joe Louis. This sort of hyperbole is continually appearing in print, as when the black writer Stanley Crouch calls Ali "a Prometheus of speech" or Michael Jordan is compared with Michelangelo on the front page of the *New York Times*.[9]

By now it is clear that the process that intellectualizes the black athlete and simultaneously athleticizes black intellect seeks to identify with only the most splendid spirits in the European pantheon: Prometheus, Shakespeare, Michelangelo, Einstein. Such is the logic of a compensatory strategy that aims at making up a deficit too painful to confront in a soberer and more practical state of mind. For those who regarded Muhammad Ali as "typical of our race in true action,"[10] as Marcus Garvey said of Joe Louis, it is certainly painful to confront the possibility that the celebration of Ali's achievements was in part an implicit denial of what everyone "knows" about black intelligence. Yet that is exactly what is suggested by the traditional inflation of black athleticism into something it is not. In his famous polemic *Soul on Ice*, Eldridge Cleaver correctly argued that Muhammad Ali was a revolutionary figure, because his independence made him the first black champion to symbolize "the Brain" more than "the Body." But what kind of brain? Leon Kamin's insinuations about Ali's "extraordinarily rapid brain activity" are countered by Charles Murray's remark to an interviewer that Ali's behavior is compatible with an IQ of only about 80.[11] The real question is why major players in the racial IQ debate were using a black athlete as evidence in the first place.

Juxtaposing black physical virtuosity with the greatest Western minds is only the most dramatic expression of the compensatory syndrome we are investigating. Attempts to find intelligence within athleticism or dance can also be found in the writings of black educational psychologists who seek to find academic potential in children. Arguing against Arthur Jensen's conclusions about black learning ability, a researcher affiliated with the District of Columbia public school system maintains that "there is an unjustified tendency by many theorists" to regard kinesthetic abilities as "crude," creating a bias that overlooks an innate dimension of the black child. Choreography, he says, demonstrates "the level of sophistication that can be reached through kinesthetic ability. The significance of movement — not just object manipulation, but learner's motion — to the acquisition and transfer of information has not been appreciated properly." The temperaments of black and white differ, he says, in that "the constantly pulsating environment in which most Black children live fosters in them a great deal of 'psychological verve,' yet such verve, which could be a natural resource for learning, is not presently capitalized upon in schools. Indeed, while society seems to value these skills in sports and dance, the traditional classroom tends to stifle them."[12] Maximizing black learning means tapping into the kinesthetic potential — the "learner's motion" — that has already developed within the body of the black child.

Another black psychologist has pursued the intellectualizing of the body along another path by claiming that preadolescent African-American boys demonstrate "cognitive processes" and "discourse modes" that are "associated with literacy" when they play basketball. The author asserts that

> a number of literacy events take place inside the discourse of basketball. For example, in my observations I noted preadolescents giving extremely close readings to local newspapers in order to make their bets on which teams would win and go to the final four of the annual National Collegiate Athletics Association (NCAA) tournament. This required that they comprehend a rather intricate scoring system, analyze complex charts, and synthesize extensive articles on all 64 teams . . . Such literacy events require intensive application of both literate behaviors and literacy skills.

This argument is less radical than the theory of kinesthetic learning in that athletic activity is seen as a stimulus to learning rather than as somehow constituting the learning process itself: "Basketball has such high motivational value that it inspires young boys to engage in a number of collateral activities, some of which have strong implications or consequences for literacy." It is easy to imagine that children who bury themselves in the sports pages will gladly absorb whatever learning experiences are to be found there. In fact, he suggests, athletic activity is superior to traditional learning in a school. "The cognitive processes and learning situations associated with the discourse of basketball differ from the passive learning styles championed by mainstream school literacy approaches."[13] In contrast to book learning, basketball is "active" learning, because it is enjoyable.

It would be simplistic to dismiss these speculations as academic exercises without wider resonance in African-American life. Indeed, we can only wonder how many African-American teachers, counselors, coaches, social workers, and psychologists have reached similar conclusions, consciously or unconsciously, about the meaning of black athletic aptitude and its possible role in the development of black intelligence. As these authors make clear, athleticizing black potential has an unmistakable Afrocentric appeal, even if the black nationalist impulse is coated in (and obscured by) a social science jargon that is meant to confer nothing less than equal status on what one writer calls "the Black mind." Having set out "to understand differences in intellectual modus operandi between Blacks and Whites," he will not disappoint his black readers by ratifying the old approach to intelligence testing. The Afrocentric alternative is to deconstruct intelligence itself through a series of invidious dichotomies (white syntax/black pragmatics, white taxonomy/black dialectics, white closure/black aperture), which confirm that "individuals of African culture seem inclined toward particular modes of functioning" that are at least as worthy as their "white" variants. Playing his strongest card, the author cites black proficiency at jazz as corroborating evidence of "African" mental flexibility. The attempt to define basketball as an educational experience employs its own form of veiled Afrocentrism in its insistence on "the richness and complexity of Black language use" and the value of "Black discourse modes."[14]

These and other Afrocentric responses to doubts about black intelligence are based on a theory of "cognitive styles" that recognizes racial differences without prejudice. A contributor to the *Negro Educational Review* thus distinguishes between "reflective" and "impulsive" cognitive styles, while insisting that children must be required to test well regardless of which style they demonstrate.[15] Black children are characteristically seen as impulsive in a physical sense, and this is why the cognitive-style approach includes, as we have seen, a persistent tendency to associate black cognitive style with the black body, its special energies, and its demonstrated aptitude for athleticism.

African-American educators who have advanced the notion of a black learning style are working in this tradition. Janice Hale-Benson, a professor of education at Cleveland State University, claims that black children require a culturally distinct learning environment: "We like soul food, rhythm and blues and jazz music. We have distinctive worship styles, distinctive artistic experiences." In a similar vein, Barbara J. Shade, an educational psychologist at the University of Wisconsin at Parkside, has claimed that black children need to see numbers literally embodied by their classmates in order to make sense of them. "It's tactile, it's body oriented, it's more personal," she says, "because they can see we're talking about different people, whereas 1 and 1 are simply symbols and symbols tend not to be in their particular culture." The theme of the body recurs in Dr. Hale-Benson's assertion that black and white children differ in physiological development, since blacks acquire motor skills and hand-eye coordination before whites do. Black physicality becomes more controversial when it is perceived as disorderly: "When black children come to the classroom and don't conform, we label them hyperactive. They elicit more discipline and are thought of as unruly."[16]

This racially dichotomizing strategy represents one response to an Afrocentric dilemma, for the Afrocentrist either creates "black" standards to banish the possibility of black deficiency, as is the case here, or acknowledges "objective," panracial norms and proceeds on the assumption that blacks will meet these norms when environmental and cultural obstacles have been removed. Even as eccentric (and biology-minded) an Afrocentrist as Frances Cress Welsing, a psychiatrist who has preached black autonomy to a mass audience for a quarter-century, has rejected the temptation to retreat from race-neutral norms. Black children, she writes, "should be taught to place academic achievement as the highest priority. Black children should be taught to read and write the oppressor's language well, before learning to sing and dance. Each neighborhood should give annual awards and prizes for the children in each age group, based upon public performance in reading and math achievement. All black children must learn that it is *knowledge and information* that are the important bases of power, along with self-respect."[17] It is no accident that Dr. Welsing demands public performances that represent an alternative to sports, for she is among the few black commentators who have understood that black athleticism under white management means confinement in a world of symbols over which blacks have little or no control.[18]

The Afrocentric approach to learning that posits innate racial traits is yet another example of African-American entrapment in an idealized notion of the black organism and its distinctive capacities. The emphasis on a separate black physicality exacts a high price, such as the alleged inability of black children to manipulate even the simplest arithmetic symbols — a defeatist view of black potential that has been disproven by countless pupils for generations. Disorderly behavior can be normalized by assuming that restlessness of uncertain origin is natural exuberance. "Psychological verve" appears to be a euphemistic term for hyperactivity, a diagnosis that has been resented by many parents, especially blacks, who do not want to medicate their children with Ritalin or other drugs.[19] In 1995 a black publication complained that the "active behavioral patterns" of black children can be unfairly designated as "hyperactive," leaving unexplained the implied claim that black children are more active than their white peers.[20]

This kind of Afrocentrism reminds us that finding racial identity in difference is a risky strategy, since racially specific traits, whether real or imagined, can be interpreted as advantageous or disadvantageous, superior or inferior, depending on the perspective of the observer. The Afrocentric strategy is made to order for the racial psychologist with doubts about black intelligence, such as Michael Levin, who is only too willing to find a bioracial essence in black behavior: "Even black educators are finding it difficult to deny that an increasing black presence in the classroom increases disorder." Levin quotes Janice Hale-Benson and Asa Hilliard to confirm that "black children are more restless than white children" and show "high levels of energy, impulsive interrupting and loud talking" uncharacteristic of white children, and he criticizes their unwillingness to recognize that such behaviors might signify an inherent black academic disability.[21] Levin's rigid view of human behavior, which dismisses historical factors as irrelevant to the development of group intelligence, rules out a cultural explanation of such behavioral differences in favor of a biological approach. Despite the different conclusions they draw, both he and the Afrocentrists are racial biologists.

Levin would certainly not challenge Hale-Benson's observation about black motor development, which has been reported in respectable scientific publications. Indeed, for Levin and other white racial psychologists over the past two centuries, black physicality has always been the authentic foundation of racial difference, and the presence or absence of athletic aptitude in blacks has long played a role in dramatizing the racial divide. During the nineteenth century, whites saw the physically deficient black organism as a sign of inferiority, while during the twentieth century the superior black organism has come to signify the same lower status. The perverse logic of this development suggests that racial biology cannot rehabilitate the black image in Western society. Efforts to convert black physicality into intelligence cannot overcome the racist tradition that has always made the body the essence of black humanity and a sign of its inferior status.

# 4

# The Suppression of the Black Male Action Figure

T HE MOST PRESTIGIOUS male archetypes in Western societies derive from what Michael Nerlich has called "the ideology of adventure," which proclaims the dynamic and aggressive male to be "the most developed and most important human being." The ideology of adventure "demands and celebrates voluntary daring, the quest for extraordinary events, i.e., adventures with (more or less) unpredictable risk, the 'enduring of danger-filled adventures,' as the highest ethical achievement." What is more, the superiority of the adventurer implies that there are two qualitatively distinct classes of men, since the role of adventurer is denied to "those deprived of rights."[1]

This distinction between the dynamic-aggressive adventurer and lesser types has always been inherent in the fundamental racial hierarchy, which places white men over blacks, who are somehow less than men. In accordance with this hierarchy, dark-skinned inhabitants of European colonies and the United States have been systematically excluded from male action roles that might confer on them the authority and prestige traditionally reserved for the most dynamic white males. Even the extensive military service of black colonial troops and African Americans has not posed a significant challenge to this hierarchy, for while white commanders have been willing to expose black soldiers to danger, they have simultaneously opposed black claims to exercise command. This stubborn refusal to allow blacks to become dynamic, charismatic figures in a military setting reflects deeply rooted ideas about black limitations that have longed permeated Western societies. "If slaves make good soldiers, our whole theory of slavery is wrong," bellowed a southern opponent of Jefferson Davis's plan to draft Negro troops toward the end of the Civil War.[2] Yet the fact that slaves and their descendants did make good soldiers in war after war did little to change the black man's status in American society. The federal government's treatment of African-American troops during World Wars I and II was a disgrace, yet it was rationalized by ideas about the deficiencies of black men that whites have found more convincing than black sacrifices on the battlefield. These stereotypes have left a disabling legacy that remains poorly understood.

Our first task is, then, to examine the black man's exclusion from the ideology of adventure and the African-American response to this exclusion. It is important for us to know that some blacks did understand what this exile portended for their own social development, and it is interesting to see how the most determined among them sought and found dynamic adventurous roles in the face of prejudice. Our central purpose, however, is to understand why the most dynamic adventurous African Americans did not become enduring role models and how the black athlete became by default the primary male action figure for black Americans. This has been a disaster for American society, and the dimensions of that disaster become evident when we compare the profound limitations of the athlete with the moral and intellectual qualities of the heroes for whom he is such an inadequate replacement.

The African-American predicament has always expressed itself as a search for "race heroes" who could expand the sense of what was possible for blacks, and it is against this standard that any role model, including the celebrity athletes of our own era, must be judged. A crucial factor in this regard is the difference between heroic physical performances and demonstrations of more complex aptitudes and ambitions that can inaugurate blacks into the modern world. In addition, the search for heroic black models has been complicated by the prestige of white norms and achievements and the resulting black dependence on the judgments of a skeptical white world. This is why in 1932 the *Negro World* declared that it was time "for the Negro to forget and cast behind him his hero worship and adoration of other races, and to start out immediately to create and emulate heroes of his own."[3]

One response to this challenge has been the reconstruction of a heroic black tradition that seeks to establish black participation in a variety of male action roles that have long been considered a white preserve. Thus in 1945 *The Negro* presented to its readers Hannibal Barca, the scourge of ancient Rome, "the Negro who almost conquered the world," a versatile adventurer who might have stepped out of the action-adventure films that today are watched by a disproportionate number of African Americans. His tutor Hamilcar, we are told, "taught him how to fence, how to ride, how to endure the privations of a bivouac with his soldiers, how to kill Romans. The Negro conqueror was a splendid athlete, lightly yet firmly built; possessed of an iron constitution." It is important that, in addition to his "excellent physique," Hannibal possessed "a quick and calculating mind" and sexual restraint, two attributes that challenge stereotypes of the black male.[4] Still, the Hannibal presented here is primarily a hater and destroyer of prodigious energy. He is offered to blacks as a kind of ancient Superfly figure who showed that black men could ravage the earth as thoroughly as their white counterparts. A 1940 article titled "Black Pirates on the Spanish Main" served up a less prestigious group of outlaws to give a black audience the same sort of gratification.[5] We can only wonder how many black readers found themselves unfulfilled by such primitive role models and hungry for more substantial fare.

The black conqueror is a coarser version of another action figure, the black explorer who can participate in the modern search for knowledge and even redefine the meaning of white exploration by eliminating its predatory racist impulse. The explorer is an unusually powerful embodiment of the adventurer in the Western tradition, because he represents both physical and intellectual power, the ability to conquer and the ability to discover what has not been known before. The role has a special resonance for blacks, because it suggests a capacity for originality and willpower as well as the physical endurance that whites have often conceded to them. The black explorer thus contradicts the racist claim that, as one southern journal presented it in 1850, "Africans have never shown to the world that they possessed any considerable degree of enterprise or invention, or any wish to distinguish themselves in the arts or sciences of peace or war."[6] The Negro, the Harvard anthropologist Earnest A. Hooton noted in 1932, was still burdened by the "educated" view that "he is responsible for no great inventions or discoveries" and thus "has subordinate place in the assemblage of races."[7] The exclusion of the Negro explorer from the annals of history thus appears to confirm the world's already low opinion of black intelligence.

In "The Negro Explorer," which appeared in the organ of the NAACP in 1940, J. A. Rogers pointed out that for all his faults, the adventurer had acquired an extraordinary and charismatic status: "The explorer, whether his motive was plunder, the spread of the gospel, knowledge, or romance, has been the pioneer, the sole pioneer, of civilization." This was why it was important for blacks to know that a black man named Matthew Henson had accompanied Admiral Peary, the white "discoverer" of the North Pole; that it was a half-black "Negro explorer of Africa," Paul DuChaillu, who had "discovered" the gorilla (the paramount symbol of black animality); that a dynamic black man named York had traveled with Lewis and Clark and played the role of superman to the hilt: "His color, kinky hair, size and prodigious strength were a revelation to the Indians and he was looked upon as a very god."[8] Still, some readers must have recognized that whatever the satisfactions offered by this black action figure, the story of York was in essence a retrograde entertainment that presented a black character in the white role of racial superior. Was it possible to imagine exploration without the drama of racial domination?

In 1974 the *Negro History Bulletin* answered in the affirmative by reinventing the explorer as a humane adventurer. Black explorers of Africa were not simply porters or "native guides" for whites, who always retained control; on the contrary, these black men, possessing both knowledge and the ability to command, were driven by ambitions that differed sharply from those of white explorers: "In a way that no white explorer could, these men sought to appreciate and understand the virtues of their black forefathers. Their expeditions . . . were pilgrimages to the motherland, and each man saw himself as potentially a fellow citizen with the natives he encountered."[9] Buried in the pages of an academic journal, this attempt to redefine the black man of action as a civilized adventurer addressed the wider world of popular entertainment, in which "blaxploitation" films, as critics noted at the time, offered nothing more than black versions of mindless white predators while black audiences were in desperate need of more edifying male role models.

It is significant that *The Crisis* conferred its special recognition on a series of unconventional black male action figures in 1940, on the eve of World War II, at a time when A. Philip Randolph and other black leaders were demanding an end to racial discrimination in the military services as the price for civil peace and full black cooperation in the war effort. The role of the soldier, and his presumed right to full citizenship, had haunted the African-American imagination ever since black men had borne arms during the Revolutionary War. Yet blacks also knew that the soldier was only one among a larger group of charismatic male role models from which they had been unjustly excluded. Just as there had been black explorers and pirates, there had once been black cowboys, such as Bill Pickett, who should have achieved the legendary status that had always been reserved for whites in American culture.

Black editors knew that their people had paid a price for their absence from this magical kingdom of male prowess and the authority it commanded in the popular imagination. Cowboys, said *The Crisis,* are usually thought of as "men of great courage, skill and ability and to give Negroes such attributes might lift them a bit too high in the minds of young Americans. So, our boys and girls, yes Negro boys and girls too, are led to believe that all the brave strong boys of the range days were pure white."[10] Today, when the power of popular culture is appreciated as never before, we can try to imagine the transformation of racial attitudes that might have granted the Negro cowboy a status comparable to that of the Lone Ranger, whose dashing style captivated a large American television audience during the 1950s. In 1940, however, African Americans were prepared to settle for much less than mythic status. Simple equality for the foot soldier would have signified epochal progress, and that is why this basic step toward full manhood and real citizenship was once again withheld from the African-American community, which continued to demand the right to go to war.

The black campaign to achieve combatant status in World War II is one of the great forgotten chapters of our social history, and it is a bitter irony that the heroism and endless humiliations of this ordeal have been driven from popular memory by white America's sentimental attachment to the integration of baseball and the lost world of the Negro Leagues. By now it should be clear that the cultic celebration of Jackie Robinson and the process he set in motion has overestimated the real social value of integrated sports and obscured black achievements that were more significant precisely because they required more than athleticism. It is time to recognize that the Jackie Robinson story has long served white America, and liberals in particular, as a deeply satisfying combination of entertainment and civic virtue that has simultaneously permitted disengagement from less tractable and more important interracial tasks, such as the pursuit of educational and military equality.

A milestone in "the Negroes' fight for the right to fight" was the publication of "It's Our Country, Too," a long and eloquent proclamation to American society by Walter White, the secretary of the NAACP, which appeared in the mass circulation *Saturday Evening Post* of December 14, 1940. "The Negro," he wrote, "insists on doing his part, and the Army and Navy want none of him."[11] The army's high-pressure enlistment drive had ignored Negro volunteers. What the *Negro History Bulletin* would later call "the black tradition of flocking to enterprises having to do with the sea" simply did not exist for whites; "the policy of not enlisting men of the colored race for any branch of the naval service except messman branch was adopted to meet the best interests of general ship efficiency," the navy's representative declared. From 1870 to 1940 not one black man had graduated from the Naval Academy, and only two had been permitted to attend. Black petty officers had been phased out after World War I. (In the U.S. merchant marine, black captains were allowed to command only ships that been named for blacks, preserving racial apartheid even at this level of symbolism.)[12] "As to pilots," declared General George C. Marshall, army chief of staff, "there is no such thing as colored aviation at the present time." The black *cause célèbre* in 1940 was not Jackie Robinson but Walter L. Robinson, a black man who finished thirteenth in a flight training class of three hundred sponsored by the Civil Aeronautics Authority. Refused admission to the U.S. Army Air Corps, he was able to join the Royal Canadian Air Force, because besieged Britain and its empire had begun to recruit black African and West Indian pilots out of sheer desperation.[13]

Because white America showed no interest in recruiting black combatants, African Americans chose to embrace black foreigners as martial role models. The majestic profile of a Senegalese soldier and his erect saber ("France's First Line of Defense") graced the cover of the March 1939 issue of *The Crisis,* while *Opportunity,* the magazine of the Urban League, romanticized the Senegalese troops who had established a daunting mystique fighting Germans during World War I. Claude McKay lauded "their hard disciplined conduct and primitive simplicity" and cited Henri Barbusse's awed account of "their ferocity in attack, their devouring passion to be in with the bayonet."[14] (The black man's alleged fondness for knife and bayonet fighting also appears in American racial folklore.) In retrospect, it is clear that the American military establishment's rejection of black combatants was rooted in a general fear that black men would acquire this kind of charisma and then a will to command that would challenge the idea of white supremacy.

The methodical defamation and devirilization of the black fighting man are among the lesser-known aspects of American and European colonial racism. Today the idea of the black man's inherent cowardice seems eccentric or perverse; fifty years ago it was a racist dogma, maintained by an American military establishment that had actually grown more racist in practice as the twentieth century progressed. During the nineteenth century, many blacks and their white sympathizers believed that honorable battle service in American wars would remove the racial stigma that was intensified by the constant humiliations and submissive rituals of slavery. When Frederick Douglass published "Why Should a

Colored Man Enlist?" (in the Union Army) in April 1863, one of his principal arguments was that "you are a member of a long enslaved and despised race. Men have set down your submission to slavery and insult, to a lack of manly courage. They point to this fact as demonstrating your fitness only to be a servile class. You should enlist and disprove the slander."[15] A month later, when colored regiments composed of "plantation hands with centuries of servitude under the lash behind them" stormed the trenches at Port Hudson, Louisiana, the point seemed to have been made. "After that," Oswald Garrison Villard wrote forty years later, "there was no more talk in that portion of the country of the 'natural cowardice' of the negro."[16] Yet this stereotype survived for many years to come, and it was still remarkably potent as late as World War II. As one black veteran of that war later recalled, "So the lie goes merrily along, perpetuated by whites, that the black man is a big zero as a fighting man; he is a coward. I find this hard to understand, since the average cracker is scared to death to tangle with a black man on a man-to-man, eyeball-to-eyeball" basis.[17]

A second charge leveled against the black soldier at this time was that he was not sufficiently intelligent to handle modern weapons, an assessment offered in 1944 by none other than Secretary of War Henry Stimson. This claim, *The Crisis* replied in language reminiscent of Douglass's, classified blacks "as morons incapable of attaining the intelligence level of the most ignorant southern cracker. What does the Negro soldier think about this? He considers it a vicious attack upon his manhood."[18] Indeed, during both world wars the American military services went to extraordinary lengths to keep black servicemen out of combat, carrying out an elaborate bureaucratic conspiracy using racial stereotypes that enjoyed official status. The War College Reports of 1936, based on unscientific surveys and interviews of white officers who had commanded black troops in World War I, concluded that the latter were "child-like," "careless," "shiftless," "irresponsible," "secretive," "superstitious," and "more likely to be guilty of moral turpitude." The Negro soldier was "a comic," "emotionally unstable," "musically inclined, with good rhythm," and "if fed, loyal and compliant." The Negro officer in particular was described as "lacking in physical courage and psychological characteristics," which made him "inherently inferior."[19] The origins of these and other damaging ideas about the Negro soldier are to be found in the racist doctrine that developed in the United States during the second half of the nineteenth century and persisted in practice for another century.

Perhaps the most intimate and candid descriptions of African-American minds and bodies came from white physicians who treated the enslaved and the indigent or studied their disorders from a racial perspective. One such portrait, by Sanford B. Hunt, M.D., surgeon to the U.S. Volunteers during the Civil War, is "The Negro as a Soldier." Hunt's cautiously optimistic assessment of Negro abilities is quite progressive for its time (1869), especially when we consider the scurrilous racial pseudo-science that was being spread by contemporary figures such as Samuel Cartwright and other southerners who thought of blacks as something like a separate species. Hunt emphasized that the very idea of the Negro soldier represented a "startling innovation" and "a grand experiment" that would reveal the capacities of the black man once and for all. Most of a century before Secretary of War Stimson concluded otherwise, Hunt decided that black soldiers had made this experiment a success, reporting that "for the purposes of the soldier, he has all the physical characteristics required, that his temperament adapts him to camp life and his morale conduces to his discipline. He is also brave and steady in action. His only disqualifications are found in his greater liability to pulmonary and exanthematous diseases and in the lack of education — perhaps of native intellect — that forbids his attainment to the rank of a commissioned officer."[20]

Hunt reached this favorable conclusion only after navigating an obstacle course consisting of contrary opinions and his own instinctive doubts about the Negro's capacity to go to war: "Had he the physique to endure hardship? Could he acquire the manual of arms and perfect himself in tactics? Had he the necessary physical courage? Would he not, when his savage blood was up in the fever-heat of battle, entail disgrace upon our cause by acts of outrage? Was not the profession of the soldier in its essence too noble and manly for this pariah of the land?" There were also doubts about black anatomy, which may sound strange to modern readers more accustomed to ideas about black physical superiority. Hunt referred to concern about the "large, flat, inelastic foot of the negro." But after he observed 1500 black troops march seventy-eight miles in seventy-six hours "with remarkable ease and without increasing the sick-list," his doubts were laid to rest. The black man marched well, Hunt said, because his "large joints and projecting apophyses of bone give a strong leverage to the muscles attached to or inserted in them" — precisely what was alleged (and then disproven) about Jesse Owens's famous feet in 1936. But the advantages of the black man's body were finally of secondary importance, since "in unfavourable circumstances there is reason to suppose that he fails to endure prolonged fatigue as well as the white man."[21] The crucial issue, as always, was the Negro's lack of what modern coaches call "mental toughness."

The racial politics of our integrated sports and military establishments will be incomprehensible to anyone who fails to appreciate the continuing influence of nineteenth-century ideas about the different capacities of whites and blacks to confront adversity. While Hunt did not openly question black toughness, his section on "Endurance of Fatigue and Hunger" quoted the opinion of two U.S. Army surgeons that the Negro "is *at present,* too animal to have moral courage or endurance." In a similar vein, a Dr. Long asserted that when blacks confront exposure or hardships, "the *morale* of the white man steps in and often aids him in overcoming the situation."[22]

Even as sympathetic an observer as Thomas Wentworth Higginson, a Union Army colonel from Massachusetts who had led black freedmen of the 1st South Carolina Volunteers, could not rid himself of these doubts and what they implied about black capacity to exercise leadership. On the one hand, Higginson debunked the idea of an inherent racial courage with candor and insight. "In almost every regiment," he wrote in 1870, "black or white, there are a score or two of men who are naturally daring, who really hunger after dangerous adventures, and are happiest when allowed to seek them. Every commander gradually finds out who these men are, and habitually uses them; certainly I had such, and I remember with delight their bearing, their coolness, and their dash." At the same time, he was never able to rid himself of certain nagging suspicions regarding black grit: "The point of inferiority that I always feared, though I never had occasion to prove it, was that they might show less fibre, less tough and dogged resistance, than whites, during a prolonged trial, — a long, disastrous march, for instance, or the hopeless defense of a besieged town. I should not be afraid of their mutinying or running away, but of their drooping and dying." His black troops had disappointed him in only one respect, in that "neither their physical nor moral temperament gave them that toughness, that obstinate purpose of living, which sustains the more materialistic Anglo-Saxon."[23]

The more primitive Samuel Cartwright made the same distinction in blunter terms: the white man was endowed with "a strong will," while the black man lacked full control over his muscles owing to "the weakness of his will." "The white men of America have performed many prodigies," he wrote, "but they have never yet been able to make a negro overwork himself."[24] By 1850 willpower had become a racial variable throughout the hierarchical world of southern plantations and

European colonies where slavery had once flourished. What is more, the lingering influence of this racial characterology is still evident in American and British sport, as well as in the German professional soccer league, which imports black African players into a society that still sees them as racial exotics.

By World War II, whites had long understood (or intuited) that racially integrated warfare would subvert the myth of white martial superiority, and this is exactly what happened when blacks saw whites in action. (The black men who played in the Negro Leagues had, of course, been making the same point about white baseball players for many years.) The performance of white troops at Anzio and Cassino, *The Crisis* said in 1944, "showed that American white troops with only one enemy to fight were hardly supermen in the face of their German opposition."[25] What was more, white military performance was now vulnerable on another front. The war in the Pacific provided blacks with even more gratifying opportunities for making racial comparisons: "This white hang-up about the infinite superiority of the white man to any man of color did not prepare the American white for the Japanese, or for Korea," said the staff sergeant quoted above. "The Japanese beat the shit out of our legendary marines . . . There were a tremendous number of mental breakdowns among the first marines to hit the Japanese-held islands."[26] Encounters with European whites provided other instructive situations. "Even the Negro soldier's policing of the German prisoners has done something to him," a black soldier told *The Negro* in early 1945. "They have seen Germans doing the dirty work — like digging latrines, putting up tents, serving officers at mess, digging graves, washing pots and pans. This has made a profound impact on the Negro — for, after all, the Germans are white, too!"[27] One German suffered a special humiliation. An American POW who had spent time in a German field hospital told of meeting a pilot whose "feelings were hurt because over Sicily he had been shot down and wounded by a Negro pilot." How, he asked the wounded prisoner, could Americans have permitted Negroes to fly and thus violate the racial purity of the skies?[28]

The defeat of a German fighter pilot by a black adversary can be seen as another version of Max Schmeling's defeat by Joe Louis in 1938. But this was a more grievous symbolic failure, in that interracial combat in the skies over Europe was not the "primitive" struggle of the boxing ring, where the black fighter supposedly enjoyed natural advantages such as dull nerves and a thick skull. For Germans in particular, performance in aerial combat was a sensitive issue, in that World War I had given their fliers "the proportions of supermen. For a great many Germans, airmen revived older martial legacies. They recalled a treasured aristocratic universe of honor and skill and distinction." At the same time, the cult of the military aviator was not simply a German preoccupation. The two decades following the Great War saw the emergence of what Peter Fritzsche has called "a vague international of fighter pilots" and an accompanying mystique that seemed to ennoble the "chivalric" warfare these heroes had conducted far above the blood and chaos of the trenches.[29] It goes without saying that this was a white international, and in this spirit the U.S. Army Air Corps "postponed military training for Negro pilots for as long as it was militarily and politically possible."[30] Without the combined pressure of the NAACP, the Negro press, and various sympathizers, the Tuskegee Negro Air Corps unit set up in January 1941 would not have come into existence. (Many years later the civilian Air Line Pilots Association had to be forced to remove its restrictions on blacks and Jews.)[31] Black fliers and other military personnel suffered constant demoralization and humiliations during the war against fascism.

Our purpose here is to understand why blacks wanted to fly and why most whites did not want them to do so. Many years after the combat successes of the 99th Pursuit Squadron and the 332nd Fighter Group, which had trained at the segregated Tuskegee base, Lieutenant Colonel Walter Downs, former leader of the 301st Fighter Squadron, recalled "the excuses made by the white military to try and keep black men out of the sky. The air force said blacks were afraid to fly; so they volunteered. Then it was said physically blacks were unable to fly because above certain altitudes they couldn't function. How they arrived at this conclusion has never been clarified. This idea was proven to be fallacious anyhow. Their last gimmick was a black man had to have education far beyond whites to comprehend the rudiments of flying."[32]

This is certainly a historically accurate account of white thinking at this time. The idea that blacks were physiologically unsuited for military aviation, whatever this meant in the early 1940s, survived for many years as a ban on carriers of sickle cell trait, on the grounds that this disorder could endanger the carrier and fellow crew members under hypoxic conditions. On May 26, 1981, however, the air force modified this policy to allow "individuals with sickle cell trait and whose red blood cells possess a hemoglobin S content of 40 percent or less to enter air crew training and perform flying duties."[33] The crucial issue here is the original motive for excluding black fliers on physiological grounds at all. Given that the medical literature had virtually eliminated sickle cell anemia as a hazard to the black aviator, it is reasonable to assume that the ban expressed the continuing desire of white officers to keep black men out of military aircraft, which had long been an almost totally white monopoly.[34] Indeed, a lawsuit and help from a congressman were required to rescind a ban that had probably originated as an invention of racist biology.

Black intelligence too, given the technical demands of flying, could not help but be an issue during the Tuskegee period and for years afterward. The first (white) administrator of the Tuskegee base, Colonel Frederick Kimble, was a segregationist and "somewhat skeptical of the black's ability to fly an aircraft." In 1943 the Army Air Corps itself directed some withering criticism against the all-Negro 99th Fighter Squadron. A report by Colonel William Momyer, their de facto commanding officer, charged that the 99th was "not of the fighting caliber of any [other] squadron in this group. They have failed to display any aggressiveness and desire for combat that are necessary to a first class fighting organization." A letter that later accompanied this report up the chain of command of the Army Air Corps stated that both commanding officers and medical staff agreed that "negroes did not possess the proper reflexes to make a first class fighter pilot."[35] But what was a "reflex" in this context? Was it to be interpreted as a mental or as a physical response? Or perhaps as a combination of the two?

Those who crafted this ambiguous phrase may well have intended to create an empty semantic space into which the least flattering stereotypes would naturally flow, and many such images were available. In 1940, for example, *The Crisis* had paraphrased racist white thinking about "the Negro's psychological evolution" in the following terms: "His so-called mental capacities to make responses to complex stimulus situations are missing or defective in some way."[36] It should be remembered that the army intelligence tests administered a generation earlier had already created fixed ideas about low black IQ, which had spread throughout the general population during the 1920s, and the idea that blacks could master the most advanced machines of the day was nothing less than a provocation to the racist mindset of many Americans. When a crowd of rural Mississippi whites saw the black pilot Cornelius Coffey expertly dismantle and then rebuild the engine of his plane in a field in 1937, they tried to distract him with remarks like "That darkie don't know what he's doin' with that airplane" — a clear case of the wish fathering the thought.[37] Blacks too "came from all around to look at the black men who actually flew an 'aireyplane,'"[38] and contemporary doubts about how blacks would handle "complex stimulus situations" make it easy to understand why. So how, then, were aviation and black self-confidence connected with each other?

As late as 1976 *Ebony* was reporting that "flying, any style, remains a lofty phenomenon in black culture." As the manager of an all-black airline put it, "Some of *us* are still wondering if it's safe to ride on *trains.*"[39] This candid observation serves as a reminder that during the 1930s many blacks saw flying as a skill that would usher black Americans out of backwardness and into the modern age via "the Gospel of Aviation." Like their far better equipped white counterparts, black aviators participated in the long-distance flying craze that literally swept the globe between the world wars. The transcontinental flight of Herman Banning and Thomas Allen in 1932 earned them celebrity and a parade through Harlem. The *New York Age* compared these race heroes to "Daniel Boone, Charles Lindbergh and other great American pioneers," thereby claiming black membership in the most exclusive white male pantheon.[40] Demonstrating a mastery of these machines would compensate for centuries of racist denigration of black heroism and intelligence. This is why the editor of *Opportunity* wrote that "aviation has tremendous and dramatic possibilities to help the race in its fight for world wide respect." Even the famous black scholar W.E.B. DuBois proclaimed that the black "race soars upward, on the wings of an aeroplane."[41] In 1934 the *Journal of Negro Education* had found that black children still preferred hymns to jazz and musicians to aviators.[42] Yet by 1936 the Negro press, civil rights organizations, and Negro aviation were advancing together in a mutually beneficial relationship that shared members, goals, and a great deal of publicity about black exploits in the air.[43]

The idea that involvement in aviation could improve the Negro mind was also taken up, belatedly and superficially, by the War Department, which had been repressing black initiative at every turn. *Wings for This Man,* a 1945 film made for the Army Air Corps and narrated by Ronald Reagan, adopted the Tuskegee airmen as model blacks who were pointing the way to better race relations and a better future for their people. They were "learning how high and how fast and how far [they] must go to reach the enemy," while the black aviator was "getting muscles in his mind — hard, keen, quick," as if the forward progress of the Negro intellect could only be imagined as the accumulation of something fibrous and athletic.[44]

Given the promotion of Joe Louis and Jesse Owens as race heroes during the 1930s, it is not surprising that an appreciation of black athleticism played a role in promoting the concept of the black aviator. The key editorial appeared not in the Negro press but in the *Chicago Tribune* of August 8, 1940, responding to General George Marshall's statement that "there is no such thing as colored aviation at this time." How could the idea of the black pilot be made most acceptable to white Americans when "an almost universal prejudice against Negroes" existed among white aviators?[45] "The first requisite of a military flyer," the *Tribune* proposed,

> is quick nervous responses. He should have a superior sense of balance, excellent muscular coordination, a good sensory apparatus, a sound body. In short, the qualities which make a good athlete are required of a flyer. Of course he should have physical and moral courage as well. In all of these qualifications Negroes have given ample demonstration of their fitness. A race which has produced, in the span of a few years, Joe Louis, Henry Armstrong, Jesse Owens, Jefferson of Northwestern, Ozzie Simmons of Iowa, and substantial number of Golden Gloves champions, and a score of other absolutely top-notch athletes, provides a rich resource which ought not to be lost to the country through prejudice. In the face of this roster of world champions the physical fitness and courage of their race cannot be questioned by any reasonable man.[46]

This endorsement was gratefully reprinted by *Opportunity* and quoted by Walter White of the NAACP in the broadside he directed at the War Department at the end of 1940.

We can only wonder how many readers understood at the time how this paean to black fitness sold short the people it was supposed to serve. For one thing, the *Tribune*'s editorial inaccurately portrayed blacks as premodern aerial neophytes at a time when any journalist in Chicago should have known otherwise. The Chicago area had been the mecca of black aviation throughout the 1930s. The Challenger Air Pilots Association, led by Cornelius Coffey, included legendary figures such as Bessie Coleman, the first black woman granted a pilot's license (in 1921) by the Fédération Aéronautique Internationale and a lecturer on aviation to black audiences; Willa Brown, a bold and charismatic woman who co-founded the National Airmen's Association of America; and John Robinson, a black pilot who flew combat missions against Mussolini's air force after the fascist attack on Ethiopia and was feted by African Americans when he returned to the United States in 1936.[47]

The athleticizing of the black man came naturally both to this white newspaper and to those at the NAACP and the Urban League who might have objected to yet another unnecessarily "premodern" portrait of black potential. Given a choice between "the Brown Condor" (John Robinson) and "the Brown Bomber" (Joe Louis), blacks as well as whites ignored the modern, politically active figure while lionizing the political innocent who spoke with his fists. When the U.S. Army released *The Negro Soldier* in 1944, a polished and highly effective propaganda film made by Frank Capra, there were Joe Louis, Jesse Owens, and a "light skinned, muscular" male lead to certify black competence to an enormous audience of blacks and whites, soldiers and civilians alike.[48] Even before black dominance in high-profile sport, the Negro athlete had become the defining symbol of African-American talent in the mind of America.

The disappearance of the black soldier and aviator as public figures in American life after 1945 was significant, because it denied an officially sanctioned modern status to black men who might otherwise have come to be identified with intellectual mastery and technological competence in the eyes of the nation. The military pilot's role had a special ideological significance, because it incarnated a masculine identity that had always been denied to blacks. An early project of the eugenicist Pioneer Fund, for example, was "cash grants to pilots in the all-white U.S. Army Air Corps to encourage them to have more children."[49] High-profile black pilots would also have challenged the traditional southern belief that "Negroes get sleepy when working with machines," a piece of folklore guaranteed to maintain blacks in their premodern state.[50] Equality for black aviators would also have made possible a black astronaut at a time when both the Mercury 7 program and the civil rights movement were becoming parts of the American landscape.

In retrospect, it is clear that the very idea of a black astronaut would have violated the racial aesthetics of this heroic elite as the media defined it. As "pioneers" and "frontiersmen," as possessors of "single combat warrior" status that made them the symbolic defenders of the nation, the early astronauts were accorded de facto status as the spiritual descendants of white Indian-hunters who helped to enforce the American racial hierarchy.[51] That the racial integration of the astronaut corps was virtually unthinkable confirms the magnitude of the loss black Americans suffered when the black aviator was not allowed to become a public icon. Compared with this modern hero, the black athlete appears as a mindless and crucially diminished version of the male action figure, whose charisma derives from his symbolic role in preserving the vitality of the nation itself. The unhappy paradox of the black athletic hero is that his celebrity confirms his role as a mere surrogate for the more substantial male figures he has replaced.

# 5

# "Writin' Is Fightin'"

## Sport and the Black Intellectuals

I F THERE IS one interest group that might have been expected to resist black America's profound attachment to athletic achievement, it is African-American intellectuals, both inside and outside the universities.[1] Yet the black male intelligentsia that has denounced almost every other form of cultural entrapment has never mounted a campaign against the sports fixation. It is important to understand why this is the case and how this abstention from serious criticism has failed to serve black educational and social development.

The dramatic exception here has been the sociologist and activist Harry Edwards. Sports, he wrote in 1973, exert a "novocain effect on the black masses" and "provide the black fan with the illusion of spiritual reinforcement in his own life struggles."[2] "When sport becomes little more than a form of black cultural exhibitionism," he said in 1988, "white America — and you have to understand that nothing moves in this society until white sentiment makes it happen — white America will come to see sport in the same vein as it sees the Harlem Globetrotters."[3]

No other black intellectual has followed Edwards onto this critical terrain, because the black athletic champion has exerted too powerful a spell on a striking number of them. This profound attachment to sport is different in scope from the sports sentimentalism and romanticism that have flourished among white intellectuals in the United States, for while the baseball and boxing cults of the white literati represent the tastes of a small group, black intellectuals regard sports as an integral part of African-American history and as a dramatization of black life itself. The knowledgeable black intellectual sees an important difference here; as Gerald Early, the best of these commentators, has noted, "The number of white intellectuals who tried to fight or who trailed behind fighters like star-struck teenagers trailing behind rock stars is remarkable: Bernard Shaw, Ernest Hemingway, A. J. Liebling, Paul Gallico, Jack London, George Plimpton, Norman Mailer, Joyce Carol Oates." The black critic's distance from these camp followers is significant, because it distinguishes between blacks, for whom the prizefighter is a race hero, and whites, for whom he is only the titillation of choice. "The boxer," says Early, "is simply the consciousness of taboo violation for the white writer."[4] Whereas white intellectuals tend to romanticize or elegize athletes as symbols of the past or for their sheer animal vitality, African-American writers romanticize athletes because they seem to incarnate the blood, sweat, and tears of black life itself.

Identification with athletes also permits the black intellectual to distinguish himself from white cultural standards and a conservative black middle-class establishment that has long been perceived as having cut itself off from the black masses.[5] This act of self-differentiation can originate in subcultures other than the sports world. Some educated blacks, the sociologist E. Franklin Frazier once pointed out, "seek escape from their frustrations by developing, for example, a serious interest in Negro music — which the respectable black bourgeoisie often pretend to despise. In this way these intellectuals achieve some identification with the Negro masses and with the traditions of Negro life."[6] In a similar vein, some black writers see stylish black athleticism as a kind of cultural avant-garde. Nelson George, for example, sees the "black athletic aesthetic" as "our music put into physical motion" — a metaphorical fusion of sport and art that has become a convention among this group of black sports fans.[7] When Michael Eric Dyson writes of Michael Jordan's "herculean cultural heroism," he is making the athlete an artist by placing him in the vanguard of modern black self-expression.[8] At a time when a flamboyant black athletic style is widely seen as opposed in spirit to a more sedate white one, the celebration of black athleticism as culture is an implicit act of resistance directed at white cultural standards that may also have black adherents.

Black athleticism can also be seen as a ritual of survival that reenacts a visceral African-American determination to persevere. Gerald Early is not alone in seeing the black fighter as a symbol of "what it means to be a black American." "One could argue," he adds, "that the three most important black figures in twentieth-century American culture were prizefighters: Jack Johnson, Joe Louis, and Muhammad Ali."[9] Indeed, the athlete's representative role is so obvious that black writers rarely pay explicit attention to athleticism as a species of survivalism.

More evident is many educated African Americans' preoccupation with the terrible physical and emotional ordeals of their ancestors and an attachment to scenarios of unnatural selection. In his memoir *Father-along,* the novelist John Edgar Wideman recites these trials: "Think of the Middle Passage — capture in African wars, forced marches to the coast, confinement in barracoons, crossing the Atlantic packed spoon-fashion in the holds of ships in unimaginably cruel, deadly conditions, sold into perpetual slavery — as a brutal threshing of the physically weak, and then the South as a test just as brutal for the mind." Is it by chance that the author refers to his father's athleticism over and over again — the man "played all sports well," the "athlete's bob, weave, and balance in the roll of his thick shoulders"? This physique is also a guarantor of male dignity: "Don't you ever assume a quarter-inch of liberty in your dealings with him that he doesn't authorize. His body speaks these words."[10]

Alvin Poussaint once offered the following description of the "brutal threshing" process: "First of all, they selected for slavery only those with a lot of brawn and ability to work hard: only the best. Second, only the strongest survived the long voyage. We may already have a very selected group of blacks in this country."[11]

While most commentators, black and white, favor this "athleticized" fantasy of the selection process, the authors of *Black Rage* present an even more dispiriting account of the winnowing process during slavery, when "the population began to be replenished by slaves who in some measure were willing to be slaves or to give the appearance of it. One might comment that even those who were newly transported from Africa had chosen to be slaves rather than die."[12] These differing stories show that the Middle Passage ordeal has become a fantasy space into which the mourner projects varying images of his people. The special appeal of the athleticized version is that it dramatizes an improbable black triumph, that "somehow in spite of terrible odds our ancestors had managed to survive."[13]

Many black intellectuals acknowledge or even celebrate the importance of physical prowess to African-American identity. One consequence of this is the writer's adoption of an athletic persona and his athleticizing of mental work, and the identity of choice is usually the prizefighter, whose authority derives from the mythic status of Jack Johnson and Joe Louis. "But let them understand," the militant Amiri Baraka (then LeRoi Jones) wrote in 1964, "that this is a fight without quarter, and I am very fast."[14] Baraka's adoption of the prizefighter persona was apparently more than metaphorical. According to Gerald Early, "Baraka has always been enchanted with the idea of being embattled, and this may explain why he has probably participated in more fistfights than any other writer in American literary history."[15]

While it is tempting to see Baraka as a black version of the Hemingway-obsessed Norman Mailer and his quest for virile fulfillment, it is important to keep in mind that Baraka's identification with physical ruggedness was only one part of a more comprehensive black machismo that required a sneering contempt for the deficient masculinity of the white male oppressor. In "American Sexual Reference: Black Male," Baraka took this racial hostility to its apparent limit: "Most American white men are trained to be fags. For this reason it is no wonder that their faces are weak and blank . . . That red flush, those silk blue faggot eyes . . . Do you understand the softness of the white man, the weakness, and again the estrangement from reality?" He sees white men as effeminate because they are separated from the realm of the physical: "The purer white, the more estranged from . . . actual physical work. Who lifts the boards and steel, who does the hardest, stupidest, most brutalizing work? . . . Can you, for a second, imagine the average middle-class white man able to do somebody harm? Alone? Without the technology that at this moment still has him rule the world?"[16]

Baraka's rage at the technologically superior (and physically inferior) white man would be no more than an artifact of his eccentric career if not for the fact that his invidious comparison between effeminate (white) technological mastery and macho (black) physicality lives on as an important factor in the lives of many black youth, who disdain intellectual development as a dishonorable form of "acting white." Far from being an obscure figure, Baraka "was the most influential black person of letters over the last twenty years, particularly influential among young blacks, and he had a striking ability to communicate to people who had never read his books. It is not likely that any black writer or intellectual will generate a similar power anytime in the near or foreseeable future."[17] As *the* charismatic black man of letters of his "revolutionary" generation, Baraka thus made a singular contribution to black anti-intellectualism by heaping scorn on white milquetoasts who "devote their energy to the nonphysical" rather than become real men like stevedores and boxers. This cult of the physical went along with a disdain for "the stunted middle-class mind, academic or popular," which he identified with the complete sterility of the educated white and black bourgeoisies.[18]

A similar theory of black vitality and white degeneracy appeared a few years later in Eldridge Cleaver's famous manifesto *Soul on Ice*. Cleaver's portraits of the (white) Omnipotent Administrator and the (black) Supermasculine Menial are an attempt to account for the division of labor in a racist society that develops the minds of some and only the bodies of others. It appears at first that he is simply describing racial stereotypes that obstruct the path to a society that has been purged of racism: "Weakness, frailty, cowardice, and effeminacy are, among other attributes, associated with the Mind. Strength, brute power, force, virility, and physical beauty are associated with the Body. Thus the upper classes, or Omnipotent Administrators, are perennially associated with physical weakness, decay, underdeveloped bodies, effeminacy, sexual impotence, and frigidity. Virility, strength, and power are associated with the lower classes, the Supermasculine Menials." It soon becomes clear, however, that Cleaver (like Baraka) believes that these racial stereotypes are grounded in a biological reality that has condemned white and black men to their respective states of incomplete manhood. The brainy white technocrat writhes in a virtually homosexual state of envy and frustration directed at "the potent bodies in the classes beneath him," while the muscular black thrall oscillates between despising and envying the physical weakness of his white master. Cleaver's racial biology culminates in a triumphant redemption in that "the [black] Supermasculine Menial and the [black female] Amazon are the least alienated from the biological chain, although their minds . . . are in a general state of underdevelopment. Still, they are the wealth of a nation, an abundant supply of unexhausted, undeessenced human raw material upon which the future of the society depends and with which, through the implacable march of history to an ever broader base of democracy and equality, the society will renew and transform itself."[19] Cleaver has both internalized the stereotype of black physical superiority and glamourized it as a symbol of black biological vigor.

The spectacular success of *Soul on Ice* tells us much about the racial politics of the late 1960s: about the paucity of articulate black voices audible to the white public, the prestige of the exotic outsider (in this case, an imprisoned rapist), and the masochistic gullibility of many white sympathizers, for whom Cleaver's crackpot biological fantasies did not constitute grounds for disqualifying him from the role of social prophet. At the same time, Cleaver was only one of the black writers who have appreciated the social significance of interracial boxing matches and used them to illuminate the black man's predicament. *Soul on Ice* thus includes a brief but lucid appreciation of the young Muhammad Ali, "the first 'free' black champion ever to confront white

America." Cleaver argues that Ali's defeat of the allegedly submissive Floyd Patterson "was a serious blow to [the white man's] self-image; because Muhammad Ali, by the very fact that he leads an autonomous private life, cannot fulfill the psychological needs of whites." Like other observers, Cleaver had good reason to wonder about the emotions that attracted white spectators to black fighters: "Through a curious psychic mechanism, the puniest white man experiences himself as a giant-killer, as a superman, a great white hunter leading a gigantic ape, the black champion tamed by the white man, around on a leash."[20]

Cleaver's mistake, like that of Amiri Baraka, was to indulge his own racial chauvinism by magnifying "the puniest white man" into a cartoonish archetype of a degenerate white masculinity. It is a long way from this kind of self-gratification to the detachment of Gerald Early, who watches the emotional entanglements that bind white intellectuals to black boxers with a combination of bemusement and genuine interest. But while Early's sophistication lies in his avoidance of chauvinistic posturing, not all of his black contemporaries have been as self-disciplined. Their hyperbolic praise of black athletes and receptiveness to ideas about black vitality should make us curious about why they feel indebted to black athletic heroism and why they are therefore unable to think about black athleticism in more critical and independent ways.

It would be interesting to know, for example, to what extent intellectual outsiders like Baraka and Cleaver set the terms of discussion that have shaped black intellectuals' treatment of sports ever since the Black Power days. How many black commentators feel obligated to follow these militants of another era by either declaring or implying the black man's physical (and sexual) superiority? How many have publicly dissented from the view that Muhammad Ali (or, more recently, Michael Jordan) is the supreme African-American achiever of his epoch? How many have openly challenged the idea that physical self-expression is the essence of being a black man?

These are important questions, because they raise the issue of whether black intellectuals are genuinely free to talk about the African-American involvement in sports and what it may have cost in terms of educational development. The intellectual's identification with the athlete can only make it more difficult for him to see how athleticism can be antithetical to the life of the mind, since he sees the life of his own mind closely bound up with athleticism and may even see his thought processes as a form of athletic effort. "It was quite generous, I thought," wrote the novelist and essayist Ishmael Reed, "for critic Mel Watkins to compare my writing style with that of [sic] Muhammad Ali's boxing style . . . If I had to compare my style with anyone's it would probably be with that of Larry Holmes."[21] Reed also titled one of his essay collections *Writin' Is Fightin': Thirty-Seven Years of Boxing on Paper*. Such formulations are not simply affectations, but rather confirm that black intellectuals make their own contributions to the athleticizing of the black mind.[22]

Exalting black athleticism has also led some intellectuals to question the value of nonphysical forms of cultural self-expression that supposedly do not dramatize black life with the immediacy of athletic competition. These writers believe that physical prowess represents the essence of the black experience in a way that other forms of expression cannot. Here too we see a fascination with the phenomenon of sheer physical struggle that can prompt the writer to confess his own shameful ineffectuality in comparison with the black athlete, who acts out the oppression of his people in real blood, sweat, and tears. "It was in a folklore moulded out of rigorous and inhuman conditions of life," Richard Wright wrote in 1938, with Joe Louis on his mind, "that the Negro achieved his most indigenous and complete expression."[23]

We have already seen the impact of these "rigorous and inhuman conditions of life," of this cruelly protracted and profoundly physical ordeal, on the African-American imagination. That is why discussions of the terrible sufferings of the Middle Passage can still incite anger when they are joined with speculations on the origins of black hypertension. In 1962 Amiri Baraka invoked this tradition of physical suffering to account for "the absence of achievement among serious Negro artists, except in Negro music." Baraka suggested, in effect, that the fine arts were simply too effete to represent the harsh conditions of black life:

> It is because of this "separation" between Negro life (as an emotional experience) and Negro art, that, say, Jack Johnson or [Sugar] Ray Robinson is a larger cultural hero than any Negro writer. It is because of this separation, even evasion, of the emotional experience of Negro life, that Jack Johnson is a more modern political symbol than most Negro writers. Johnson's life, as proposed, certainly, by his career, reflects much more accurately the symbolic yearnings for singular values among the great masses of Negroes than any black novelist has managed to convey. Where is the Negro-ness of a literature written in imitation of the meanest of social intelligences to be found in American culture, *i.e.*, the white middle class?[24]

It is important to recognize this denigration of literature as the act of emotional blackmail it is. Baraka virtually dares the black intelligentsia to choose between pugilism and art, between the authority of the body and that of the mind, between masculinity and effeminacy, implying all the while that only music and sports fall within the magic circle of authentically black self-expression. The reckless iconoclasm of this demand makes even the firebrand author of *Soul on Ice* sound like a moderate. "Haven't you ever wondered," Cleaver asks, "why the white man genuinely applauds a black man who achieves excellence with his body in the field of sports, while he hates to see a black man achieve excellence with his brain?"[25] For all of his racial militancy, Cleaver was open-minded enough not to dictate the parameters of artistic life to other blacks. Yet how many young intellectuals have been held hostage to the blackmailing tactics of Baraka and the racial chauvinists who have followed in his wake? Where, indeed, we might ask, is the "Negroness" of the middle-class black academics who have succeeded Baraka and Cleaver as commentators on race and sports? How can such people establish their racial credentials to the satisfaction of black nationalists and their demands for authenticity? Consider, for example, the predicament of a young black academic who is tormented by the apparent contradiction between being a professor and being a homeboy and who may also be concerned about the impression he makes on the basketball court.

Here we confront a seldom-discussed obstacle to intellectual development that originates in profound feelings about physical ability as the guarantor of black survival. "The scholar finds himself especially torn," say the authors of *Black Rage,* since he must choose between his family's ambitions for him and an instinctive sense that he must not outperform his parents. In addition, the black intellectual has had to stand comparison with the legendary "bad niggers" who "provided the measure of manhood for all black men and stood in ultimate masculine opposition to the feminine counterpart who sought protection from the foe by turning to education. Thus any man who turned from violent confrontation of the white enemy and instead followed academic pursuits would have to feel deep inside, in his heart of hearts, that he had retreated from the battle. It was his secret, this cowardice, and there was an emptiness where his manhood might have been."[26]

This is the heritage to which Amiri Baraka and Eldridge Cleaver brought new life in the 1960s. Baraka invoked the athlete precisely because he cannot be trumped as *the* dramatic symbol of black suffering, and the visceral force of this spectacle has bound black intellectuals to sports in a unique way. Cultural critics who remain confined within this legacy, held hostage by the false dichotomy between the martyred black athlete and the effete black thinker who "acts white," will find it difficult to assess the costs and benefits of the black athletic subculture with the dispassion this analysis requires.

The black intelligentsia's response to the sports fixation has always been ambivalent, because it has been held captive by this melodrama of the suffering black body and the idea that it articulates the deepest stratum of black experience. A second source of ambivalence has been uneasiness about the political value of athletic achievement, which is an ambiguous form of self-expression in that it can signify either self-abasement or self-assertion. Cleaver, an early and aggressive critic of the coopted black athlete, cited in 1968 "the historical fact that the only Negro Americans allowed to attain national or international fame have been the puppets and lackeys of the white power structure — and entertainers and athletes . . . By crushing black leaders, while inflating the images of Uncle Toms and celebrities from the apolitical world of sport and play, the mass media were able to channel and control the aspirations and goals of the black masses." Cleaver was one of the few commentators historically minded enough to make the point that white authorities have traditionally granted black celebrities more influence than dynamic black men of greater intellectual ability: "When the question of segregation in the armed services arose during the '40s, the then heavyweight champion of the world, Joe Louis, and Louis Satchmo Armstrong, who was also noted for blowing a trumpet, were more likely to be quoted on the subject than A. Philip Randolph or W.E.B. Du-Bois."[27] Yet even Cleaver was ambivalent about black involvement in sports, in that his oft-repeated scorn for "entertainers and athletes" was countered by a belief that a heroic black athleticism could ultimately transform the image of black humanity. "The white man wants to be the *brain* and he wants us to be the muscle, the *body*," he wrote. But "Muhammad Ali, the Brain," had confounded this formula by means of his religious conversion and political revolt, demonstrating that the Supermasculine Menial might someday recover the mind that a racist society had taken from him.[28]

Ishmael Reed, who has published essays on Muhammad Ali and Mike Tyson, athleticizes his own identity even though he understands how sports have damaged his people. Like some other writers, black and white, he dignifies athleticism by blurring the boundary between physicality and artistic creation. "Writing poetry," he says, "is the hard manual labor of the imagination." And, "To be a good black poet in the '60s meant capturing the rhythms of Ali and Malcolm X on the page."[29] "The task of adequately describing the blues," says Houston Baker, "is equivalent to the labor of describing a world class athlete's awesome gymnastics."[30] Metaphorical exercises of this kind are meant to elevate the cultural status of athleticism, which many African Americans regard as a prime black art form, by making poetic creativity and athletic grace flow from the same source.

Yet Reed also understands that black athleticism provides an unending flow of disastrous images that are eagerly disseminated by the white-dominated media industry: "In the print and electronic media, pictures of blacks are associated with social pathology, while whites are represented as society's stewards." Sports become a part of this pathology, "since the typical image of blacks on television is that of a violent or physical people, involved in criminal activity or athletics." Reed is properly suspicious of the white image factory, which is constantly producing "blacks who always seem to be poised for a jump shot." He resents the fact that black children are presented with "buffoonish entertainers and athletes as role models." He salutes the poet Gwendolyn Brooks, who "will not tolerate the fools who cry 'Africa!' only to go home and watch 'Gunsmoke,' 'Gilligan's Island,' and the NFL"[31] — which might prompt us to ask whether a black *male* writer has ever counseled abstinence from the National Football League as a way of escaping the corrosive inanities of white popular culture.

Black critiques of sports tend to lack coherence, because they cannot reconcile a deep attachment to athleticism and its charismatic black hero with the inevitable exploitation of black athletes by white image-makers and the white financial interests they serve. One result of this unresolved conflict is a surprising lack of interest in the relationship between the sports fixation and the anti-intellectual attitudes that flourish among black youth. Reed, for example, who objects with good reason to the image of blacks as "physical people," has little more to offer than a collection of inchoate resentments as opposed to a philosophy of action that might move the black image in a more cerebral direction. When he claims that it is rappers and not educators who have succeeded "in motivating inner-city youth to take as much interest in language as they do in basketball," he does not mention that black boys' preoccupation with basketball might be one part of the problem.[32] It is curious that his real insights into the effects of this preoccupation do not add up to a resolve to confront the addiction to athleticism as the social pathology it is.

A similar lack of focus on sports and educational issues is evident in Cornel West's best-selling manifesto *Race Matters,* although here the root of the problem is a lack of familiarity with athletes rather than an identification with them. West is clearly a sporting neophyte who, as a black intellectual, feels obligated to address a subject that does not really interest him in more than a peripheral way. In fact, his only thesis about sport is that it promotes racial integration through cultural borrowing: "The Afro-Americanization of white youth — given the disproportionate black role in popular music and athletics — has put white kids in closer contact with their own bodies and facilitated more human interaction with black people . . . This process results in white youth — male and female — imitating and emulating black male styles of walking, talking, dressing, and gesticulating in relation to others."[33] It is a measure of West's estrangement from the realities of the black sports world that he addresses the stylistic impact of black athletes on young whites rather than their more baneful influence on the career aspirations of young blacks.

What West does have to offer, however, are some general observations about the black male predicament, which he could link to involvement with sports but does not. One of his favorite themes is the power of corporate interests and advertising experts to impose "market forces and market moralities" on black life: "The reduction of individuals to objects of pleasure is especially evident in the culture industries — television, radio, video, music — in which gestures of sexual foreplay and orgiastic pleasure flood the marketplace. Like all Americans, African-Americans are influenced greatly by the images of comfort, convenience, machismo, femininity, violence, and sexual stimulation that bombard consumers." It is striking that West does not mention the ubiquitous and often subliminally racist images of professional athletes that occupy a place in this perverse consumer paradise. Again without mentioning the sports world, he refers to "a black tragedy of major proportions: the refusal of white and black America to entertain seriously new stylistic options for black men caught in the deadly endeavor of rejecting black machismo identities."[34] Here too he does not point out that popular black athletes are a major source of the black male identities he deplores. Equally striking is the fact that West invokes "visceral feelings about black bodies fed by racist myths and promoted by market-driven quests for stimulation" without saying a word about the role of black athleticism in maintaining this traffic in racial mythology.[35]

If Cornel West does not really engage with the issue of black athleticism, another commentator embraces it with such fervor that he becomes conceptually disoriented in the process. The most credulous of the academic apologists for the cultural importance of the black athlete is Michael Eric Dyson, a professor of communications who has been called upon to interpret rap music for the predominantly white readership of the *New York Times*.[36] In his essay "Be Like Mike? Michael Jordan and the Pedagogy of Desire," Dyson transforms "the best, and best-known, athlete in the world today" into a towering redemptive figure in the messianic tradition of Joe Louis. In the process of formulating his paean, he makes claims about black culture that should arrest the attention of every reader, including the galaxy of African-American academic stars who endorsed his book (including Cornel West as well as Henry Louis Gates, Jr. and William Julius Wilson). Basketball, he says, has become "the metaphoric center of black cultural imagination"; hence "the Olympian sum of Jordan's cultural meaning," "the herculean cultural heroism he has come to embody," and his "cultural canonization."[37]

To be sure, Dyson is aware that black athleticism is vulnerable to exploitation. He knows, for example, that "the African-American aspects of Jordan's game [spontaneity, improvisation, deceptiveness] are indissolubly linked to the culture of consumption and the commodification of black culture," and he is candid enough to fault Jordan himself for his indifference to the consequences of his advertising appeals to young blacks. The moral force of these doubts dissolves, however, in the dazzling brilliance of Jordan's "unparalleled cultural status" and the fact that his achievements "have furthered the cultural acceptance of at least the athletic black body."[38] But how can Dyson fail to understand the meagerness of this achievement, since accepting "the athletic black body" has always been the path of least resistance for whites who will not recognize black people as fully human?

Dyson's determination to make Jordan an emblem of social progress requires an inflation of his symbolic value that is achieved by ignoring historical change, for while it is true that black athletes have in the past "acquired a heroic dimension" and served as "icons of cultural excellence," their stature originated in the needs of black people who lived in a segregated society. Dyson's attempt to make Michael Jordan a worthy successor to Joe Louis and Jackie Robinson fails because Jordan has never confronted a segregated society or the white authorities of his own era. What he does confront is an advertising market that cannot get enough of him. Fixated on the idea of Jordan's redemptive mission, Dyson transforms this super-commercialized athlete into "a public pedagogue, a figure of estimable public moral authority" and "the supreme symbol of black creativity" — an endorsement that amounts to a remarkable transfer of authority from the mind to the body.[39]

It is important to recognize that this extravagant rhetoric derives from a tradition that has equated black athleticism with black creativity in the widest sense, "extending the scope and expressive range of black humanity in mainstream culture," as Gerald Early has put it.[40] Even Ralph Ellison, who was as immune to cultural chauvinism as anyone can be, called Joe Louis "as elegant as the finest of ballet dancers"[41] and saw an athletic dimension in jazz. "It is an orgiastic art," he wrote in 1958, "which demands great physical stamina of its practitioners, and many of its most talented creators die young."[42]

The connection between athleticism and black music is in fact a favorite theme of black writers. James Baldwin compared the "miraculously tough and tender" heavyweight champion Floyd Patterson to the great jazz trumpeter Miles Davis, who was given to "presenting himself, in alter ego guise, as a prizefighter."[43] "One could say," the critic Stanley Crouch wrote in 1979, "that Muhammad Ali comes close to jazz and his art says some things about innovation in particularly American terms . . . Performing sports are arts of the moment. Like the jazzman, the training of the great athlete has prepared him to manhandle the moment."[44] Joe Louis, says Gerald Early, "was the greatest, the most expansive and mythical blues hero in twentieth-century America, nothing less."[45] "Like a streamlined athlete's awesomely dazzling explosions of prowess," writes Houston Baker, "the blues song erupts, creating a veritable playful festival of meaning."[46]

While there is no question that such analogies show the creative imagination at work, we must again ask whether this identification with athleticism has also precluded serious work on the racial politics of sport. What is certain is that some very able black writers have adopted the athletic idiom to express their most serious thoughts about how blacks should live. "If there is any job before us," Stanley Crouch said in a memorial service for a departed friend, "it is to decide whether we shall go to the gym and train for the professional championships, or sloppily train, never move toward a professional contest but will demand prize monies and trophies on the basis of sentimental manipulation."[47]

Today the least conflicted black critic of the sports fixation tends to be the so-called conservative, for whom the celebration of black athleticism appears as one more diversion from the most serious and intractable problems facing black people. It is therefore appropriate that the most persuasive critique of the sports fixation appears in the context of a discussion of black educational underachievement. In *The Content of Our Character,* Shelby Steele's best-selling treatise on the damaging emotional complexities of the African-American psyche, the author sees the focus on athletic achievement as a self-defeating defensive strategy, a way of staving off self-doubts that are continually being generated by academic failure. "Across the country thousands of young black males take every opportunity and make every effort to reach the elite ranks of the NBA or NFL," Steele writes. "But in the classroom, where racial vulnerability is a hidden terror, they and many of their classmates put forth the meagerest effort and show a virtual indifference to the genuine opportunity that is education." Steele regards athleticism as an example of "compensatory grandiosity," even including "the magnificent egotism of a Muhammad Ali." While such grandiosity has enriched American culture, it "can become too much of an escape from diminishment, too much of a self-delusion. It can become a form of dependency, a posture of personal or racial specialness that we rely on to keep the demons of doubt at bay. In this lower form, beauty and grace change into self-advertisement, a stance of superiority that we take on for promotional purposes." Steele refuses to romanticize the black body, and he insists on recognizing the pathos that always lurked inside the doggerel and the exhibitionist swagger of a popular black hero like Ali. On a smaller scale, he finds the same complex at work at the integrated high school he attended, where "one of the worst sins a black student could be guilty of was not dancing well."[48]

It is worth noting that Steele's treatment of this kind of black chauvinism could have been much blunter and even crueler if he had felt so inclined. The Jamaican-born sociologist Orlando Patterson has offered a less sparing portrait of such Afrocentric vanities in his description of the "survivalist" school of black history. "One unfortunate aspect of survivalism," he wrote in 1971, "is that, so often, it so easily degenerates into a vulgar exoticism in which there is not only an obsessive glorification of one's 'soul' but all sorts of inverted racist claims of superior sexual potency and greater zest and passion for life, a crass wallowing in none too 'noble savagery.'"[49]

This analysis can easily be applied to certain celebrations of black athleticism. The economist and social critic Glenn Loury, for example, has criticized "the pernicious chauvinism that leads a black to feel himself superior in view of the demographic composition of the NBA."[50] Yet notwithstanding the painstaking diplomacy of Steele's book, he has been branded a black conservative, and I have heard black academics dismiss him as a traitor to the race. Steele's critics should remember that it was the left-wing African-American hero Paul Robeson who said in 1949, "We Negroes must begin to realize that there is more to life than singing, dancing, and playing ball. We have to speak out for our people."[51]

How black intellectuals deal with athleticism is important because of athleticism's role in the ongoing cultural civil war that has pitted African-American defenders of "middle-class" values against a loose coalition of "gangsta rappers," flamboyant athletes, their various apologists, and white-owned corporate and media interests that profit from the production of black male stereotypes. Members of the black intelligentsia are found on both sides of this conflict, and the same critic may assess the value of athletes and rappers in very different ways. Stanley Crouch, a lionizer of Muhammad Ali, has called rap "either an infantile self-celebration or anarchic glamourization of criminal behavior." Rappers "are not rebelling against anything," he adds. "They are a bunch of opportunists who are appealing to an appetite that America has for vulgarity, violence and anarchy inside Afro America."[52] "Most blacks," an African-American journalism professor wrote in 1993, "feel that hip-hoppers, vulgar comedians and movie makers are doing a great disservice to the black cause." A year earlier, he reported, "many members of the National Association of Black Journalists walked out of a workshop session with rap artists to protest the use of the terms 'bitches' and 'ho's.'"[53] "This new wave of rap music," says a writer who specializes in covering the rap scene, "has influenced black children in a bad way. It's made us think that being hard is the sole definition of being black in the 1990's."[54] "Gangsta rappers," a black minister wrote during the media backlash of late 1993, "have slipped to a level of base behavior that is not recognized within African and African-American cultures."[55]

Michael Eric Dyson, by contrast, has defended even the more aggressive forms of rap music as uniquely informative about "complex dimensions of ghetto life" and against what he regards as hypocritical attacks from the black middle class.[56] Gangster rap, he wrote in 1994, "is largely an indictment of bourgeois black cultural institutions by young people who do not find conventional methods of addressing personal and social calamity useful." His most interesting argument is that a misogynistic and sexist black church has forfeited its moral authority to criticize the "verbal sexual misconduct" of foul-mouthed rappers: "Gangster rap's greatest sin, in the eyes of many critics, is that it tells the truth about practices and beliefs that rappers hold in common with the black elite. This music has embarrassed black bourgeois culture and exposed its polite sexism and its disregard for gay men and lesbians."[57]

Dyson sees rap as a predominantly positive force in black life, praising its "productive and healthy moments" and claiming that it has "provided a healthy and flourishing alternative to a burgeoning juvenocracy in the urban inner city." He embraces "the possibility for expanding the didactic functions, the teaching functions of rap music — people are now talking about adopting rap music in the classroom, and it's primarily because of the powerful positive messages that these groups convey."[58] He explains the cultural division that rap has provoked as the result of generational and class differences rather than the bad taste or warped values of younger blacks. Indeed, his repeated use of the word *healthy* to describe the effects of rap is an implicit refutation of its pathological reputation.

Dyson finesses the effects of gangster rap with the same evenhandedness he brings to black athleticism, and the verdict once again favors the culture of the street. While the rap group N.W.A. (Niggaz With Attitudes) needs to develop "an ethical perspective" on drug gangs, it and other rap artists are "truly urban griots dispensing social and cultural critique, verbal shamans exorcising the demons of cultural amnesia."[59] Like the "public pedagogue" Michael Jordan, the rap star is an educator who conveys the lore of black history to his young admirers.

The most obvious problems with this doctrine derive from the cultural illiteracy of the rappers and the fact that attempts to squeeze "education" out of popular culture are usually signs of desperation rather than hope. But behind the problem of determining whether harnessing the wisdom of rappers' minds and athletes' bodies actually makes sense, there is the problem of motive. Why does the progressive African-American professor make such a point of criticizing and baiting the black bourgeoisie and its conception of middle-class respectability?

Black intellectuals have taken anti-bourgeois positions in the African-American cultural wars when they have found middle-class taste to be intolerably narrow and "white" in a way that denies the legitimacy of black cultural achievements. The classic conflict of this kind was the internecine struggle over the blues, which pitted clergymen and other "quality" black men against "primitive" black artists.[60] "Only Negro music," Amiri Baraka wrote in *Blues People,* "has been able to survive the constant and willful dilutions of the black middle class," since "the emotional significance and vitality at its core remain, to this day, unaltered. It was the one vector out of African culture impossible to eradicate."[61] Michael Eric Dyson has adopted this argument to make an analogous case for rap: "The blues functioned for another generation of blacks much as rap functions for young blacks today: as a source of racial identity, permitting forms of boasting and asserting machismo for devalued black men suffering from social degradation, allowing commentary on social and personal conditions in uncensored language, and fostering the ability to transform hurt and anguish into art and commerce."[62] Here as elsewhere, Dyson raises questions about his ability to discriminate between higher and lower cultural productions. The larger point, however, is that opposing factions have defined black achievement in different ways, and it is here that our inquiry into black athleticism's cultural status must begin. Has black athleticism succeeded black music as an insurgent culture that challenges "respectable" norms?

The black middle class and its educated progeny have never achieved full independence from white cultural standards, and this lack of autonomy has complicated the problem of defining what black achievement, and therefore black identity, actually are. In addition, some of the children of what Harold Cruse calls this "culturally imitative and unimaginative" class have repudiated the conservatism of their parents and made common cause with the cultural productions of "ordinary" blacks.[63] The black middle class, as Baraka once pointed out, "wanted no subculture, nothing that could connect them with the poor black man or the slave."[64] Black middle-class children who embrace ghetto rappers are thus repeating a perennial black bourgeois trauma. It is interesting to learn that even as revered a figure as Joe Louis once caused this sort of pain. "Of course," Gerald Early writes, "the black bourgeoisie rejected Louis at first, rejecting the idea of having the 'genius' of the Negro race represented by a mere prizefighter in much the same way that whites rejected him at first as representative of American manhood and masculinity."[65] Even more interesting, however, is how Early handles the issue of black athleticism and the "genius" of the race. Early has no patience for the "black philistines" who looked down on the black fighter, because he believes they had no standards of their own by which to make such judgments. Their disapproval, he says, was "the black philistine's cry for standards and achievements that whites would be bound to respect because the black philistine never wanted freedom for blacks, only the right and access to be absorbed by a massive white philistinism." During the civil rights era, the symbolically diverse careers of the bourgeois Floyd Patterson, the thuggish Sonny Liston, and the rebellious Muhammad Ali made "blacks as a group examine to some considerable degree the epistemological core of black achievement, social uplift, and race pride. Not every black who achieves in this culture should be a symbol of race pride, and perhaps none should; but if there are to be such, then they should by their example tell us something remarkable about what being a black American is."[66]

Early's analysis is clearly formulated yet tantalizingly incomplete.

For one thing, he does not explore "the epistemological core of black achievement" beyond implying that it must not be held hostage to white standards. Repelled by the "ungracious and graceless self-consciousness" of the black bourgeoisie, he gravitates naturally toward the athlete's supposed humility and lack of pretense. He feels no obligation here to determine whether athleticism deserves the same status as artistry in the traditional (white) sense, or to think about whether the extraordinary prestige of black athleticism might have deleterious effects on black educational ambitions. Indeed, by requiring the person who symbolizes race pride to express the essence of the African-American experience, he guarantees a place for the athlete in the black pantheon of culture heroes, for if the sweat of the athlete and the sweat of the bluesman issue from the same pool of suffering, then they are self-expressive branches of the same experiential tree. It thus appears that Early is so intent on honoring the physical ordeal of his people that he is willing to suspend any disbelief about the cultural value and social consequences of black athleticism. But the price of this loyalty to the sufferings of the black body may well be a disengagement from certain cultural controversies that periodically rock the black community.

The reception of the former heavyweight champion Mike Tyson after his release from prison in March 1995 is a case in point. The nearly all-male "welcoming committee" that put on a somewhat anticlimactic "salute" to Tyson on June 20 was criticized by black writers such as Bob Herbert of the *New York Times,* the columnist Clarence Page, and Jill Nelson of African-Americans Against Violence, all of them representing the bourgeois respectability scorned by Tyson's entourage. As Dyson might have predicted, Tyson's reception in Harlem drew a crowd of forgiving black preachers who proclaimed him "the prodigal son."[67] (Ishmael Reed saw Tyson as the victim of "a lynching fest.")[68] It was perhaps inevitable that the ideological conflict at the core of this clash received so little coverage in the press. That, however, simply demonstrates the invisibility of the black middle class and its desperate struggle against the media's glorification of the deviant black male. "What blacks who achieve prominence in this culture should be admired?" Early asks in his discussion of middle-class blacks' anxieties about their unruly racial brethren. It is tempting to reply that criminals, at the least, should be excluded from this select group. Yet this sort of exclusivity ignores the fact that as a cultural figure, Mike Tyson is a direct descendant of Joe Louis, and that the charisma of his athleticism will certainly prevail over "middle-class" disapproval of his "uncivilized" conduct, in part because white media interests have a vested interest in restoring him to stardom. But if Tyson is an embarrassment to respectable blacks, then who among them will disavow the cult of black athleticism that has preserved his stature as a cultural icon?

Even as mature a writer as John Edgar Wideman has served up the pathological Dennis Rodman as an example of creative black resistance to white domination. Rodman, he says, is "a perpetual work in progress, compelling, outrageous, amoral," a Caliban who cannot be tamed by the Prosperos who pay him: "The czar and his minions can make these syncretic outlaw creatures, but can't break them. Somewhere just out of sight, Dennis the Menace, the Worm, the Gangsta Rapper, the Rebel Robot plot their revenge."[69] Seduced by Rodman's unique proficiency at the game he himself loves, Wideman embraces the black rebel on his own self-indulgent, juvenile terms, siding with the athletic exhibitionist against the respectable norms of black people who regard Rodman as an embarrassment.

If there are members of the black intelligentsia who might begin to reshape the role of sports in the imaginations of young people, black and white, they would be filmmakers such as Spike Lee and John Singleton, the latter of whom in 1994 said, "Enough of basketball. Our children need assets like technology that will lead us into the next century. And they need to learn that it's *cool* to learn this technology."[70] This is not, however, the public viewpoint of Spike Lee. As the highly visible companion of Michael Jordan, a defender of their televised Nike ads, a conspicuous fan of the New York Knicks, and a regular visitor to Mike Tyson during his imprisonment for rape, Lee is not inclined to ask probing questions about the negative effects of black athleticism.[71]

To be sure, Lee's highly public involvement with black athletes is one kind of response to Cornel West's complaint about "the widespread refusal of black intellectuals to remain, in some visible way, organically linked with African-American cultural life." Yet the mere fact of "organic linkage" does not guarantee constructive results. As Michael Bérubé has pointed out, intellectuals who engage with popular culture "need not settle for the role of fan, disk jockey, or press agent" in the manner of Spike Lee's engagement with sport, which includes a measure of political fatalism.[72] "Today's Afro-American athlete," he said in 1993, "is not going to stick his neck out, jeopardize a contract or a sneaker deal."[73] This resignation (and Lee's cheerleader status in the arena) are hardly compatible with Houston Baker's claim that Lee has taken aim at "a complicitous black silence before white, Western courts of power and desire."[74]

The key question is whether the black intellectual is prepared to

criticize the iconic status of physical culture in black life. This is unlikely
in that the male bonding exemplified by Lee's exhibitionistic fandom
will continue to be a formidable obstacle. "Several decades ago," wrote
the psychiatrists Grier and Cobbs, "observers were impressed by the
black community's adulation of Joe Louis . . . Educated and sophisticated Negroes also participated in this hero worship, since all black men
swim in the same sea."[75] Precisely because this male bonding inhibits
criticism, the cultural deflation of black athleticism will have to be the
work of black feminists such as Bell Hooks, who has criticized Lee's
"exotification of phallocentric black masculinity" and the "pugilistic
eroticism" of the actor Eddie Murphy. "On the terms set by white
supremacist patriarchy," she writes, "black men can name their pain
only by talking about themselves in crude ways that reinscribe them in a
context of primitivism." But these are the very terms on which the
world of black athleticism exists. Small wonder, then, that the black
intellectuals who are best able to escape disabling identifications with
athletes are women. Not all black women, however, take a critical view
of the sports fixation. In her story "The Fight," an inspirational retelling
of Joe Louis's victory over Primo Carnera, Maya Angelou credits the
"Brown Bomber" with refuting the racist idea "that we were lower
types of human beings," and proving "that we were the strongest people
in the world."[70]

*What does Hobetman mean by "black athleticism," and why does he find "inherently racist in destructive of race relations in a multiracial society?*

# PART II

# Prospero and Caliban

---

## Sport As Racial Competition

# 6

# Wonders Out of Africa

THE ASCENDANCY of the black athlete over the past century and the growing Western belief in his biological superiority represent a historic reversal of roles in the racial encounter between Africans and the West. White European preeminence during the nineteenth century included the presumption of physical as well as intellectual and characterological superiority over other races, and athletic ability played a significant role in establishing white male authority in colonial societies. The British Empire was the *locus classicus* of this masculine style, and sporting encounters between colonial masters and native subjects became symbolic racial competitions, which have continued to the present day.

The development of sport during the postcolonial period has transformed the colonial racial constellation of "white" and "colored" into a far more complex global subculture of elite competitions. The significance of the 1996 World Cup cricket matches, for example, was not that the result demonstrated "colored" (Sri Lankan) supremacy; black West Indians, after all, have won cricket competitions for the past two decades with a vengeance. The new element was that the Indian subcontinent had now become the center of an English sport, and the fierce enmity that marked the India-Pakistan matches showed that skin color had lost the meaning it possessed in different historical and political circumstances.[1] In 1982, as *The Guardian* noted, England's cricketers had "travelled unwillingly to Colombo, believing that such a match was beneath their strutting dignity."[2] Now their reluctance to confront Asians on the cricket pitch was rooted in the fear of defeat. After England was humiliated by the Sri Lankans at the 1996 world championship, the chairman of the English Test and County Cricket Board offered a dire prediction: "If our team keeps going the way it has been going, then our game will die."[3]

This new world order has also led to a racial integration of European sports teams that would have been unimaginable, much less permissible, in the colonial age. At the same time, global multiracialism has brought with it a globalization of the racial folklore that is always generated by multiethnic sports. A fateful consequence of this folklore has been the growing demoralization of many white athletes, who in recent years have found themselves unable to cope with their darker-skinned competitors around the world.

The European sense of superiority vis-à-vis other races that developed during centuries of exploration rested on a self-conscious pride in a whole range of achievements: technological innovations, military proficiency, the Christian religion, literacy, the habit of wearing clothes (which promoted sexual self-control), and even the machine-regulated time sense made possible by clocks. In addition, there was a broad consensus that Europeans were both physically superior to and more courageous than the "savages" they met in remote places. Throughout the nineteenth century, which saw the first comparative measurements of racial aptitudes, sport (like war) was an arena in which Caucasian men displayed both physical mastery and the masculine qualities of character that established their right to command the other races. In particular, Anglo-Saxon racial self-confidence was built on an athleticism of both physique and temperament, and the conquered or submissive inferior played a role in confirming the masculinity of the explorer or colonist, whose toughness and self-confidence made him a charismatic and athletic figure who was in most cases contemptuous of Africans and Asians as well as of whites who could not keep up with him.

The greatest of these explorers, Richard Francis Burton, exemplified the athletic dimension of his role. His legendary achievements in Africa and Asia owed not a little to his tremendous capacity for physical and mental suffering. This superhuman stoicism was made possible by sheer force of will and gave Burton an aura: Arthur Symons wrote of his "tremendous animalism," while Frank Harris said he "looked like a prize-fighter."[4] Burton's "ferocity" also enabled him to anticipate the pitiless ethos of modern high-performance sport. After climbing one of the highest peaks in the Cameroon mountains, he wrote, "To be first in such matters is everything, to be second nothing."[5] This infatuation with achievement went hand in hand with the Victorian mania for measuring and comparing racial aptitudes of mind and body, a mania that expressed, in addition to scientific curiosity, an interest in power. "I soon acquired the reputation of being the strongest man in Zayla," Burton boasted in 1854. "This is perhaps the easiest way of winning respect from a barbarous people, who honour body and degrade mind to mere cunning."[6] The same strategy was recommended at the end of the century by the French explorer Èdouard Foa, who warned that the white man who lacked the requisite physical skills and endurance — and thus permitted himself to be intimidated — would lose his authority and perhaps his life if he did not maintain *la supériorité physique.*[7]

European superiority was in fact regarded more as a matter of character than of physique, and no one promoted this theme more insistently than the British governing class, for whom the administration of colonial subjects was quite literally a matter of life and death. (Indeed, their urgent emotional need for this sort of personal superiority required invidious comparisons between themselves and other white Europeans, the Germans and French in particular, quite apart from the comparisons with "racial aliens," or nonwhites.)[8] While the capacity for courage was seen as the indispensable basis of masculine dignity, the British need to distinguish between distinct black and white masculinities actually split the phenomenon of courage along racial lines. While less racist observers could see Africans as "naturally courageous," others saw their courage as somehow degenerate or inauthentic. The Zulu warrior was "daring" but not "brave"; he possessed only "the courage of maniacs and drunkards," or his bravery came from the intoxicants he ingested before going into battle.[9] Many years later, the white Kenyan torturers of Mau Mau suspects saw the tenacity of their victims as a stubbornness that was somehow less than genuine courage: "Detainees were sometimes beaten until they were unconscious, or dead, without screaming or pleading for mercy. The screeners were maddened by this stoicism, which they saw as mute animal obstinacy rather than courage, and eventually the beatings that were to have cleansed the Mau Mau cleansed the screeners instead."[10]

That the colonial mentality simply could not grant full manhood to nonwhites confirms that the cult of masculinity was an integral part of the entire colonial enterprise. In a similar vein, the reluctance of many white Americans to grant administrative authority or "immortal" status to black athletes such as Henry Aaron, who surpassed the "legendary" Babe Ruth, implies that neocolonialist assumptions about racial character persist in today's "integrated" sports establishment.

Europeans felt a profound ambivalence toward the physically vital African, which expressed itself as a conflict between the Caucasian observer's racial narcissism and the simultaneous need to find in the "primitive" an idealized male type, an athleticized "noble savage" who possessed all of the masculine virtues except the aura of command. This ambivalence is evident in the attitudes of Lord Baden-Powell, an eminent Edwardian who was the founder of the Boy Scout movement (in 1908) and a rather typical racist of his era. Despite his published reference to "the stupid inertness of the puzzled negro," Baden-Powell's fascination with and respect for Zulus and American Indians, their vitality and their outdoor skills, have entered the culture of the West through the Boy Scout handbook. In fact, Baden-Powell saw the admiration of muscles as a mutual preoccupation of blacks and whites. Thus he was pleased to report that a party of African chiefs who visited Britain in the 1890s had been smitten by a group of well-built British gymnastics instructors and "were not fully satisfied until they had the men stripped and had examined for themselves their muscular development."[11] This was a rare instance of whites being undressed to satisfy the curiosity of blacks. In almost all other cases whites undressed and examined blacks, sometimes including their blood and their semen, in the context of "scientific" or "ethnological" investigations which they did not recognize as indirectly introspective procedures. Like the undressing games of preadolescent children, these examinations allowed "civilized" whites to explore their own sexual and "barbarian" parts.

The ambivalent relationship to the "primitive" was a part of the Western imagination a century before Baden-Powell made it an official part of acquiring imperial manhood, and it lives on in the world of interracial sport. The Texas coach who in 1992 screamed out a racial epithet to motivate her black athlete (thereby causing a scandal) was reenacting this fascination with the racial exotic, in that her denigration also expressed admiration for a prodigious (and atavistic) athleticism. Provoked beyond the restraints of racial politesse, the coach made a desperate attempt to catalyze the athlete's racial soul and its special energies.[12]

While some early-nineteenth-century Europeans expressed disappointment that the black African was inferior in strength to the chimpanzee and the orangutan,[13] later assessments bore witness to the physical vitality of these "grand specimens of savage humanity."[14] Europeans who penetrated into the African interior found indigenous physical cultures that could be both exotic and deadly. Richard Burton witnessed battles to the death between wrestlers intoxicated with opium and marijuana. The Scottish explorer Hugh Clapperton, having organized a boxing match among the Hausa, prohibited serious fighting when he learned that some of the combatants faced certain death. His colleague Dixon Denham attended wrestling matches between slaves whose owners threatened to shoot them if they lost, while snapped spines, dislocated limbs, and death were par for the course.[15]

African dances also prompted Europeans to compare their own physical capacities with those of the performers. Whereas a disdainful visitor
to the Colonial Exposition in Paris in 1931 described African dancing
as nothing more than "frenetic agitation and epileptic convulsions,"
earlier observers were literally awed by what they saw Africans do
with their bodies.[16] Europeans were amazed by the athletic agility of
Zulu dancers. A missionary who visited Zululand in 1835 saw young
women perform moves that "would cause a European female to go
upon crutches for the remainder of her life." Another British missionary, who visited the Ibos in 1920, described their dances as follows:
"The physical strength required is tremendous. The body movements
are extremely difficult and would probably kill a European."[17] Indeed,
some of the dancers drugged themselves in order "to exert themselves
abnormally. Under its influence they are capable of feats beyond anything they would attempt to do under natural conditions."[18]

In their own way, these observations responded to a suggestion offered in the "Manual of Ethnological Inquiry," published in England
in 1854, that the racial aliens might have "dances and games exhibiting agility, strength, or skill."[19] The discovery that they did held out
the possibility that they might possess supernormal physiologies as
well. There was already a variety of evidence to support such an assumption, including numerous accounts of extraordinary physical endurance. An English ship's surgeon sent to New Zealand in 1834 saw a
Maori chief who had suffered wounds that would have "killed outright
any man with a European constitution," yet they caused him "little
inconvenience beyond the weakness incidental to excessive haemor-
rhage."[20] Similar thinking about the special self-healing powers of Africans appeared over a century later in the report of an Austrian physiologist who journeyed to Uganda in 1911–1912 to pursue studies in
comparative racial biology.[21] Such views anticipate the supposedly
scientific ideas about the supernormal physiologies of African athletes
that haunt white athletes around the world today.

Scientific speculation about what we would call the athletic potential
of non-Western people has been a part of the Western racial imagination for at least two centuries. Even before the modern age of sport
began in Europe during the last decades of the nineteenth century,
observations of the physical and cultural characteristics of remote peoples had become a natural theme of travelers' accounts of their experiences at the far ends of the earth. The origins of physical anthropology
can thus be traced back to the European voyages of discovery that
made such observations possible. In particular, the European ethnologists of the nineteenth century, who sought to produce a portrait of the

human organism that included a full inventory of its physical capacities, recorded many observations of the physical strength, endurance, and quasi-athletic skills of Australian Aborigines, black Africans, American Indians, Eskimos, Polynesians, and others. By the beginning of that century, at least one of these amateur investigators was using a primitive dynamometer to measure the hand-grip strength of "savages."[22] From that point on, the scientizing of anthropological measurements increased along with the growing sophistication of scientific instruments that measured anatomical features, physiological variables, and sensory aptitudes. These measurements of the human body occurred simultaneously with the growth of scientific racism in Europe and the United States during the latter half of the 1800s.

In a colonial context or on a slave plantation, the physical capacities of the racial alien were of implicitly political as well as economic and scientific interest. Comparative ranking of the physical aptitudes of the different races could serve as a way of measuring the biological or even cultural vitality of competing racial groups. In fact, European ethnologists simultaneously admired and condescended to the physically impressive "savages," whom they regarded as cultural (if not always physical) inferiors. The European discovery of black African physical aptitudes must be understood in the context of a larger anthropological project that collected observations of a multiracial population spread across the globe. At the same time, Africans *were* unique in that they were invariably ranked lowest on the cultural scale and were assumed to be the racial antithesis of white Europeans. Associating black Africans with primates like the gorilla confirmed their low evolutionary status and at the same time suggested an unusual physical strength, which was eventually interpreted in sportive terms.

It is important to keep in mind that nineteenth-century Europeans who admired the bodies of black Africans (and other "aboriginal" or "primitive" people) did not see them as potential athletes; that is why we must speak of quasi- or proto-athletic traits and abilities at this time.[23] White anxieties about black African athletic potential appeared only at the end of the nineteenth century in the United States and during the 1920s in Germany. Today, the twilight of the Caucasian athlete is a regular feature of sports commentary in Germany, where public speculations about racial physiology can be carried on in the absence of a black population who might object to unsubstantiated talk about racially distinct muscle fiber percentages and "the ancient heritage of Mother Africa."[24]

In summary, today's speculations about racial physiology and anatomy continue a nineteenth-century tradition in a scientific idiom that deserves careful scrutiny. In this context it is important to determine the roles that old fantasies continue to play in ostensibly scientific work about racial differences. The Western search for anatomical and physiological differences bearing on proto-athletic and sportive aptitudes has been under way for two centuries and has by no means concluded its speculations and researches.

How have Europeans reacted to the unsettling idea that black Africans might be anatomically or physiologically superior to themselves? How have anthropological encounters affected the European self-image, once grounded in a profound sense of racial superiority? The historical record suggests that modern anxieties about white athletic competitiveness are only the most recent versions of concerns that appeared throughout the anthropological and ethnological literature of the nineteenth century. Indeed, the Western anthropological project that has pursued comparative studies of white and black bodies for the past two centuries has always included a competitive dimension. The study of differences leads naturally to invidious comparisons, and the judgments they produce have always been a staple of Western racial commentary. The interesting point here is that the Europeans' effortless sense of cultural and intellectual superiority did not insulate them from concerns about their own physical vitality when they were confronted with physically impressive people of other races. These anxieties are still alive, and today popular and scientific curiosity about African athletic aptitude plays a significant role in perpetuating archaic ideas about racial differences. Indeed, the rise of the black athlete during our own century has revived nineteenth-century racial physiology in new and more scientific forms.[25]

The racial competition of the later nineteenth century included comparisons of physical ability that sometimes took the form of physical contests.[26] Charles Darwin was only one of many who assumed that Europeans were generally stronger than darker-skinned people and that the performances of their explorers had confirmed this. In *The Descent of Man,* he stated that "civilised men [have] been found, wherever compared, to be physically stronger than savages. They appear also to have equal powers of endurance, as has been proved in many adventurous expeditions."[27]

Even before the appearance of Darwin's influential book in 1871, the German anthropologist Theodor Waitz had made the same point. In addition, he made an important distinction between vitality and muscular force that is characteristic of nineteenth-century racial anthropology: "The greatest energy of physical life is generally found, as indeed may be expected, among peoples in a primitive state; but the longer duration of life, a more extended power of acclimatization, a lesser destruction of life by diseases, and greater muscular strength, is found among civilized nations, owing to their protecting themselves from injurious influences of all kinds, in combination with superior nutrition and regular exercise."[28]

A British traveler to Africa reported in 1864 that "the stature of the negro is stunted; the knees are bent; the calves weak; the upper part of the thigh is thin; the head large, and sunk between the shoulders; and the whole form angular and badly shaped," all of this signifying "the feebleness of his muscles."[29] When in 1869 the British physician John Davy told an audience at the Anthropological Society of London that "the average negro [has] muscles as well developed as any European," his claim was refuted by a Mr. Tate ("He never saw a Negro run") and a Mr. Dendy, who referred to "the recent cricket matches, at Kennington Oval, between Englishmen and [Aboriginal] Australians. The latter batted well, but they lost every game because they could not run."[30] But not all British observers were so judgmental. "It must not be inferred," *Sporting Life* generously commented, "that they are savages."[31]

This distinction between the savage and the better-disciplined (and therefore better-trained) European helped to preserve the latter's athletic self-image and thus his sense of authority. At the same time, the superiority complex based on the white man's physical and characterological strength was always being challenged by positive impressions of African physicality. These sometimes took the form of awestruck wonder, as when Westerners responded to African dances. On a larger scale, the Zulu War of 1879 provided a dramatic demonstration of black African physical ability and courage to Europeans who had often doubted both. "We could not but admire the perfect manner in which these Zulus skirmished," said one British soldier.[32] While Europeans frequently saw "savage" existence as a form of "training" that conferred physiological advantages (such as physical endurance),[33] they might also see training as a technique that could preserve their own physical superiority vis-à-vis the "savage." "Civilised athletes" who have undergone "a course of training," one British physician wrote in 1888, can reach "the highest state of physical perfection a human being can attain to . . . a super-recuperative bodily vitality" which is "far beyond that of the standard of either the savage, or of the civilised typical man living in a rude state."[34]

At a time when the word *race* was often synonymous with nationality,

racial athletic competition came to include invidious comparisons between pale and scrawny Englishmen and the tough white colonials of
Anglo-Saxon heritage who had conquered the wilderness tracts of Australia, New Zealand, the United States, and Canada.[35] "On the river, the
running path, and the cricket field our distant cousins have already
sufficiently proved that they are no degenerate descendants of the old
stock," the *Manchester Examiner* said in 1892, and this was putting it
mildly.[36] Indeed, by this time "the physical splendour of the young
Australians was already a legend," while the Boers "were so stringy and
spare, like the biltong that hung from their saddles, that they made their
imperial opponents seem flabby by comparison."[37]

The Victorian idea that physical and mental toughness meant national superiority came back to haunt the British when the outstanding
performances of Australian and New Zealand soldiers in both the Boer
War and World War I were contrasted with the alleged passivity of
troops raised in the cramped and anemic environment of the mother
country. Australian energy and roughness contrasted starkly with English enervation and refinement in the racial imagination of this period.
Today this contrast between hard and soft whites has been replaced by
the dichotomy between the vital black and the depleted white. The
decline of the European empires has thus meant the decline of the
white male, and the world of sport is still adjusting to the psychological
dislocations brought about by this loss of prestige.

# 7

## The World of Colonial Sport

SPORT IN THE COLONIAL CONTEXT has been both an instrument of cultural domination and a field of racial conflict. The Anglo-Saxons' self-image of "an energetic people" endowed with "dynamic, violent qualities" required them to display their physical prowess and implied an unequal competition with subject peoples. The British in particular saw athletic competence (in the widest sense of the term) as identical to the ability to govern racial inferiors.[1] Europeans in general believed that they possessed an energy that animated only the man "who plays 'against the clock.'" "The bodily discipline that the Europeans displayed in their work, military training, and athletic competitions was seen as a key factor in their dominance over less controlled, less well-organized, less goal-oriented peoples."[2] Similarly, in the American South, "the white naturally assumed command in play and sport owing to superior genetic endowment, and the black naturally learned the proper role of subordinate."[3] In Australia, doubts about the whites' ability to labor in the extreme heat could provoke the touchy reply that "white men are physically capable to do whatever coloured men can do."[4] This defensive attitude extended to the running track, prompting the Queensland home secretary to write in 1897 that "the whites complained of the superior capabilities of the blacks at Fraser Island, and asked me to stop them competing with the whites."[5] A century later, ambivalent feelings about supernormal black athletes represent new variations on these old anxieties.

The European colonialist's emotional stake in his sense of physical vitality made the issue of racial athletic competition a sensitive one. On the one hand, sport became a vehicle of cultural imperialism and imported a predominantly British system of values into Africa, Asia, Australia, and New Zealand. At the same time, sport was an arena in which racial subordinates could win victories signifying some kind of parity with whites. Some colonialist thinkers, such as the founder of the modern Olympic movement, the French baron Pierre de Coubertin, reasoned that a few victories on the cricket pitch might divert native energies in a politically useful way.[6] Still, colonial administrators had to debate the wisdom of transferring *any* skills and ideas to subject peoples, who might use them to redress the imbalance of power. "After the Russo-Japanese War," a racist American professor wrote in 1911, "a vague rumor that a white race somewhere had been beaten in a war by a colored people filtered into very remote portions of Africa."[7] Small wonder that European officers who fell ill on troop ships did not appear before their colored men, since "an officer off-color is an anomaly."[8] Even the spread of Christianity was a calculated risk, in that it might produce an interest in democracy.

Sportive competitions were opening the door to genuinely personal confrontations that raised questions about the carefully cultivated mystique of authority that surrounded white colonials. Hence in 1904 Australian authorities decided to put an end to the practice of allowing Aboriginal sprinters to run against whites after a group of natives became too "cheeky" after competing in cricket matches.[9] This hunger for self-display or revenge was always present. When an Indian soccer team beat the British in 1911, a journalist wrote, "It fills every Indian with pride and joy to know that rice-eating, malaria-ridden, bare-footed Bengalis have got the better of beef-eating, Herculean, booted John Bull in that peculiarly British sport."[10] This drama of sport as cultural and political resistance is still being enacted in various ways in the neocolonial worlds of the Olympic Games, World Cup soccer tournaments, international cricket matches, and professional and college sports leagues in the United States.

International cricket, as we have seen, has served as a dramatic and often politicized theater of white athletic decline. The interracial drama of cricket began in the Australian outback during the first half of the nineteenth century, when an Aborigine named Shiney made three consecutive "ducks" in 1835. In 1872, Billy the Blackboy supposedly threw a cricket ball 140 yards — an improbable feat that ranks among the first stories of miraculous performances by black men. In 1868 a team composed of Aborigines with nicknames like Dick-a-Dick, Red Cap, and Jim Crow made their famous tour of England, drawing nineteen matches while winning fourteen and losing the same number.[11] Expectations in England were high, in that "no arrival [had] been anticipated with so much curiosity and interest" since an American Indian named Deerfoot had competed against the English long-distance walk-ers known as pedestrians. Contemporary English appraisals of this "im-possible coffee-coloured team" anticipate in every respect the discourse of racial difference that was flourishing by the turn of the century. Despite "their slight peculiarity of build," the Aborigines displayed "an almost English width across the shoulder." The star batter was credited with "an all-round capacity in cricket, with something of a personality to back it," even if he had also shown an "aversion to hard running."[12] Together these judgments constitute a fine précis of incomplete savage manhood, identifying defects of body, soul, and willpower.

Eventually, however, black men resolved to use the game to repair this image of deficient masculinity. In January 1894 the first English cricket team to tour the Caribbean solved the problem of interracial competition by simply refusing to play any team that included a black man.[13] Yet even at this time the process of racial integration had begun in the Caribbean, on the multicultural island of Trinidad. According to the 1898 edition of the standard cricket reference work known as Wis-den, "black men add considerably to the strength of a side, while their inclusion makes the game more popular locally and tends to instil a great and universal enthusiasm among all classes of the population. The black men are especially fine fieldsmen; they throw very well and sel-dom miss a catch."[14] Seen in retrospect, this innocent commentary on black ability and popular enthusiasm was prophetic.

Characterological judgments of dark-skinned sportsmen are modern versions of colonial assessments of dark-skinned military recruits. To set the scene, let us turn back the clock to Queen Victoria's Diamond Jubilee procession through London, in 1897. The military parade fea-tured African and Indian soldiers as well as British home regiments and units of the white colonial forces — as the *Daily Mail* put it, men of "every colour, every contingent, every race, every speech."[15] These men were not, however, considered equal in their capacities to fight and lead. Whereas black soldiers had served in the British Army since the seven-teenth century, they had rarely been made officers; in fact, the first "man of colour" did not receive a king's commission until World War II. Even as the multiracial might of the empire marched through the streets of London, nonwhite members of the paramilitary Sierra Leone Frontier Force were being "denounced by Europeans as 'morally inferior' and lacking gentlemanly or 'officer-like' qualities." The first African to re-ceive a king's commission was Seth K. Anthony, a member of the Ewe tribe, from what is now Ghana. Called "blondie" in the officers' mess, Anthony earned the respect of his peers "by his success at sports, at which he happened to be pre-eminent, and later in battle."[16]

The theory of the "martial races" is generally credited to Lord Roberts of Kandahar, who wrote in the year of the Diamond Jubilee that the Madras and Bombay armies "could no longer be pitted with safety against warlike races." Philip Mason has argued that this scheme for assessing the various "races" of India was actually based on indigenous fantasies about the defects of native character: "The division of the people into 'martial' and 'non-martial' was not an invention of the British; it was the recognition of something already implicit in the Indian social system. But it was extremely convenient to a conqueror."[17] Most convenient of all was the opportunity such a theory offered for implementing a policy of divide and rule. But underlying the entire project, and presented with the absolute confidence of the Herrenvolk mentality, are two unquestioned propositions. The first is that compared with whites, dark-skinned males can be assumed to be deficient in courage until they prove otherwise. The second is that a few native populations are superior to the others in this respect.

The classic exposition of this racial psychology appears in the books of General Sir George Fletcher MacMunn (1869–1952), a despiser of the pacifist (and thus effeminate) Gandhi, a colonel commandant in the Royal Artillery, and a highly opinionated analyst of Indian military prowess. In *The Armies of India,* MacMunn lays out his racial dichotomy with characteristic self-confidence: "It is one of the essential differences between the East and the West, that in the East, with certain exceptions, only certain clans and classes can bear arms; the others have not the physical courage necessary for the warrior. In Europe, as we know, every able-bodied man, given food and arms, is a fighting man of some sort, some better, some worse, but still as capable of bearing arms as any other of his nationality. In the East, or certainly in India, this is not so." His explanation for the decadence of the East is based not on biology but on the force of acquired habits: "Only certain races were permitted to bear arms, and in course of time only certain races remained fit to bear arms." Nor can social status or even athletic appearance be relied on as indicators of male virtue: "It is extraordinary that the well-born race of the upper classes in Bengal should be hopeless poltroons, while it is absurd that the great, merry, powerful Kashmiri should have not an ounce of physical courage in his constitution, but it is so. Nor are appearances of any use as a criterion. Some of the most manly-looking people in India are in this respect the most despicable."[18] What counts for the imperialist is not form but function, not the shape of the body but the willpower that gets things done.

Twenty years later General MacMunn refined and expanded this theory in *The Martial Races of India,* and once again his point of depar-

ture was the contrast between European masculinity and Indian effeminacy: "We do not speak of the martial races of Britain as distinct from
the non-martial, nor of Germany, nor of France. But in India we speak
of the martial races as a thing apart because the mass of the people have
neither martial aptitude nor . . . the courage that we talk of colloquially
as 'guts.'" The general's physical typology expresses the military man's
anthropological curiosity about the diverse human material at his dis-
posal. There is "the square-shouldered athletic Musselman of the Pun-
jab"; the Muslims, who are "hardy, muscular, powerful, enduring and
yet pusillanimous beyond belief"; "the great muscular, hardworking,
rather stupid yeoman farmer[s]" called the Jats. The "agile little men"
known as Mahrattas possess "the active litheness of the wildcat," while
the similarly undersized Gurkhas are of a "squat diminutive pug-dog
build."[19]

Here too it is character rather than physique that determines the
worth of a man, and one way to find it is to look for evidence of the
British élan that is so prized on the fields of sport. This is why the "wild
highlanders" called the Pathans, who are "sporting, high-spirited, adventurous, and jaunty," appeal so strongly to most British officers. Similarly, in the early nineteenth century the British Army had "fraternized
easily with the hard-riding sporting Afghan quality" of the native soldiers. Yet even this sort of camaraderie did not signify racial equality.
For all his appreciation of "the sturdy little tykes we associate with the
name Gurkha," who "play happily at drilling each other for hours at a
time," it is their childlike loyalty rather than authentic manhood that
appeals to General MacMunn. Only the Sikh grenadier fights with "the
majesty with which the British soldier fights," yet even this kind of performance cannot invest him with the authority of his British masters.[20]

The crucial distinction between these higher and lower masculine
categories remains curiously intangible, as MacMunn celebrates more
than one example of interracial fellowship that manages to preserve
racial difference. This ostensible paradox survives even the closest encounters with male equality. When serving with the best of the Rajputs,
we are told, British officers "have the feeling that they are with men
whose doings and feelings are always moved by a code of honour, not
always the same as theirs, but one demanding a certain class of action,
demeanour and integrity, which will not fail." In the end it becomes
clear that British and Indian males inhabit parallel universes that can
share everything but a common status, and the key to this inequality
appears to be the mastery of rational technique itself. Confirming the
importance of stereotypes based on the ideal of national productivity,

General MacMunn contrasts "the efficiency of Western military ways" with "that streak of inefficiency" that is part of the Indian character.[21] In the last analysis, not even British-style courage could secure the colored man a place at the controls of modern civilization.[22]

This sense of white military superiority has survived many colonial wars against tenacious "coloured" adversaries, from the Zulu War of 1879 to the Mau Mau insurrection of the 1950s, persisting even beyond the French and American debacles in Vietnam. (Just as Sylvester Stallone's *Rocky* is an attempt to restore white male honor in the ring, so his *Rambo* films are white male action fantasies that seek to reestablish a military hegemony that was lost in the jungles of Indochina.) "I don't mean to be racist," a German mercenary in Africa said in 1977, "but I don't think much of the blacks as fighters. Sure, there are two or three hundred in the [Rhodesian] Selous Scouts, but those are the Super-blacks."[23]

This sort of racial contempt fed the perverse impulse to treat killing as sport, and the most vicious aspect of the colonial world was the emergence of Negro-killing as a sportive exercise. "Man-shooting is the finest sport of all," said General Wolseley, who (like others) saw the Zulus as "dangerous black game that made the hunt especially exhilarating."[24] Like the South African Bushmen, Australian Aborigines were hunted like animals, a frontier routine known as "shooting off the black stuff."[25] In 1883 the British high commissioner complained that white men "of culture and refinement" spoke of murdering Aborigines "exactly as they would talk of a day's sport, or of having to kill some troubling animal."[26] The contemporary pursuit of the Zulu could also be seen as being "of the same high grade as lion-hunting."[27] During the Mau Mau uprising in Kenya in the 1950s, some professional hunters, emulating the "nigger hunts" of the 1890s, stalked Kikuyu as if they were dangerous game animals. Even the torture of Mau Mau suspects was sometimes rationalized as sport. "It's all just like a good clean rugger scrum," said the officer in charge of one detention camp, even if, as we have seen, this could be a frustrating "sport" even for hardened colonial interrogators.[28] Over time these terrible struggles played their own role in refashioning white attitudes toward African masculinity.

The racial self-confidence of "the more hell-for-leather class of colonist" was based on the legacy of this masculine superiority and on advantages in military technology that whites have taken for granted for the past four hundred years.[29] But another type of white male supremacy could not survive the rigors of interracial athletic competition, and that is one reason such contests became symbolic encounters of such importance for race relations in colonial societies. For the white athletes of the world, the past century can be seen as an ordeal whose essential drama has derived from harrowing encounters with a superior black physicality. The most dramatic arena of this struggle, apart from the boxing ring, has been the cricket competitions of the British Empire. The temper tantrums that marred the Britain-Pakistan series during the summer of 1992 showed that these encounters are still colonial dramas, as the winning Pakistanis "fumed over what they regarded as a kind of 19th-century imperial indignation, as if the British were really arguing that the only way a former colonial side could beat them was by cheating."[30]

What the dispassionate observer may regard as the disproportionate significance of these matches turns out to be an unresolved colonial conflict that is somehow thriving in a postcolonial age. Unaffected by more strategic national disparities in technology, education, and per capita income, these games create the proverbial level playing field for civilized interracial competition. But the consequences of such games cannot always be described as harmless.

# 8

# The New Multiracial World Order

RACIAL IMAGES of athletic aptitude or ineptitude address qualities of body and mind that are believed to determine the fates of nations in military and economic competition. For this reason, images of athletic aptitude belong to a larger category of stereotypes that constitute myths of national character and efficiency. Images of maximally efficient Asian workers on the Pacific Rim commingle with images of coolly effective Swedish tennis players in the global media. Success or failure inside the soccer stadium can symbolize national renewal or decline. The most surprising aspect of this kaleidoscopic world of images is the order that has persisted amid its complexity. For these images, as Hugh O'Donnell has admirably demonstrated, form "a discursive network" that expresses both the value system of modern technological civilization and the racial hierarchy that colonial relationships and industrial competition have done so much to create.

The power of these sportive stereotypes derives from the athleticizing of races and nation-states that occurred during the later decades of the nineteenth century. Physical comparisons, as we have seen, could imply more comprehensive assessments of racial fitness. Observing the natives of New Zealand in 1849, a British army surgeon thus found comfort in the discovery that "in physical strength they are much inferior to men drawn from a country where machinery and civilization have produced changes in the manner and habits of the people to an extent unknown among other civilized races."[1] The coexistence of technological and physical superiority in a European "race" gave the lie to fears that "savages" had a monopoly on racial vigor.

The "emotional characteristics of different nations" also included their "athletic characters," and there was much talk of English "energy" in particular.[2] Colonialized Indians, intimidated by the British masculine ideal, internalized an English educator's maxim that "weaklings are despised and a weakling nation is doomed."[3] Another Englishman maintained that "the vital energies of a people had a great deal to do with the state of the body, and that the capacity of the chest should count for something very considerable as an indication of national power."[4] The astonishing persistence of sportive nationalism in our own age, when real power flows from electronic circuits rather than muscle fibers, shows how much influence these old images of national vigor have retained.[5]

The theory of sportive stereotypes depicts a Eurocentric discourse that identifies northwestern Europe as the principal site (the Center) of efficiency and productivity and Africa as the exemplary sinkhole of inefficiency and underdevelopment. Europe itself includes an industrious north and a lethargic south, while countries such as Spain and Italy subdivide themselves in exactly the same manner into northern and southern zones of productivity and lethargy. It is the athletes of the north who monopolize brain power and self-control. As Hugh O'Donnell points out, a Swedish golfer displays "his cool frame of mind, even by Swedish standards." "Everything in their sporting culture," a Scottish newspaper says of the Swedes, "seems to hinge on the cerebral dimension." What is more, the Scandinavian traits of "coolness and clinical rationality" can be acquired, at least temporarily, by southern athletes who meet northern standards. "When the Spanish athlete Fermin Cacho won the gold medal in the 1500 meters in the Barcelona Olympics, the Spanish sports daily *El Mundo Deportivo* (9 August 1992) described his performance as 'cold, calculating, more Nordic than Iberian'" — a fine example of the internalized ethnic stereotype and the self-contempt it implies.[6]

The dominant stereotype of German national character "combines the idea of strong mental control with discipline, efficiency, reliability and hard work." Boris Becker's serve is thus "a triumph of natural genetics and Germanic efficiency," according to the English *Observer*. Perpetuating an image dating from the Franco-Prussian War, the Norwegian tabloid *Verdens Gang* depicted German soccer players as "German machines." The dominant stereotype of the French athlete "is best represented by terms such as 'flamboyance', 'flair', 'inspiration', 'charm', even 'style.'"[7] The cerebral quality of the French sportsman is soft rather than hard, all fluff and lacking in tenacity. If French toughness exists at all, it has apparently been effectively banished from the

mind of Europe by French romanticism, Left Bank intellectuals wearing berets, and several calamitous encounters with German military
might.

The southern stereotype, comprising Mediterranean Europe and
Latin America, is based on the idea of "the temperamental Latin," its
essential themes being "passion, hot temper, frivolity, sensuality, even
hedonism." Situated midway between the affluence of the north and the
misery of tropical Africa, the southern athlete is an ambiguous figure
who can be undone by the turmoil of his own emotional effervescence.
"The 'fieriness' of the Latin carries with it notions of unpredictable,
even uncontrolled creativity. For all its entertainment value, however,
this creativity — which is often described as 'magic', particularly in the
case of Latin Americans — is viewed unfavourably if it does not bring
results." As O'Donnell makes clear, the damage done by the Latin
stereotype is a direct result of its ambiguity. The sportswriter who might
balk at (or be prohibited from) employing a denigrating Latin stereotype may feel that its inherently positive reference to magical creativity
justifies its dissemination to a potential audience of millions. The negative underside of this stereotype is the "notions of indiscipline, irration-
ality and recklessness," which we associate with hyperinflation, banana
republics, and the soccer hysteria that appears to grip entire populations
like a voodoo cult.[8]

At the very bottom of this hierarchy are the Africans, whose soccer players participate in the Latin stereotype as "football magicians."
Their true (if often unspoken) status was vocalized by the French sports
newspaper *L'Equipe* when it called African soccer "a victory for the
irrational."[9] It is difficult to exaggerate the importance of such phrases
and their power to perpetuate the image of underdevelopment. Centuries of European speculation about the African brain — its size, the
number of its convolutions, its arrested development — are condensed
here into a single image of African retardation. Immune to United
Nations resolutions, ignored by the Organization for African Unity,
unregulated by the media that employ it, this colonial idiom has been
granted complete autonomy in the postcolonial world of international
sport.

The ideological function of this hierarchy of images, or what O'Donnell calls their "centre of gravity," is the "mythologizing of collective
fitness for *work*."[10] Dynamic athletic images are important for the corporations and governments of technologically advanced societies, because they dramatize the power and efficiency of modern organizations
and machines. Over the past decade this kind of imagery has achieved

iconic status in global advertising. Any system of stereotypes that calls into question the rationality and efficiency of dark-skinned Mediterraneans or Africans thus reproduces the basic colonialist critique of "lazy" subject peoples.

As Michael Adas has shown, the technology gap between Europeans and non-Europeans during the age of European conquest and colonization may have done more than racist doctrine itself to encourage European contempt for the "primitives" of Asia and Africa. We have already seen that sportive images can convey judgments about progress and backwardness with an almost poetic efficiency, and this is why the "discursive network" of global sport is so powerful. At the heart of the Center are "international economic muscle" and the "entrepreneurial capitalism . . . which is constructed as dynamic, energetic, aggressive and internationally important."[11] And the traditional center of the symbolic Center is Britain, whose people created both the industrial revolution and modern sport as we know it.

White fatalism about racial athletic aptitude marks the end of a certain kind of racial prestige that was originally vested in the colonial male. In the United States, the slogan "white men can't jump" — an idea that has been widely broadcast by the eponymous film — exemplifies a gallows humor that acknowledges the twilight of white athleticism and whatever this portends for the supposedly beleaguered Caucasian male. The scenario of white decline can have a seductive appeal for those of liberal temperament, because it seems to represent at least a minimal redistribution of status amounting to compensation for centuries of racial oppression. Further reflection makes it clear, however, that the spectacle of white failure in the world of sport, while real enough inside the stadium, has not been accompanied by any significant change in the traditional imbalance of power between white Euroamerica and those of African descent. On the contrary, today's concurrent crises in sub-Saharan Africa and Afro-America are so severe that public discussion of them is still inhibited by doubts about addressing unequal competitions between racial groups.

Given the continuing subordinate status of black people, we must ask why black athletic victories matter to white people at all. This book argues that current white responses to white athletic decline are of psychological importance because they are indicators of anxiety about social and economic status in relation to black progress, and because racial disparities in athletic performance encourage unscientific thinking about racial biology in enormous numbers of people. From a historical perspective, some of the symbolic power of interracial contests is rooted in our tendency to conflate the importance of physical prowess during the "heroic" era of colonial domination with the meaning of athletic dominance today. Hence the importance of O'Donnell's discursive network of national and racial stereotypes, which address labor efficiency as well as athletic competence, since this network tends to preserve the status of the former colonial powers in a world of black athletic dominance by exalting images of rationality and technology. During the colonial period, the myth of white physical superiority helped to sustain the power of Europeans who viewed physical and emotional toughness as prerequisites for survival. Today, in the age of the global cognitive elite, athletic superiority is, in a Darwinian sense, a vestigial trait that possesses ornamental rather than strategic value for nations whose stereotyped racial identities bar their membership in what O'Donnell calls the "entrepreneurial capitalism" of the Center. Today Kenyan and Ethiopian runners conquer the descendants of Europeans who colonized and oppressed their forefathers, but the misery of East Africa and the symbolic exclusion of blacks from the productive world of rational efficiency continues unabated.[12] Understanding why athletic victories cannot alleviate the black exile from modernity requires us to examine how interracial sports function as a cultural and economic system around the world.

High-performance sports are one of the defining traits of modern civilization, and black athletes monopolize some of their most conspicuous elites. Yet athletic achievement has done little to transform the premodern image of black people. Where, for example, is the postcolonial African athlete who represents a clean break with the colonial past? Where is the postmodern African-American athlete who represents the black man's breakthrough into the computerized world of rational efficiency that is so effectively symbolized by the images of dynamic athleticism that suffuse modern advertising? The fact that public images of such people do not exist suggests, first, that blacks do not have the power to interpret black athleticism for its global audience, and second, that black athleticism as we know it cannot be modernized in such a way as to dissolve traditional stereotypes of black physicality. The first predicament was addressed in 1995 by the organizer of an African film festival held in the impoverished country of Burkino Faso. "We have a lot to say," he declared, "but that begins by controlling our own images."[13] The second problem presents a far more difficult challenge. Indeed, the apparent intractability of our images of African physicality suggests that destroying the myth of the black body will require eliminating the black athlete as a charismatic role model, precisely because he will always be a creature of the colonial imagination.

The benign image of global multiracial sports has effectively diverted attention from the Eurocentric political and economic interest groups that plan and control its far-flung operations and its most prestigious events. Three transnational bodies are particularly important in this regard. The International Olympic Committee (IOC), the International Soccer Federation (FIFA), and the international governing body of track and field (IAAF) are headed by a trio of very wealthy men — a Spaniard, a Brazilian, and an Italian — whose checkered pasts and corrupt practices need not concern us here.[14] The larger point is that the world of interracial sport is a neocolonialist enterprise, both as an economic operation and as a cultural time capsule in which the colonial ideology of race lives on in ways that may surprise consumers of Olympic rhetoric about the brotherhood of man.

From an economic standpoint, elite sports are a merciless labor market that offers limited opportunities to large numbers of financially desperate athletes from Third World countries and from the newly impoverished societies of the former Communist empire. African teenagers and middle-aged Russian women compete with many others for hard currency (and the occasional Mercedes) in the West.[15] In a development reminiscent of the educational disaster now occurring among African-American youth, dreams of wealth have begun to affect the academic prospects of the most athletically gifted African children. "I have heard," one of the great Kenyan runners said in 1994, "that some of our national heroes are now telling parents that running is more important than school. That is a catastrophe."[16]

When a Ghanaian team won the world soccer championship for players under the age of seventeen in 1991, deeply rooted Western ideas about African precocity took even firmer root in the minds of European talent scouts. Their appetites whetted by fantasies of natural African talent, professional soccer teams in Germany recruited fifteen-year-old boys off the dusty streets of Ghanaian villages, installed them in apartments in German cities, and then released them when their African "genius" for playing the game did not live up to expectations.[17] Of the many young African stars who have been bought by European clubs, most simply disappear after management discovers that young black athletes, like their white counterparts, need to go through a developmental phase.[18]

European agents and coaches, who sometimes talk of taking "foreign aid" to the underdeveloped world, may take their own agendas to Africa instead. Clemens Westerhof, a Dutchman who resigned as head coach of the Nigerian national soccer team after the 1994 World Cup tournament, told an interviewer that there are "two kinds of Nigerians: the ones who play soccer, and the others who deal drugs all over the world." Arriving in Dallas for the World Cup, Westerhof effectively placed his African charges under house arrest. "I know them," he said, "they are immature and easily diverted." Eschewing the standard clichés about international understanding, he declared that his purpose in training Africans was "to make an international name for myself." "We know that he is a racist and a militarist," said one Nigerian admirer of his national team, "but he does a good job."[19]

The presence of African athletes in Germany is a cultural anomaly that has given rise to a minor genre of racially awkward situations that appear to confirm ideas about the vulnerability, instability, and general undesirability of the African character. The German Soccer Federation's official claim (in 1995) that importing athletic "black gold" exemplifies "problem-free integration" is self-delusion.[20] In a vignette that would be unthinkable in countries with large black minorities, like the United States and Britain, the Social Democratic politician Oskar Lafontaine publicly stated that the Ghanaian soccer star Anthony Yeboah was "the only black I like." This favored status did not help Yeboah when it came time for him to reenact the timeless, pathetic drama of the bewildered colonial subject who comes to grief in metropolitan Europe. As the league-leading scorer for Frankfurt Eintracht and the only African captain of a German professional club, he was riding high in the fall of 1994, until he refused to participate in a disciplinary exercise ordered by his German coach. Yeboah — "as sensitive as a mimosa," as one journalist described him — was offended when the coach called him overweight and commented on his "problems with expressing himself" (Yeboah had learned enough German to refuse the services of an interpreter when he had appeared before the soccer federation appeals board). When asked two years earlier about how it felt to be compared to gazelles and seals in the German press, Yeboah had simply said, "I can live with that." He was well acquainted with the folklore about African athletes: they were undisciplined, malarial, and couldn't take the winter. Now, however, the cup had run over, and Yeboah demanded that the club release him or the coach. Within weeks he had been sold to an English team, for which he became a major star.[21]

German athletes who compete with blacks abroad also sometimes play roles in neocolonial minidramas that are absorbed by the public back home. German fans have been able to follow the multicultural adventures of Detlef Schrempf, a successful player for the Seattle Supersonics basketball team, and his adaptation to the most celebrated black subculture in American sports. According to Germany's leading newsmagazine, Schrempf "walks the way NBA pros walk. The feet seem to roll, the shoulders swing, everything relaxed, demonstratively cool." But the German athlete's assimilation to this black world does not go beyond body language. As a white man, his German public is told, his function in the NBA is to be the head coach's right-hand man, helping to discipline his unruly black teammates. With five Schrempfs, says his coach, "we would have won." "I hate showiness and egotism," says Schrempf, the ambassador of "the German work ethic," which fits perfectly into the racially stereotyped division of labor in the NBA that sportswriters continue to present in coded language to the American public.[22] When Schrempf was named to the NBA All-Star Team in 1995, some black players wondered out loud why he had been honored at all.[23] Two other top German players, Henning Harnisch and Uwe Blab, did not survive long in the NBA, in part because their teammates made them look bad in games in order to hold on to their own jobs. In 1993 Harnisch told a German interviewer that success in the NBA was diffi-cult because of the physical superiority of the black talent pool. "Their bodies are much stronger and more athletic," he said, thereby con-firming what many whites already believed.[24]

Universal access to global media has made interracial athletic compe-tition a standard entertainment even for European societies that lack racial diversity on a significant scale. The development of attitudes in Germany is especially interesting, because the dark-skinned citizen-ath-lete is still an exotic figure in a society that has only recently begun to absorb large numbers of people whose appearance differs markedly from the Caucasian model. In conformity with the stereotype of the natural African athlete, the world-class eight-hundred-meter runner Nico Motchebon has been presented as a biracial German who has succeeded "without serious training, and without the help of doctors and scientists," unlike his pampered white teammates. In fact, his suc-cess has been built on six years of training as a modern pentathlete, but this sort of information is suppressed by the appeal of the stereotype.[25]

In the wider world, media saturation means that every modern soci-ety generates its own racial subcultures of sport, including its own ver-sion of the Western folklore about racial athletic aptitudes. In England, where many years of immigration from former colonial territories have led to large communities of West Indian blacks, Pakistanis, and Indians, the racial politics of sport is more complex and has a far greater impact on national life than in more homogenous societies like Germany's. As in any modern society, racial integration has been accompanied by public demonstrations of chauvinism rooted in issues of cultural identity. Yorkshire cricket in particular has been jealously preserved as a "white" sport even in recent years, because race-based claims to identity have been preserved intact: "In a post-imperial era, where much of the chauvinism of Empire and nation has been transferred to a regional or city jingoism . . . the notion of the Yorkshire 'birthright', far from withering away, has grown stronger." When the West Indian star Viv Richards played in front of a Yorkshire crowd in 1986, he reported, "They called me nigger, black bastard, sambo, monkey, gorilla, they threw bananas and I had to take these insults."[26] In a society where half the track-and-field athletes and boxers are black, Yorkshire cricket fans are still known to chant, "We're so white it's unbelievable!" As of 1993, Everton was the only all-white soccer team left in the Premier League; its fans, who routinely greeted visiting black players with grunts and bananas, went so far as to welcome one black goalkeeper with a flaming cross in the style of the Ku Klux Klan.[27] Race consciousness can also be converted into lighter forms of entertainment for the sporting public. Following Linford Christie's gold-medal performance in the hundred-meter dash at the 1992 Barcelona Olympic Games, British television commentators had endless fun referring to the genitalia that bulged beneath Christie's spandex tights as "Linford's lunchbox."

The race factor can also assume less obvious forms. For example, British admiration of Indian cricket players tends to be limited to the subtlety rather than the physical prowess of their play, reflecting the lingering effects of deeply rooted colonial ideas about the effeminacy of most Indian men. Another example of compulsive racial thinking concerns Ryan Giggs, the young offensive star of the Manchester United Football Club. In 1994 an unfounded rumor held that his (estranged or absent) father was black. The public simply assumed that the most expensive, and thus the most gifted, player in Britain had to be of African descent.

Coexisting with such phenomena, however, is a distinctly British code of sporting conduct that insists on acknowledging personal stature on the basis of colorblind standards. Great black sportsmen such as Pele, Muhammad Ali, and the cricket immortal Gary Sobers are regarded as "absolute gentlemen" by all but the racist fringe. Black athletes and announcers are frequently considered more articulate than their white counterparts, a striking reversal of the stereotype that prevails in the United States.[28] The black heavyweight Frank Bruno, a clever (and now wealthy) man who has feigned being "thick" for his white audience, represents a miraculous racial paradox. He is "our Frank," a "broad British oak," the embodiment of a "muscular black English masculinity" who has achieved a "conspicuous 'trans-racial' popularity."[29] A less persuasive example of transracial British identity is the boxer Chris Eubanks, whose stylish monocle and cane have discomfited other British blacks, recalling those "African chiefs of savage splendour [who decked] themselves in the fineries of imperial Britain."[30]

Racial folklore about athletic aptitudes is shaped by the prominence or absence of ethnic groups in certain major sports. Popular beliefs about racial anatomy combine impressions based on actual performances with the almost medieval credulity about alien life forms one finds in the worst tabloid newspapers. "On our playing fields," a British sportswriter wrote in 1990, "you might still hear that blacks possess an extra bone in the heel."[31] The same year a report on racism in British sport described the most widespread stereotypes: "Afro-Caribbeans are good sprinters; Asian girls are unable to adopt certain postures; Afro-Caribbeans are sinkers in water; Asian men have double-jointed wrists enabling them to play stick sports."[32] Such beliefs are anything but immutable, adapting easily to whichever fantasy objects present themselves at the time. In 1928, for example, the London *Times* reported that the black Caribbean cricket star W. H. St. Hill "performs amazing apparently double-jointed tricks with his wrists and arms."[33]

It is important to recognize that such ideas about racial difference are not simply inflicted on minorities by whites; the seldom acknowledged truth is that significant numbers of people in all racial communities absorb these stereotypes and collaborate in preserving them for a variety of reasons. Spectators at Everton who yelled "Kick the nigger!" whenever a black player tested their team's defense were expressing their attachment to the traditional colonial fantasy of white physical supremacy and all it once implied about Britain's mastery of a multiracial empire.[34] Southeast Asian girls in Britain "believe that they lack sportive ability, and to some extent begin to internalize a self-image of passivity and frailty."[35] When a white sociologist argued in 1982 that widespread belief in the natural superiority of black athletes was damaging their social progress, "the response from some areas of the black community in Britain was that the book destroyed vestiges of pride."[36] These people had embraced the stereotype of black physicality to find a distinctive identity of which they could be proud. "We don't do very well at reading and writing," the black boxer Jimmy Dublin once said, "but we're made for physical things."[37] This identification with a crypto-racist self-image is one example of the fateful entrapment in a mythic black physicality that Franz Fanon described in his famous study of colonial psychology, *Black Skin, White Masks.*

Racist colonial psychology also expresses itself when blacks and whites are assigned contrasting characters reflecting subordinate and dominant personalities. Over the past few decades, the colonial rigidity of this distribution of roles has softened to the point where blacks do not have to occupy subordinate positions. In postwar Britain the range of black athletic temperament has been defined by the symbolic exploits of two men who are remembered for fulfilling black potential in directly contrary ways. The first and sadder tale concerns a black South African soccer player named Albert Johanneson, imported in the 1960s to play as a winger for Leeds United. Johanneson was "a mercurial performer, full of craft and daring one moment, but likely to be cowed by a ferocious opponent, or simply by his sudden projection into a white man's world. After he left Leeds his marriage fell apart and he was last seen as a hobo wandering the canal walks. Around Johanneson grew the myth of a black stereotype . . . suggesting that black athletes have in-built grace and fluidity that no white man could match."[38]

The charismatic role made possible by natural "grace and fluidity" eventually fell to an Englishman named John Barnes, who in 1984 scored a miraculous goal against the famed Brazilian national team in Rio de Janeiro. This feat, as one British sportswriter put it, "proved that there was an English player who could fight Brazilian flair with his own very special flair. He also happened to be black." The mysterious process whereby a black man can represent the essence of England to his otherwise race-conscious white countrymen, as in the case of Frank Bruno, has never been explained. Yet Barnes's goal, replayed over and over on British television screens ever since, became "a totem of the theory that blacks are something special in our national game. A moment of soccer magic has been invested with the power to transform society."[39]

The presumed instability of the African personality and its related capacity to produce "soccer magic" are the bipolar stereotypes that confirm the essential abnormality of black potential in a white man's world. Black magic cancels black failure. The wreckage of Albert Johanneson's life is counterbalanced by the supernormal achievement of John Barnes and its value to the self-image of a white nation.

The primary function of colonial psychology has always been to produce invidious comparisons between racial temperaments that justify white male authority, and interracial sport has been contributing to this process for a hundred years. Athletes who occupy "white" positions in team sports must, according to one British study, display "leadership, intelligence, emotional control and the ability to make decisions under pressure," while "black" positions require "strength, speed, quickness, high emotion and good instinct," in conformity with the traditional stereotype of African character.[40]

This basic dichotomy now prevails around the world. In New Zealand, brown-skinned Maori and other Polynesian athletes, influenced in part by televised images of African-American stars, are in the process of taking over rugby, netball, and basketball, in the context of a Polynesian cultural renaissance that has been accompanied by the steady decline of white sports traditions (like rugby), which are historically linked to the image of robust colonial masculinity.[41] Just as in Britain, Germany, and the United States, New Zealanders' doubts about the darker-skinned athlete focus on the mysteries of the non-European personality. As an Auckland sports administrator put it in 1993, "In the early days, coaches were never too sure what to make of the Polynesian element — not too sure where the head was at." A star rugby player of European descent who finished his career in 1980 recalls, "Polynesian players were naturally superior to us in talent, but a lot of them aren't there now because they didn't have the discipline for physical conditioning. They lacked the right kind of mental attitude. They'd just turn up and play." A rugby player who is part Tongan, Maori, and European offers an assessment that bears an uncanny resemblance to the damning European verdict on nonwhite soldiers over the past two hundred years: "Ten years ago your typical Polynesian rugby team would have just lost their head in a pressure situation. It was almost as if it was the Polynesian way to do something really stupid that gave the game away. They were always good in the first 20 minutes or so because they ran on pure adrenalin. But when it came down to tactical thinking they'd lose their way and get thrashed in the last 20 minutes."[42] More recently, New Zealanders have been presented with a theory that the Polynesian surge in sport is due to their "obvious assets: natural muscularity, hand-to-eye co-ordination and sense of rhythm," which evolved as their ancestors adapted to cold-weather Pacific crossings over the ages.[43]

Several years earlier, and halfway around the world, a similar appraisal of defective black character caused a firestorm in British sport. In August 1991 the chairman of the Crystal Palace soccer club, one of the most racially integrated teams in the First Division, told a television interviewer, "When you're getting in to midwinter in England you need the hard white man to carry the artistic black players through."[44] Since British soccer clubs without black players were already regarded as racist enclaves, his remark caused a scandal and nearly provoked a walkout by his offended black players. In a wonderfully ironic evocation of the game's Victorian (and lily-white) heritage, the head of the players' union stated, "We feel we have no alternative but to refer to the Football Association under their Rule 26 which deals with ungentlemanly, insulting remarks or improper behaviour likely to bring the game into disrepute."[45] The Crystal Palace chairman, representing "a white-owned industry whose collective directorship amounts to a stronghold of Little England Toryism," was forced to apologize to dark-skinned men for whom the term *gentlemen* would have been unthinkable a century earlier. His publicly expressed regrets notwithstanding, it was clear following the public outcry that he did not understand the racial meaning of what he had said. What is more, he had gone well beyond diagnosing the demoralizing effects of cold weather on tropical constitutions. "I don't think too many of them can read the game," he had gone on. "You get an awful lot, great pace, great athletes, love to play with the ball in front of them," but "when it's behind them, it's chaos."[46] There were no black managers in the league, he said, because they did not sign up for coaching courses and were unwilling to attend games for the purpose of studying tactics.[47] Stunned by the hostility he had provoked, he could only console himself with the knowledge that, as one sportswriter noted, his remarks were "the kind of casually expressed opinion[s] about black sportsmen and women that you could hear a dozen times a week down at your local [pub]."[48]

The midfield of a soccer pitch is called "the engine room," because it is where strength, tenacity, and tactical intelligence decide the course of a game. It is, in a word, the space within which the decisive drama of the game unfolds, and in Britain it remained "a virtual white man's preserve" until the early 1980s.[49] The machine image confirms the truth of O'Donnell's "discursive network" by fusing industrial productivity with the performance of a highly skilled group of athletes and their need for coordinated action. The racial implications of combining leadership and technological competence within a single role will be clear to anyone familiar with the colonial world of the European empires. Keeping dark-skinned men out of "the engine room" was one of the classic racist caveats of the nineteenth century and a theme that has been immortalized in one of the most influential works of modern literature, Joseph Conrad's *Heart of Darkness*. Readers of this racist novella with a humanitarian reputation will recall how the narrator heaps good-natured ridicule on the mechanical illiteracy of his African helper, who is awed by the steam engine and the explosive god that dwells inside it. For the Western imagination, an African who combines technological skill and a capacity for leadership is unthinkable. In the world of sport, which does not require engineering skills, even the burdens of leadership have been considered too much for black men to bear until very recent times. In 1975, for example, twelve of fourteen English First Division soccer managers stated that they would not recruit black players because "they lack bottle [courage], are no good in the mud and have no stamina."[50]

Ten years earlier the unfortunate Albert Johanneson, an expatriate whose shyness had been bred into him by the constant intimidations of apartheid, had somehow earned "a reputation for being easily cowed by defenders."[51] This sense of the black man's deficient courage and re-solve had long been internalized by many colonial subjects throughout the empire, who accepted the regnant British conception of masculinity that was famously rejected by the gentle Mahatma Gandhi. After the West Indian cricket team's second English tour, in 1933, one editorial writer back home, as if anticipating the Albert Johannesons of the future, regretted that these young black men had shown "a mercurial disposition that precluded any show of fighting qualities when faced with difficult situations." The irony is that colonial authorities had intro-duced sport in order to cure the "mercurial" temperament of the na-tives.[52] Decades would pass before this biracial consensus on black inferiority began to break up under the pressure of decolonization and demonstrated black leadership on the field. The emotional price paid by cross-cultural players such as Albert Johanneson, Anthony Yeboah, and many others has not been factored into racial folklore about black character and its inability to take command. (Cross-cultural migration is also a feature of interracial life in the United States, where the minus-cule number of black quarterbacks in the National Football League demonstrates the residual effects of the same ideas about the black man's inability to lead.)

The belief that black men can throw a cricket ball at abnormal speeds and impart to it abnormal motions has existed for over a hundred years. One consequence of this "fast bowling" technique has been a long-standing controversy over whether it represents an intolerable threat to the tradition of the game.[53] In 1900 the great Aboriginal fast bowler Jack Marsh submitted to a special procedure to demonstrate the fair-ness of his throwing motion. According to the *Sydney Morning Herald,* "He caused a piece of wood to be tightly fixed along the arm, and bowled as fast as ever." The Englishmen who faced his fellow Aborigine Albert Henry during a tour in 1903–04 judged him to be the fastest bowler they had ever seen, but they agreed that his technique was "not above suspicion."[54]

Over the past quarter-century, fast bowling has become the specialty of the black West Indies team, which has not lost a five-day series in almost twenty years — a phenomenal record of superiority over many worthy opponents spread across the former British Empire. Facing West Indian fast bowlers has thus become a kind of white man's ordeal for the cricketers who take them on, and press accounts of these uneven contests sometimes convey a sense of almost pathetic helplessness on the part of the British batsmen. Surveying the recent history of West Indian throwers in 1994, the *Guardian* reported that they "never let batsmen off the hook and achieved an almost total dominance over successive English teams. They perfected the 'seek-and-destroy' technique, singling out the two main batsmen in the opposing ranks and setting about demoralising them, ultimately dismissing them, and thus deflating other more impressionable and less experienced members of the batting line-up." The fast bowler Curtly Ambrose, considered the best in the world by many batsmen, was described as follows: "Releasing the ball from a height of more than 8 ft. with a deceptive wave of the front arm in delivery — this is not a welcoming hello — at a speed to tingle the reflexes, he is a frightening proposition. Ambrose is mean, dislikes batsmen, hates giving them runs and delights in taking wickets, evidenced by the most frenetic display of shadow boxing since Muhammad Ali graced the ring."[55]

The diplomatic, even courtly tone of this language stands in stark contrast to the pugnacity of the Great White Hope idiom of a century ago. Such decorum suggests that the white man's predicament in the 1990s is not what it was in the 1890s — that the political significance of white athletic demoralization has either diminished or been converted into more up-to-date fears about psychologically comparable figures, such as the physically imposing black criminal. In accordance with the unofficial rules of liberal racial discourse, such commentaries make a point of not addressing the race factor in an explicit way. Blackness and latent political content are conceded obliquely by the reference to Muhammad Ali, but the issue of racial athletic aptitude is avoided altogether. Defining racial athletic aptitude as unfit for public discussion is a modern version of that chivalrous approach to gentlemen's competitions that once required that all political baggage be temporarily left at the door. But suppressing discussion of race and performance precludes our asking why there are so many black athletes in the first place and discourages critical thinking about the colonial stereotypes and relationships that flourish in the sports world. Even more important than these missed opportunities is the fact that public interest in racial biology cannot be suppressed beyond a certain point. Indeed, curiosity about racial difference is inseparable from interracial competitions that reproduce the human diversity of the colonial expositions that displayed dark-skinned "natives" to white audiences in the not so distant past.

In this sense, the modern world of multiracial sport can be understood as a kind of Darwinian theater, which has preserved like no other public forum the evolutionary drama that transformed the human image during the nineteenth century. Today, when the laws of natural selection are losing their hold over human evolution and the creation of a global gene pool is gradually precluding further evolutionary change in response to the challenges of nature, the spectacle of interracial athletic competition stands out as a unique reenactment of evolutionary struggle, as if the rigors of sport were all that separated the human species from the end of its natural history.[56] Precisely because the predominantly white inhabitants of technologically advanced societies sense their own removal from the processes of nature, they are drawn to black athletes as fantasy objects who serve as symbols of racial health. For the African sports specialist at the *Süddeutsche Zeitung* in Munich, the innately superior African athlete combines a "legendary hardness" with an inner state of relaxation deriving from "the ancient heritage of Mother Africa." Sports scientists, he says, should explain to the public why Western sports medicine has been unable to stem "the tide of black victors." Sports psychology too is just a pathetic attempt to boost the confidence of white athletes by teaching them "positive thinking," as if psychotherapy could compete with generations of natural selection.[57]

This response to the dynamic-athletic African developed during the last decades of the nineteenth century. For example, let us consider one notable scene in Conrad's *Heart of Darkness*. For all his impatience with the African temperament, Conrad paid sincere homage to the biological force of the savage African. As a canoe propelled by the exuberant strength of its dark paddlers approaches his ship, Conrad's narrator can only marvel at what he sees: "They had bone, muscle, a wild vitality, an intense energy of movement, that was . . . natural and true."

A century later, this racial romanticism has been both preserved and enriched by a better-informed layman's view of evolutionary processes. In the most interesting (and self-revealing) of the many paeans to the "magisterial" distance runners of the Kenyan highlands, the American journalist Kenny Moore enumerated the cultural factors that account for their overwhelming dominance: ritual circumcision, which teaches a stoic attitude toward pain, and a cattle-raiding tradition, which has selected for wiry bodies that can cover hundreds of miles on minimal nourishment. As valid as such explanations may be, they do not answer the profound Western need for Darwinian drama in the wild. For this reason the author awakes one morning in Kenya and finds himself "thinking about how Africa can seem a sieve of afflictions through which only the hardy may pass. The largest, fastest, wildest, strangest beasts are here. Every poisonous bug, screaming bird and thorned shrub has arrived at this moment through the most severe competition." Set against the backdrop of this merciless selective process, the struggles of athletes are mere figments of violent death and triumphant survival: "Sport is a pale shadow of the competitive life that has gone on forever across this high, fierce, first continent. Is it any wonder that frail European varieties feel threatened?"[58]

Conceding this sort of evolutionary superiority to Africans has both intended and unintended consequences. On the one hand, the cause of racial fraternity appears to be served by a master-disciple relationship that inverts the traditional hierarchy of colonial origin. Western runners who go to East Africa to train with the black prodigies sometimes speak of a newfound humility. When the German marathoner Herbert Steffny returned home in 1988 from five weeks in Kenya, he brought back nothing less than the elements of a new philosophy of life.[59] Such experiences are both physical ordeals and exercises in cross-cultural exchange, and they belong to an honorable tradition of finding wisdom far from home among strangers who have access to undreamed-of sources of knowledge about human potential.

The problem with this sort of discipleship is that it promotes both a black biological mystique and, however inadvertently, the fact of underdevelopment. Such exercises in awestruck wonder at African athleticism are compromised by the polite silence they require about the catastrophic economic and political conditions that have long shaped our sense of sub-Saharan Africa. Visions of superhealthy black runners compete with more familiar images of African bodies with distended bellies, sticklike limbs, and the enormous vacant eyes that convey racial dependency far more effectively than submissive gestures toward the World Bank. The world knows far more about the celebrated dominance of Kenyan distance runners than about the destruction of Kenyan universities by the country's dictator president.[60] In a word, the white man's breathless admiration, which sometimes conveys an unmistakable hint of masochism, stands in stark contrast to the actual balance of power between blacks and whites after centuries of more serious racial competitions that have devastated the "dark continent." Indeed, the opportunity to ponder the secrets of East African biology can provide welcome relief from the problems of conscience that haunt Westerners as they agonize over the demoralizing complexities of "aid to development."

Romanticizing human potential while tracing its origins to a primeval vitality is thus an exercise in colonial anthropology which makes the black organism into a specimen while preserving the white scientist's authority to situate this organism, implicitly or explicitly, within an evolutionary hierarchy that has always signified black inferiority. The paradoxical moments of this project occur when white scientists appear to understand less than their black subjects, or when the athletically superior black subject appears to invalidate Western science by confounding its predictions or refusing its purported benefits.

For example, in September 1991 Yobes Ondieki, who later became the first man to run ten thousand meters in less than twenty-seven minutes, was a recent world champion. When he visited Canberra after his triumph in Tokyo, Australian sports scientists begged him to submit to lactic-acid testing, which would tell him (and his benefactors) more than they knew about his level of fitness. But Ondieki refused this offer on the grounds that "I would no longer be mentally free."[61] An examination of his response to this overture can tell us much about elite sport as a kind of interracial encounter, for among the poignant moments that have resulted from the intermingling of Europeans and Africans within the world of sport, this was surely one of the most interesting, even if much depends on who is interpreting its significance. For the scientist, Ondieki's response was a lost opportunity to collect exotic data. For the racial romantic interested in preserving premodern African innocence, it was an act of defiance on the part of the physiologically noble savage. But for Ondieki, who also refused to look at stadium clocks to pace himself during races, it was a practical decision rather than romantic defiance. Integration into the Western scientific project would have meant losing the personal autonomy that sustains him through the ordeal of long-distance running. And his rejection of Western techniques may also have been scientifically sound: "sports science" is still a rudimentary discipline, whose benefits for the elite athlete (apart from certain drugs) are routinely exaggerated by the practitioners and journalists who have created and sustained its public image, and its powers of prediction are limited at best.[62] Before Anthony Yeboah became the top scorer in German soccer during the early 1990s, he failed a lactic-acid test, and the team that had him tested sent him down to an inferior league. Like white athletes who have had the same experience, Yeboah was demoralized by his lactate readings, and his career went into temporary eclipse.[63]

The failures of sports science have a bearing on racial politics because colonial domination has always been synonymous with European mastery of science and technology.[64] Like the sporting victories of colonial subjects, doubts about Western applied science can raise destabilizing questions about the foundations of authority, and the doubters may even be Europeans. Otto Pfister, a German who was coaching the Ghanaian national soccer team in 1992, is such a doubter who exemplifies the coexistence of colonial and anticolonial forces in African sport. The fact that Ghana imported a European to take charge of a politically significant team suggests that the nation suffers from a lack of native expertise; in this sense, the white coach is equivalent to a foreign military adviser who can explain the latest armaments. But it is also possible for the European adviser to sympathize with his charges to the point where he wants to demystify the colonial ideology he represents, including its denigrating ideas about Africans.

Pfister became a celebrity when his Ghanaian youth team won the junior world championship in 1991, and this experience made him, like some other outsiders, a believer in the fabulous potential of African athletes. "My fifteen-year-olds," he said provocatively, "are technically more advanced than any mid-level player in the Bundesliga." What made Pfister different was his insistence on praising the minds as well as the bodies of his players. The traditional stereotype of the undisciplined African, he said, was "racist nonsense." "Because they have to exert themselves twice as hard as the whites, they develop a tremendous motivation and mental stability" — a claim that flew in the face of centuries of folklore about the African personality. In the world of modern soccer, Pfister suggested, such ideas were meant to divert attention from the fact of European decline, and he proceeded to link this decline to the scientific pretensions of the West. White men's doubts that Africans could be integrated into the strict tactical concepts of the elite European teams, he commented acerbically, were "a sign of helplessness, because European soccer is so over-regimented and over-scientized that it has reached a dead end. There are always new fads: stretching, tapering off, recovery pools, psychological tricks or calf-blood treatments." In the end, Pfister confounded his interviewers by claiming that his players were both miraculous and modern. "They make passes that defy logic, that almost give me a heart attack as I'm sitting on the bench. And suddenly I realize that it's brilliant, brilliant and creative."[65] Then, as if anticipating the bipolar stereotype that joins African soccer genius with characterological instability, he insisted that blacks could indeed function within an organization. What did *not* interest them was functioning within an organization that had been rendered sclerotic by the futile scientism of the West.

# 9

# The Fastest White Man
# in the World

I N AUGUST 1993, the president of the German Track and Field
Federation, Dr. Helmut Digel, made an extraordinary public comment about the demoralized state of white athletes around the
world. "In the developed countries," he said, "track and field is caught
in a deep crisis: the athletes see the superiority of the Africans in the
distance races, and many simply give up. No young person is going to
train for the title of 'the world's fastest white man.'"[1]

In fact, Dr. Digel's portrait of Caucasian athletic inferiority did not
portray its full dimensions, since his remarks referred only to the long-
time hegemony of East African distance runners and, more recently, the
achievements of North Africans such as Noureddine Morceli, the invincible Algerian middle-distance specialist, and Khalid Skah, the Moroc-
can distance star who has himself been defeated by squads of tireless
Kenyans. He did not point out that the racial performance gap has
spread throughout the running and jumping events in track and field
and far beyond. Today the white male sprinter is all but extinct, and
even the last remaining "white" world record has been called into question in a way that emphasizes the race consciousness of modern sport.[2]
According to his former coach, Pietro Mennea's two-hundred-meter
time of 19.72 seconds owes something to the black African blood that
flows through his veins.[3]

Nor have the white sprinter's female counterparts done much better.
With the demise of the steroid-assisted East German women, it is now
the Russian Irina Primalova who has declared that she "will be the
fastest woman in the world"; she too, like many athletes from the
impoverished regions of Eastern Europe (and some Africans), may be

using illegal drugs to survive in the pitiless world of professional track and field in the post-Communist age.[4] France and Great Britain have run all-black sprint relay teams in international competitions, while other citizen-athletes of African descent, like the flamboyantly African tennis star Yannick Noah, have become familiar figures across the face of Europe.

In the United States, the high-profile sports are dominated by black athletes at both the college and professional levels. There is not a white star left in the National Basketball Association, nor a white running back worth mentioning in the National Football League; the idea of a white cornerback in today's NFL has become virtually unthinkable; a high and increasing percentage of the batting stars in major league baseball are African Americans. In summary, the dramatic ascent of the black athlete during the twentieth century has been a linear development, and it will continue into the foreseeable future, because there are no cultural or political forces to inhibit it.

Having understated the dimensions of black athletic dominance, Dr. Digel proceeded to overestimate the resolve of many white athletes to remain competitive with their black counterparts. A year after his prediction that white athletes would never resign themselves to an inferior intraracial competition, the Norwegian sprinter Geir Moen, a member of the European elite, told an interviewer that he was looking forward to being "the first white man who manages to run 100 meters in less than 10 seconds."[5] One man who will not beat him to it is Andreas Berger of Austria. The world's fastest white sprinter of 1993, with an excellent time of 10.15 seconds, Berger's career as a white hope fell victim to the doping police that summer, even as one tabloid celebrated him as "an unappreciated hero."[6]

The racial isolation of German sprinters and distance runners is often noted by the sportswriters who cover their attempts to keep up with faster black athletes. Florian Schwarthoff is presented not only as the solitary white man in a field of hurdlers but as the only German high-hurdler of any stature whatsoever; similarly, the sprinter Marc Blume is introduced as the only white athlete entered in the hundred-meter dash at another meet. Dieter Baumann, the great star of German track and field since his gold medal in the five-thousand-meter run at the 1992 Barcelona Olympic Games, is often depicted as a beleaguered white hero holding the fort against the Africans who outnumber and usually outrun him.

To his credit, Baumann has refrained from playing to the intense German fantasies about African physiology that have been so evident over the past century, and he has even tried to defuse the racial issue in his public statements. "I am a white Kenyan," he said just before the 1992 Olympic Games, conveying to his devoted German public a deep respect for Africans which they are unlikely to share. In further pursuit of the chimera of racial equality, he has exhorted his fellow whites to throw off the chains of their self-inflicted complexes about African athletes. "We Europeans," he said after his victory in Barcelona, "are just as good as them and no less suited" for distance running. "I don't see myself on the defensive, because the Africans are simply normal opponents."[7]

A year later Baumann's teammate Stephane Franke expressed his own feelings about the growing fatalism regarding white runners. "What I just can't stand to hear is talk about how the Europeans don't have it in them anymore," he said in exasperation.[8] Eamonn Coghlan, the Irish runner whose indoor mile mark of 3:49.78 is one of only two middle-distance records still held by white runners, speaks of the profoundly opposed mindsets of athletes who have been shaped by different cultural worlds. The African, he said in 1993, "runs with no fear. Runners in the Western world have a tendency to create psychological barriers for themselves. [Noureddine] Morceli runs at will, with no inhibitions."[9]

These issues receive limited coverage in the press, in part because racial athletic aptitude remains a delicate topic for public discussion in predominantly white societies. In addition, there is widespread resignation about closing the performance gap. We do not know how many white athletes can bring themselves to believe what Dieter Baumann once claimed regarding the physiological parity of the races. Indeed, his own sense of resignation in the face of African superiority has grown stronger in recent years.[10]

On the European road-racing circuit, which stretches from the Baltic to the Pyrenees, it is clear that the large numbers of first-class African runners have had a demoralizing effect on many white competitors. "When you are trying to earn your living on the road it is getting silly," one top British runner said in 1992. "There are 10 or 15 Kenyans everywhere." Spanish athletes have shown open resentment of the Africans, and the Belgian track-and-field federation has responded by establishing a lucrative cross-challenge that is limited to Belgian runners — in effect, a racially segregated event that provides financial incentives to the country's best runners. The strongest white Europeans understand that they need to test themselves against the Africans simply because their countrymen cannot push them hard enough. But the attitude of second-tier Europeans who try to survive as professionals tends to be less ambitious and more practical.[11]

Yet it is not only white athletes who feel disadvantaged in multiracial competitions. Racial inferiority complexes are an even more serious problem among Asian athletes and those who train them to compete in the Western sports that monopolize Olympic competition. During the 1988 Seoul Olympic Games, the head of the Sri Lankan gymnastics association argued for a eugenic solution, declaring that Asians would have to breed with Europeans, Americans, or Soviet citizens if they were to have any chance of becoming world-class athletes.[12]

For the Chinese, who have mounted a serious drive to become a world sports power, a principal problem is the black athlete and his alleged natural advantages. During preparations for the Seoul games, one Chinese track coach admitted that "Chinese coaches and athletes are not very liberal. One of our most popular notions is that physiologically black people are more talented than Chinese, so there's no way we can even get close." Belief in physiological inferiority, he said, had created psychological obstacles to performance.[13] Some Japanese who participate in competitive sailing are similarly convinced that their performance is impaired by a physiological deficit.[14]

By 1994 the Chinese sports establishment had put into effect a policy of avoiding sports such as basketball, boxing, and sprinting, in which black athletes are dominant. They decided instead to concentrate on sports such as distance running, swimming, gymnastics, and diving, to which people with small torsos are better adapted. The rationale for this policy includes a racial biology of athletic aptitude that is both uniquely Chinese and, like some related ideas of Western origin, pseudo-scientific. According to Professor Tian Maijiu, vice president of the Beijing Institute of Physical Education, sprinting aptitude is linked to both blood type and body type. Seventy to 90 percent of blacks but only 30 percent of Asians, he claims, have blood type O, and "O-type people get excited very easily, and that is why they make very good sprinters." In addition, "black people have very good genetics. Compared with them, the people in Asia are very inferior. The buttocks the blacks have in very high position. The whites, a little bit lower. The Asians, even lower. Because of that, muscles [in blacks] are longer, [and have] more power. That forms a very good lever."[15]

Such ideas are typical of the tabloid-style racial science examined later in this book. While the blood-group theory is simply nonsense, the anatomical thesis caricatures reliable anthropometric data about small average racial differences which may or may not be relevant to elite

performance. We will investigate the political and biological significance of these data in due course. What matters here is the role of
fantasy and scientific illiteracy in the construction of ideas about racial
difference. Such ideas can focus on less tangible attributes than the
position of the buttocks. Chinese ambitions to progress up through the
ranks of World Cup soccer, for example, have prompted the national
federation to put its most talented young athletes in the hands of highly
qualified foreign tutors with whom Chinese officials can feel something resembling racial affinity. Finding European soccer too "power-
oriented and awkward," they send their best and brightest to Brazil,
since South Americans are "small and agile and have the body proportions and mentality of the Chinese." The banner that stretches across
the entrance to their spartan training camp southwest of São Paulo
reads FASTER, HIGHER, STRONGER, and here the young Asians are
learning a whole new somatic style. "The Chinese are fast but still much
too stiff," says their Brazilian trainer, who has hired a samba teacher
and an expert in Brazilian martial arts to loosen them up. If they learn
their lessons well, then the Chinese will have acquired the art of *ginga,*
the Brazilian technique of dribbling the ball around an opponent like a
dancer. Their goal is to win at least one game in major international
competition by the year 2000.[16]

The evidence shows that the globalization of modern sport has
brought about a simultaneous globalization of racial folklore about
athletic performance. The standard repertory of stereotypes — gazelle-
like Africans, fiery Latins, tenacious Finns, emotional Italians, impassive Slavs — has proven to be remarkably stable throughout the twentieth century. Yet it is also clear, as the Chinese pilgrimage to Brazil
suggests, that influence — and anxiety — tend to flow in certain directions and not in others. These gradients of strength and weakness, of
competence and incompetence, have been shaped by our most powerful
racial images. The inequalities they imply account for the fact that
comparable athletic achievements do not necessarily create comparable
international images of racial superiority or inferiority.

For example, in the many commentaries that have been devoted to
the astonishing performances of China's female runners and swimmers
during 1993 and 1994, there is a conspicuous absence of theorizing
about racial anatomy and physiology. Many foreign observers have
assumed that these achievements were made possible by illicit drugs,
and subsequent drug testing of Chinese swimmers appeared to confirm that thesis. At the same time, we must keep in mind that cross-
cultural suspicions about the origins of record-breaking athletic per-

formances transcend purely scientific issues and focus inevitably on myths of national character and capacity. Westerners are prepared to accept the idea of Chinese deceit, but we do not associate Asians with supernormal athletic ability. The stellar Olympic performances of Japanese and native Hawaiian swimmers before World War II are remembered by aficionados of the sport, but they did not create an enduring image of racial fortitude. The image of Japanese males was dramatically improved by their smashing victory in the Russo-Japanese War of 1904–5. Conversely, positive images of victorious Japanese swimmers at the 1932 Los Angeles Olympic Games may have been erased by American propaganda about subhuman Japanese during World War II.

This law of deficient returns can also apply to those who are racially identified as Africans. In 1974 a young black woman from Curaçao was the fastest female swimmer in the world, but her performances and those of other swimmers of African descent have hardly made a dent in the universal image of blacks as a race that can barely stay afloat, appearing to confirm the African proverb that "water is the enemy of man."[17] In short, every racial myth of athletic aptitude — or athletic inadequacy, as in the case of big-boned African "sinkers" or uncoordinated Jews — results from the interplay of what athletes actually do and the powerful racial or ethnic stereotypes that shape popular interpretations of their performances.

Responses to fatalism about white athletic decline will be a useful barometer of race relations for the foreseeable future. Months after Geir Moen's disappointing sixth-place finish in the two-hundred-meter race in the 1995 World Championships ("He was the only white man in the final"), the major Oslo paper devoted most of a page to a postmortem — "Blacks Have the Speed and the Strength" — that recapitulated the past sixty years of theorizing for its readers. And here too there was a note of Caucasian impatience. According to this writer, a combination of "astonishment, admiration, and irritation" has created a demand among spectators, athletes, and scientists for an explanation of "black dominance."[18]

The rampant commercialization of track and field has also been affected, in that advertisers find themselves wondering how to make black African athletes into marketing vehicles that can appeal to white audiences.[19] "In every race," Dieter Baumann lamented before the 1996 Atlanta Olympic Games, "I am supposed to defend the honor of the West against each and every African."[20] Knowledgeable observers, including Baumann himself, recognize the sheer impossibility of such a challenge. "Right now," as one German journalist dryly noted, "there are only the white also-rans who may, perhaps, be able to learn something from the Africans. Whatever that is they will have to find out for themselves."[21] In the absence of such salvational knowledge, there remains the hope that Western science will eventually be able to explain the physiological secrets of the black body.

# PART III

# Dissecting John Henry

---

## The Search for
## Racial Athletic Aptitude

# 10

# Imagining the Black Organism

O N SEPTEMBER 13, 1995, Sir Roger Bannister delivered a
speech on the athletic limits of the human organism to the
British Association for the Advancement of Science. Now a
prominent neurologist, Sir Roger is best known as the first man to run a
mile in less than four minutes, a feat he accomplished to global acclaim
in 1954. His topic on this occasion was, by contrast, undramatic; indeed,
speculations about human limits have been an avocation for numerous
scientists throughout the twentieth century, and they have never stirred
real controversy. Yet Sir Roger's commentary on human athletic performance became international news because he indulged in what he
called "political incorrectness," in this case a willingness to muse out
loud about the natural advantages of black athletes.

"It is perfectly obvious," Sir Roger stated, "when you see an all-black
sprint final that there must be something rather special about their
anatomy or physiology which produces these outstanding successes, and
indeed there may be — but we don't know quite what it is." This combination of curiosity and scientific imprecision typifies the history of
thinking about racial athletic aptitude, and for this reason Sir Roger's
remarks offered nothing new. More surprising, however, was the fact
that this distinguished speaker was uninformed about ideas he appeared
to be tossing off the top of his head. "It may be their heel bone is a bit
longer," he continued, recycling an idea that had been put to rest in
1936, "or it may be that because of their adaptation to warm climates
they have a lower subcutaneous fat [sic], so their power-to-weight ratio
is better. Maybe they have an elasticity or capacity innately of the
muscle fibers which contract quickly, which is some adaptation of the
warmer environment."[1] Sir Roger seemed unaware that the racial difference in body fat is no longer just hypothetical, or that even the

confirmation of such average differences between racial populations tells us nothing intelligible about the origins of superior athletic performance. His brief meditation on muscle fibers betrayed no current knowledge of a complex and controversial topic. "Perhaps," he said, "there are anatomical advantages in the length of the Achilles' tendon, the longest tendon in the body" — an idea that has seldom been heard since it first appeared in a 1930 study of black and white cadavers. "I do not know the true reasons," he confessed.[2] This was, in short, a strikingly amateurish performance by a professional scientist on a topic that has long provoked acrimony between blacks and whites.

The relationship between scientific curiosity and racial biology has been fraught with ambiguity for most of the twentieth century. The unscientific character and cultural chauvinism of nineteenth-century racial anthropology, as well as Nazi perversions of this kind of racialism, have demonstrated to most observers the virtual impossibility of a race-neutral science of human behavior. In fact, racial science is problematic for two reasons. First, curiosity about racial difference originates in minds that have already absorbed ideas about the meaning of race and its significance in human relations; curiosity is not, therefore, a wholly autonomous instrument of scientific inquiry into human variation. Second, racial biology incorporates cultural as well as biological factors that affect human anatomy, physiology, health — and athletic potential. These two points challenge the claim that "race biology, pursued with 'cool curiosity', can be separated from racism."[3]

Yet it was to this ideal that Dr. Bannister aspired in his remarks on race. "As a scientist rather than a sociologist," he declared, "I am prepared to risk political incorrectness by drawing attention to the seemingly obvious but understressed fact that black sprinters and black athletes in general all seem to have natural anatomical advantages."[4] Like others who have attempted to locate the source of "natural" racial differences, Dr. Bannister legitimized his speculations by claiming that he could separate the scientific from the sociological. But his insistence on rescuing "obvious" racial differences from undeserved obscurity expressed his own socially conditioned list of which human differences deserve systematic attention in the first place. In addition, he overlooked the fact that what is obvious is black performance rather than black anatomy. Finally, he overlooked the fact that science endeavors to show that phenomena that may appear to be obvious in nature are often nothing of the kind.

A critique of the search for racial athletic aptitude can be legitimized on both scientific and humanitarian grounds. It is easy enough to show that a great deal of naive speculation about purported racial differences has appeared in scientific and medical journals; indeed, many examples of such biased thinking are presented in this book. We can also point to the malign role that racial science has often played in human affairs over the past two centuries. Yet it is also the case that these arguments can take the form of a disingenuous (and unscientific) opposition to the investigation of racial differences per se on the grounds that they are either too trivial or too potentially dangerous to examine.

The claim that observable differences are too insignificant to warrant understanding is as vulnerable as the claim that certain causal relationships are too obvious to doubt, since scientists should refuse to judge what is insignificant and what is obvious until they have looked more deeply into causes and effects. Such disingenuousness can also involve a premature suppression of biological thinking; as one American sociologist pointed out, it is a fallacy to insist that "one must know the specific nature of a physiological mechanism before one may suspect that such a mechanism exists."[5] Such antibiological puritanism is rooted in an ideological phobia rather than in scientific curiosity.

Similarly, the argument that the investigation of racial differences is too hazardous to pursue turns out to be less an objection to what might be done than a belated protest against what has already been done, the effects of which are often difficult to assess. Indeed, a large volume of peer-reviewed work on anatomical and physiological differences of a racial character has been published without having had any discernible effects on the public's thinking about race. Problems tend to arise only when scientific work is publicized as "tabloid science" — melodramatic reporting that is consumed by people attracted to simplistic explanations of complex phenomena.

The superiority of black runners, whether they are sprinters of West African descent or East African distance specialists, is now so overwhelming that only the naive can claim that their performances are of no legitimate scientific interest. It is equally naive to embrace with pseudo-scientific certainty the plausible but unproven thesis that such superior performances are unrelated to genetic factors, since the fact is that we do not know whether this is true. What we do know is that there is growing racist interest in racial athletic aptitude. "Obviously," the neo-Nazi politician David Duke said in 1989, "blacks have a natural affinity to sporting activities that require quick bursts of speed."[6] This effortless conflation of performance and racial type expresses an impatience with the ambiguous nature of evidence and often signals an eagerness to find racial differences that has no basis in scientific motives. The controversial molecular geneticist Vincent Sarich, who has declared his belief in the inequality of the races, is only one of a number of intellectuals who have seized upon black athleticism as prima facie evidence of significant racial difference. "If you can believe that individuals of recent African ancestry are not genetically advantaged over those of European and Asian ancestry in certain athletic endeavours," he told his students at Berkeley, "then you probably could be led to believe just about anything."[7]

The idea of black athletic superiority has also been absorbed by the white population at large. Half of the respondents to an American poll in 1991 agreed with the idea that "blacks have more natural physical ability," and we may assume that this assessment is still widely linked to derogatory ideas about black intelligence.[8] As the almost simultaneous publication of *The Bell Curve* and the election of a Republican Congress made clear in late 1994, a resurgent interest in racial difference can develop in tandem with or even catalyze social policies that express white doubts about black potential. The search for racial athletic aptitude is important precisely because it threatens to transform the spectacle of black athleticism into a highly public image of black retardation.

Half a century ago, however, it was still possible to think of racial athletic aptitude as evidence of human equality. On May 24, 1941, a thought-provoking article on race and physical fitness appeared in the *Journal of the American Medical Association*. Its author was an exercise physiologist named Ernst Jokl, who during the 1920s had been one of several first-rate Jewish sprinters competing in Weimar Germany. In 1935 Nazi persecution of the Jews prompted him to emigrate to South Africa, where he became head of the Department of Physical Education at Witwatersrand Technical College and consultant on medical aspects of physical education to the South African Defense Force. It was thus from the heartland of apartheid that he delivered a physiologist's testimony to the fundamental unity of the human species. Jokl and his colleagues performed a series of tests on the physical skill, strength, and endurance of a racial cross-section of South African children — English, Afrikaner, Jewish, Bantu, Cape Colored, Indian, and Chinese — and the results surprised the investigators. "We were impressed," Jokl wrote, "with the similarity between the standards of physical performance found in the different racial groups. No more impressive evidence for the basic equality of man has ever been adduced."[9]

The claim that tests of physical performance had established the parity of the races was a most unusual dissent from a long tradition of thinking about race and athletic aptitude. Western thinking has for the past two centuries maintained that there are significant physical differences, both anatomical and physiological, between blacks and whites, and that these differences express themselves in the physical superiority or inferiority of one group in relation to the other. While racial thinking has focused primarily on alleged differences in intelligence, anatomy and physiology have also served to preserve our culture's sense of racial difference.

Although whites have been the primary promoters of ideas about racial distinctiveness, African Americans too have often adopted racial biology for their own purposes, and this has long included ideas about black athletic superiority. Nevertheless, it is the white fixation on black biology that has established the basic framework in which we continue to discuss racial differences and what they mean. This profound interest in maintaining a sense of racial difference does not always insist that differences mean white superiority. While this is usually the case, white attitudes toward real or imagined black traits can also accommodate black superiority, if the trait in question implies a kind of inferiority at the same time. It was once common, for example, to assert that blacks around the world possessed keener eyesight and hearing than whites, but this "superiority" came at the price of being labeled a more primitive human type.

Our receptiveness to the idea of a biologically grounded black athletic aptitude is rooted ultimately in the belief that there are distinct racial subspecies which have evolved special traits and capacities — anatomical, physiological, and temperamental — to adapt to varying climates, landscapes, and ways of life. What is more, this belief played an important role in justifying the southern view of racial hierarchy. "A major tenet of the institution of slavery was the belief that biological differences existed between slaves and whites. Slaves were viewed as a distinct species which was immune to certain diseases, yet inferior biologically and mentally to whites. These real and fabricated biological differences offered to the slave owner partial justification for the institution of slavery."[10] A seminal formulation of this doctrine by a well-known racist southern physician, Samuel Cartwright, appeared in 1851 in a publication read by many slaveholders: "It is not only in the skin that a difference of color exists between the negro and the white man, but in the membranes, the muscles, the tendons, and in all the fluids and secretions. Even the negro brain and nerves, the chyle and all the humors, are tintured with a shade of the pervading darkness. His bile is of a deeper color, and his blood is blacker than the white man's."[11]

Not all of Cartwright's contemporaries accepted this view. One physician, commenting anonymously in the *Charleston Medical Journal and Review,* pointed sardonically to the role of wish fulfillment in the formulation of this dichotomizing racial physiology. Cartwright's findings, he said, were "the fruit of the imaginative brain of some . . . aspirant in the race for fame, rather than the actual demonstration of the scalpel."[12] Yet this clarity of vision was the exception rather than the rule until well into the twentieth century. The standard medical view throughout the 1800s was much closer to Cartwright's version of anatomical apartheid than to the enlightened skepticism of his anonymous critic. The Association of American Anatomists went so far as to distribute a questionnaire asking physicians to "keep a careful record of all variations and anomalies" between whites and blacks.[13]

This energetic search for racial differences served both the emotional and the political needs of a white supremacist culture that required a congenial fantasy of the Negro organism: "Medical science and Southern nationalism, reinforcing each other in the thought of the physician, created a fictitious Negro type whose attributes were accepted as having real substance." Medical thinking thus continued the traditional construction of black and white as opposite types. Physicians believed that black and white illnesses oscillated seasonally but in opposite phases; blacks were more susceptible to diseases of the winter and spring, while whites were more vulnerable during the summer and autumn.[14] But this need for a physiologically exotic (and in most respects inferior) Negro type was not confined to the South. To be sure, the slave culture intensified feelings about black minds and bodies to the point where some southern physicians and lay people were literally "seeing things" rather than observing real traits and behaviors. Yet these eccentric perceptions were only magnified versions of a racial folklore that prevailed throughout Western societies (and their medical establishments) long past the turn of the twentieth century.

The persistence of this "southern" fixation on racial biology in modern Western cultures is one of the least discussed aspects of our own engagement with the issue of race, and its focus on the alleged peculiarities of the black body has long provided the emotional and conceptual foundation for speculations about racial athletic aptitude. While it can be difficult to follow the evolution of these ideas in the public sphere, it is easier to trace them in the medical literature, where popular ideas about racial difference have often commingled and sometimes coalesced with the clinical observations of physicians who have been quite unaware of how the popular attitudes they have absorbed from their social milieu have affected their own perceptions of the black organism.

A survey of medical opinion during the first half of this century demonstrates how firmly entrenched racial separatism has been in the minds of American physicians confronting a human type they came to call "the Negro patient." "I do not believe," one doctor wrote in 1932, "that any physician who does not include in his practice a large number of negroes, and especially a large number of Southern negroes, can possibly realize the peculiar medical problems which the colored race presents."[15] "There is much evidence to show," another contributor to the *Southern Medical Journal* wrote in 1934, "that syphilis behaves differently in the white and the negro, and attacks the various organs and systems of the body with different force." One can only wonder, he notes, "how much of the negro's reaction to disease is different from the Caucasian because of native endowments, structural and functional."[16] "That the negro has anatomical peculiarities, is prone to certain diseases and relatively free of others is well recognized," a dermatologist wrote in 1939. "In our own field of dermatology important anatomic, physiologic and pathologic variations have been noted."[17] A proctologist from Dallas claimed in 1925 that there were "urologic idiosyncrasies" in the Negro, while a psychiatrist from South Carolina found in 1943 that an anticonvulsant drug used to treat epileptics was "more effective in Negroes" than in white patients.[18]

Nor were these differences limited to pathological conditions. The influential eugenicist Charles B. Davenport concluded in 1929 that "there are differences in the structure of the sense organs and the nervous system of negroes and whites, such that the negroes are superior in some respects, the whites in others." Biological difference led in turn to cultural difference. "Rhythm," Davenport argued, "probably depends upon some structural peculiarity of the hearing mechanism, and it seems probable that this mechanism is superior in the blacks to the whites. The conclusion has, therefore, to be drawn that there is a racial difference in discrimination of capacity for rhythm between the negroes and the whites."[19] This theory reflects the fact that numerous investigations of Negro musical ability appeared in the psychological literature in Davenport's time.[20]

These purported differences were, as we shall see, only a few of many traits that physicians regarded as black deviations from a healthy white norm. A generation after the public triumphs of the civil rights movement, which put overt medical racism beyond the pale, we should realize that the racial biology of this period expressed deeply rooted cultural habits of thought and behavior that pervaded the most respectable medical and scholarly circles. At the same time, concurrent scientific developments produced an unprecedented deracializing of human biology in the fields of physical anthropology and medicine.

These conflicting developments sometimes produced interesting combinations of pseudo-science and medical enlightenment in the pages of professional journals. The Dallas proctologist who in 1925 compared blacks with "anthropoid apes" also warned against theorizing about organic racial differences "on a purely phylogenetic or atavistic basis," arguing in effect that those who wished to put blacks in their phylogenetic place had to observe certain scientific standards.[21] Even as the *Journal of the American Medical Association* was publishing clinical papers that would be unacceptable by today's standards of racial discourse, the editors were dispensing modern advice to doctors whose queries reflected a deep ignorance of racial biology. "There is no way at present known to determine by blood test whether or not a person has negro blood," the editors replied to a pair of correspondents in 1921. In 1935 an M.D. from Idaho wanted to know whether "telegony" was fact or fiction: "That is, if a Negro raped a white woman, who gave birth to a mulatto, and later she marries a white man, would their children be liable to have Negro characteristics?" No, the editors assured him, there was "no scientific evidence for and considerable evidence against telegony." A year later the journal told a doctor from California that there was no scientific way to identify a Gypsy. In 1939 the blood-test issue reappeared. "Several of us," an M.D. from Alabama wrote, "are anxious to know whether any work has been done to differentiate by the precipitin test the blood of Negroes from the blood of white persons." On this occasion too the editors had to respond that authorities on the subject unanimously agreed that "at the present time" no such test was available. In 1940 the question was whether the sweat of the Negro differed from that of the white. As late as 1955 a physician wanted to know whether "there are any differences between the Negro and white race in their responses to antibiotic therapy." And once again the answer was no: "The results have been more or less uniform with respect to efficacy and reactions in all parts of the world." As far as the editors of *JAMA* were concerned, the family of man remained physiologically intact.[22]

# 11

# The Negro as a Defective Type

THE MEDICAL QUERIES of the early twentieth century pointed to a prodigious appetite for a confirmation of racial differences that would establish the inferiority of the Negro once and for all. Regardless of the scientific idiom in which they were posed, questions about blood, sweat, and telegony were prompted by racial anxiety and a transparent desire to establish physiological apartheid. Racial differences implied defects in blacks precisely because a deep attachment to the traditional racial hierarchy animated an ostensibly scientific enterprise. That these black defects included physical inferiority is likely to surprise modern readers, who have seen so much evidence of black athletic superiority. Still, as counter-intuitive as it may seem, this white fixation on the defective Negro organism represented an important dimension of the racism of this period, combining pity and scorn with the authority of medical science. In this context, medical candor expressed racial contempt by promoting an image of the black as a degenerate and dilapidated creature whose improvement appeared to be a hopeless task, even for modern medicine and other agents of white benevolence. That much of this was the result of fallacious or wishful thinking tells us something important about the sheer depth of the racist feelings that created images of organismic decrepitude. Eventually, however, the image of the physically defective black was erased in the minds of whites by more powerful images of black athletic vigor and violent black criminality, which were associated with characterological and cultural defects rather than physical ones.

Ideas about black anatomical and physiological inferiority have always served the slave-based or colonial societies that formulate them by assigning certain capacities to blacks and denying that they possess whatever other capacities would enable them to transcend their lowly or even subhuman status. White characterizations of black racial biology have thus been a balancing act that concedes to slaves or servants the aptitudes that make them functional members of the social order they serve while withholding aptitudes that are reserved for whites alone. This dualistic portrait is clearly evident in the writings of the southern physician Samuel Cartwright, whose proslavery polemics are a valuable record of racist medical ambivalence, responding to the black's dual role as indispensable slave and potential rebel.

For Cartwright, the Negro problem was the old story of Prospero and Caliban: how could the white master control a savage creature ruled by appetites that signified a potentially ungovernable energy? He answered this question in 1851 by offering a reassuring physiological explanation of the black organism: "The great development of the nervous system, and the profuse distribution of nervous matter to the stomach, liver and genital organs, would make the Ethiopian race unmanageable, if it were not that this excessive nervous development is associated with a deficiency of red blood in the pulmonary and arterial systems." Such biological deficiencies were "the true cause of that debasement of mind, which has rendered the people of Africa unable to take care of themselves. It is the true cause of their indolence and apathy."[1] This physiological equilibrium was thus crucial to the preservation of political equilibrium. "The vulgar error that there is no difference in the negro's organization, physiology and psychology," Cartwright asserted, "and that all the apparent difference arises from Southern slavery, is the cause of all those political agitations which are threatening to dissolve our Union."[2] Pseudo-scientific talk about this "defective hematosis, or atmospherization of the blood," was thus an implicitly political stratagem that pointed to the symbolic significance of Negro sickness and health. Stigmatizing the Negro organism as deviant and defective permitted an apologist like Cartwright to argue that slavery neither caused nor exacerbated black inferiority, which was firmly rooted in the biology of the African.

At the same time, the doctrine of black inferiority had to be compatible with the labor requirements of North American and colonial plantations that subjected blacks to severe physiological stress. Southerners like Cartwright as well as European colonialists were thus practical-minded enough to credit blacks with the physiological capacity to do the work that was required of them. Along with many others, Cartwright believed that the alleged Negro affinity for a hot environment was an "ethnical peculiarity" which was "in harmony with their efficiency as laborers in hot, damp, close, suffocating atmospheres — where instead of suffering and dying, as the white man would, they are healthier, happier and more prolific than in their native Africa."[3] That blacks were, as another author put it in 1850, "capable of great endurance under a burning sun"[4] became one of the great racial truisms of the modern age, and was as convenient for the operators of South African gold mines as it was for the cotton-growers of the American South.

Cartwright was not averse to crediting blacks with certain other signs of organismic vitality. "The negro's hearing is better," he wrote, "his sight stronger, and he seldom needs spectacles."[5] Yet apart from these concessions to the idea of Negro health, his analysis was categorically negative, in a way that directly contradicts the familiar image of the physically imposing black male slave. He was particularly adamant about the black's inherent inability to perform physical labor unless he was animated by the white man's will: "Under the compulsive power of the white man, they are made to labor or exercise, which makes the lungs perform the duty of vitalizing the blood more perfectly than is done when they are left free to indulge in idleness." Indeed, it is "the want of a sufficiency of red, vital blood" that accounts for the black man's confinement within "unalterable physiological laws," such that "his will is too weak to command his muscles" beyond his inborn limits.[6]

By the end of the nineteenth century the idea of Negro infirmity had become a firmly entrenched part of an intense racism. Despite the fact that the African-American population continued to grow, "the belief in the Negro's extinction became one of the most pervasive ideas in American medical and anthropological thought during the late nineteenth century. It was also a fitting culmination to the concept of racial inferiority in American life." The extinction thesis served to establish the disastrous consequences of emancipation for the black population. A half-century earlier, a southern physician had already argued that the "unparalleled deterioration [of the free blacks], their frequent insanity, dementia, blindness, deafness, pauperism, premature death, their decrease, or minimized rate of increase, their physical degeneration and tendency to extinction," made slavery, as one historian has put it, "an ethical as well as medical necessity."[7] This emphasis on Negro disorders continued long after it had become clear to the most diehard southern racists that emancipation was an irrevocable fact of life.

Such accounts of black pathology were often realistic enough, given the miserable circumstances in which most blacks lived during the age of Jim Crow. They are most interesting, however, as evidence of the sheer tenacity of the racial folklore that continued to express the worldview and serve the emotional needs of white people. Even the extinction theory appears in the medical literature as late as 1923, invoked by an Alabama physician who reported on widespread malnutrition among black infants and children and predicted dire consequences for both races. "If these conclusions are correct," he wrote, "a few more years and the negro race in the South will be so weakened that it will rot because of its low resistance to disease. From an economic standpoint can we afford this? For our own health assurance and for our own protection can we allow this to go on?" Another pernicious factor was the Negro midwife, whose "gross ignorance regarding the laws and the principles of asepsis and antisepsis combined with her superstitions make her a very potent force looking toward the extermination of the race." The wholly unsentimental message from this healer was that black disease threatened white health, and that unfounded white fears of "social equality" between the races must no longer retard white initiatives to improve the health of blacks. "With disease rampant among the negroes, with abundant evidence of their general race deterioration, it is time for the white race of the South to lay aside its perverse obstinacy and foolish sensitiveness."[8] Like the slaveowners of the Old South, who had often monitored the health of their human chattel with self-interested care, the many whites who now employed blacks as paid servants could not afford to be indifferent to the continuing biological deterioration of the Negro race.

During the twentieth century the doctrine of biological Negro inferiority was slowly transformed into a somewhat more humane approach to black health problems, which combined pity and contempt in varying proportions. "The future of the negro," an expert on syphilis wrote in the *Journal of the American Medical Asssociation* in 1910, "lies more in the research laboratory than in the schools. This strange and pitiable creature, whose mind and body are traveling in different directions, is an ever-changing type, and new ideas have to be evolved to meet him at his different stages of mingled development and retrogression." The Negro, said Dr. Thomas W. Murrell, was "as a rule, but a sorry specimen, for disease and dissipation have done their work only too well," and the only remedy for this medical and social disaster was "a paternal government" that might bring health to the helpless.[9] Nearly half a century after Emancipation, the dehumanizing ethos of plantation medicine was alive and well in the pages of the flagship journal of American medicine.

A more humane discussion of "Syphilis in the American Negro" appeared in the same journal in 1914. The author, who held appointments in the medical departments of both Georgetown University and

Howard University, a venerable African-American institution, wrote without the racist exasperation of Murrell (whom he cited as an authority) but with evident concern about sexual promiscuity among the "poorer class of negroes," to whom he contrasted another class composed of "colored people who are trying to make something of themselves, who have become responsible physicians, lawyers, teachers and business men, and who live a life not materially different from the same type of whites."[10] This physician, who saw the "responsible" Negroes of Howard University on a regular basis, clearly understood that it was important to remove the stigma of disease from the tiny and struggling black middle class of his era.

By noting the relationship between disease and class, this more sympathetic treatment partly succeeded in removing the issue of race from a notorious scourge that had done considerable damage to the campaign to achieve respectability and first-class citizenship for African Americans. Negro sexual behavior, W.E.B. Du Bois wrote in 1897, "compels us to plead guilty to the shameful fact that sexual impurity among Negro men and Negro women of America is the crying disgrace of the American republic," and it is of interest to us that he recommended "athletic sports" as an antidote to licentiousness.[11] It is important, however, that Du Bois, unlike some of his contemporaries, saw sport as a socially rather than biologically significant activity for demonstrating the normality of the black man. Like every other African-American intellectual of his time, Du Bois had no choice but to grapple with the biological meaning of race in an era when biological determinism shaped mainstream thinking about racial identity. It is thus a measure of his progressive outlook that he did not think of athleticism in biological terms. As Kwame Anthony Appiah has pointed out, Du Bois moved "away from the 'scientific' — that is, biological and anthropological — conception of race to a sociohistorical notion."[12]

In fact, Du Bois employed an interesting rhetorical strategy to deal with the issue of racial difference. On the one hand, he noted that the American Negro had felt an urgent need "to deprecate and minimize race distinctions," which had done him great harm. While making a point of his own more open-minded acknowledgement of physical differences separating "the two most extreme types of the world's races," Du Bois then proceeded to show that "the grosser physical differences of color, hair and bone go but a short way to explaining the different roles which groups of men have played in Human Progress . . . The deeper differences," he argued, "are spiritual, psychical, differences — undoubtedly based on the physical, but transcending them."[13] Deemphasizing racial biology was a defensive strategy that aimed at making it more difficult for racists to seize on the defective Negro body as proof of racial inferiority.

Concern for the image of African Americans was seldom evident within the American medical establishment during the first half of this century, and much uninhibited commentary on purported Negro defects and potential therapies for them appears in the medical and anthropological literature of this period. "The negro," the prominent American biologist Raymond Pearl wrote in 1929, "reacts differently to diseases than the white, in a great many ways, including incidence, organological distribution of pathological lesions, etc. In some respects these racial differences in pathology are so great as to make it seem reasonable that they should be taken into account in planning health programs for the negro . . . Is it unreasonable to suggest that specific health activities be directed toward helping him in regard to his specific biological disabilities?"[14]

Pearl's crucial assumption was that racial difference was synonymous with Negro deficiency. Yet he was also aware of the biological balance sheet that had always accompanied comparisons of whites and blacks and that had frequently accorded a greater vitality to the black organism. "In some particulars," he said, the Negro "appears to enjoy a greater biological fitness than the white race, while in other respects he is apparently distinctly less well adapted to the general environment in which he must live and have his being."[15] Yet despite his acknowledgement of this biological parity and his own finding that whites were more vulnerable to cancer than blacks, it was the "specific biological disabilities" of the Negro that he featured in his report. This bias permeated the racial biology of the time and was expressed in a vague but suggestive pseudo-scientific idiom that referred to "the negro's weakness" (1921), his "general race deterioration" (1923), "the inferior organism of the race" (1925), and so on.[16]

Racial biology was (and remains) an inherently judgmental and hierarchical project that made clinical objectivity the least common response to difference among those who should have practiced such self-control. If, for example, scientists thought in 1937 that they had observed "racial peculiarities in . . . response to endocrine products," the "peculiar" patients were certain to be black.[17] Another example of the black-pathology bias appeared in a 1928 commentary on an unknown factor supposedly involved in the high incidence of heart disease among American blacks: "That is something which is hard to define but which seems quite definite, the fact that the negro has probably inherited a defective cardiovascular apparatus, which begins to break down sooner than that of the [white] man."[18] It was irrelevant to Dr. C. T. Stone of Galveston, Texas, that he had swaddled the "fact" of Negro deficiency in a thick blanket of qualifiers, because the medical ethnocentrist regarded the "biological disabilities" of the Negro as a law of nature. More surprising, perhaps, is the fact that the doctor did not refer to the contemporary myth of the black man's "natural cardiac strength," an equally fictitious piece of medico-racial folklore discussed later in this book.[19]

Commentaries on black biological inferiority also appear in some unexpected sources. Gunnar Myrdal's famous study of race in America, *An American Dilemma,* published in 1944, offers a remarkably enlightened treatment of the racial biology of the time. It is therefore interesting that Myrdal reported that the black man's "body is more often deformed" than that of the white, especially given the fact that here too there was a countervailing myth of Negro physical perfection. Myrdal was also capable of thinking of blacks as human specimens whose future, as one of our racist physicians put it in 1910, was to be found in the research laboratory. "Controlled biological experiments on the Negro are not out of the question," Myrdal wrote. "Concentrated [vitamin] $B_1$ has been administered to white persons and the effects of greater energy and optimism and lesser susceptibility to fatigue noted. Is it not a reasonable and verifiable hypothesis that the administration of concentrated doses of vitamins would have even greater effects on Negroes, whose diets are, on the average, even more deficient than those of whites?"[20] Myrdal's combination of clinical remoteness and humanitarian intent reminds us that this kind of paternalistic scientism toward "the Negro patient" was standard medical practice until very recently.

The traumatized state of African Americans promoted the special focus on their alleged biological inferiority and legitimized the exploration of specific disorders and anomalies. Indeed, the extent of these traumas seemed to demand an intimate portrait of the damage so that reparative work could begin. This link between the black ordeal and the identification of "racial" quirks and deficiencies is exemplified by a comparative study of mortality in blacks and whites during anesthesia, obstetrics, and surgery that appeared in 1957 in the journal of the National Medical Association, the African-American equivalent of the better-known American Medical Association. In this clinical report, Dr. Robert A. Hingson, an obstetrician at the Western Reserve University School of Medicine, set the stage by recalling the traumas of the African-American experience. "We shall leave it to the sociologist," he wrote, "to determine the damage the scars of history have left upon the black man. The historians have already recorded the fact that the Negro was torn from his native tropical home and transported against his will into an environment encompassing a new climate, a new diet, a new pathogenic bacteriology, a new language and a new psychology quite different from the sun of Africa and the centuries-old customs of his native habitat." The medical cost of this complex ordeal was nothing less than "a racial melancholia, associated with suprarenal hypertension, cardiovascular crises, and eclamptogenic toxemia with convulsions, that have greatly increased rates of morbidity and mortality." And here too racial difference meant black deficiency. "Biochemists," said Dr. Hingson, "have noticed that the endocrine 'make-up' of Africans differs from that of Europeans," suggesting "a cortical hormone deficiency in Africans . . . A low level of the cortical hormones is certainly associated with a poor response to stress and may account for the difference between the colored and white patient's reaction to surgical procedures." Contrary to the myth concerning a special black tolerance for surgery, black patients were dying in greater numbers than their white counterparts. More interesting than the clinical data, however, is that in 1957 the idea of race-specific disorders was still inseparable from the habitual paternalism that aimed at treating it. What is more, this endorsement of "the Negro's need for special attention" appeared in a black-edited publication, along with the assertion that Negro survival itself had been made possible by "the humanitarian and scientific ministrations of a compassionate nation."[21]

It is interesting to note that a similar exercise in speculative endocrinology had occurred a generation earlier. As modern endocrinology took shape during the 1920s, the British anthropologist Arthur Keith proposed a hormonal theory of racial difference (or "gland theory") that lives on today in the work of the Canadian racial psychologist J. Philippe Rushton. Keith's theory of racial origins, in the words of a contemporary, held that "the dissimilarities in the average bodily structure of the two races are explained in terms of the functioning of the endocrine glands . . . The long 'storklike' legs of some Negroid types have been thought by some to be due to abeyance of the interstitial gland action."[22]

The problem with the gland theory was that it contained an internal contradiction. Keith associated an adrenal cortex deficiency with dark skin color. But as one endocrinologist noted in 1933, "adrenal deficiency is especially characterized by bodily weakness and some of the Negro tribes are notable for their strength. An over-supply of the cortical hormone is one cause of precocious puberty, hence deficiency of this hormone would presumably result in delayed puberty. Such is not characteristic of Negroes; the dark races tend to mature earlier than the light."[23] In a word, adrenal deficiency theory could not displace better-established ideas about the robust Negro and his precocious development.

Such speculations about racial difference gravitated naturally to the idea of the defective black organism. Like the Caucasian acromegalic of Neanderthal appearance, the Negro could be seen as the product of abnormal endocrine functioning and thus as a kind of freak of nature. Once again, difference was synonymous with pathology. From time to time, however, the fundamental premise of black biological inferiority ran up against some very different ideas about black physicality, which pointed in the direction of superior athletic potential. The foundering of Keith's "gland theory" on the shoals of black strength and physical precocity was not the only case in which an alleged lack of vigor looks very curious in light of the athletic performances achieved by African Americans during and after the 1920s. Small wonder that one anesthesiologist noted with surprise in 1949 that "even physically fit Negroes are bad risks" in surgery; it was, after all, only natural to expect a robust black man to demonstrate all-round vitality.[24]

Perhaps the most perplexing scientific observation regarding black organismic inferiority concerned "vital capacity," or the amount of air a subject could exhale in a single effort. A scientist and a physician studying the effects of hookworm infection on black and white children found the latter to possess superior pulmonary capacity and proposed in 1926 "that low vital capacity is a racial characteristic, and that vital capacity standards which may be applied to white people cannot be directly applied to the negro race."[25] This view became one of the unchallenged dogmas of racial biology. The prominent anthropologist Otto Klineberg reported in 1935 (without specific reference to blacks) that scientific opinion generally held that "low vital capacity is due not to race or nationality, but to the warm climate, smaller amount of exercise, low metabolism and poor chest expansion," and that physical training improved it.[26] Yet credible scientific reports that blacks in particular were endowed with a low vital capacity appeared well into the 1960s.[27]

These conflicting assessments of vital capacity exemplify the problematic status of racial biology as a science of man, since the original questions that are asked and the observations that follow are rarely immune to the influence of racial folklore. It is significant, for example, that the idea of black pulmonary inferiority played a prominent role in the eccentric racial physiology of Dr. Cartwright.[28] This claim was inseparable from older ideas about black susceptibility to pneumonia and tuberculosis and an innate black tendency to have "weak" lungs.[29] The hookworm specialists from Alabama also noted that "negroes have longer limbs and shorter trunks than white children, and this fact may explain, in part at least, their lower vital capacity."[30] Yet this was the body build that came to be associated (however dubiously) with the allegedly superior running ability of black athletes. How, we may ask, did the idea of inferior black lungs survive the spectacular careers of Jesse Owens and many other black champions?

This conundrum leads back to the striking conflict between the image of the defective black organism and its increasingly impressive athletic achievements during the twentieth century. People suffering from vitamin deficiencies, low vital capacity, a defective cardiovascular system, physical defects, and poorly developed calves would appear to be poor candidates for athletic prominence.[31] It was impossible, Dr. S. W. Douglas of Eudora, Arkansas, wrote in 1926, to get black people to "take proper exercise."[32] Yet this medical echo of southern talk about "lazy" or "indolent" blacks flew in the face of common knowledge that the vast majority of black Americans survived only by the sweat of their brows, and that many performed countless feats of strength and endurance outside as well as inside the stadium.

Finally, the idea of black biological inferiority reminds us that the trauma of slavery and racial oppression has been interpreted in two contradictory ways, as either weakening or strengthening the African-American population, and that adherence to these competing viewpoints has divided along racial lines. White racists, along with the many whites who passively absorb images of black inferiority, have a vested interest in a theory of innate black defects, which makes social action on behalf of African Americans look ineffectual and pointless, while blacks have drawn strength from a doctrine (or myth) of black survival that emphasizes physical as well as mental suffering and has given African-American athletic achievement its unique symbolic importance. This conflict over the state of African-American health and the need for a black response to centuries of traumatic experience have enlisted only a handful of African-American scientists and scholars in their unequal struggle with white thinking about racial difference. Let us now see how ideas about physical vitality and athletic aptitude came to play an important role in the struggle to define the biological meaning of being black.

# 12

# African-American Responses
# to Racial Biology

O VER THE PAST CENTURY, a constant stream of publications
on "the biology of the Negro" has forced African Americans to
develop their own scientific interpretations of racial biology in
order to contest the racist or otherwise unscientific premises on which
so much of this writing has been based. One important example is *The
Health and Physique of the Negro American,* by the prolific scholar
W.E.B. Du Bois. The purpose of his treatise was nothing less than to
establish the biological normality of black human beings. It is poignant
to see Du Bois arguing that "in all physical characteristics the Negro
race cannot be set off by itself as absolutely different," that "what has
been described as being peculiar in the size, shape, and anatomy of the
Negro brain is not true of all Negro brains," that the Negro is "by far the
most prolific" American group rather than a race in decline, that "there
is much uncertainty as to the purely racial differences in human liability
to disease," that "the Negro death rate and sickness are largely matters
of condition and not due to racial traits and tendencies."[1]

The author took this last phrase from Frederick L. Hoffman's *Race
Traits and Tendencies of the American Negro,* described by George M.
Frederickson as "the most influential discussion of the race question to
appear in the late nineteenth century."[2] Hoffman's statistics-laden treatise became well known for its prediction that the Negro's biological
decline "must in the end cause the extinction of the race." "It is sufficient to know," Hoffman wrote, "that in the struggle for race supremacy the black race is not holding its own; and this fact once recognized,
all danger from a possible numerical supremacy of the race vanishes. Its
extreme liability to consumption alone would suffice to seal its fate as
a race."[3]

The theory of black degeneration and decline propounded by Hoffman and others provides a historical perspective that may help to account for the stark contrast between the portrait of black physical inferiority and the images of black physical vitality with which we have become so familiar. The degeneration theory was rooted implicitly or explicitly in the belief that the emancipation of the slaves, or at least the manner in which they had been freed, was a social disaster that southern race discipline could have prevented had it prevailed. Demonstrating the validity of this claim required an invidious comparison between the diseased and profligate emancipated Negro and the healthier and better-disciplined slave he once had been.

Hoffman presented abundant evidence that this physical deterioration had actually occurred. While whites had gained in vitality, he reported, "we have abundant proof of the physical deterioration of the colored race. Before emancipation he presented in many respects a most excellent physical type even superior to the average white man examined for military service under similar conditions." One Kentucky physician described black men he had encountered in the 1860s in the following terms: "For symmetry, muscular strength and endurance, I do not think the Kentucky negro can be surpassed by any people on earth. The stoutest and most muscular men I ever examined were the negroes of this office." Dr. John Streeter of Boston reported that the colored men he had seen "compare favorably in intelligence and aptitude for military service with white recruits. In muscular development and freedom from physical disqualifications they are superior to the average white men I have examined." These and other testimonials presented "an almost perfect agreement of widely separated authorities and investigators, that the negro of thirty years ago was physically the equal if not the superior of the white."[4] Contrasted with the sheer vitality of this idealized black "buck" of yesteryear was the "lower vital power of the negro of the present time." Hoffman took pains to counter "the prevailing notion that the average negro possesses superior physical strength," and he took pleasure in refuting the "opinion that the negro is on the whole more capable of enduring physical exercise." Lower vital capacity was in itself "proof of an inferior physical organism."[5]

Variations on the theme of the decrepit Negro persisted well past the turn of the century. The Richmond, Virginia, physician who called the Negro of 1910 a "strange and pitiable creature" explained why his counterpart of a half-century earlier had been a better physical specimen: "The negro of 1859 was not a free agent, and valuable only as a form of energy. He was a business proposition and, to get an interest on his investment, it was the business of his owner that this machine should be able to run at a proper potentiality. To this end the negro was not allowed to abuse his body, but, on the contrary, was made to preserve it." Sexual profligacy had also played a role in the process of degeneration, when, after Emancipation, "the birth-rate became a plaything of sexual impulse" rather than the reproductive discipline of the plantation. The children who had resulted from "this carnival" were "degenerates as compared to their forbears."[6] According to another breeding theory, which appeared in 1923, the decline of the black race was directly related to the declining quality of the white genes that were being infused into it. Whereas "the best blood" had impregnated black women around the time of the Civil War, in recent years these superior types had been replaced by mere boys and "old, broken-down, worn-out men" who were unfit to beget children.[7]

Another view held that social misery and degraded habits had spoiled a once robust physical organism. "Nature," an Arkansas physician wrote, also in 1923, "endows the negro with strong passions, strong muscles, and a vigorous constitution. Poor housing conditions, irregularity in eating and sleeping, venereal diseases, sexual excesses, and other abuses have deprived him of a greater part of this heritage."[8] A second environmental theory also took up the theme of natural endowment and saw the ruination of a physiologically noble savage by civilization itself: "Three hundred years of life in the environment for which he was not primarily bred," a New Orleans physician wrote in 1932, "have destroyed in him the strength of the primitive race, have implanted in him all the weaknesses of a civilization that is far from effete, but that certainly has its enervating moods. The pure strain of the native negro has been largely lost."[9]

It is important for us to understand how these white observers felt about the process of black degeneration they described. First of all, it is clear that the specter of black decline aroused little alarm or humanitarian concern. What we find is a profoundly segregationist view of the two "most extreme" racial types and the hierarchical relationship in which they belonged. Hoffman's observation that the Negro was losing "the struggle for race supremacy" and would never pose a demographic threat to the white population sounds very much like a wish in the process of being fulfilled, and other white commentators did not exercise as much self-restraint as they contemplated the Negro's demise. Dr. Charles S. Bacon of Detroit expressed the view in 1903 that white society should "help along the process of extinction," while Dr. Louis S. Pedrigo of Roanoke, Virginia, maintained that "the only hope for the southern end of the United States, is just these forces that are tending to exterminate the negro."[10] (Widespread suspicions among African Americans today that there is a white conspiracy to exterminate them should be evaluated against the historical background of this earlier medical racism and its large white constituency.)[11]

The inhumanity of this sort of reasoning was rationalized in accordance with the social Darwinism of the era and its ethos of a competitive racial fight to the finish. If blacks were, in Hoffman's phrase, "unsuited for the battle of life," if anatomical differences reduced "the social and economic efficiency of the colored man," then there was little to be done but let nature take its course.[12] The physicians of the late nineteenth century thus saw racial competition not as a spur to the evolution of a stronger Negro type but as a process whereby blacks surrendered to "the laws of nature and slowly succumb[ed] to the rigors of competition."[13]

The more interesting white response to black biology is represented most eloquently by the physician who judged the muscular development of Kentucky black men to be superior to that of "any people on earth." We have already seen that colonial encounters around the globe produced many similar assessments of black male physicality and that these appreciations of well-endowed black bodies were emotionally complex responses, stimulating the wishes, fears, and competitive feelings of admiring whites. The muscular black male for whom certain white men felt a kind of nostalgia long after Emancipation can thus be seen as a kind of domesticated noble savage, and it is likely that our own culture's taste for *Mandingo*-style images of the black man is to some degree a legacy of this; an idealized black muscularity that was once safely confined by whips and chains is now financially controlled by the white businessmen who own and operate the professional sports leagues. The classic view of the black man's dual nature was that "he was docile and amiable when enslaved, ferocious and murderous when free."[14] The statuesque black military recruit, like the modern black athlete, who is promoted to white children as a racially neutered cartoon figure, represented muscularity without ferocity.[15] It was his presumed docility that made him unfit to advance the interests of his people against theories of black inferiority. This daunting task fell to a small number of educated black men, who could dispute the claims of the scientific racists in their own language.

The most important African-American response to Hoffman's theory of gradual black extinction was a review of *Race Traits and Tendencies* by the sociologist Kelly Miller, a critique that was "the first paper to be published by the newly founded American Negro Academy, established in 1897 in Washington, D.C., as a forum for intellectual discussion, and more specifically to refute or challenge the assertions of white scientists."[16] Miller referred dismissively to Hoffman's concept of "race traits and tendencies" as "a blind force recently discovered and named by him" and found it "passing strange" that he had not noticed that black population growth had exceeded the white increase over the preceding decade. Miller also pointed out that white notions about the eventual fate of the black population had nothing to do with scientific deliberation. Public opinion had responded in a "rhythmical" fashion to a series of mass emotional factors: "In 1870 it was extermination; in 1880 it was dreaded that the whole country would be Africanized because of the prolificness of a barbarous race; in 1890 the doctrine of extinction was preached once more; what will be the outcry in 1900 can only be divined at this stage, but we may rest assured that it will be something startling."[17] Confronting the irrational urges that drove white opinion from one extreme to another, the beleaguered black scholar could only do his best "to use science to point out the errors, the questionable data, and the specious logic of the discourses on human difference and inequality." Gunnar Myrdal believed that these efforts helped to sustain the morale of the black community.[18]

An important consequence of refuting the idea of Negro disease was to embrace with equal fervor the idea of black physical vitality. Miller had no choice but to defend the integrity of the black organism by emphasizing its vigor. "Does it not require much fuller demonstration than [Hoffman] anywhere presents," he asked incredulously in his review, "to convince the ordinary mind that a people that has shown such physical vitality for so long a period, has all at once, in a single decade, become comparatively infecund and threatened with extinction?" Elsewhere, Miller intensified his rhetoric by implying that those of African descent constituted a kind of physiological elite. "If history teaches any clear lesson," he wrote, "it is that civilization is communicable to the tougher and hardier breeds of men, whose physical stamina can endure the awful stress of transmission."[19] Miller challenged "the traditional and prevalent belief" regarding the Negro's low vital capacity and even played the surgical toughness card, reporting that the surgeon-in-chief of the Freedmen's Hospital in Washington, D.C., after three thousand operations on whites and blacks, had found "unmistakable evidence of higher vital power among the colored patients."[20]

This use of surgery as an index of racial vitality was, to say the least, a problematic ploy on the part of an author bent on rescuing racial science from the vagaries of hearsay evidence. At the same time, however, Miller's claim that nature had given the black man a tougher organism illustrates the predicament of the black intellectual of his era, whose task was to rehabilitate the image of his people. Both the racist attack on the biological integrity of the black organism and the paucity of black cultural achievement that could impress whites virtually demanded an emphasis on physical health and strength, and that emphasis eventually escalated into various forms of physiological and athletic chauvinism as the sport-obsessed twentieth century progressed.

It is also important to recognize that the black scholars who challenged white racial doctrines were demonstrating their own conflicted feelings about racial difference. On the one hand, their task was to affirm the monogenist view of a single human family, yet at the same time they felt obliged to demonstrate the existence of a supernormal black vigor that would give to African Americans that vague but indispensable glow of all-round health the racists had denied them. Even Du Bois, who showed little interest in biological arguments, boasted in 1913 that African Americans were "the only race which has held at bay the life destroying forces of the tropics."[21] When he wanted to document the physical robustness of one subject in his 1906 treatise, he noted that the man was a baseball player.[22]

The crucial point is that all of these arguments tended to identify the black man with the state of his body. When Kelly Miller endowed black men with "a higher vital power," he was increasing the African-American stake in racial biology and helping to prepare the way for the fixation on athletic achievement, which began to take hold during the 1920s.

This unstable combination of African-American contestation of racial biology and the increasing attachment to athleticism culminated in the career of William Montague Cobb, M.D., Ph.D., the only African American to hold a doctorate in physical anthropology prior to 1950.[23] Cobb, born in 1904, began his career as a public spokesman on racial biology by demonstrating that the world-record-holding sprinter and long jumper Jesse Owens possessed none of the anatomical traits to which white commentators attributed the success of black athletes. More generally, Cobb argued, there was no evidence "to indicate that Negroid physical characters are anatomically concerned with the present dominance of Negro athletes in national competition in the short dashes and the broad jump. There is not a single physical characteristic which all the Negro stars have in common which would definitely identify them as Negroes. Jesse Owens, who has run faster and leaped farther than a human being has done before, does not have what is considered the Negroid type of calf, foot, and heel bone."[24] Six years later Cobb reiterated that "in all those characters presumptively associated with race or physical ability, Owens was Caucasoid rather than Negroid in type. Thus his heel bone was relatively short, instead of long; his calf muscles had very long instead of short bellies; and his arches were high and strong instead of being low and weak."[25]

Refuting the idea that Owens was an anomalous creature was only one part of a more comprehensive effort to demonstrate the normality of the African American. "The popular stereotype of the Negro as a biological inferior," Cobb declared, "has neither scientific origin nor usefulness." Like Miller and Du Bois before him, he made his contribution to putting the extinction theory to rest, reporting in 1939 that "by all acceptable criteria of fertility the Negro is now reproducing more rapidly than his white competitor."[26] He gently ridiculed a New York doctor's assertion that blacks could be identified by means of an examination of their nasal cartilage.[27] He dismissed the voluminous "pseudo-scientific comment [that] has been devoted to allegation of marked generalized thickness in the Negro skin." He refuted the notion that blacks enjoyed a special "inward serenity" and consequently low blood pressure. He called into question an unpublished claim that blacks had thicker webbing on the backs of their hands, reminding his readers that "the Negro has given objective evidence of development of the most difficult digital skills," presumably referring to the African sculptures that inspired Picasso and Negro mastery of the blues guitar. To the claim that blacks had smaller vital viscera (heart, lungs, kidneys, liver, spleen), Cobb replied that "the Negro's established abilities in hard labor and in athletics make it appear that if he really does have relatively smaller viscera, this is an asset."[28]

The suggestion that black anatomy might offer a physiological advantage to the athlete points to Cobb's ambivalent attitude toward the significance of racial athletic aptitude. On the one hand, he cited a lack of evidence for "superiority in Negro anatomy or physiology" and referred to his own work on Jesse Owens's bodily dimensions to deny any relationship between ability and race. "The margins separating the performances of White and Negro stars," he asserted, "have been insignificant from an anthropological standpoint." But Cobb was also a passionate subscriber to the survivalist view of African-American history, in which paeans to Negro hardiness contain at least a hint of racial triumphalism. The Negro, he writes, "is *physically strong,* showing great endurance at strenuous labor under severe climatic and nutritional hardships, and producing a disproportionately large number of champions in representative fields of athletics." Cobb believed all his life that the ordeal of slavery had been a brutal but ultimately eugenic process of selection and that this was confirmed by black athletic achievement. "No other group of Americans in such large numbers," he wrote in 1939, "has had to pass such rigorous tests of survival fitness as has the Negro. From this standpoint he is the most highly selected stock in America."[29]

Twenty-five years later, in his inaugural address to the National Medical Association, Cobb repeated his claim that African Americans were "the most highly selected stock" in the United States and added that blacks had benefited from the infusion of "white genes . . . from the privileged upper levels" of American society. "How else," he asked, "can one explain the fact that in the few short years since competition in professional sports has been open, Negroes have risen to dominant positions in every field?"[30] In a lecture he delivered in 1974 at Georgetown University Medical School, Cobb reiterated that "every African who landed on these shores had undergone a more rigid biological selection than any group in the history of mankind."[31]

Cobb's fixation on black toughness can only have made him curious about the "mysterious" sources of this special "hardihood." He was clearly intrigued by scientific work on "speed in energy change, which is, with training, the essence of athletic superiority. Researches of this nature should be very enlightening if conducted upon Negro athletes and non-athletes, and might possibly be decisive in determining the relationship of race to athletic ability."[32] This comment alone makes it clear that he had not resolved the issue of racial athletic aptitude in his own mind.

Nor were these the idle speculations of a nonathlete. In fact, Cobb's attachment to the world of sport lasted his entire adult lifetime. As one of a handful of athletically and academically gifted black students at Amherst College, he had won collegiate championships in boxing and cross-country running.[33] In the twilight of his life, Cobb invoked the world of athletics for a banquet audience at the Howard University College of Medicine, alluding to the failure of his aging cohort to have produced more people like themselves. "My generation," Cobb said, "has been like the offensive linemen on a football team whose job it is to make holes for fastbacks to run through. The linemen get battered, but they don't mind, if the fastbacks are there. When they aren't, the holes close up. Unfortunately, we do not have enough fastbacks today. You must recruit them, starting at the cradle."[34]

# 13

# Black "Hardiness" and the Origins of Medical Racism

W E HAVE SEEN that the idea of Negro biological inferiority served to reinforce the subordinate status of African Americans by impugning both their health and, by implication, their ability to hold their own in the fateful competition with their white fellow citizens. This idea of interracial competition was inherently perverse, in that it was grounded in a specious notion of equal opportunity and fair play. Indeed, the popularity of the extinction theory throughout the 1800s suggests that many whites eagerly awaited, consciously or unconsciously, the unequal contest that would relieve them of the race problem once and for all. George M. Fredrickson has rightly noted "the callousness implicit in the notion that a race degraded by slavery and suspected to be biologically inferior should simply be given its formal rights and then forced to compete in a capitalistic free-labor society." Even sympathetic white observers could entertain few doubts about the outcome of this struggle. "If [the black man] is, as is claimed, an inferior being and unable to compete with the white man on terms of equality," the Radical Republican Ignatius Donnelly proclaimed in 1866, "surely you will not add to the injustice of nature by casting him beneath the feet of the white man."[1]

But there were also doubts about the degree to which nature had been unjust in its distribution of racial favors. We have seen that assertions of Negro weakness were sometimes linked with diametrically opposed evidence of a special black vitality, which has now become the dominant paradigm in white thinking about the black body and what it can do. No single term can adequately convey this sense of a specially endowed, superpotentiated organism and its heightened powers, which has now culminated in the figure of the invincible black athlete. On the contrary, this idea has been highly elastic, corresponding to the inventive powers of the minds that have observed or imagined it.

What is more, the construction of black physical vitality as a cultural theme has been a biracial enterprise, enlisting the needs and fantasies of both blacks and whites. While the overwhelming power of white-dominated cultural institutions has tended to marginalize black contributions to this process in the public mind, it is important to recognize that the African-American investment in racial biology that is documented throughout this book is as tenacious as other forms of racial folklore, and that it has continued to meet the needs of people who must deal with antiblack stereotypes in their daily lives. Consider, for example, the following passage, which appeared in an African-American newspaper in 1994: "When massa was ill he had a big, strong buck that would lie on the floor so he could rest the soles of his feet on him to pass the illness from his body into the slave's, and simultaneously draw the buck's great strength into his."[2] Assuming that this story is not simply a recent invention, it would be fascinating to know its origin and follow its transmission from the era of slavery down to the present day. Did such a medical superstition actually exist among whites? Its depiction of an inherently unfair exchange between master and slave certainly suggests it is of African-American origin. Its reference to the black man's "great strength" in the context of an ordeal recalls the many variations on the late nineteenth-century story of John Henry, the most important saga of black physical power prior to the age of sport.

Finally, it is significant that the black superiority depicted here is not specifically athletic. Like so much of the terminology bearing on the theme of racial vitality, the phrase "great strength" is ultimately impossible to define, suggesting anything from bulging biceps to abundant health or fortitude of character. "The history of the Negro race," Frederick Douglass wrote in 1854, "proves them to be wonderfully adapted to all countries, all climates, and all conditions. Their tenacity of life, their powers of endurance, their malleable toughness, would almost imply especial interposition on their behalf."[3] With this paean to black fortitude Douglass established a tradition. "Blacks," an army chaplain told *Jet* magazine in 1977, "have an inborn ability to adjust much better than whites have."[4] This narrative of survival became one of the archetypal African-American stories and has been invoked unceasingly. "Blacks," Gerald Early wrote with exasperation, "love to wallow in the sentimentality of their myth of endurance."[5] No one, however, would question the fundamental importance of a myth that was also translated into explicitly biological terms. "The Negro," *Opportunity* told its readers in 1924, "possesses 'biologic fitness.'"[6] This is a story black people have been telling themselves since the time of slavery, and such tales of endurance survive because they play a role in the emotional life of the community that preserves them.

White imaginations have had other reasons to idealize the powers of the black organism. We have already seen that an appreciation of the muscular black bodies of the 1860s could serve to highlight the alleged decrepitude of the black bodies of the 1890s and thus impugn the state of Negro health during a virulently racist period of American history. The image of black hardiness could also promote in retrospect the benevolence of the slaveowners of the Old South. "There is a common belief," Felice Swados wrote in 1941, "that slaves on antebellum plantations enjoyed bounding good health. It would seem, offhand, only reasonable that a planter keep his field hands at the height of their vigor, for they were his machines, and represented an investment of thousands of dollars." But accurate assessments of the frequency of disease among the slaves would have undermined this humane image of plantation life. "The popular conception of the slaves as a sleek, robust, hearty group, enjoying a high degree of welfare on the old plantations, is false."[7] "The slave of tradition," Kenneth Stampp wrote in 1956, "was a physically robust specimen who suffered from few of the ailments which beset the white man. A tradition with less substance to it has seldom existed."[8]

The "biological fitness" argument also legitimated slave labor by endowing blacks with a special capacity for exertion in a hot and humid climate. "Negroes," said a southern treatise published in 1829, "are not only healthy people, but robust and durable even in the swamps."[9] This theme had a long career on southern plantations and in South African gold mines and eventually established itself as medical folklore. "Colored children," a contributor to the *Journal of the American Medical Association* reported in 1899, "are much more sensitive to heat than white children, which probably means that their power of discrimination is better, and not that they suffer more from heat." Shortly thereafter the journal reported on French research confirming that "the grease in the skin of the negro reflects the rays" of the sun.[10]

Employing the same archetype of supernormal vitality, white commentators could rationalize hard black labor on other physiological grounds; thus the *Journal of the American Medical Association* announced in 1915 that "the natural cardiac strength of the negro" enabled him "to continue work at very hard labor."[11] The image of robust slave health also appeared to resolve the still controversial question of how adequately the slaves had been fed; what whites told themselves about black nutrition, as Gunnar Myrdal pointed out in 1944, remained an issue long after Emancipation: "The belief that they have so much of the foods they desire seems to have the opportunistic purpose of hiding the fact that Negroes are too poor to buy all the foods they actually need."[12]

Another argument held that forced labor itself had physically improved the slaves. Plantation life, a South Carolina novelist wrote in 1837, had increased the black man's "health and strength" and improved "his physical symmetry and organization."[13] A century later the same reasoning was endorsed by an African-American sportswriter, thereby turning black survivalist doctrine into an endorsement of slavery. "The 250 years that slaves of the South worked in the cotton fields and on the plantation accounts for the splendid physique of the race today," wrote A. A. Duckett in the New York Age, as though the athletic development of the race were all that mattered.[14] All of these claims about physical potency were used to rationalize black suffering and exploitation in the past. At the same time, constant focus on them preserved the deep cultural premise that the black man's body was his essential self. As one American physician put it in 1910, "everything tended to make the negro of that time a physical man."[15]

Our receptiveness to the idea of black athletic aptitude originates in a racial folklore that has always accentuated the physicality and the "hardy" or "robust" qualities of the black organism. "Most colored people live strenuously," a University of Chicago pathologist wrote in 1942, expressing an inchoate feeling about black durability that has buffered white sensibilities for centuries.[16] Western thinking about blacks has traditionally imagined them in terms of their bodies and corporeal performances rather than their mental and cultural complexity. It is therefore not surprising that an innovative study of National Geographic magazine, a powerful cultural institution that has infused colonialist attitudes into the racial thinking of generations of Americans, found that dark-skinned peoples have been "most likely to be depicted in high levels of activity — engaged in strenuous work or athletics," while whites "were most likely to be engaged in low-level activity — seated or reclining, perhaps manipulating something with their hands, but rarely exerting themselves." Dark-skinned males "were far more likely than those coded white to appear bare-chested in the pages of the magazine — often in poses that drew attention to musculature and strength." As the authors of this study point out, these color-coded images of physical energy and contemplative repose grow out of our ideas about the relationship between race and labor: "While people of color were inherently suited to labor, they never wanted to work hard enough in the fields of their white masters. *The image of a tremendous capacity for work,* coupled with an unwillingness to actually work, gave rise to contradictory stereotypes. The heritage of these stereotypes and the labor relations that gave rise to them can be traced in the strenuously employed black bodies portrayed in the pages of *National Geographic* [emphasis added]."[17] Here too is the racial folklore of interracial sport throughout the former British Empire, including the United States. Indeed, one of the ideological functions of *National Geographic* has been to situate the physically endowed black body beyond our shores and thereby divert attention from the domestic colonialism that has always characterized race relations in the worlds of American labor and sport.

The idea of black hardiness and vitality is a system of interrelated subthemes that are finally all related to the theme of the primitive human type who is biologically different from civilized man. "They have different kinds of instincts," as one author paraphrases the antebellum conception of the black slave. "They can better stand the hot sun. They mate promiscuously like the animals. Their women breed like animals and give birth to offspring without pain. Indeed, they are all highly insensitive to pain. It is impossible to read the expressions on their faces. They seem to die on short notice or without any notice at all."[18] Hardiness is the natural endowment of an instinct-driven and impassive creature who is less a man than an automaton.

This image has endured in a variety of medical, anthropological, and popular versions (including the athlete) far longer than is generally understood. In 1925 a contributor to the *Journal of the American Medical Association* declared that the Negro was "stranded in a primitive stage" and approached "the anthropoid apes in the essential physical characteristics in which he differs anatomically from the rest of mankind."[19] The presumed antithesis between savage and civilized life provided a useful framework for the construction of a dichotomous racial biology. "It has been asserted more than once," a contributor to the prestigious journal *Science* wrote in 1929, "that cardiovascular diseases are correlated with civilized life, a reaction to the nervous strain." Low blood pressure and the rarity of hypertrophy of the heart among African Negroes thus appeared to be biological evidence of their cultural retardation.[20] In 1955 a contributor to the *Journal of the National Medical Association* tried to put to rest the culturally archaic (and thus very powerful) idea that "due to the rigors of natural selection," earlier versions of "savage" humanity had been "biologically more fit" than the "civilized" types of more recent history. "In short," he wrote, "the assumption that all people in earlier times were healthy, vigorous, and fit, simply has no foundation in fact."[21]

Our belief in "the strength of the primitive race" has survived to this day because it has become associated with each of the interrelated subthemes that together constitute the doctrine of primitive hardiness.[22] Some investigators with scientific credentials have argued, for example, that black skin, "the 'resistant ectoderm' of the Negro," signifies a primitive toughness.[23] In 1925 the proctologist from Dallas previously mentioned approvingly cited a French study published in 1887 that had ascribed to the Negro a "lessened sensibility of the general nervous system to pain and shock, which he believed to be associated with a histologic difference in the development and shape of the tactile pupil-lae of the skin. This fact is in harmony with the inferior organism of the race; it is not peculiar to the negro, but common to all 'stoic' savage races." The alleged rarity of hemorrhoids in the Negro made it appear to be "an immunity common to primitive races" and the lower mam-mals.[24] An article that appeared in 1937 in the *American Journal of Physical Anthropology,* the flagship journal of the field, announced that a demonstration of the racial uniqueness of Negro skin would "prove that the negro race is phylogenetically a closer approach to primitive man than the white race."[25]

Skin was, in addition, a richly symbolic corporeal medium that stimu-lated curiosity even as it established racial difference. Years after one former slave had been subjected to experimental tests of his heat endur-ance, he told of how his relentless tormentor had blistered him "to ascertain how deep my black skin went."[26] The hideous deformities of elephantiasis, often involving the breasts or external genitalia, afflicted far more blacks than whites and became a powerful sign of the deviant black body.[27] Less serious skin diseases, Charles B. Davenport reported in 1919, affected black soldiers less than white ones. This relative immu-nity to abscesses, boils, dermatitis, venomous bites, and stings consti-tuted one aspect of biological toughness, which prompted Davenport to call the black troops he studied "constitutionally better physiological machines than the white men."[28] The alleged thickness of black skin was credited with an increased resistance to both infection and diseases such as scarlet fever, erysipelas, and measles.[29] As late as 1985 the "mystery" of black resistance to yellow fever was being explained in the same way, in that "the thicker, darker skin of the Negro may decrease the number, or penetration, of mosquito bites."[30] But this epidermal hardiness, like the slave's ability to endure heat, was also a potential hazard to the black worker. "It is well known in industry," Julian Herman Lewis wrote in *The Biology of the Negro,* "that the Negro is less sensitive to the action of skin irritants than the white man,"[31] and we can only wonder how many accidental burns resulted from this sort of confidence in the Negro epidermis.

The alleged toughness of black skin and its special healing properties could also play a role in the politics of racial pride. Whereas a curiously judgmental medical outlook took for granted "the inherent tendency of the dark skinned races to form fibrous tissue in excess,"[32] a commentator in the African-American medical journal reacted to this kind of thinking by advocating a physiological universalism regarding the scar tissue most often associated with blacks. "Keloid formation," he wrote, is not a stigma inflicted on the black man alone but "a healing, protective and reparative process designed by nature for all mankind."[33] Black skin can also inspire a form of racial chauvinism. "I'll never have plastic surgery," an African-American woman wrote in the *New York Times Magazine* in 1995, "because I know that I won't have to. My dark-mahogany skin is one of the most wonderful parts of my legacy."[34]

This cacophony of interpretations confirms that black skin has always possessed the inherent elasticity of any other medical or cultural construct. It may be ugly or beautiful, a medical asset or liability, but it is never anything but tough. The "special hazards" of black skin, one physician wrote in 1957, lie precisely in its blank inexpressiveness, which "camouflages cyanosis during anesthesia, surgery and childbirth and infant resuscitation; that masks anemia during physical examination; that obscures the veins and makes more difficult venipuncture, so necessary for instantaneous transfusions during major surgery, shock and following traumatic or obstetrical hemorrhage."[35] As an unintentional aesthetic assessment of the black organism, this reading of black skin is comparable to the traditional axiom of racist anatomy that faults the Negro face for its lack of the fine musculature that facilitates delicacy of expression. Even as a medical liability, then, black skin does not demonstrate softness or weakness, because it cannot possess the sensitivity that is reserved for whites alone.

The toughness of black skin is directly related to one of the fundamental themes of Western racial biology — the idea that blacks do not feel pain as easily as whites do. Like the doctrine of black immunity to heat, this pseudo-neurological dogma ascribed a special resiliency to blacks so as to rationalize their exploitation and brutalization. Their primitive biological status meant that black people were able to endure "with few expressions of pain, the accidents of nature, which agonize white people."[36] At least one antebellum physician concluded that blacks possessed less sensitive nervous systems on the grounds that they endured whippings without feeling pain.[37] In 1860 a southern lady novelist "not only argued that Negroes could not be overworked but claimed that it was physically impossible for a master to knock a slave 'senseless to the ground' — as he was so often knocked in abolitionist writings — because the Negro skull was so thick that such an effort would bruise or break a white man's fist."[38]

This conception of the pain-resistant Negro organism unquestionably facilitated medical experimentation on blacks as well. It has been claimed that the first complete anesthesia was carried out on a black boy in 1839.[39] The famous treatment for vesicovaginal fistula devised by Dr. J. Marion Sims in Alabama during the 1840s and 1850s was made possible only by the heroic endurance of the black women who submitted, unanesthetized, to his experimental surgeries, since he "discovered that Caucasian patients often failed to persevere as well as Negroes during the painful and uncomfortable procedure."[40] These terrible ordeals, during which black women suffered painful vaginal surgery at the hands of a white surgeon and at times before an audience of white doctors, must have been both physically and emotionally traumatic.

The question of why black women could apparently endure pain that white women could not leads us to the deeply problematic status of "racial" capacities as biological traits. It is now understood that the sensation of pain is a highly subjective experience that varies by culture as well as by individual temperament and situation, since different cultural communities create differing expectations about what constitutes pain and how it is to be resisted or endured. The African-American experience offers unusually interesting opportunities to study the cultural status of pain, both because this group has long been classified as a relatively anesthetic "race" and because it has suffered so many painful ordeals. We can assume that the emotional state of the black women who submitted to Marion Sims's procedures had already been shaped by the humiliations of chattel slavery, possibly including sexual assaults by white men in positions of authority. These were, in addition, miserable people, some of whom had been ostracized by their own families because of the odor that resulted from their fistulas. Who can say to what degree these women endured Sims's interventions out of sheer desperation, how many saw him as an unfeeling tormentor, or whether they shared W. Montague Cobb's view that "Sims' unswerving persistence must be regarded as one of the great humanitarian as well as scientific landmarks of American surgery"? To what degree had they internalized the stereotype of their own immunity to pain? When Ephraim McDowell performed eleven ovariotomies during the early years of the nineteenth century, the editor of the *London Medical and Chirurical Review* commented derisively, "When we come to reflect that all the women operated on in Kentucky, except one, were Negresses, and that these people will bear cutting with nearly, if not quite, as much impunity as dogs and rabbits, our wonder is lessened."[41] Given the stresses of their lives and the universal belief among whites that blacks enjoyed a degree of immunity to pain, it is hard to imagine that African-American slaves did not construct some kind of emotional armor to deal with the traumatic pain experiences of their time and place.

The racist mythology of pain remained a part of the Western imagination long after the end of slavery. Antebellum ideas about diminished pain sensitivity and the surgical hardiness of the Negro remained essentially intact, along with a corresponding portrait of his emotional vacuity. "The average negro," a contributor to the *Southern Medical Journal* said in 1932, "because of his duller perceptions, is an excellent subject for any sort of anesthesia, and perhaps his traditional confidence in the white man gives him a feeling of security which the more highly organized white patient sometimes lacks. I am repeatedly struck with the attitude of the negro prior to operation, an attitude which may perhaps be stoicism, but which more strongly impresses one as a total lack of interest in what is going to happen."[42] "Surgeons who have had considerable clinical experience with Negroes," the University of Chicago pathologist wrote ten years later, "commend them as excellent surgical risks. They are stoic in their reaction to pain and discomfiture, do not easily go into shock, take anesthesia well, resist infection, and show remarkable powers of recovery."[43] The idea of a higher pain threshold also appears in the medical literature about cardiac disease in blacks. "I am interested in explaining the absence of pain during coronary occlusion in the Negro," a physician wrote in 1946. "The rarity of angina in the Negro is well known and is commonly ascribed to lack of stress or to inability of the Negro to feel or express pain."[44] In 1934 another author had wondered whether the Negro seldom had angina because of "his less highly organized nervous system."[45]

An emotionally charged exchange over glaucoma and pain among an interracial panel of nine physicians occurred in 1952 in the journal of the African-American medical association. To a white ophthalmologist's claim that glaucoma causes black patients little or no pain, an African-American physician replied, "I do not believe that pain is a symptom that can be used to distinguish between the races." This blunt response expressed the generic African-American anger that can erupt when whites propose a biological segregation of the races on ostensibly scientific grounds. "The eye of the Negro is physiologically no different from the eyes of other people," Dr. Roosevelt Brooks flatly stated, and others have reacted in similar fashion to theories of black athletic superiority based on anatomical or physiological differences.[46]

Reproductive power is another symbolic form of black vitality that is related to pain immunity and other allegedly racial traits that make up black hardiness. It is an elastic idea that has both macro and micro forms, encompassing reproductive dynamism or the fabled sexual athleticism of the black male, which is tied to the image of Negro fecundity.[47] ("His sexual powers are those of a specialist in a chosen field," as one American physician put it a century ago.[48]) Black fertility also means venereal hardiness. "To the negro, gonorrhea is no more than a cold," a white doctor wrote in 1926;[49] nor does he fear syphilis.[50] The African explorer David Livingstone was convinced that black fecundity conferred a near immunity to syphilis.[51] Fertility is symbolically associated with the primitive stage of biological development. "The simpler the organism," a Georgia physician wrote in 1887, "the simpler the genesis and the greater the prolificness."[52]

Whites have also associated the "natural fecundity" of the African with painless childbirth. "It is generally believed," says *The Biology of the Negro*, "that women living under primitive conditions, as do most native Africans, go through pregnancy and delivery with comparative ease and little inconvenience. Most of the writings that express this opinion are of an old date, however, and are chiefly by nonmedical people, mainly anthropologists. Marchand, more recently, marveled at the natives' vitality and power of recovery after delivery" and "recounted pathological conditions ending in recovery under which European women would have died."[53] The dramatic comparison of durable African and vulnerable European became a standard refrain of colonial medicine and is also found in the medical literature about American blacks and whites. "The colored woman," the *Southern Medical Journal* reported in 1932, "because of her lessened sensibility to pain, is willing to endure a prolonged natural labor when a white woman would hours before be demanding relief."[54] This is why "the European requires assistance at delivery more often than the Bantu," as a report phrased it in 1947.[55] Ease of birth was linked in turn to a low rate of birth injuries among blacks.[56]

The genital hardiness of the black female is also manifested in her response to pelvic disease, including cases where "the upper genital tract is the site sometimes of incredible pathological conditions ... One marvels how these women have lived, let alone how they have remained, as very many of them do remain, in comparatively good condition."[57] In 1951 the *Journal of the American Medical Association* speculated that the rarity of pelvic endometriosis in black women might be due to "a constitutional racial factor."[58] In 1966 it was reported that "genital prolapse is much more frequent among Caucasian women than among Negro women," a circumstance the racially sensitive author tied to the fact that "the southern Negro woman has generally performed heavy physical work from earliest existence." In contradistinction to the symbolic (and thus potentially demagogic) use of racial biology, here genital hardiness and the athleticism of hard labor turn out to be related aspects of a way of life quite independent of bioracial factors. "From a lifetime of study and thought concerning racial contrast," he concludes, "I have become convinced that almost all of the so-called 'racial differences' are apparent and not real."[59]

Abundant reproductive powers and the universal belief that sexual activity among blacks began early in life pointed to various forms of black precocity, both behavioral and biological, that were regarded paradoxically as signs of arrested development.[60] (The presumed conflict between intelligence and fertility, the civilized and the savage, the refined and the primal, is yet another aspect of racial hardiness.[61]) In the late nineteenth century, physicians "often emphasized the extreme precocity and early mental arrest of Negro youths. Growing to maturity much faster than white children, Negroes exhibited sexual passion at an earlier age and then, because of mental atrophy, remained through life seemingly enslaved to the sexual impulse."[62] The idea of precocity, like the act of childbirth, had long offered opportunities for racial comparison and competition. Young Negro children, the prominent British ethnologist James Hunt wrote in 1864, "exhibit, when young, an animal liveliness for play and tricks far surpassing the European child."[63]

The idea of a black physical precocity that might portend supernormal athletic feats has lived on in medical and scientific journals as a set of credible observations with uncertain implications regarding adult physical performance.[64] The differing rates of motor development among black and white infants, meaning the ability to walk, hold the head erect, and stand alone, have become part of the larger nature-nurture controversy about racial differences. "Gross motor acceleration," an American pediatrician and a child psychologist noted in 1953, "has often been one of the stereotypes attributed to the Negro child and the implication has been made in the [medical] literature as well as in the folklore that motor functioning among Negroes is advanced while the rest of mental development lags behind."[65] While these authors found that motor acceleration is related to child-rearing practices and is a socioeconomic rather than a racial characteristic, the publication of a more influential series of studies lay only a few years in the future.

The studies of precocity in Ugandan infants by the French physician Marcelle Geber and her colleagues belong among the romantic narratives that fall under the category of "Wonders Out of Africa." "From birth," Geber wrote in 1957, "the muscular tone of the African infant is different from that of the European, and the head is held better. The lesser degree of flexion may explain why there is in the African earlier standing, prehension [seizing] and manipulation." What is more, and reversing the traditional stereotype, physical precocity appeared to be positively linked to mental precocity. "The most remarkable finding was the precocity of the younger infants. The motor development was greatly in advance of that of European infants of the same age, but was not an isolated phenomenon; it was paralleled by advanced adaptivity, language, and personal-social behaviour."[66] Such precocity was also a form of African infantile hardiness, in that it was "well recognised that African children whose weight at birth would by ordinary standards cause them to be classed as 'premature', are often sturdy and active and can be reared without the special care that has to be lavished on European children of the same weight."[67] A team of American anthropologists confirmed these results in 1970, reporting that "one infant was running at fifteen and one-half months, and there were no infants nineteen months or older who could not run."[68]

Given the astonishing performances of black African runners in recent years, such a vignette has special symbolic resonance for Western spectators, who grasp at explanations for white inferiority in these tests of endurance. Yet it is just this seductive appearance of cause and effect, and the temptation to interpret such infantile performances as representative of total human potential, that must be resisted on scientific grounds. As one investigator who conceded the superiority of many Ugandan infants pointed out in 1958, "It is important to caution against equating motor activity with intellectual potential. It is even more important to caution against attributing the reported startling differences to genetic and cultural factors rather than to difficulties in the interpretation and evaluation of behavior itself."[69] Such wariness is mandated by the roles played by fear and desire in the interpretation of "racial" behaviors and by the potential consequences of disseminating inconclusive data about racial differences. It is worth noting that the psychologist Frank McGurk, who in 1956 was arguing against racially integrated education on the grounds that blacks were less intelligent than whites, was discussing precocious black motor development in the pages of a racist magazine as late as 1978.[70]

Heat tolerance is another allegedly racial trait inherent in black hardiness. "Mere survival in tropical Africa," the Harvard anthropologist Earnest A. Hooton told an African-American audience in 1932, "is a great human achievement"[71] — a dubious compliment coming from a man whose views on black athleticism and criminality tended to harden stereotypes rather than dissolve them. "It appears," a New York physician wrote the same year, "that Negroes tolerate high temperatures better than do whites, but it is not altogether clear whether this is a racial characteristic or whether it depends on environmental factors such as acclimatization or training. Negroes tolerate stoke-room temperatures better than whites."[72]

This was the logic of the slaveholders brought into the modern industrial age, and the same reasoning appeared eight years later as the United States prepared for possible entry into World War II. "National defense plans," the *Science News Letter* told its readers in June 1940, "call for Negro tank troops and Negro submarine crews," because studies conducted by staff scientists at the Harvard Fatigue Laboratory confirmed the Negro's superior ability to endure labor in hot, humid conditions. A treadmill experiment carried out on white and Negro sharecroppers in Mississippi had shown that "the Negroes lost less salt and water from their bodies in sweat than the whites" and had lower heart rates. The lead scientist also found inspiration in the fact that Negroes had enabled the United States to win the track-and-field competition at the 1936 Berlin Olympic Games.[73]

Whatever its scientific value, this experiment in racial physiology was wasted effort so far as war preparedness was concerned. The racism of the U.S. armed services would not have permitted black tank or submarine crews in the first place, since War Department policy was to deny combat roles to black military personnel at almost any cost. Racist practice did not, however, inhibit fantasies about getting the greatest military value out of America's own racial exotics. In 1941 two scientists at Fort Bragg, North Carolina, announced that blacks could see far better at night than whites. "This may lead us to conclusions never before dreamed of," they said. "It may result in changes in our military setup on land, sea, and in the air."[74] Needless to say, such a scheme would have been utterly impractical in a segregated military establishment.

The finding that the black subjects of the treadmill experiment conserved salt better than their white counterparts leads to the most controversial topic pertaining to black hardiness — the "slave-ship hypothesis" of hypertension. This theory proposes that "abnormally" high levels of blood pressure in African Americans are the result of a selective process that operated during the African slave trade. Those who were better able to retain salt in their bodies had a better chance of surviving the dehydration resulting from hunger, thirst, perspiration, seasickness, and diarrhea. This ordeal, which resulted in the "survival of the fittest" slaves, has caused medical problems for their descendants, who are accustomed to modern salt-rich diets that elevate blood pressure beyond safe levels.[75]

This theory is controversial because it appears to force a choice between genetic and environmental explanations of black hypertension. The selection hypothesis assumes that the surviving slave ancestors of modern African Americans passed on a gene or genes that somehow code for the salt retention that promoted survival during the physiological misery of the Middle Passage. The environmental argument holds that black hypertension results from race-related stress, possibly including "a hormonal 'fight or flight' response that boosts heart rate and blood pressure."[76] Its supporters offer three supporting arguments. The first is that the genetic theory encourages the medical racism that can result when African-American health problems are mistakenly assumed to be of biological rather than socioeconomic origin. The second is that the natural selection idea is unrealistic: "To attribute that magnitude of evolutionary change to a fairly brief period is a kind of fantasy," as one dissenting researcher put it.[77] The third and least focused claim is that talk about natural selection among blacks is too reminiscent of traditional theories of black intellectual inferiority.

It is probable that both genetic and environmental factors are active in producing black hypertension. In addition to highly suggestive historical findings and data on differences in West African and African-American blood pressure, it has been shown that high blood pressure in African Americans of low socioeconomic status is correlated with darker skin color, thereby suggesting the presence of a susceptible gene that may act in concert with environmental stress factors.[78] At the same time, we must recognize that any resolution of this scientific mystery is complicated by our desire to find exotic or dramatic physiological events in racial aliens. It is indeed possible that an explanation of black hypertension that compresses evolutionary change into a relatively short timespan fulfills a fantasy need in people who have been culturally conditioned to expect wonders out of Africa. Yet it is also possible that the physiological process that fulfills the fantasy need is both real and scientifically verifiable. While every assertion of racial difference is prompted by a motive, not all motives serve the desire to find racial difference.

The human catastrophe of the Middle Passage is both the focus of African-American mourning and the primal myth of black hardiness. A central thesis of this book is that the Middle Passage has produced a complex aftermath in which the theme of black toughness and resiliency has played a profound and often unappreciated role in the formation of black identity. One part of this legacy is what we can call the medical tragedy of black hardiness, an insensibility or self-neglect that caused uncounted numbers of black men and women to ignore or discount symptoms of illness that should have prompted them to seek medical treatment. This symptom-aversive behavior only deepened the racist attitudes of the physicians who treated blacks, and their descriptions of "the Negro patient" in the medical literature alternately express wry sarcasm, exasperation, and martyred patience.[79] "One thing you cannot do," a physician wrote in 1910, "is to convince the negro that he has any disease that he cannot see or feel."[80] "Those of us who have to do with the care of negro patients," two doctors wrote in 1928, "will readily appreciate the difficulty which one experiences in any attempt to obtain an accurate history, particularly as to the duration of symptoms, of almost any disability. This type of individual is usually one who complains very little and who notices his symptoms very little, unless they are of sufficient degree to cause complete or total disability."[81] "And, worst of all," another added in 1932, "his tendency to disregard slight symptoms, his willingness to endure discomfort and inconvenience until pain forces him to seek relief, frequently mean that his pathology is of a very advanced degree."[82] "Sudden loss of vision is frightening it is true," an ophthalmologist wrote in 1952, "but unless it is accompanied by pain the Negro patient procrastinates."[83]

There can be little doubt that these commentaries describe real behavior that frustrated the medical treatment of black patients, who were often demonstrating a kind of dysfunctional hardiness. But determining the origins of this behavior and assigning responsibility for it are another matter. Were the opthalmologist's glaucoma patients really ignoring their symptoms, or was this the fault of "unskilled practitioners, the charity clinics and optometrists to whom these people are forced to go because of economic privation"? Or, alternatively, was it actually "a clinical fact" that procrastination led to a situation in which blacks did not "respond or react well in comparison to other racial groups"? Or did gloomy assessments of glaucoma operations performed on blacks amount to "a defeatist attitude," introduced into the clinical relationship by cynical or demoralized white surgeons?[84] What, indeed, *is* the nature of a "clinical fact," as distinct from the command-response relationship of doctor and patient?

Today we know that the systematic neglect of black patients has been a part of modern medicine. "Compared to Whites, Blacks are far less likely to be seen by a cardiologist, to have coronary angiography performed, and to undergo coronary artery bypass surgery. These differences persist even among hospitalized patients, controlling for the clinical severity of disease." This is an arresting observation that cries out for clarification. Do white medical personnel simply act out a culturally sanctioned conviction that black life is cheap? Do they approach disease in black people on the unspoken premise that these patients are endowed with a special organismic hardiness? Indeed, do not these attitudes in the last analysis express a single approach to treating "the Negro patient"? And then there is the mental world of these patients themselves: "Blacks may be less likely to perceive chest pain as serious enough to warrant immediate medical attention," suggesting that "the meaning of pain may vary by race."[85] As, in fact, it can vary if "race" is understood to be a way of life. "It matters not how thoroughly one speaks to these [black] individuals of the danger of over-exertion, of exercise, and of straining, in the causation of cardiac failure. As soon as they recover a fair degree of compensation, they consider themselves well, and resume their normal physical activities."[86]

Such has always been the credo of manual laborers, just as today it is the credo of professional athletes. But the ascription of hardiness to blacks has applied to the race as a whole. "Many white physicians with whom I trained," an African-American doctor wrote in 1973,

> preferred black patients because they believed the black patient was less likely to be critical and to express dissatisfaction or to question procedures. Most white physicians interpreted the master-servant relationship as a good doctor-patient relationship. Their patients were "happy." Black patients are almost invariably called by their first names and they are frequently exploited for teaching sessions. One black woman related to me that she had had nine pelvic examinations by physicians and students and had never been told whether her pelvis was normal or abnormal.[87]

We may conclude that organismic hardiness becomes a "racial" trait when white physicians treat black patients like colonial subjects.

Black hardiness has shown itself to be a strikingly — indeed, a suspiciously — diverse collection of supernormal traits. This range of endowments once included a supposed absence of physical deformities, an idea that has since been refuted by modern research.[88] Southern Negroes, the dean of the Scientific School of Harvard University wrote in 1900, are "in excellent physical condition. They are of curiously even, serviceable size, dwarfs and giants being very rare — much rarer than among the whites. The percentage of deformed persons is, so far as the eye can determine it, very low," an impression that was repeated in a medical journal in 1945.[89] But the alleged superiority comes at the price of the purported uniformity of the lower race.

The idea of black geriatric toughness draws on the African-American survivalist tradition as well as an element of the fantastic, hence the modern notion that only black life expectancy increases with advancing age, or a report that appeared in an African-American newspaper in 1904: "Rachel Taylor, the oldest Negro woman in Missouri, and perhaps in the world, died at New London, Mo., last week. Her second sight had come to her. At the time of her death she had cut an entire new set of teeth."[90] It would be interesting to know whether such reports of black geriatric heroism focus primarily on women, given the stereotype of the black woman as a paragon of emotional strength and endurance.[91]

Finally, several forms of hardiness are linked to the theme of food. Gastric hardiness means that blacks have "a stronger digestion" than whites,[92] an idea that can be linked with mental inferiority. The racist Dr. Cartwright refused to believe that dyspepsia occurred in blacks, since it was "a disease that selects its victims from the most intellectual of mankind, passing by the ignorant and unreflecting."[93] Nutritional hardiness is a fantasy of black health that derives from the image of black athleticism. In 1984 Dr. George E. Graham, professor of international health and pediatrics at Johns Hopkins University and a member of President Reagan's Task Force on Food Assistance, stated that black children were probably "the best-nourished group in the United States," and he cited the large numbers of black sports stars as proof of his assertion.[94] This remark continued a long tradition of ignorant or self-excusing white comments about black diet since the time of slavery.

Perhaps the most interesting story of black gastric hardiness is a more credible variant of Cartwright's dyspepsia theory. This is the alleged nonexistence of eating disorders among African Americans. When, for example, a visiting physician gave a talk on anorexia nervosa at the Howard University Hospital in 1984, "the vast majority of the audience considered this an esoteric disease that they would probably never encounter in their practice" serving a black clientele.[95] The rarity of observed eating disorders among blacks is a particularly good example of a biological phenomenon that is in all likelihood a complex social artifact. Relevant social factors include the prevalence of these disorders in upper and middle socioeconomic classes, black avoidance of psychiatric services, greater black acceptance of obesity, and a less compulsive attitude toward dieting. Nor can one rule out the possibility that eating disorders, like many other diseases, have been chronically underreported in the black community.[96]

In summary, the sheer variety of these forms of hardiness demonstrates that an intuitive sense of the toughness of the African organism has soaked into our conception of the black human being, and that the effects of this belief in black hardiness can damage African Americans in a variety of ways.

# 14

# Theories of
# Racial Athletic Aptitude

T HE MYTH of black hardiness and supernormal vitality has been the crucible of our thinking about racial athletic aptitude, which can include toughness to the point of masochism and endurance to the point of impassivity.[1] Here were people who, according to the melodramatic (and sometimes contradictory) doctrines of a pervasive racial folklore, had survived the physiological hazards of the Middle Passage, who stoically endured pain and heat that whites could not, who were physically precocious, whose thick skin formed impenetrable keloids after being cut, who ignored postsurgical trauma and gave birth without stress, whose thick skulls absorbed all but the most vicious blows, whose teeth did not decay, whose appendices did not burst, who almost never died the hemophiliac's death by bleeding, who were sexual and dancing machines.[2] The sometimes jocular tone of these popular beliefs is captured perfectly in an interview with a white physician that was published in 1924 by the black editor of *Opportunity:* "I remember one young buck. His thumb had been nearly torn off when a firecracker exploded in his hands. If he had been a white man I should have amputated at once, but as he was a nigger I went to work and sewed it up. It was a pretty hard job, but it healed up so fine you could hardly see the scar. Oh yes, a nigger's resistance to disease is less than a white man's but his repairative [*sic*] power is much greater."[3]

All of these assumptions about the black organism signified its special hardiness, and it was only natural that this casual attitude toward black pain eventually carried over into the newly integrated world of American sports during the 1950s and 1960s. As inheritors of a standard racist dogma about the black nervous system, many white coaches and trainers saw black athletes as largely immune to injury, and this sort of thinking still exists to one degree or another.[4] In his 1968 report on the status of black college athletes, Jack Olsen presented dramatic testimony about popular belief in black hardiness: "The double standard applies to injuries. 'They figure that the Negro is Superman,' says a Negro back. 'We can't get hurt,' says an esteemed basketball player. 'We're supposed to be made of stone.' This is a view aired by every dissident group of black athletes that has publicly made an issue of its grievances in recent months."[5]

Nor is it surprising that this tradition has continued. The scandal that ousted Pat Dye from his position as head coach of the Auburn University football team in 1992 included the allegation that a coach who would not think of kicking a white player found it easy to kick a black one.[6] Cultural continuities of this kind pervade the history of ideas about racial athletic aptitude, and twentieth-century thinking about racial biology has often preserved and recycled nineteenth-century ideas about black anatomy and physiology.

Popular and scientific speculation about black athletic aptitude originated in crude Darwinian ideas about the retarded evolutionary status of Africans and the disproportionate development of certain bodily traits and lower human faculties. The first black athletes to become racial symbols in the United States were the prizefighters who fought each other and some white boxers during the 1890s. The racial-anthropological framework was already well established when their interracial encounters occurred, and the principal themes were differences in bone structure and the Negro's primitive nervous system. "The skeleton of the Negro is heavier, the bones thicker and larger in proportion to the muscles than in the European," the prominent German anthropologist Theodor Waitz wrote in 1859. "This is especially the case with regard to the skull, which is hard and unusually thick, so that in fighting, Negroes, men and women, butt each other like rams without exhibiting much sensibility." His distinguished compatriot Carl Vogt agreed that the Negro, "like a ram, uses his hard skull in a fight."[7]

Such ideas about black bone density reached far beyond the scientific literature into racial folklore. A John Henry–like hero known among the African-American population of Jacksonville, Florida, was Henry Peterson, "familiarly known as Old Pete, who had prodigious strength when he was young, at the turn of the century. For a nickel he allowed coconuts to be broken open on his skull, and for fifty cents he had butting contests with billy goats, whom he invariably bested."[8] It is hardly surprising that this image of the black skull came to play a role in the interracial prizefighting milieu. "Being a warm admirer of [the white boxer] Jim Jeffries," the black fighter Allen Johnson wrote in 1905, "I am sorry to see him make the public declaration that he does not want to fight Jack Johnson because his head is too hard. Such a statement may cause a good laugh among the ignorant class of colored people, but the majority of our race take it as an insult . . . I can say that it does not take a harder blow to knock out a Negro than a white man."[9]

Juxtaposing the legend of Henry Peterson with black resentment of racial lore about the skull illustrates once again the profound ambivalence toward racial difference that has marked the African-American experience. The idea of black hardiness can be embraced or rejected, and these contrasting attitudes, according to Allen Johnson, are determined by one's level of sophistication. Black anger directed at the idea of the thick Negro skull was rooted in its symbolic relationship to intelligence. The skull of the white man, the French anthropologist Gratiolet wrote in 1856, "is a temple divine but that of brutish races is merely a helmet constructed to ward off heavy blows."[10] In 1908 the black sociologist Kelly Miller commented acerbically on the same tradition: "Do you recall the school of pro-slavery scientists who demonstrated beyond doubt that the Negro's skull was too thick to comprehend the substance of Aryan knowledge?"[11] Today, however, observations about the deleterious effects of displaying black hardiness in the boxing ring are conspicuous by their absence.

Another late-nineteenth-century claim alleged that a racial difference between the nervous systems of blacks and whites accounted for the success of black prizefighters. In 1892 the American psychologist Joseph Jastrow argued that "lowly organized creatures" such as the "inferior races" were "guided almost entirely by reflex actions" such as those displayed by boxers.[12] This idea was developed further by another psychologist, R. Meade Bache, who in 1895 interpreted racial ability in boxing as an example of the Darwinian "law of compensation," which postulated an inverse relationship between brain and brawn, between "intelligence" and "primitive constitution." While Bache assumed on these grounds that the faster reflexes (or "reaction times") of black fighters guaranteed both their athletic superiority and their racial inferiority, he also knew that the chauvinism of many of his white compatriots made them incapable of viewing interracial competitions with such scientific objectivity, and he appears to have taken a cynical pleasure in his own detachment. "Pride of race obscures the view of the white with reference to the relative automatic quickness of the negro," he wrote. "That the negro is, in the truest sense, a race inferior to that of the white can be proved by many facts, and among these by the quickness of his automatic movements as compared with those of the white. Many men, however, resent any claim for him of superiority, even in the low sphere of automatic movements." Unlike his fellow racists, who could not stomach the notion of black athletic superiority, the more scientific Bache took consolation in the fact that the Negro was "more of an automaton than the white man."[13]

The "scientific" search for the racial secrets of elite athletic performance is thus inseparable from the legacy of racial folklore, which has always viewed the African as the biological as well as cultural opposite of the white European. The belief that blacks and whites constitute the primary racial polarity within the human species has generated a profound urge to find differences that fulfill the original desire for exotic discoveries about the bodies of racial aliens. The combination of this desire and race-neutral scientific curiosity has produced an extensive literature on racial athletic aptitude, which should be divided into two separate categories. The first consists of scientific publications that attempt to make comparisons of anatomical features or physiological processes that may be relevant to athletic performance; while these studies usually appear in refereed journals, readers should always be alert to the influence of folkloric themes. The second type of commentary presents a credulous and incongruous mixture of folklore and brief accounts of what is assumed to be scientific progress in unraveling the mysteries of racial biology.

It is this genre of "tabloid science" that has reached the enormous public in the United States that is receptive to news about racial differences. Widespread curiosity about the biological basis of black athletic achievement dates from the successes of Jesse Owens and other African-American runners during the 1930s. "One of the most interesting athletic phenomena of our time," the popular historian Frederick Lewis Allen wrote in August 1936, "is the emergence of American Negroes as the best sprinters and jumpers in the world." While Allen had no real way to explain their prominence, he was astute enough to assume that "their recent rise to supremacy is chiefly a sociological phenomenon," thereby demonstrating an uncommon ability to resist contemporary anatomical arguments about black limb length, projecting heel bones, and allegedly stronger Achilles tendons.[14]

The widespread belief that black athletes benefited from anatomical advantages was directly contradicted by W. Montague Cobb in January 1936, following Jesse Owens's world-record feats of May 1935 but well in advance of his four gold medals at the 1936 Berlin Olympic Games.

Cobb's article "Race and Runners" is best known for demonstrating that "Owens' foot presents none of the characteristics commonly but often erroneously designated as Negroid" and that his calf structure "is of the Caucasoid type rather than the Negroid." The larger purpose of Cobb's courteous and systematic argument, as his conclusions about Owens's anatomy make clear, was to subvert the idea of well-defined racial types and to refute the idea that such types corresponded to different levels of athletic ability. What is more, Cobb had the sagacity to make a point about the scientific analysis of elite athletic perform-ance that most observers are still unable to absorb: "The personal histo-ries and constitutions of our sprinters have not yet been sufficiently analyzed for the formula for the perfect sprinter or jumper to be given. We are not able to say what measure of natural capacity is due to physical proportions, or to physiological efficiency or to forceful per-sonality. Nor can we weight capacity and training scientifically." And the same uncertainty applied to racial athletic aptitude: "There is not one single physical feature, including skin color, which all our Negro champions have in common which would identify them as Negroes."[15]

The irony of Cobb's argument is that he was and remained, as we have seen, a passionate subscriber to a doctrine of black hardiness that could not have met the standard of scientific rigor he sets in "Race and Runners." This incompatibility between science and racial pride was evident since the natural selection theory of black hardiness leads straight to biological mysticism of one kind or another. The African-American sportswriter Edwin Bancroft Henderson provided an exam-ple of this sort of reasoning several months before Jesse Owens's tri-umphs in Berlin:

> When one recalls that it is estimated that only one Negro slave in five was able to live through the rigors of the "Middle Passage," and that the horrible conditions of slavery took toll of many slaves who could make biological adjustments in a hostile environment, one finds the Darwinian theory of the survival of the fit operating among Negroes as rigorously as any selective process ever operated among human beings. *There is just a likelihood that some very vital elements persist in the histological tissues of the glands or muscles of Negro athletes* [emphasis added].[16]

Quasi-scientific thinking of this kind gradually became a part of West-ern discourse about black athletic aptitude. "I think," a British physi-cian (with a knighthood) wrote in *The Eugenics Review* in 1952, "there is some special quality in his muscles — a more rapid contractility or viscosity. Alternatively, there may be a superior co-ordination related to his nervous system."[17] While such speculations were attempts to think scientifically, they give further evidence of the core belief in the hardiness of the black organism. In 1941 the exercise physiologist Ernst Jokl had found "a striking similarity between the standards of physiologic performance of the different racial groups." A third of a century later, however, Jokl was settled in the United States and had become a believer in the "innate capacity" (as opposed to "innate ability") of the black athlete. "You must make a distinction between the two," he asserted. "I think that, on the whole, Negroes have enormously underdeveloped capacity (for athletics) due to their late coming into emancipation. With his emancipation, the Negro discovered by trial and error where his abilities lay — and once he discovered that, he cultivated those abilities. Where you have Negro boys, they will run and they will play basketball. By trial and error they find out what they do best. From capacity comes the ability."[18]

It is only too clear that Jokl's concept of "innate capacity" is little more than a pseudo-scientific construct that anticipates the racial paternalism of *The Bell Curve,* which proposes that most blacks should content themselves with developing "innate capacities" that have nothing to do with becoming viable citizens of a modern society. Small wonder that Charles Murray has commented acerbically that "it is impossible to speak straightforwardly about the dominance of many black athletes without being subject to accusations that one is being backhandedly anti-black."[19] While Murray does understand that proposing an inverse relationship between black athletic ability and intelligence will be widely resented, he does not understand the nonscientific character of his intuitions about black athletic aptitude. Fixated on his belief that the "truth" about racial differences has been systematically suppressed, he assumes that there are untold secrets about racial athletic aptitude, comparable to the secrets of racial intelligence he purports to reveal in his book. Murray's melodramatic scenario of concealment and revelation — as if the study of race were not already dramatic enough — is only one small episode in the recent history of ideas about race and athletic ability.

The idea that scientific investigation of racial athletic aptitude defies a powerful social taboo is a standard theme of the journalistic treatments of this topic. The first of these popularizations, Marshall Smith's "Giving the Olympics an Anthropological Once-Over," appeared in the October 23, 1964, issue of *Life.* Smith began his narrative by representing the Olympic athletes assembled in Tokyo as a kind of human zoo, where the physical anthropologist could find "the world's most varied and superbly conditioned assortment of the human species, in all shapes, sizes and colors." Having discerned an "anthropological" pattern of achievement by the "Mongoloid," "Negroid," and "Caucasoid" branches of the human family, and having announced "the scientific fact that there are, in general, basic physical differences between races of people," he noted that "there are those who refuse to argue the question at all because of the hotly controversial implications" of such an inquiry. His expert witnesses on the existence and athletic significance of racial differences in anatomy were the American physical anthropologists Carleton S. Coon and Edward E. Hunt, Jr. For the most part, Smith was content to record the opinions of a mixed group of scientists and coaches, including W. Montague Cobb, and to present respectable published data on small average differences in arm, leg, and trunk length found in American blacks and whites that might play a role in sport. He also presented data indicating that black skeletons are heavier than white ones and that blacks have significantly less body fat than whites, suggesting that blacks are less buoyant and thus at a disadvantage in swimming competitions. At the conclusion of his essay he noted the "scientific contradictions, if not total confusion" that lurk within the "fascinating data" about racial difference.[20]

The best-known of the popular treatments was published in the January 18, 1971, issue of *Sports Illustrated* by Martin Kane, a senior editor of the magazine, who wrote of the "fascinating" but "controversial" theories he was about to make public. Whereas Smith had merely invoked the indisputable "scientific fact" of physical differences between the races and left their athletic significance unresolved, Kane went a step further by claiming there was "an increasing body of scientific opinion which suggests that physical differences in the races might well have enhanced the athletic potential of the Negro in certain events."[21] The method employed by popularizing white journalists is to accumulate suggestive but scientifically invalid or inconclusive evidence of black athletic superiority. The collective impact of this material on an audience already primed to believe in the exotic potential of African biology is likely to be substantial.

Kane's most irresponsible assertion illustrates perfectly how this culturally constructed appetite for sensational news about racial physiology can predominate over a more circumspect approach to the selection of evidence that winds up in the public domain. There is, he wrote, "a trifle of evidence — this aspect has been studied so little that it is still in the highly speculative state — that the black man's adrenal glands, a vital factor in many sports, are larger than the white man's." Kane's groping after a hormonal basis to account for racial differences in performances derived, whether he knew it or not, from the teachings of plantation physicians and Arthur Keith's long-discredited theory, dating from an early period in the development of endocrinology, that racial characteristics were produced by the glands.[22] This uncritical approach to evidence is the basic method of tabloid science.

Kane next cited *The Physique of the Olympic Athlete,* by the reputable anthropologist J. M. Tanner, as follows: "Amongst competitors in both track and field events there are large significant racial differences in leg length, arm length and hip width." But are these racial differences athletically significant? It is a task for the physical educationist, Tanner said, to determine the athletic value of specific anatomical features. Elsewhere, Kane discussed the black athlete's alleged ability to "relax under pressure," the precocious motor development of Ugandan infants, and the allegedly deficient buoyancy of the black swimmer, and he introduced the important topic of muscle fiber type. "I believe that the black athlete has more white muscle fibers," announced James E. Counsilman of Indiana University, the U.S. swimming coach at the Tokyo Olympics. "Oversimplifying it, every muscle has two types of fibers — white fibers and red fibers. The white muscle fibers are adapted for speed of movement, otherwise power. The red muscle fibers are adapted for endurance . . . I think the difference in muscle fibers is the reason the black athlete is a better sprinter."[23]

Finally, Kane embraced the dramatic Middle Passage theory of black toughness to help account for black athletic success: "Of all the physical and psychological theories about the American black's excellence in sport, none has proved more controversial than one of the least discussed: that slavery weeded out the weak." Most of the transported slaves were, he claims, "warriors captured from other tribes, therefore physically superior," while the traders "dickered for the fittest."[24] Kane cited no source for his account of a brutal selective process applied to the hardiest of an African physical elite. In *The Myth of the Negro Past,* Melville Herskovits argued, to the contrary, that the slavers kidnapped neither the best nor the worst of the West African populations: "It has been shown that the history of slavery gives little evidence of any kind of selectivity in the capture of Negroes."[25]

It is reasonable to assume that the version of events favored by the less scholarly and more credulous Kane responded to a need for melodrama that the professional anthropologist did not feel. What is more, Kane was able to quote black athletes who were as convinced by the Middle Passage theory as he was. "We were bred for it," said Lee Evans, the Olympic champion and world record holder in the four-hundred-meter dash. "Certainly the black people who survived in the slave ships must have contained a high proportion of the strongest. Then, on the plantations, a strong black man was mated with a strong black woman. We were simply bred for physical qualities."[26] Kane seems to accord this sort of ignorant commentary the same authority he grants to physicians and anthropologists. That Everyman gets his chance to theorize along with the professionals is, after all, part of the appeal of tabloid science. And of all the tabloid-style fascinations that dress up irrational drives as scientific theories, racial science is the game that virtually anyone can play.

African-American responses to Kane's article accepted the fact of black athletic superiority but challenged its biological basis and identified sociocultural and socioeconomic factors that channeled a disproportionate amount of black energy into competitive sport. As Harry Edwards pointed out in November 1971, Kane's motley collection of arguments did not even approach the standards of real science for two reasons. First, the evidence he had presented was essentially anecdotal, since none of it employed random sampling or control groups; second, he had used a hopelessly outdated notion of "race" to compare blacks and whites who in fact shared many genes as the result of interbreeding over hundreds of years. Writing three decades after Cobb, Edwards reminded his readers that black athletes demonstrated "a wide range of physical builds, body proportions, and other highly diverse anatomical, physiological, and biological features, as do other groups including the so-called white race." He was particularly critical of Kane's recruitment of "well-meaning but uninformed and unthinking black athletes" such as Lee Evans and Calvin Hill (of the Dallas Cowboys) as expert witnesses concerning the Middle Passage ordeal and the alleged breeding of slaves. Edwards rightly emphasized the persisting Darwinian context in which black athletic performances were still interpreted as evidence of retarded development: "So by asserting that blacks are physically superior, whites at best reinforce some old stereotypes long held about Afro-Americans — to wit, that they are little removed from the apes in their evolutionary development."[27] An ironic effect of this racist dogma, as he noted, is that by accepting the stereotype of black athletic superiority, white athletes inflict a crippling psychological handicap on themselves.[28] Finally, by arguing for a cultural rather than a biological interpretation of "race," Edwards proposed that black athletic superiority results from "a complex of societal conditions" that channels a disproportionate number of talented blacks into athletic careers.[29]

Three years later the young African-American sportswriter Bill Rhoden, who is now a columnist for the *New York Times,* analyzed the issue of racial athletic aptitude for the readers of *Ebony.* By this time there was a standard repertory of expert opinions on the subject, and Rhoden presented them without comment. Whereas Cobb had debunked the idea of racial physique, the physical educator Eleanor Metheny and the anthropologist J. M. Tanner had established in 1939 and 1964, respectively, that blacks had on average longer arms and legs, shorter trunks, narrower hips, and heavier bones than whites. Rhoden pitted Harry Edwards against Ernst Jokl's theory of innate capacity and Kane's theory of the survival of the fittest, while the black psychiatrist Alvin Poussaint called sport a prime outlet for "black aggression."[30]

Conspicuous by their absence from this public discussion were black scientists and historians of science who could have offered more expert commentary on matters pertaining to race and human biology. During the 1930s, *The Journal of Negro Education* had published "The Investigation of Racial Differences Prior to 1910," coauthored by the prominent black scholar Horace Mann Bond, and Cobb had performed his famous examination of Jesse Owens in his unique role as an African-American public scientific intellectual.[31] Their efforts to look critically at white ideas about black bodies were well crafted but short-lived, and since that time the dearth of African-American scientists has ensured that scientifically informed discussions of racial athletic aptitude have been conducted among white physiologists and anthropologists. Some of what these scientists have been willing to say about racial biology has then been interpreted by white journalists for the general public.

Scientific speculation about racial athletic aptitude has thus led a double life, in that the peer-reviewed scientific literature is more cautious than journalistic stories, which tend to ignore the limitations of the evidence in favor of romanticizing black athletic potential. The distortions and omissions endemic to tabloid science necessitate a careful separation of experimental results from what is reported in the lay press. A minor complication is that some of the modern anthropometric data do roughly correspond to claims that functioned as racist dogmas during the nineteenth century. "The skeleton of the Negro is heavier, the bones thicker and larger in proportion to the muscles than in the European," Theodor Waitz wrote in 1859, and this is essentially correct.[32] Blacks do in fact have greater bone density than whites; whether this also applies to the subpopulation of elite athletes, and whether such a difference might be of athletic significance, is not known.[33] While nineteenth-century observations about the "peculiarities" or "weakness" of the African calf anticipated the finding of smaller calf muscles in modern blacks, it should be obvious by now that these smaller muscles are not the inferior trait some observers once thought they were.[34] Apparently reliable anthropometric data also confirm that blacks have on average longer arms and legs and narrower hips than whites.[35] These data are, however, problematic in that they can give rise to culture-bound speculations. Metheny, for example, assumes that the narrower hip of the black athlete is anatomically advantageous, yet it is difficult to tell whether her argument is based on valid biomechanical reasoning or the widely presumed (but unexplained) biomechanical efficiency of the black body. Indeed, her own assessment of the anatomical evidence bearing on racial differences concedes that such evidence is wholly inconclusive.[36]

Every theory of racial athletic aptitude, being vulnerable to the expectations created by racial folklore, consists of varying proportions of scientific reasoning and unscientific thinking about racial difference. Such problems belong to a larger class of problems in the world of medical research. As a gynecologist once pointed out, every observed racial contrast in obstetrics and gynecology belongs in "one of two categories: folklore or real difference . . . It becomes obvious that many racial contrasts depend upon such factors as custom, social and financial station, rather than race. Finally, there remain a few real differences."[37] This, in effect, is the procedure we must apply to the problem of real and imagined anatomical and physiological differences that might affect athletic aptitude. The athlete can make his presence felt in the laboratory by presenting researchers with this tangle of scientific and cultural factors.

An interesting example of how scientific thinking can be influenced by the phenomenon (and perhaps the symbolism) of black athleticism appeared in the journal of the African-American medical group two decades ago. At issue was an observed difference in the hemoglobin levels of blacks and whites, with the former showing significantly lower levels than the latter. This discrepancy raised the possibility that separate racial norms for hemoglobin might be required on medical grounds. This idea raised in turn the question of how blacks managed to cope so well with their "deficiency," and it was at this point that the researchers introduced athletes (of both races) into their reasoning process, as extreme physiological cases that confirmed the reality of difference. "Studies of athletes who tend to higher hemoglobins and hematocrits," they wrote, "still show evidence of differences between blacks and whites," even if on a smaller scale. Here the athlete's role as a (deviant) representative of his group appears to be scientifically valid. His more symbolic role appeared when the researchers speculated on whether the observed discrepancy was of environmental or genetic origin. If it was the latter, then this "would also raise the possibility of mechanisms for oxygen transport beyond those provided by the respiratory pigments" — in a word, an exotic physiological pathway reserved for black athletes alone.[38]

The same logic was offered two years later by another team of researchers. "Surely," they wrote, "some compensatory mechanisms must exist to counteract this relative deficiency of hemoglobin, since a significant difference has even been demonstrated in healthy athletes."[39] While this may actually be the case, we must also wonder whether data that offered a physiological rationale for black athletic superiority was more attractive than environmental factors precisely because they confirmed a preexisting conception of the hardy black organism possessing special adaptive powers.

In fact, speculation about superior energy metabolism in blacks had appeared a decade earlier, and here too a response to black athletic performance clearly shaped scientific thinking. "Physiological factors," wrote the Harvard anthropologist Albert Damon in 1966, "are more likely than anthropometric ones to explain the much greater success of Negroes in track events requiring short bursts of power . . . One can only speculate that the Negro-white differences in lung function reported here may in some way relate to corresponding differences in athletic performance."[40]

It is important to note that this relationship between athletics and physiology reverses the more familiar (and cautious) approach to cause and effect in exercise physiology, where one first confirms the existence of a physiological mechanism and then speculates about its role in determining performance. The speculative exercises described above reverse this relationship by presuming the existence of an "exotic" black (athletic) metabolism that points in turn to a physiological mechanism that remains unidentified. Such episodes demonstrate the influence of fixed ideas about black athleticism inside as well as outside the laboratory.[41]

Examining the historical development of theories of racial athletic aptitude permits us to see how scientific and folkloric elements can be incorporated into a hypothesis about organismic "superiority" of racial origin, and how science and folklore compete for influence in the wider world of popular thinking about race and athletic performance. If we begin with the least credible theory and proceed in ascending order of scientific value, then the first such idea is that the black athlete has a special ability to achieve a relaxed state that improves performance, a notion that derives from a long tradition of racist thinking about the primitive character of the black nervous system and its alleged stability.[42] Belief in a special black capacity for relaxation has also corresponded to the thoroughly discredited idea that blacks have lower blood pressures than whites.[43] Such findings, a disapproving W. Montague Cobb pointed out in 1942, were taken as "indicative of greater inward serenity and less disturbance at outer circumstances, in contrast with worrying habits of the White engendered by the fitful pace of modern lives which causes the pressure to mount."[44] As Cobb clearly understood, lower blood pressure and the relaxed state it made possible signified the premodern mentality from which most whites believed blacks would never emerge.

The improbable notion of the black person's special immunity to stress also appears in the medical literature. Addressing the alleged rarity of diabetes mellitus in blacks, a New Orleans physician pointed in 1921 to the role of nervous stress in precipitating the onset of the disease and the black person's freedom from experiences such as "intense application to business" and "mental shock and worry." "I do not mean that the race is without the finer sensibilities," he wrote, "but that its nervous burden is light and its nervous toll is small aside from the ravages of [syphilis]."[45] The same reasoning was also applied to cardiac pain. "The rarity of angina in the Negro," a physician wrote in 1946, "is well known and is commonly ascribed to lack of stress or to inability of the Negro to feel or to express pain."[46] Given its prophylactic role in buffering the black organism from pain and disease, the special capacity for relaxation thus belongs to the larger repertory of mysterious physiological mechanisms that constitute black hardiness.

The relaxation thesis has enjoyed a long career in the racial folklore of sports because it is a variation on the idea of the black primitive, which still suffuses Western culture. The mindset once common among white track-and-field coaches appears in undiluted form in a book by Dean Cromwell, the head coach of the U.S. Olympic team at the 1936 games in Berlin. In *Championship Technique in Track and Field,* Jesse Owens's Olympic mentor offered his own Darwinian theory, to the effect that "the Negro excels in the events he does because he is closer to the primitive than the white man. It was not so long ago that his ability to sprint and jump was a life-and-death matter to him in the jungle. His muscles are pliable, and his easy-going disposition is a valuable aid to the mental and physical relaxation that a runner and jumper must have."[47]

Three decades later, in his controversial article on racial differences for *Sports Illustrated,* Kane accorded the relaxation theory the same status as speculations about more tangible phenomena, such as limb lengths and muscle fibers, and here too the special plasticity of the black athlete encompassed both mind and body.[48] Whereas Cromwell referred to pliable black muscles, here the anthropologist Edward E. Hunt, Jr., claimed that the black athlete had "hyperextensibility — or what the layman might call being double-jointed." But the real focus of interest was an athletic variation on that special looseness of temperament that has been celebrated by racist humorists for the past two centuries. Black athletes, said Lloyd (Bud) Winter, former coach of Olympic medalists such as Tommie Smith and John Carlos, "are far ahead of the whites in that one factor — relaxation under pressure. It is their secret." "What heritage or heredity brought the black athlete this ability to keep out tension, no one knows," Winter continued. "In white athletes the conscious mind often takes over and the tensions mount." Another coach who had worked with world-class black sprinters went on in the same vein: "The black athletes have an ability to let their bodies go — you know, they hang everything loose. They walk loose, they dance loose, they *are* loose. You see it easily in their dancing . . . I think it is linked with the suppressed life of the black man in America. Their emotions come out in their bodies, and we notice this kind of expression develops body muscle control. Have you noticed how, when they're dancing or playing games, their heads seem to flop around? It's magnificent."[49]

This appreciative testimonial to the eloquence of black body language recalls a long tradition of Western ambivalence toward the black primitive, who can be culturally retrograde, temperamentally mysterious, and physically appealing all at the same time.[50] Speaking not long after the crest of the civil rights movement, these coaches reflexively juxtaposed the mind of the white with the instinct of the black, the conscious feelings of the former with the corporeal emotions of the latter. Such naively well intended comments testify to the sheer tenacity of the original "lazy" African stereotype, which has survived by adapting to a succession of black types in modern societies. Winter's notion of the black athlete's immunity to tension is indistinguishable from the physician's observation, published fifty years earlier, that the "happy-go-lucky" Negro was protected from diabetes by his exemption from "nervous strain."[51]

While the relaxation theory thus preserves in altered form the old idea of African indolence and passivity, it is also tied to racial folklore about how well blacks sleep. Thomas Jefferson combined these two themes in his belief that blacks needed less sleep than whites but grew somnolent when confronted with work.[52] Having studied the blacks of Uganda just before World War I, the Austrian physician Robert Stigler concluded that blacks sleep more deeply than whites.[53] A century ago American racial folklore held that a black man "could sleep soundly under conditions that would have made sleep impossible for a white man."[54] Here is the physiological noble savage par excellence, for implicit in the capacity to sleep especially deeply are the powers of recovery inherent in the myth of black hardiness.

The idea that blacks have larger nerve cells than whites appears as early as a German treatise "On the Physical Differences Between the Negro and the European," published in 1785.[55] The plantation doctor Samuel Cartwright held the same view, claiming in 1851 that all of the nerves in a Negro's body, except for those going to the muscles, "are larger in proportion than in the white man."[56] This purported anomaly was sufficiently well known to appear in popular fiction. In a story published in the *Atlantic Monthly* in 1862, one white character tells another that "there are nerves in these black carcasses, thicker, more quickly stung to madness than yours."[57] This is an interesting claim, because it contradicts the prevailing image of the somnolent Negro in favor of the more volatile neurological one that reappears in Bache's 1895 report of the black prizefighter's quick reaction time. Having ascribed fast reflexes to the black body, Bache had no choice but to divorce athletic reaction time from intelligence, and he duly announced that "the reflective [white] man" is "the slower being" in the boxing ring.[58]

During the twentieth century this distinction between reaction time and the measurement of intelligence remained largely intact until the 1960s. The relationship between reaction time, race, and sport reappeared in 1987, when Leon Kamin referred to black athletes' visual mastery of the basketball court to challenge the results of intelligence tests that indicated slower reaction times to complex stimuli (and thus lower intelligence) in black subjects.[59]

An associated neurological problem that also bears on athletic performance concerns the cross-sectional area of nerve fibers and the assumption that a thicker nerve conducts the nerve impulse more quickly. In fact, "speed of nerve conduction" is the second of two sequential processes that constitute the "reaction time" required to respond to such stimuli as the configuration of players on a basketball court or the strategy of an opponent in the boxing ring. The first phase is mental processing of what is perceived, and the second is the execution of a physical movement in response to the visual cues presented by the scenario to which the athlete must react. The auditory cue represented by the firing of a starter's gun to begin a sprinting race is a less complex scenario in which an athlete's reaction time is also of crucial importance.

Speculation about speed of nerve conduction as a racial trait enjoyed a brief career during the 1930s. *The Journal of Comparative Neurology* published a paper in 1930 reporting greater cross-sectional nerve areas in black subjects. Given evidence that the speed of the nerve impulse should increase with the diameter of the fiber, the author concluded that "a slightly more rapid impulse rate in the male negroes is to be expected" — a result with implications for the capacity to produce quick athletic movements.[60] Of greater importance, however, was the relationship between speed of conduction and intelligence, which was debated during this period by the opposing sides in an ideological conflict regarding race and intelligence testing. The contending factions were the environmentalists, including the prominent psychologist Otto Klineberg, and those who argued for a biological interpretation of test results that indicated faster reaction times in white subjects.

Klineberg maintained in 1928 that "environmental factors — culture, custom, education, contact and relationship with other peoples — are much more tangible than the factor of race, psychologically speaking."[61] Another investigator phrased the cultural-environmental thesis as follows: "The white man's concern for speed and punctuality may be an acquired trait, we feel. If this be so, then one racial group, being more set than another on speed of performance alone or on accuracy alone disregarding speed, might react to psychological tests with resulting differences of achievement."[62]

To more biologically oriented psychologists, this sort of environmentalism was both sentimental and intellectually irresponsible. "There is no immediately apparent *a priori* reason why the race equality principle should have found such favor in sociological circles," two of the better-known authors wrote, "unless one assumes that the doctrine of the universal brotherhood of man still motivates the earnest but often misguided efforts of workers in this field." Employing a "speed index" to reflect performance on a "Rational Learning Test," these researchers found a speed difference they described as "a temperamental difference, a difference in social 'sensitivity,' rather than in facility in handling the 'rational' aspects of the problem . . . The whites seemed to the examiner to be more alert, over-anxious, whereas the Negroes were lethargic."[63]

Klineberg's response to the biological thesis was to situate reaction time beyond mere biology. "There are so many factors which may enter into reflex latent time," he wrote in 1935, "that any direct relation to intelligence is hardly to be expected. It is known that speed of nerve conduction depends not only on the actual rate of transmission in the nerve fiber, but also upon the inhibiting effect of the higher nervous centers."[64] By claiming that reaction time has an emotional dimension, he was refusing to hardwire speed of conduction into the human body as a reliably measurable racial trait.

A year later W. Montague Cobb noted that research on nerve fibers and race had been conducted, and he reported that the "tapping test" he had administered to Jesse Owens had shown the champion sprinter to be "exceptionally fast with his right arm and above average with his left." Three years later Cobb was debunking the significance of cross-sectional nerve areas and claiming, rather curiously, that Jesse Owens's tapping reflexes "were no speedier than those of the average person."[65] This abrupt change of perspective indicates Cobb's fundamental ambivalence toward the issue of black athletic ability. Even though he was proud of black athleticism, he recognized the hazards of establishing different nervous systems for blacks and whites, and caution prevailed. His response to the racial neurology of the 1930s put him in the same camp as Klineberg, whose "attitude of special pleading" on behalf of racial equality had excited the contempt of his opponents. The significance of this "debiologizing" of human potential is that it runs directly contrary to the ambition of tabloid science to establish an exotic biology as the explanation for black athletic superiority.

The search for racial differences in muscle fiber proportions has revived the anatomical inquiry into neuromotor differences, which faded away more than half a century ago. Kane's public presentation of the issue in 1971 relied entirely on the anecdotal testimony of the swimming coach James Counsilman, whose claims about differing racial proportions of white ("fast-twitch") and red ("slow-twitch") fibers coincided with a burst of commentary on muscle fiber types in the scientific literature that did not address the racial issue at all.[66] By this time scientists had identified type I (slow) and two variations of type II (fast) skeletal muscle fibers of potential athletic significance; it was assumed that distance runners would show a higher proportion of slow-twitch fibers, while sprinters would have more of the fast-twitch variety that generates "explosive" movement. It was also believed that specific types of physical training could convert white fibers into red ones and vice versa.[67]

The publication in 1986 of a comparative study of small groups of

West African and French Canadian nonathletes introduced the racial factor into the discussion of fiber types. After analyzing muscle samples from their black and Caucasian groups, a team of scientists at Laval University concluded that their results were "compatible with the notion that Black male individuals are well endowed to perform in sports events of short duration," even though the observed racial difference in type I fibers (8 percent) exceeded the relevant margin of error (7 percent) by a single point. The authors also found that the largest physiological difference between the racial groups, bearing on the muscle enzyme activities of anaerobic energy metabolism, lent support to "a presumed advantage of Black males" in short running events.[68] In 1990 the same research team failed to find significant differences between nonathletic black and white males in brief tests of muscular exertion, a result that contradicted, as they pointed out, "the common observation that Black athletes are generally more successful in running events of short duration." Their finding that their black subjects became fatigued more quickly than whites after thirty seconds of all-out effort appeared to the researchers to confirm the hypothesis that black Africans have "slightly more" fast-twitch muscle fibers than whites.[69]

Two popular feature articles on racial athletic aptitude that appeared in 1988 addressed the issue of race and muscle fiber types but did not mention the Canadian research, confirming that widespread interest in racial physiology flourishes even in the absence of peer-reviewed scientific evidence. John Underwood's article in *Life* cites the belief of the biomechanician Gideon Ariel that black athletes' faster reaction times derive from their fiber-type profile.[70] (Ariel and his "force plate" jumping experiments reappeared on NBC-TV's *Black Athletes — Fact and Fiction,* hosted by Tom Brokaw and broadcast on April 25, 1989, to a very large American audience.) Michael Sokolove's article in the *Philadelphia Inquirer Magazine* was the first skeptical treatment of the subject. "The fast-twitch/slow-twitch theory has reached the status of a dogma in the track-and-field community," he reported, "where coaches tend to be much more up-to-date on the latest scientific research." A scientist at the Human Performance Lab at Ball State University revealed that public awareness of muscle fibers had already reached the point where some parents wanted their children to undergo muscle biopsies to assess their prospects in various sports: "People call all the time and want their children biopsied. We've had them ask for children as young as five. They think if they know, they can shortcut the process and pick a sport for their kid. We don't do it because we have never believed fiber type is a good predictor of performance."[71] Another re-

searcher expressed surprise that biopsies of sixty black and white subjects, including ten black sprinters, had produced undramatic results.
"The blacks had the same spreads," said Dr. Drew Gaffney, of the
University of Texas Southwestern Medical Center in Houston. "The
sprinters may have been a little higher, but not much. They were not out
of the range of the rest of the group." In his opinion, the fiber-type
hypothesis was a long way from being proven.[72]

Such doubts about fiber typing were less decisive, however, than the
sheer appeal of a technique that promised to distinguish whites from
blacks with the sort of scientific rigor that population genetics had
seemed to put out of reach. The muscle fiber story thus reappeared in
the cover story of the August 1992 issue of *Runner's World,* which
carried the provocative title "White Men Can't Run."

Amby Burfoot's announced purpose here was to pierce the "shroud
of silence" that enforces "our societal taboo against discussing racial
differences" — a taboo whose power he exaggerated to add drama to
his narrative of scientific revelation. This was tabloid journalism, because the article presented evidence that had been purged of uncertainty, ambiguity, and in some cases the sort of modest scientific pedi-
gree not likely to inspire confidence in a reasonably sophisticated
reader. Its driving theme was that disbelievers in biologically grounded
racial athletic aptitude have been overtaken by scientific advances with
which they do not want to contend. Americans, we read, "aren't ready
for the genetics revolution that's already sweeping over us" — a revolution that even three years later had not produced a single effective gene
therapy for human disease. A rhetorical staple of tabloid science is to
assume that such future knowledge will inevitably appear, so we are told
that the Human Genome Project will eventually "tell us more about
ourselves than we are prepared to know," including the secrets of elite
athletic performance. The scientific exhibits are the familiar anatomical
data about narrower hips and longer legs among blacks; a 1935 test of
reflex time whose author (unlike Burfoot) called its results "only suggestive"[73]; Claude Bouchard's 1986 study of muscle fiber types; an exercise physiologist who found no racial difference in laboratory tests of
anaerobic power; and a study showing that a high percentage of South
African blacks can exercise at a higher percentage of their maximum
oxygen capacity than whites.[74] The author's strategy is to offer this uneven collection as a demonstration of black physiological superiority
that amounts to more than the sum of its parts.

The most significant evidence presented in "White Men Can't Run"
was at that point unpublished research on Kenyan and Swedish runners

carried out by the physiologist Bengt Saltin, work that can be described as the first and only credible research on the physiology of elite athletes involving racial comparisons. The published results differ from Burfoot's version in that they raise more questions than they answer. In 1992 Saltin dealt a blow to the muscle fiber theory by calling into question the representative character of any given muscle biopsy sample, thereby making the identification of fiber type a problematic exercise to begin with. He pointed out repeatedly that the physiological values found in Kenyan runners relating to enzyme levels, capillaries serving muscle fibers, and oxygen uptake did not differ from those of other accomplished endurance athletes, even if he had not studied the very best Kenyans. What he did find was Kenyan muscle fibers whose smaller cross-sectional area presumably facilitated exchanges between their centers and a relatively dense network of capillaries surrounding the muscle.[75] In 1995 Saltin deflated the muscle fiber hypothesis again: "A key finding of this study is that the Kenyan runners had a muscle fiber type distribution very similar to that of successful European runners."[76] There were also suggestive physiological differences, in that ammonia and lactic acid accumulated more slowly in the blood of the Kenyan runners, presumably delaying the onset of fatigue. In the last analysis, however, defining the nature of Kenyan superiority proved to be an elusive exercise. While "the Kenyans run faster because they have better running efficiency," the origin of good running efficiency remained unknown.[77]

The difference between tabloid science and genuine science is that real scientists do not streamline their presentations and feign omniscience in order to excite their readers. Burfoot's article never mentions the well-known uncertainties associated with muscle fiber typing.[73] Saltin's pioneering studies, by contrast, contain repeated confessions of ignorance. Even the effects of training on enzyme levels and capillaries, he conceded in 1992, cannot explain the Kenyans' running ability. "The Kenyan runners," he wrote three years later, "have fascinated the world for decades. What makes them run so well? What is the secret behind new runners repeatedly entering the scene and capturing medals at major events? The results of this study bring no sensational dimensions to what makes a great runner." It is not Saltin's purpose either to suppress or to promote the idea of biological difference. He did find interesting differences in certain physiological variables, and he is perfectly willing to speculate that the tendons around the knee joints of "long and slender" Kenyan legs might offer a mechanical advantage, even if this remains only "an intriguing possibility." In the last analysis, we still confront the mysterious interface between culture and biology: "Can the regular physical activity from early childhood explain the Africans' superiority, or do they have a genetic endowment pre-disposing them for enhancing oxygen transport and utilization?"[78] The fact is that we do not yet (and may never) know.

The idea that life itself is a form of athletic training for some Africans is many years old; at the same time, we must wonder why the physically demanding lives of many white men around the world, such as Norwegians and Australians, have not been linked to their athletic achievements in quite the same way. It remains a cultural fact that Africans have a special place in the Western imagination as fantasy objects associated with physical vitality, and this makes them especially attractive to those in search of biological distinctions between the races. Tabloid science is dangerous because it can function as a potent carrier of pseudo-scientific ideas about racial difference, feeding the appetite for such revelations, which is a major legacy of our racist past. These dangers have been most evident when whites have gone in search of the biological sources of black criminality.

# 15

# Athleticizing
# the Black Criminal

THE INVESTIGATION of black athletic aptitude during this century has coincided with two related and fateful developments: the athleticizing of the black criminal and theorizing about the biological causes of violent behavior. Biomedical speculations about violence have usually pointed to the disproportionate number of violent crimes committed by African-American males and raised the question of whether black criminals may be biologically anomalous people. The extensive publicity accorded to black athletes in recent decades has played a significant role in public thinking about race and crime by merging the black athlete and the black criminal into a single threatening figure in two ways: first, by dramatizing two physically dynamic black male types which are often presumed to be both culturally and biologically deviant; and second, by putting the violent or otherwise deviant behavior of black athletes on constant public display so as to reinforce the idea of the black male's characterological instability. This continuous barrage of highly selective evidence about black male behavior amounts to an ongoing media show that effectively criminalizes the black athlete even as it athleticizes the black criminal in the minds of an enormous audience.

The cultural construction of the physically dynamic and aggressive black male has proceeded concurrently in the popular imagination and in the scientific literature. This highly physicalized criminal type can be regarded as the deviant and dangerous expression of hardiness as a racial trait. By the turn of the century, the idea of the Negro as beast and rapist was firmly established in the United States and was being popularized in the novels of Thomas Dixon, including *The Leopard's Spots*

(1902) and *The Clansman* (1905), as well as in diverse other publications.[1] Nor was the idea of an entire racial population gone out of control simply a fantasy disseminated by southern racists. In "The Conservation of Races," W.E.B. Du Bois himself declared, "Unless we conquer our present vices they will conquer us; we are diseased, we are developing criminal tendencies, and an alarmingly large percentage of our women are sexually impure"[2] — his final point coinciding with the virtually unanimous opinion of white physicians writing for years after the turn of the century. This sense of racial anarchy appeared as late as 1939 in the work of the African-American sociologist E. Franklin Frazier: "When the yoke of slavery was lifted, the drifting masses were left without any restraint upon their vagrant impulses and wild desires."[3] And it was from these unrestrained and libidinous masses that the black male emerged as a special threat to the safety of white women in particular.

Demonizing the muscular Negro offered a Darwinian drama par excellence, in that portraying the black male as an undisciplined savage confirmed both his primitive nature and his inevitable failure in the competition with civilized whites in a modern society. In *The Descent of Man,* Darwin had compared the respective advantages of a powerful physique and gentler social qualities for human survival and concluded that "an animal possessing great size, strength, and ferocity" would have probably failed to develop the "higher mental qualities" required for civilized life.[4] This failure to evolve could also be presented as sportive underdevelopment. In Booth Tarkington's 1914 novel *Penrod,* a white bully who is routed by two tougher black boys learns about "the danger of colliding with beings in one of those lower states of evolution wherein theories about 'hitting below the belt' have not yet made their appearance." Observing this unequal struggle, the eleven-year-old Penrod and his friend know better than to challenge the law of the jungle: "Primal forces operated here, and the two blanched, slightly higher products of evolution, Sam and Penrod, no more thought of interfering than they would have thought of interfering with an earthquake."[5]

This Darwinian drama has been kept alive by black athleticism in general and by black prizefighters in particular. What the public career of Mike Tyson has cost black Americans is incalculable in the literal sense of the term, but it is reasonable to assume that his well-publicized brutalities in and out of the ring have helped to preserve pseudo-evolutionary fantasies about black ferocity that are still of commercial value to fight promoters and their business partners in the media.

Our sense that this stereotype of untamed black muscularity has always predominated is wrong. The plantation physicians who tended black slaves emphasized not their robust qualities but their medical disorders and bodily defects. Samuel Cartwright never represented the black man as physically impressive; on the contrary, he was physiologically hobbled by the inferiority of his lungs and his blood, and his muscles were slack unless goaded into action by the white man's will.[6] And there were good political reasons not to make the animalistic Negro a conspicuous type: "Because the pro-slavery authors were anxious to prove that slavery had been a benefit to the Negro in removing him from savagery to Christianity, the stereotype of the 'brute Negro' was relatively insignificant in antebellum days."[7] Post-Reconstruction hysteria about the criminal impulses of the "Negro as beast" was clearly a complex emotional response to Emancipation and to the uncertain future of race relations and economic competition.

This is not to say that the idea of black supermuscularity did not exist before the 1890s. The black villain of Rebecca Harding Davis's 1862 story "John Lamar," for example, is "a gigantic fellow, with a gladiator's muscles. Stronger than that Yankee captain, he thought, — than either of them: better breathed — drawing the air into his brawny chest" — an interesting touch that disputes Cartwright's unceasing disparagements of Negro lungs.[8] But the dangerous Negro giant as a type existed primarily in fiction. Still, the "great stealthy body" of John Lamar confirms the continuity of an important racial obsession addressed by scholars such as Winthrop Jordan and George M. Fredrickson: "There is little reason to doubt the conventional notion that a fear of oversexed 'brute' Negroes has been a constant and deeply rooted feature of the white racist imagination. But it remains true that this image came to the surface in a new and spectacular way around the turn of the century."[9] The "spectacular" response to this image was a wave of public lynchings and tortures of black men that continued well into this century.

Another, less public response to black male physicality came from academic men with scientific pretensions. Nathaniel Southgate Shaler, a geologist and dean of the Scientific School of Harvard University, described two physically superior black types in 1900. The "real or Guinea negro[es]" were "generally burly fellows, attaining at a relatively early age a massive trunk and strong thighs," while "the Southern negroes" were "in excellent physical condition" and almost always free of bodily deformities.[10] This interest in racial physique, and some of its vocabulary, established itself as an increasingly marginal, reactionary, but still visible part of modern physical anthropology during the twentieth century, which sometimes retained a distinctly nineteenth-century flavor.

The organizing in 1926 of a "Committee on the Negro," jointly sponsored by the American Association of Physical Anthropology and the National Research Council, institutionalized an interest in Negro anatomy that expressed the racism of the era. Ales Hrdlicka, a member of the committee and founder of the *American Journal of Physical Anthropology,* inaugurated the committee's work with a document that included the following statement: "The real problem of the American negro lies in his brain, and it would seem, therefore, that this organ above all others would have received scientific attention."[11] In 1927 he endorsed a comparison of African babies with young apes.[12] In 1937 the *AJPA* published an attempt "to prove that the negro race is phylogenetically a closer approach to primitive man than the white race."[13] As late as 1954 an anthropologist writing elsewhere was echoing Shaler's language by referring to "the exaggerated development of muscle so characteristic of the burly Negro."[14] The continuing presence of the muscular black as a racial type in the anthropological imagination encouraged the racist faction to retain the traditional neo-Darwinian concept of the black primitive, which found its fulfillment in the persons of black athletes and criminals.

The most important academic mediator of the black athletic and criminal types was Earnest Albert Hooton, who taught at Harvard from 1913 until the year of his death, 1954. Hooton has been described as "the most influential physical anthropologist in the country during the interwar years," a position that makes his approach to race all the more significant.[15] For our purposes, the most salient fact is that Hooton was a believer in the constitutional approach to human biology, a consummately nineteenth-century outlook that saw correspondences between physique and temperament that could be found in the apparently random disorder of human genetic variation.[16]

From 1926, the year he was appointed to the Committee on the Negro (along with Hrdlicka and the eugenist Charles B. Davenport, among others), Hooton's major research focused on finding a biological basis for criminal behavior. The fruit of his labors, which involved examining seventeen thousand criminals and noncriminals, was *Crime and the Man,* a book that shows how easy it is to absorb racial stereotypes into an anthropological framework that equates bodily and behavioral traits at an ultimately mysterious level of functioning. "It is sufficiently obvious," wrote Hooton,

> that as yet undefined anatomical and physiological qualities of the Negro organism are responsible for Negro preeminence in sprinting and jump-

ing, that the larynx of the Negro is constructed in some peculiar way which permits or facilitates the production of a different voice quality from that ordinarily characteristic of Whites, that a certain fluidity of muscular movement and a hypersensitivity to rhythm are responsible for the racial individuality of Negro music and art, et cetera. In general, the behavior which arises from the Negro organism differs from that emanating from the Whites, either subtilely or crassly, and there is nothing invidious in the distinction.[17]

Hooton's final remark, disclaiming any invidious intent, was echoed fifty-five years later by the authors of *The Bell Curve,* whose disingenuous approach to racial egalitarianism has been met with the widespread skepticism it deserves.[18] It is quite possible that Hooton was more sincere in his disclaimer, if only because he was writing at a less politically correct time and was less expert in the art of ideological self-camouflage than a modern neoconservative such as Charles Murray; indeed, in the judgment of Elazar Barkan, Hooton's "cynicism and bad taste often exceeded acceptable bounds for scholarly work."[19]

There is certainly no question that Hooton regarded black athletic aptitude as a defining racial trait. "No one who follows sports news," he wrote in 1941,

> can fail to be impressed with the apparent supremacy of Negroes in certain types of contest — notably sprinting, middle-distance running, high- and broad-jumping, boxing. Here there would seem to be certain advantages in body build, reaction time, or other morphological and functional characters which are factors in Negro success. This subject has not been explored and I cannot develop here the possibilities of Negroid variations which may be involved . . . The Negro, for aught I know, may have superior, all-round athletic ability.[20]

Hooton's two short passages on black athleticism epitomize the casual disorder and groundless certainties that characterize the impressionistic racial biology of any period. What is clear is that he believed the "undefined anatomical and physiological qualities of the Negro organism" were manifested as a racial trait in the black athlete.

The real focus of Hooton's book, however, was the criminal, and here too the anthropologist fused racial and physical characteristics. Observation of thousands of men had persuaded Hooton that Negro criminals "appear to be more strongly built and to possess more vigorous physiques than their law-abiding relatives." But he was not satisfied with identifying race and physique; his even more radical step was to identify race and criminality itself. Observed differences among the lawbreakers, he wrote, "suggest that the criminals represent racially a more fully developed Negro type than do the civilians, but not a physically inferior type — rather the reverse."[21]

While this was an astonishing claim, it was not without precedent. Samuel Cartwright had also argued that the intensification of Negroid physical traits — black skin, thick lips, flat nose — corresponded to an intensification of vitality and physical strength. "All negroes are not equally black," he wrote in 1851; "the blacker, the healthier and stronger; and deviation from the black color, in the pure race, is a mark of feebleness or ill health."[22] And Cartwright, like Hooton, would have acknowledged the analogous correlation between Negroid traits and savage instincts described by another writer in 1850, who proclaimed that "ferocity and stupidity are the characteristics of those tribes in which the peculiar negro features are found most developed."[23]

In fact, Hooton did not even try to conceal his nineteenth-century mindset. "The study of Negro criminality in the United States," he wrote, "offers an excellent opportunity for the testing of the Lombrosian hypothesis that criminals represent a class of men who not only retain many primitive physical characters such as are more commonly encountered in savages, but who also manifest types of behavior which may be called atavistic or reversionary."[24] Nor did this view make him an eccentric by the standards of the prewar era. "It is commonly believed," the sociologist Thorsten Sellin wrote in 1928, "that the Negro in our country is more criminal than the white. This condition is commonly laid at the door of inherited racial characteristics, ranging from an 'inferior mentality' to what a recent writer on 'criminal science' has called 'inherited recollections,' presumably handed down from the jungles of Africa."[25]

However influential this climate of opinion may have been, it is astonishing that the most powerful physical anthropologist in the country could have advanced such a view, for the theoretical core of Hooton's claim was that criminality, like athleticism, represented a fulfillment of the black man's racial essence. The law of correspondence that underlies this kind of thinking might be called the King Kong principle, in recognition of the enormous symbolic power of the 1933 film that created our major (obscene) icon of black physical strength allied with unbridled rage and lust. This film confronted its audience with the unspoken problem of how an enormous black ape might achieve sexual congress with the tiny blond rag doll he claimed as his true love.

Hooton's interest in black athleticism expressed the more regressive side of his thinking about racial differences, and it brought out the anthropological primitive in a prominent colleague as well. Carleton Coon taught anthropology at Harvard from 1927 to 1948, and his intellectual career, like that of his mentor Hooton, included the awkward transition from the racial dogmas of the nineteenth century to the less picturesque study of human variation that eventually drove such neo-Darwinian fantasies out of respectable academic discourse. (Darwin had conjoined muscularity and "the lower races" in *The Descent of Man.*)[26] As Pat Shipman has pointed out, Coon "was the last of a type of flamboyant anthropologist-explorer, the sort epitomized by men of the nineteenth and early twentieth centuries like Richard Burton, the explorer of Africa and Arabia, or T. E. Lawrence of Arabia." His swashbuckling temperament went hand in hand with an unrestrained approach to classifying the impressive variety of the human family, "a habit that became more than distinctly unfashionable and, to some, offensive."[27]

To men like Hooton and Coon, for whom human variation was both a form of entertainment and an intellectual challenge, the topic of racial athletic aptitude offered a conceptual playground on which to let their minds run free. In 1964 Coon and yet another Harvard anthropologist, Edward E. Hunt, Jr., told *Life* magazine that "inherited physical adaptations seem to play a part in the abilities of members of different races to excel in different sports. That is one reason why Negro athletes have achieved such outstanding success in certain fields — in addition to whatever social factors or motivation may be involved." Coon associated the supposedly loose-jointed appearance of blacks with that of fast animals such as the cheetah, and he described the Negro foot as "a marvelous organ for mobility, leaping, jumping and landing with a minimum of shock," dealing another blow to the long-standing idea that blacks had flat feet.[28] While Coon and Hunt declared that none of their claims had any bearing on the question of racial superiority or inferiority, the fact is that their remarks simply recycled the anatomical speculations of the 1930s and gave vivid life once again to that harsh and primal African landscape in which blacks and animals evolve together in the Western imagination.

Implicit in Hooton's idea of the physically superior Negro criminal is the familiar combination of black athleticism and unstable temperament, which has become integral to the ongoing public discussion about black male behavior and what can be done to improve it. Here too the traditional image of the young black has developed from the Victorian period into distinctly modern forms that often merge physical vitality and deviant tendencies into a single racial syndrome. The "hyperactive" black schoolchild, for example, was already evident in 1869 to a British doctor who observed that "the constant animal restlessness" of the black children he tended at a school in New York made them very different from their white counterparts.[29] And here too popular and scientific ideas about black behavior developed in parallel and often independent ways, which are difficult to chart. Even if the man in the street did not need Hooton to provide him with an image of black criminality, the fact is that Hooton sometimes did reach general audiences, and public discussions of black crime or athleticism provided a medium in which his ideas could take on a measure of public life.

Other academics demonstrated a similar rapport with public thinking about racial differences. The authors of a reaction time study published in 1933 wondered whether "the Negro might represent a more 'primitive,' less differentiated type of organization of behavior traits."[30] Gunnar Myrdal noted in 1944 that the stereotype most often applied to blacks was "a tendency to be aggressive," and he agreed that this claim, while exaggerated, was not entirely unfounded: "Both the lack of a strong cultural tradition and the caste-fostered trait of cynical bitterness combine to make the Negro less inhibited in a way which may be dangerous to his fellows." Many young blacks, in fact, reminded him of Bigger Thomas, the troubled hero of Richard Wright's novel *Native Son:* "They have a bearing of the whole body, a way of carrying their hats, a way of looking cheeky and talking coolly, and a general recklessness about their own and others' personal security and property, which gives one a feeling that carelessness, asociality, and fear have reached their zenith. In some cities they are known in the Negro community by the appropriate epithet 'cats.'"[31]

That someone as progressive as Myrdal had recourse to descriptions of body language, cheeky looks, and his own feelings about black recklessness shows how difficult it can be to distinguish between the language of racial defamation and unsparing portraits of black lives that have somehow gone out of control. It is in fact the difficulties involved in making this distinction that have haunted public discussions of black social "pathology," and it is easy enough to follow this conundrum in the social science literature. A decade after Myrdal's famous book and almost forty years before the police beating of Rodney King, the *American Journal of Sociology* was reporting a police commander's view that "as a group, Negroes are more pugnacious when they're arrested . . . Some of the Negro leaders know it, too, although some of them don't want to know."[32] But where did this "contentiousness and belligerency" come from? Was it due to diminished "emotional potential," as Abraham Kardiner claimed in his 1962 book *The Mark of Oppression,* or did it result from an understandable fear of white policemen?[33]

A constant theme running through a century's worth of white commentary on black behavior has been that this racial group lacks both self-control and the ability to defer gratification in pursuit of long-range goals, a deficiency that is associated with criminal behavior.[34] Social scientists have even offered experimental evidence (of dubious value) showing that blacks and whites prefer different sports activities, on the grounds that "reactive" black children are less inclined than white children to delay gratification on behalf of "self-paced" play.[35]

This sort of thinking has been influential enough to produce some strange bedfellows. When the black activist Ron Karenga describes "a high level of present time orientation"[36] as characteristic of young black males, he is seconded by the racial psychologist Michael Levin, a believer in black intellectual inferiority, who quotes black educators on the "high levels of energy, impulsive interrupting and loud talking"[37] that distinguish black children from their white peers. The crucial difference is that Karenga ascribes this behavior to societal factors, while Levin adheres to a biological interpretation of racial behavior that is indebted to the controversial Canadian psychologist J. Philippe Rushton, who regards "Mongoloids," "Caucasoids," and "Negroids" as different human subspecies.[38] For Levin it is axiomatic that "higher Negroid levels of [physiologically based] reactivity most simply explain black proneness to 'crimes of violence,'" and that "Negroid levels of aggression were also presumably adaptive in the environments in which Negroids evolved."[39]

The challenge here, beyond separating sense from nonsense, is to determine how ideas about blacks and self-control are created and disseminated both inside and outside the academy and how such ideas are kept alive by media interest in black athletes. While Levin remains a marginal figure both on and off campus in the public discussion of race, Rushton's work has been promoted by the authors of *The Bell Curve* to a readership of hundreds of thousands. But to what effect in the wider world in which racial stereotypes play a role in shaping the behavior of blacks and whites alike?

Hooton's merging of black muscularity and criminal temperament reappeared many years later in *Crime and Human Nature,* a major study published in 1985 by two prominent Harvard academics, the political scientist James Q. Wilson and the psychologist Richard J. Herrnstein. *Crime and Human Nature* caused a stir by arguing (unfashionably) that "constitutional factors" should be taken seriously as possible causes of criminal behavior, and the most conspicuous factor of all, represented by a term proposed by the Harvard psychologist William H. Sheldon, was "a mesomorphic build, toward heavy-boned muscularity." Having exhumed and partially rehabilitated both Lombroso and Hooton, the authors presented the following conclusion: "The general thrust of the evidence should be apparent. Wherever it has been examined, criminals on the average differ in physique from the population at large. They tend to be more mesomorphic (muscular) . . . Where it has been assessed, the 'masculine' configuration called andromorphy also characterizes the average criminal." Less clear, the authors said, is whether the greater mesomorphism of the young black male is related to the rate at which he commits crimes.[40]

This renovated version of the muscular black criminal did not enter public discourse as a theory of racial body types. Indeed, in *Crime and Human Nature* black mesomorphism is less an established fact than a haunting image left to echo through the corridors of our racial imagination. As the nation's leading criminologist, Wilson was primarily interested in deviant behavior, and in subsequent statements he has addressed several issues that become controversial when combined: genetically determined behavior, lack of self-control, and the black crime rate. "Unfortunately," he wrote in 1993, "since temperament is to a significant degree under genetic control, there is an elevated probability that difficult children will be born to incompetent parents." One group of incompetent parents was all too familiar: "Children of teenage black mothers are less able to control their impulses, have a lower tolerance for frustration, are more likely to be hyperactive, have more difficulty adapting to school, and, if boys, are more likely to be hostile, assertive, and willful than children of older mothers."[41] The underclass, he noted a year earlier, "is perceived to be a black phenomenon. So long as black men commit violent crimes at a rate that is six to eight times higher than the rate found among whites, that perception will persist."[42]

The biological dimension of Wilson's thinking about black delinquency was publicized by the conservative columnist George Will, whose rendering of Wilson's views brings us to the threshold of the sports world, where the sometimes violent behavior of athletic black males is constantly on display. Society's problem with male violence, Will wrote in 1991, is of hormonal origin in that it has "a biological basis in neurochemical stuff like testosterone. Socialization must contend against biology . . . Many male traits," he continued, "such as aggressiveness and hyperactivity, were useful many millennia ago when there were woolly mammoths to be hunted, or during the Thirty Years' War. But those traits are ruinous in today's cities. Aggression is no longer an adaptive trait in bureaucratized societies that require conformity to many norms, and technical competence more than boldness and physical prowess." This sort of prowess, Wilson had said, had become a way of life for a whole subpopulation of young black men. "We do know how to wage war on idleness, idleness that is the breeding ground of selfishness and the arena for *pointless masculine display* [emphasis added]"[43] — a formula that sums up a widespread and resentful white attitude toward the demonstrative gestures and dancing routines that some professional black athletes have turned into a signature style. These exhibitionistic athletes dramatize in their domesticated but still unsettling way the warrior class decried by Wilson and Will.

Biological speculation along Darwinian lines achieved national notoriety in February 1992, when Dr. Frederick Goodwin, head of the Alcoholism, Drug Abuse, and Mental Health Administration, delivered some remarks on behalf of the Violence Initiative then under development by the Department of Health and Human Services. This program aimed at studying male violence as a public health problem that could be remedied by means of drugs or other therapeutic interventions. Speculating out loud about the origins of inner-city violence, Goodwin stepped into a time capsule and emerged in the guise of a Victorian ethnologist just back from a tour through the Heart of Darkness: "If you look, for example, at male monkeys, especially in the wild, roughly half of them survive to adulthood. The other half die by violence. That is the natural way of it for males, to knock each other off, and, in fact, there are some interesting evolutionary implications of that because the same hyperaggressive monkeys who kill each other are also hypersexual, so they copulate more and therefore they reproduce more to offset the fact that half of them are dying." Goodwin then argued that the black ghetto represented an untimely reversion back to a primitive and chaotic state of nature: "Now, one could say that if some of the loss of social structure in this society, and particularly within high impact inner city areas, has removed some of the civilizing evolutionary things that we have built up and that maybe it isn't just a careless use of the word when people call certain areas of certain cities jungles, that we may have gone back to what might be more natural, without all of the social controls that we have imposed upon ourselves as a civilization over thousands of years in our own evolution."[44]

This was an extraordinary self-revelatory moment for the white policymaking community, which had been practicing the art of racial euphemism since Daniel Patrick Moynihan's identification of a black "tangle of pathology" had caused a public firestorm back in 1965. Following calls for his dismissal by the Congressional Black Caucus and other groups, Goodwin was reassigned by the Bush administration as director of the National Institute of Mental Health. The irony of the Violence Initiative scandal was that its chief sponsor was Dr. Louis Sullivan, an African-American physician who was at that time director of the Department of Health and Human Services. The rising rate of homicide among young black men, he said, required a medical approach to violence as a matter of public policy.

In fact, the sudden notoriety of Frederick Goodwin had the unfortunate effect of making African-American concern about black male behavior even less visible than it already was. White policy experts like James Q. Wilson were not the only people looking for noninflammatory terms to describe black children who were perceived to be more "restless" than their white peers. An article on black male academies published in the NAACP's *Crisis* only a few months after George Will's column also addressed the gender issue and racial differences in classroom behavior: "As originally set up, the male academies were to train teachers to understand how males interact using their motor skills development, which many behaviorists have established is different than female motor skills development." The black educator administering these academies in Detroit believed that "black males ought not be labeled as hyperactive when that activity is a part of their motor skills development, and in some cases their self-expression."[45]

Diagnosing black children as hyperactive has been a matter of concern to the African-American community since the early 1970s. The widespread use of stimulants such as Ritalin to treat this condition, also known as attention deficit hyperactivity disorder (ADHD), was and continues to be seen by some black observers as a white strategy to suppress the development of black children by pacifying them.[46] "Parents complain," *Destiny Magazine* noted in 1995, "that black children, because of their active behavioral patterns, are being unfairly labeled hyperactive."[47] Left unresolved were the origins of "active behavioral patterns," which are of concern to blacks and whites alike, and the consistent focus of this concern was the young and unruly black male, both in and out of the classroom. In 1994, for example, the white attorney for a Cincinnati school district dealing with racial disparities in discipline raised the possibility that "some black males are more physical," a formula that preserves with exquisite ambiguity traditional uncertainties about the biological and/or social origins of young and "restless" behavior.[48]

Hyperactivity has served as a kind of Rorschach test onto which observers have projected their biological or environmental interpretations of human behavior, and it was virtually inevitable that the hyperactive syndrome would eventually absorb the racial stereotype that euphemistically distinguishes between active black and more self-controlled white children. We should also keep in mind that the racial drama that is being played out in our public schools is actually less publicized than the better regulated and commercialized racial theater of professional and college sports.

Prominent people have regularly violated the taboo that proscribes the public discussion of blacks as biologically anomalous people. The psychologist Arthur Jensen, famed for his views on racial intelligence, has embraced both the Middle Passage and discredited breeding theories of black development. When his famous article appeared in the *Harvard Educational Review* in 1969, Jensen said that it was "likely, though speculative, of course, that Negroes brought here as slaves were selected for docility and strength rather than mental ability, and that through selective mating the mental qualities never had a chance to flourish."[49] In an article on "Crime and Race" published in 1989, the ultraconservative columnist Patrick Buchanan expressed his own visceral revulsion at black biology by calling black crime "the ugliest expression of racism in America," which "is, like sickle cell anemia, a ghetto sickness, a malady afflicting the black underclass, not a suburban phenomenon" — a rare instance of medical defamation in our racial discourse.[50] Senator Daniel Patrick Moynihan referred in 1994 to out-of-wedlock births among (presumably black) teenage mothers as the beginning of what biologists call speciation, showing once again that the most powerful figures in a modern society are quite capable of interpreting the black organism in the most naked Darwinian terms.[51]

Faced with the instinctive biological thinking of the American elite, African-American participants in the public debate about race have reacted warily to the trend to treat violence as a medical matter inherent in the ongoing federal Violence Initiative. The depth of this fear is evident in a comment by a prominent opponent of the initiative, the Howard University political scientist Ronald Walters. "There are types of research that shouldn't be done," he told an interviewer, "because the danger to society is so great. We are on the precipice of something very important and very dangerous."[52] This fear of racial science also underlies the angry resistance to research into racial athletic aptitudes.

# 16

# The Fear of Racial Biology

THE INVESTIGATION of racial athletic aptitude inspires fear in whites and blacks alike because it suggests other, more intimate racial differences pertaining to intellectual and emotional capacity. The anxiety level within both groups persists because scientists and the general public share the habit of concealing much of what they really think about racial anatomy and physiology, and this silence allows racial folklore and pseudo-science to flourish unchecked, satisfying the fantasy needs of both blacks and whites. A powerful and generally unspoken assumption is that human biologists are hiding a terrible truth about racial difference, and despite the official antiracist proclamations of modern science, there is a profound disinclination to believe that such research might confirm not only the diversity but also the unity of the human species.

White physiologists generally avoid this subject because an interest in racial differences is sometimes interpreted as the product of a racist mindset. The long history of amateurish and offensive pronouncements on this topic and the well-founded indignation they have often provoked are a disincentive to scientists whose curiosity may run in this direction. While black commentators emphasize the racist motives or reckless ignorance of white investigators, these accusations also serve to camouflage their own deep anxieties about what research into the intimate world of tissues and secretions might reveal about the meaning of racial traits that are supposedly only skin deep.

Another reason blacks feel threatened by racial biology is that African Americans have produced too few scientists to carry on the campaign against bioracial apartheid once waged by a handful of black researchers such as W. Montague Cobb. Confronting a white scientific establishment and its contending factions, which debate topics such

as racial intelligence and biomedical difference as though black researchers scarcely existed, blacks have good reason to feel that they are
at the mercy of investigations into human biology such as the Human
Genome Project, which proceed without any recognition of perceived
black interests. The humiliating legacy of white medical racism has only
intensified this feeling of vulnerability.

Eventually, however, every citizen of a modern, science-based society
must deal in one way or another with the accepted results of scientific
research, and a reckoning with the meaning of race on a molecular level
is one of the issues that will occupy a prominent position at the top of
this agenda over the next century.

An eloquent example of the raw fear that genetic research can inspire
is Ronald Walters's insistence that "there are types of research that
shouldn't be done." This demand to suppress scientific inquiry into
racial differences exposes a lack of faith in the species unity that anti-
racists claim to be defending and reveals the expectation of a disastrous outcome — scientific confirmation of black inferiority in relation
to white racial norms. The terrifying premise of this fear is the existence of a dirty little secret that will confirm centuries of folklore about
blacks. But the problem with suppressing public discussion of anatomical and physiological differences is that such evasiveness only encourages the public's ill-defined suspicions that profound differences are
being covered up. The disarming candor of Professor Walters's warning
thus raises a tantalizing question: What must not be known in order to
preserve the fully human status of black people? This is an important
question, and how we answer it will have a profound impact on the
theory and practice of human biology as a scientific endeavor.

The destructive effects of racism have made most scientists self-conscious about doing research on racial biology. One medical scientist,
stunned by her discovery that biomedical racial differences actually
existed, posed the following questions in 1986: "What are the biologic
or genetic differences among racial or ethnic groups? Should we shrink
from the possibility of a biologic/genetic influence?" Her response was
that "we need a research agenda that can go beyond what we now know
to address racial and ethnic differences. There is growing evidence of
different intrauterine growth patterns for blacks and whites. Do such
differences exist for other groups as well?"[1]

Six years later two physicians presented a detailed and critical response to the research agenda that was already under way. "Is racial
research in medicine racist?" they asked, pointing to three distinct issues associated with the investigation of racial difference: scientific accuracy, personal motive, and social repercussions. First, they argued

that "race as a research category seriously compromises the objectivity of scientific inquiry. When race is a study variable, the likelihood increases that the scientific merits of the investigation will suffer." This judgment is certainly borne out by the racially oriented medical research of the last hundred years, which has shown a pronounced tendency to find illusory differences more often than it has discovered real ones. Second, the authors alluded to a difference between warranted and unwarranted types of intellectual curiosity. "There may indeed be legitimate reasons for looking at arbitrary variables without any prior hypothesis," they wrote, "merely to identify areas where more intensive scrutiny is likely to be fruitful." The grudging tone of this carefully formulated concession to scientific ambition signals a wariness about their third concern, which is the foreseeable consequences of such research: "When authors study racial correlations in this manner, they need to take steps to avoid using medical research to support, condone, or justify racist attitudes in society."[2]

In this spirit of social responsibility, publications dealing with bioracial difference may include pledges of humanitarian concern. Racial labels are justified, two authors have written, "when they help us understand biological processes and thus serve human needs," since "populations may be characterized as much by differences in biochemistry, physiology, or pathology as by anatomical differences."[3] Such pledges, however, are not always made by racial egalitarians.[4]

At times, sheer intellectual exuberance can overpower politically correct inhibitions. "Although it is manifestly true that under the skin we are far more alike than we are different," writes Robert P. Heaney, M.D., "such ethnic differences as we can find are still irresistibly interesting because they provide chinks into which we can insert the pry bars of our science and attempt to lift the lid on nature's secrets."[5] In fact, medical interest in biological racial differences is an important restraint on the view propounded by many anthropologists that race is not a scientifically meaningful category. "Medical researchers, unlike the anthropologists, seem to have little question about the reality of racial categories," because they are useful for organizing data.[6] For this reason, the fact that it is impossible to define race in a wholly consistent way complicates but does not invalidate the biological idea of race. This conflict over the meaning of race is in part an ideological struggle, bound up with ideas about superiority and inferiority that belong to our colonial heritage. Consequently, some people believe that subverting the very idea of race can help alter the racial imbalance of power by eliminating racial categories and thus the idea of inferiority itself.

A militantly environmentalist approach to the health problems of

African Americans simply denies the existence of racial differences of genetic origin. "Despite overwhelming evidence to the contrary," two authors have asserted, "the theory that 'race' is primarily a biological category and that black-white differences in health are genetically determined continues to exert profound influence on both medical thinking and popular ideology." These authors correctly point out that observed racial differences in disease incidence can be illusory and that controls are not always chosen well enough to attribute observed differences reliably to an underlying genetic structure. The problem with their formulation is that it is too polemical, in that it categorically dismisses the role of genetic factors in physiological phenomena that may actually have a racial dimension. The political dogmatism and sheer obscurantism that drive this antigenetic argument are evident in the assertion that "the genetic model — newly dressed in the language of molecular genetics — continues to divert attention from the class origin of disease."[7] But it is intellectually dishonest to suggest that studying the racial dimension of disease forces us to make a choice between molecular genetics and social class analysis, since we need both to make sense of how medical disorders are distributed in a multiracial population. The more practical disadvantage of this strategy is that it rules out the production of certain kinds of scientific knowledge and complicates medical practice in potentially dangerous ways.

Learning how to distinguish between real and illusory biomedical racial differences has been an important task of twentieth-century medicine. On the one hand, medical racism has harmed or endangered many African-American patients by making false assumptions about racial differences. Even in recent years, physicians "have, for example, failed to order appropriate tests to detect macrosomia or intrauterine growth retardation because 'black women are less apt to know they are pregnant early in pregnancy than white women.'" Black heart attack patients have tended to receive less medical treatment than whites.[8]

But it can also be medically hazardous to assume that differences in racial physiology do not exist at all. Ethnic differences in drug metabolism suggest differences in receptor sensitivity that are relevant to appropriate dosing.[9] Racial differences in bone density "might mistakenly be thought to represent a disease process" if they are not recognized for what they are.[10] Separate hemoglobin norms for whites and blacks are widely accepted, if still controversial.[11] Glaucoma "is both more common and more aggressive in blacks . . . Responses to medical, laser, and surgical therapy also seem to be influenced by race,"[12] and it is generally assumed that special black vulnerability to glaucoma has a genetic basis.[13] It is clear that effective screening for this disease has to be race-conscious in order to be as effective as possible. Kidney transplants are race-sensitive to some degree, because "profound racial differences exist in antigen expression."[14] The antigenetic authors cited above ridicule the conclusion of a U.S. government report that blacks do not "exhibit the same immunologic reactions to cancerous processes."[15] But environmental factors alone cannot at this point explain why cancerous breast tumors grow faster in black women than in white women. "There is a difference and I don't think we can ignore it," according to Dr. Brenda K. Edwards, associate director of the surveillance program at the National Cancer Institute.[16] While the motive for ignoring such differences may well be justifiable anger over the inferior health care available to most African Americans, it is black patients who will eventually pay for the kind of political correctness that puts the study of racial physiology beyond the pale.

Even if all of these phenomena prove to be of genetic origin, this information presents no evident threat to race relations, because it does not appear to bear on fundamental human capacities. Because its specialized status permits it to be safely contained within the world of clinical medicine, it has not, in Marek Kohn's words, broken through "the firebreak between modern population genetics and political controversy."[17] What, then, is "dangerous" biomedical knowledge in a multiracial society, and how is it relevant to racial athletic aptitude?

To answer these questions we must recognize that black athletic achievement is still haunted by the Law of Compensation, which postulates an inverse relationship between mind and muscle, between athletic and intellectual development. In this sense, the idea of racial equality is being held hostage by a crude nineteenth-century formula. As the authors of *The Bell Curve* once gingerly observed, "It is impossible to speak straightforwardly about the dominance of many black athletes without being subject to accusations that one is being backhandedly anti-black."[18] In fact, neither man had a clue about how to make biological sense of what they were insinuating.[19] Yet this was less important than their canny sense that simply raising the issue of black athletic dominance might well intimidate those who deny the biological meaning of race.

Potentially dangerous knowledge about racial biology would have to activate latent cultural fantasies about "primitive" or "retarded" human development, and black athleticism has served throughout this century as the most dramatic vehicle in which such ideas can ride into public consciousness. Joe Louis, who was granted messianic status by his fellow blacks, was also depicted as a savage brute to his white audience. "It is a doubtful compliment to the Negro athlete," the popular columnist Westbrook Pegler wrote in 1936, to suggest "that he is still so close to the primitive that whenever he runs a foot-race in a formal meet between schools his civilization vanishes and he becomes again for the moment an African savage in breechcloth and nose ring legging it through the jungle."[20] A more recent observer has suggested that black athletic dominance "does perhaps support the impression that blacks are 'a breed' apart," an idea that "may be incorrect."[21] It is safe to assume that this highly educated (and scientifically naive) person's uncertainty about racial difference is shared by many of his less sophisticated fellow citizens.

While the overtly racist sportswriting of the 1930s is gone, the fact that racial athletic aptitude remains a delicate issue confirms that modern thinking is still haunted by evolutionary fantasies about black physicality or sensory capacities, which we imagine as adaptational changes to a physically challenging and "primitive" environment that was more rigorous than the environments encountered by other racial populations. One example of this imaginative approach to the natural selection of human beings involves observed racial differences in auditory acuity and hearing loss. There is some evidence that hearing sensitivity is slightly better and the rate of otosclerosis, a middle-ear hearing disorder, is dramatically lower among blacks than among whites.[22] It should be emphasized that this kind of work inhabits the classic terra infirma of racial physiology, where culture and biology commingle in confounding ways and causal relationships are difficult or impossible to verify. The sheer indeterminacy of such nature-nurture entanglements invites imaginative interpretations that inevitably reveal the culturally acquired assumptions of the observer.

This is evident in a reading of some auditory data that appeared in the *Eugenics Quarterly* in 1964. Black men, we are told, "show a rather marked superiority at the higher pitches and age levels. This superiority tends to increase with both ascending pitch and greater age."[23] The apparent black advantage at higher frequencies prompts this author to hypothesize that "Negroes have evolved in habitats where very faint sounds are more important to survival than in the white populations' habitats." He proceeds to elaborate this evolutionary scenario in the following terms:

Perhaps sounds such as the "swish" of grass under the stealthy feet of predators and human enemies, or of branches of trees and shrubs as light breezes blow or a stalking body passes by, are apt to produce sounds of higher tones. Such important sounds as the whispered voice, the flights of arrows, the "hiss" of certain snakes and insects are known to be of higher tones. These assumptions are supported by the marked superiority of several other mammals to man, especially at the highest tonal frequencies, such as dogs, cats, and rats.[24]

This portrait of the "Negro habitat," which is closer to a Tarzan film than to evolutionary thinking, embodies the author's deepest assumption about racial evolution: whites and blacks have diverged because they have faced different adaptational challenges; having left behind their "more primitive habitat" before blacks, whites have experienced a "relaxation" of evolutionary pressures such as the need to detect predators moving through tall grass.

The same logic can apply to other capacities, as when the same author theorizes about the alleged superiority of black draftees during World War II: "American Negroes must be slightly more highly selected, robust, healthy, etc., in general than their white compatriots simply in order to attain the ages of drafted men, because of the greater ardors of their environment."[25] While it is possible this superiority was real, it is equally important to examine the retrospective mental process that shapes such judgments. More specifically, which themes and concepts do we bring to the reconstruction of scenarios that feature the adaptational adventures of black and white human beings? And how can we athleticize evolutionary development in scientific terms so as to make black people into Darwin's authentic modern athletes?

The most dangerous strategy for establishing racial athletic superiority on a physiological basis would be to establish hormonal differences that translate into physical advantages (and associated intellectual disadvantages) for a racially specific population. As we have seen, the idea that racial characteristics are of hormonal origin was promoted by the prominent British anthropologist Arthur Keith early in this century, and speculation about race and hormones has shown up both inside and outside the medical literature ever since.[26] Keith argued that the "long, stork-like legs" of the Nilotic black African type resulted from an abeyance of glandular action. In a similar vein, he believed that the predominance of the pituitary had created the gorilla and an overactive thyroid would produce an orangutan. The same principle applied to the bone growth disorder known as acromegaly. "The rational interpretation of acromegaly," he wrote in 1919, "is that it is a pathological disorder of the mechanism of adaptational response" that reacts to "the burden thrown on the body" in the form of stress.[27] Contemplating the skulls of a Neanderthal and a modern acromegalic in a museum case, Keith concluded in 1911 that the pituitary disorder that had produced the latter must have produced the former as well: "When this gland becomes enlarged, as it occasionally does in the disease known as acromegaly, the Neanderthal characters are developed in the subjects of the disease in an exaggerated and bizarre form. The functions of the pituitary seem to afford a key to Neanderthal characteristics."[28] Racial physiology was now linked to a large-boned, heavily muscled human type, which would eventually take on the contours of the modern black male.

Although Keith's various inheritors do not remember him, they have nonetheless created an up-to-date version of his synthesis of racial traits and hormonal functioning. These investigators can be divided into purely clinical scientists and those who are promoting a particular theory of racial evolution. We might think of these groups as ideologically disinterested and ideologically motivated factions.

The first group has reported that black men have higher levels of both testosterone and human growth hormone than white men. This research was undertaken to help account for the fact that African-American men have the world's highest rate of prostate cancer, a rate that is almost double that of white American men.[29] A significant difference in testosterone levels could be athletically significant, in that testosterone is known to promote the growth of lean muscle mass, hence the illicit use by many athletes of the synthetic testosterone compounds known as anabolic-androgenic steroids. Growth hormone (GH) has similar effects: "The anabolic effects of GH increase both muscle mass and strength, which has a consequent effect on the skeleton."[30] In other words, a significant difference in growth hormone levels is interesting because of the established racial difference in bone density, which differential growth hormone levels may promote.[31] "American (and many African) blacks have larger, denser bones than do whites and Asians. Why? Blacks reach and maintain this difference despite lactase nonpersistence and a calcium intake that is substantially lower than that of whites, at least in the United States."[32] Denser bones are of potential importance to athletic performance because bone density may be positively correlated with muscle mass.[33] All in all, this highly suggestive information seems to indicate a black athletic advantage, although scientific confirmation remains tantalizingly vague.

The evolutionary implications of these data preoccupy the investigators, whose theoretical agenda goes well beyond clinical data and their bearing on black health. The hormonal theorists Ellis and Nyborg confirm the racial difference in testosterone levels and explore its implications in areas well outside their stated interest in the elevated rate of black prostate cancer. "With regard to racially linked genetic factors," they have written, "recent evidence has shown that black men exhibit biochemical responses to stress that are, on average, distinct from white men, i.e., black men produce higher beta-endorphin levels in response to stress." Responding in advance to "the concern that may be raised about the propriety of probing into this sensitive area of research," the authors noted that they "are aware that average racial/ethnic differences in testosterone levels may not only help to explain group variations in disease, but could also be relevant to group differences in behavior patterns, given that testosterone and its metabolites are neurologically very active."[34] The threat of prostate cancer to black men turns out to have been only a prologue to a more ambitious theory of hormonal effects and the racial character traits to which they supposedly contribute.

A hormonal theory linking black physical superiority and intellectual inferiority is presented in Nyborg's 1994 tract, *Hormones, Sex and Society*. His method is a case study in adapting racial biology to an antiracist climate of opinion that must be propitiated to some degree if such theorizing is to stand a chance of being taken seriously. In their testosterone paper, Nyborg and Ellis had sternly reminded readers that "scientists should be on guard against even the hint of any misuse of research findings in this area," and here too Nyborg asserts that "the many factors involved in hormone actions and the genetic diversity remind us to be cautious at all times."[35] These cautionary words are, however, a misleading prologue to a bold theory of hormonal (and, implicitly, racial) character, even if Nyborg treats race as an irritating distraction rather than as a topic for serious discussion. His aim is to establish a science of "physicology" that "redefines the study of culture/race/ethnicity." This research program "disarms the hotly debated racist controversy by boiling the matter down to a question of geo-climatically dictated differences in physico-chemistry and individual differences within borders," thereby "circumvent[ing] the danger of generalized racism sometimes associated with population statistics." In other words, according to Nyborg, the study of human adaptation to selective pressures "does not boil down to racism" because there is genetic variation in every racial population.[36]

This oblique approach to racial biology employs "androtypes" rather than racial ones, since Nyborg classifies males by testosterone level and females by estrogen level. While low-testosterone males "are predicted to show a higher level of brain-based, so-called intellectual activity," high-testosterone males are "physically more active" than their more cerebral friends and neighbors. Nyborg views the male organism in general as the product of a particularly harsh selective ordeal and as the eventual victim of its high-octane physiology, since the price of high testosterone is "a male metabolic burnout phenomenon" that produces aggressiveness, criminality, and a shorter lifespan.[37]

The core of Nyborg's ambitious and ominous project, however, is to resurrect the Law of Compensation in the form of a zero-sum physiological economy in which "the fast sex hormonal promotion of full sexual differentiation of the body is accompanied by fast maturation of the brain." And this model leads straight to the classic muscle/mind tradeoff Darwin presented in *The Descent of Man.* "The economy principle," says Nyborg, "implies that this [body-brain relationship] requires intrasystemic energy resources that detract from complete brain development (larger body, thicker bones, and relatively smaller head/brain)." A "much less sophisticated formula," he notes, is "the old saying: 'Too much muscles, too little brains.'"[38] Or, as his colleague Philippe Rushton once put it, less elegantly, "Even if you take something like athletic ability or sexuality — not to reinforce stereotypes or some such thing — but, you know, it's a trade-off: more brain or more penis. You can't have everything."[39] While both writers invoke the image of the "more physical" black male, the difference between Nyborg and Rushton is that the latter is far more candid about his belief in black intellectual inferiority and the athletic superiority that is its necessary complement. It does not require much imagination to see that this is *The Bell Curve* dressed up in hormonal costume, and that is why Nyborg launches a preemptive strike against the charge of racism at the outset.

This and other versions of the Law of Compensation are traditionally paired with ideas about precocious black mental development followed by early mental decline, and Nyborg offers a hormonal version of this old racial doctrine along with the tradeoff hypothesis. "There is some evidence," he writes, citing his own work, "to support the notion that early-maturing children enjoy a brief period of covariantly accelerated body, brain, and intellectual growth relative to late maturing children, but that after puberty they will be intellectually outperformed by late-maturing children."[40] In other words, high hormone levels close down the capacity to learn even as early as adolescence, an idea that has a long tradition in Western thinking about race. More than a century ago, the president of the Anthropological Society of London, James Hunt, offered essentially the same theory minus the hormonal window-dressing: "From all the evidence we have examined, we see no reason to believe that the pure Negro even advances further in intellect than an intelligent European boy of fourteen years of age . . . As he grows up, his intelligence seems to be dulled or diminished: he has no genius for discovery, and though apt in acquiring rudiments, he is incapable of generalising."[41]

A more scientific approach to black African precocity appeared in the scholarly literature during the 1950s, driven by reports of remarkable Ugandan infants whose physical development at two or three weeks "was equal to that of European children twice or three times that age. The results were not altogether unexpected, because clinical observation of African children in the first year of life had already shown that the accepted 'milestones' of development — raising the head, sitting, standing, walking, and so on — were passed at an earlier age than in European children."[42] Similar reports also found African-American and Jamaican black infants to be advanced in motor development.[43] Unlike Nyborg, however, these investigators did not couple precocious motor development with early mental decline. "Gross motor acceleration," two of these authors pointed out, "has often been one of the stereotypes attributed to the Negro child and the implication has been made in the literature as well as in the folklore that motor functioning among Negroes is advanced while the rest of mental development lags behind." What is more, their investigation suggested that "acceleration of gross motor development is not a 'racial' characteristic but is, to an extent, related to the way in which a child is cared for and handled" and thus "a function of socio-economic level."[44] But this rejection of nineteenth-century thinking has not been embraced by all twentieth-century investigators of racial difference.

The principal modernizer of nineteenth-century racial physiology is the Canadian psychologist J. Philippe Rushton, a professor at the University of Western Ontario, who has been buffeted by student demonstrations, vilified by colleagues, investigated by a provincial pornography and hate literature squad, reprimanded for conducting a survey of racial sex habits at a shopping mall, and told by the attorney general of Ontario that his theories are "loony" if not quite indictable.[45] Rushton's public notoriety, which has been almost entirely confined to Canada despite an appearance on the Geraldo Rivera show in February 1989, derives from a theory of racial variation that he presented at the annual meeting of the American Association for the Advancement of Science a month before he faced his American television audience.[46] Like Nyborg, Rushton claims to have left the race issue behind. "For scientific progress to be made," he has written, "it is necessary to rise above both 'racist' and 'antiracist' ideology," despite the fact that "the evolutionary psychology of race differences has become the most politically incorrect topic in the world today."[47]

Rushton's "life-history" theory regards the major races as separate human subspecies that have adapted to different kinds of selective pressures. His hierarchy makes "Mongoloids" the most intelligent and the least sexual and "Negroids" the least intelligent and the most sexual, while "Caucasoids" occupy the intermediate position. He too finds a "trade-off between brain size, speed of maturation, and reproductive potency" and believes in black physiological precocity, such as the "superior muscular strength and eye-hand coordination" of black babies. His magnum opus includes a brief, amateurish, and ineffectual argument on behalf of black athletic superiority as well as the claim that "reliable differences among the races in testosterone" may underlie many differences. And it is here that Rushton plays what he regards as the biggest genetic trump card of all, predicting that the Human Genome Project will tell us "more about ourselves than many of us are prepared to know"[48] — a claim that has become a mantra among those who believe in the sovereign power of the gene to determine human potential. "This knowledge," according to Rushton, "will include why ethnic and racial groups are disproportionately represented in various spheres of activity" — why whites and Asians become mathematicians and blacks monopolize the sprints and jumps.[49]

The career of Philippe Rushton can teach us a great deal about what Marek Kohn has called "the return of racial science" to public discussion and how unprepared modern societies are to deal with scientific racism. Rushton's tenured position and Guggenheim Fellowship (1988–89) show that it is still possible for an eccentric to publish his way into a secure academic niche despite a quirky obsession with race, private right-wing financing (from the eugenist Pioneer Fund), and articles in what a distinguished historian of science, Robert Proctor, has called "one of three of the most far-right and extremist journals now being published in the world" (Mankind Quarterly).[50] "How did Rushton's shoddy research slip through the mechanisms of academic self-governance in the first place?" asked one observer when the storm broke in early 1989.[51] Was it a coincidence that Rushton had never failed his annual performance review until 1990, the year after he became a pariah?[52]

In fact, Rushton's academic career should occasion less outrage than curiosity about the procedures by which science attempts to advance and regulate itself at the same time. When Rushton produced a paper in 1986 arguing that Hitler's army had fought effectively on account of its genetic purity, no audible alarm bells went off.[53] Indeed, academic freedom limits this sort of alarm as a matter of principle, and there have been few outright calls for Rushton's dismissal, the most inappropriate coming from the premier of Ontario, on the grounds that Rushton's research is "morally offensive to the way Ontario thinks."[54] The president of the University of Western Ontario, George Pedersen, properly defended Rushton's right to free speech. Even an outraged spokesman for the African Association of London (Ontario) said he did not expect Rushton to be fired.

What is vexing about the case is that unlike the vast majority of his fellow academics, Rushton has been permitted to operate for a long time on the fine line that separates sense from nonsense, thereby creating a dilemma for his colleagues. On the one hand, it is both impossible and self-defeating for the intellectual establishment to ban cutting-edge work because it may be wrong or offensive to some. Yet there is also a real need to prevent what Emeka Njoku of the African Association called "garbage research."[55] We might expect such distinctions to be made before academic tenure is granted and before bad science is given an opportunity to cause public scandal. "A strong case for investigating Rushton's competence as a scholar," four York University psychologists wrote later in 1989, "could be based on the numerous public claims by his peers that his work is incompetent, that he has misunderstood or misrepresented the studies he uses to support his theory, that he is highly selective in his use of evidence, largely ignoring counter-evidence, and that he violates the standards of scientific investigation. Academic freedom does not protect such incompetence." But by then it was too late, for Rushton had beaten the peer-review system by publishing often in obscure journals edited by sympathetic colleagues.[56]

Effective critiques of Rushton-style research examine either the quality of the methodology or the quality of the data. While numerous qualified critics have found Rushton's research strategies wanting, too little attention has been paid to his credulous approach to whatever is published in a wide array of scientific journals, and this is a problem to which he has even alluded himself.[57] With a charming fecklessness, he offered a scientist's true confession to Geraldo Rivera's audience. "I admit a lot of the data sets leave a lot to be desired," he said, "but they all converge in the same direction." Detecting such convergences is, in fact, the norm in science. Research disciplines such as meta-analysis aim at extracting signs of the truth from combinations of studies that cannot possibly be conclusive on an individual basis.[58] But such procedures require an objectivity that does not characterize Rushton's work, which relies instead on fitting data onto the procrustean bed of his racial theory. His response to criticism is to blame the timidity of less intrepid colleagues: "The quality of the science is poor, relatively speaking, because people are afraid to do this kind of research."[59]

It is a shame that Malcolm Browne, the *New York Times* science reporter who reviewed Rushton's book along with *The Bell Curve* for his newspaper, was not tuned in to *Geraldo* when Rushton made these candid remarks. "The writers of these works are recognized by colleagues as serious scholars," Browne assured the readers of America's most influential book review, oblivious (like most Americans) to anything that happens north of the border.[60] In fact, Rushton's book was eventually savaged in the professional journals.[61] And where had Browne confirmed Rushton's stature as a scientist? From a passage that appears toward the end of *The Bell Curve*, where the authors commend Rushton to their many readers with the almost comical note of solemnity that often appears in their book. "Rushton's work," they intone, "is not that of a crackpot or a bigot, as many of his critics are given to charging . . . He is not alone in seeking an evolutionary explanation of the observed differences among the races."[62] Conceptually unequipped for the task and intimidated by the erudition of *The Bell Curve*, Browne allowed Rushton's cockleshell to sail boldly forth in the wake of the grander vessel.

It was left to more expert reviewers to point out Rushton's indiscriminate approach to data about human biology and behavior. That approach "proceeds by skimming the surface of countless studies of grab groups, and what is to be found on that surface is not always cream," wrote *Nature*'s reviewer, who concluded that *Race, Evolution, and Behavior* is "an intellectual jumble sale posing as a haute couture collection" that "does a major disservice to the serious study of the biological basis of behaviour." *The Nation*'s reviewer, a biocultural anthropologist, was less self-restrained. "It is an index of how far right this country has gone in recent years," she wrote, "that the *New York Times*'s own reviewer gave this racist trash an accolade."[63]

Rushton's sociopolitical significance derives from his insertion of hormone-based evolutionary thinking into the neoeugenism of *The Bell Curve* and the neoconservative biocriminology that pays attention to black male muscularity and hormone levels. "One advantage of an evolutionary perspective," he wrote, "is the focus it brings to underlying physiology, including the endocrine system." Indeed, his insistence on "reliable differences among the races in testosterone" is fundamental to his theory of racial variation in behaviors such as sexual drive, aggression, and (by implication) athletic performance.[64]

But there is a great deal about testosterone levels and experimental procedure that Rushton has not reported. Neither of the two published studies on which he relies offers quality control data with regard to intra-assay variance (pipetting technique) or inter-assay variance (consistently produced samples); this is important because replicating values obtained in the laboratory can be problematic. Neither of these studies uses scientifically sampled data that represent the respective groups in an unbiased way. Rushton did not point out that the average testosterone levels found for blacks and whites in both studies fall well within the normal range.[65] Neither did he recognize the sheer complexity of hormonal physiology, including the fact that the effects of circulating testosterone are dependent upon the regulation of receptors in the target tissues.

Most important, Rushton's empowering of testosterone — like that of Ellis and Nyborg — has been naively reductionistic in its one-dimensional focus on quantities of circulating hormone and their presumed genetic basis. This trio of ideologically affined researchers has thus ignored three well-known nongenetic factors that can influence testosterone level, namely, diet, exercise, and emotional state. Different eating habits can affect testosterone levels, but Ellis and Nyborg do not mention this. Hormone levels are also affected by physical exercise, but these studies do not control for this factor. Testosterone levels are related to emotion in complex ways, but none of these authors confronts Theodore Kemper's thesis that "T level is under psychological and social control."[66] Intense emotions elevate testosterone levels through an adrenal effect, and this could be particularly relevant when taking blood samples from black subjects in a medical setting. Prestress arousal before getting stuck with a hypodermic needle could well be relatively higher in blacks because of their traditional estrangement from the white medical establishment.[67] "You may persuade a negro to take one hypodermic," an Arkansas physician wryly noted in 1926, "but you will hardly have an opportunity of giving the second one."[68]

Such racist humor from a doctor reminds us that medical data originate in a sociological as well as a physiological context. Indeed, Rushton's inability to take historical experience and the human factor into account recalls the lack of feeling that seems to afflict his American counterpart, Michael Levin. "I'm probably very deficient as a person," Levin told an interviewer in 1994, "in that I have no desire or need to be liked by anybody."[69] More important than this sort of misanthropy, however, is our modern tendency to endow sex hormones with a power they do not always possess.[70] Rushton is only one of countless people who are vulnerable to the idea of hyperpotent androgenic substances.[71] This mythic dimension of our engagement with sex hormones makes data like Rushton's socially powerful not because they are convincing but because they are attractive. The social agenda they serve became evident when in 1994 the arch-conservative *National Review* presented Rushton as a kind of misunderstood genius.[72]

Rushton's grasp of the factors involved in racial athletic aptitude is based on a single lay publication and is thus wholly inadequate. Nor do his own observations inspire confidence in how he uses what he thinks he knows, as when he refers to the small heads of "high-speed runners from, say, Kenya," a country that happens to be renowned for low-speed distance men.[73] But such foibles count less than the thematic use of the black athlete by racial theorists to demonstrate black mental inferiority. The presumed anatomical and physiological superiority of African and African-American athletes is now firmly established in right-wing doctrines of racial difference. Like Rushton, Dinesh D'Souza recites the contents of Amby Burfoot's *Runner's World* article "White Men Can't Run" in *The End of Racism* in order to raise the possibility of more significant intellectual and psychological differences that set the races apart.[74] The controversial molecular anthropologist Vincent Sarich is another racial thinker who regards black athleticism as prima facie evidence of biological racial difference.[75] "If you can believe that individuals of recent African ancestry are not genetically advantaged over those of European and Asian ancestry in certain athletic endeavours," he told his students at Berkeley, "then you could probably be led to believe just about anything." Here, as Marek Kohn points out, "the importance of sport as a precedent for race differences in other domains was explicit and provocative."[76] Charles Murray's interest in "the dominance of many black athletes" and Arthur Jensen's thoughts on the natural selection of African-American slaves have already been noted.

This interest in racial athletic aptitude is also related to biological thinking about black criminality, as in Rushton's appreciation of Wilson and Herrnstein's "magisterial" *Crime and Human Nature*.[77] Like the thinkers he has analyzed, even Kohn has ingested Burfoot's popular scientific potpourri and finds the evolutionary origin of athletic ability a "reasonable" hypothesis, even in the absence of more specific knowledge about plausible mechanisms. There is, he has noted, an "intuitive appeal" to the idea that lean Kenyans evolved over time to run long distances. This is an important observation about how almost all of us are taught to think about race. But Kohn is also aware that such intuitions can come at a high price to racial egalitarianism. "To make it possible to talk about physical differences without reiterating the old racist subtext," he wrote, "physiology needs to be uncoupled from psychology."[78] The fact that science cannot at present achieve this uncoupling means that Darwinian interpretations of racial athletic aptitude will affect thinking about racial intelligence into the foreseeable future.

The evolution of racial differences is a difficult topic, because we can only imagine most of what actually took place in the distant past. As Nyborg has conceded, "Evolutionary theory presents a serious problem in that we can only guess about the precise physico-chemical nature of the selective pressure of the past."[79] The study of athletic performance is especially appealing in this context, because it appears to circumvent the complications of cultural influences on performance. Running is presented by Burfoot as "the perfect laboratory" for measuring racial athletic aptitude because it seems to be a basic human behavior.[80] Sarich too has adopted this approach to argue for a Rushton-style model of racial evolution. It is mistaken, he has said, to assume that fundamental human abilities such as intelligence and bipedal locomotion, which includes athletic skills like running and jumping, were simply too important for all evolving human beings to differ by racial group. "One of the cleanest tests" of differential evolution, he wrote, "comes in the realm of athletic competition." Here he complicated matters by pointing to the black majority in the National Basketball Association to confirm the reality of racial difference, thereby overlooking the cultural dimension that leads the game to attract a disproportionately large and committed number of talented blacks.[78] He would have been more convincing reciting vertical jump or sprinting data, but that is not really the point. What Sarich and many others do not grasp is how many factors contribute to the origins of elite athletic performance and how impossible it is to control for many of the relevant variables in a scientifically convincing way.[81]

Sarich's problem is not that his theory is impossible but that he is too quick to accept athletic data as scientifically unambiguous. It does not occur to Rushton or Sarich to ask whether acculturation into a race-conscious society might predispose people to treat culturally race-loaded performances (such as running and jumping) as less complex than they actually are. Sarich has attempted to trump his opponents by noting that there has never been a white Michael Jordan, to which the molecular anthropologist Jonathan Marks has properly replied that "until quite recently there was no black Michael Jordan either."[82] Expressing no sense of athleticism's historical and cultural dimensions, Sarich has presented the extraordinary Jordan as a representative African American, unaware that like almost all whites, and in unwitting obedience to a long tradition, he perceives blacks as a superhomogenous population, because his culture has taught him to do so. Raised like other Americans on Tarzan movies and the NBA, Sarich has been well prepared to see black athleticism as a way to cut the Gordian knot of nature-nurture complexities. And for the racial inegalitarian, inequality in bipedal locomotion points directly to a more ominous disparity. "The extension to brain size," he has written, "is obvious."[83]

The evolutionary past is thus a fantasy space in which modern stereotypes can find a new primordial life. When the president of the American Anthropological Association saw the "centripetal movements" of an Ainu climbing a pole in 1904, his first thought was of "a tree-climbing ancestry."[84] Like the hormonally minded Arthur Keith, Rushton has referred to the extinct superathletes *Homo sapiens* left behind on the ash heap of natural history: "Neanderthals have dense skeletal bones and thick skulls with projecting brow ridges, and both sexes are extraordinarily muscular . . . Robust hind limbs and dense bone suggests [sic ] high levels of endurance and an adaptation to long hours of walking."[85] While Rushton is free to "suggest" which adaptations nature had in mind, the truth about Neanderthal athleticism is likely to remain a mystery. In the meantime, every night is amateur night at the Evolutionary Café when the crowd wants developmental stories to come true. There is "a classic biological theory," wrote Amby Burfoot, to the effect that "faster reflexes will tend to create stronger muscles, which will tend to create denser bones."[86] This is one way to make sense of muscular black sprinters, their impressive reaction times, and their somewhat denser bones, but the facts are that Burfoot's "classic theory" is a verbal confection and bone-muscle interaction remains poorly understood. All we know is that "blacks make denser bone to ensure that ordinary use produces less bending," but how and why this adaptation occurred is unknown.[87] The result of this and many other uncertainties is that "evolutionary history is a game everybody feels able to play."[88]

The appeal of this game is rooted in the fact that the evolutionary model appeals to us all on such a deep level that it is almost impregnable to critical thinking. More than a century after their publication, Darwin's classic works still set the terms for how we think about racial differences. It was unresolved doubts about the biological foundations of racial equality that made possible the great debate about race that began at the end of 1994. "In the world of ideas," Philippe Rushton wrote two years later, "*The Bell Curve* is a blockbuster with the capacity to alter the way we view the world — a fact not lost on its critics."[89] "In the public mind," one such critic remarked the same year, "it has not nearly been debunked."[90] Rushton's role in this project has been that of the intrepid scout who probes dangerous territory in advance of more respectable allies. (Charles Murray spent the last days of 1995 as one of twelve hundred guests at President Clinton's Renaissance Weekend in South Carolina.) The triumphant note we hear from Murray, Sarich, and Rushton derives from their faith in the Human Genome Project and what they expect it to reveal about the sources of human variation. These partisans of the racial right are anticipating indisputable confirmation of the traditional stereotypes. In the meantime, their ideological opponents cannot (and should not) match this premature confidence in what will be known years or decades into the future. Faced with an accelerating series of genetic discoveries about human traits and disorders, the antiracist left is on the defensive, and the bioracialists can smell their fear of what might be coming.

Marek Kohn's attempt to referee this contest demonstrates the power of the current biologizing trend. The primary message of his 1995 book *The Race Gallery* is that the postwar "UNESCO scheme of human diversity" is now on its last legs and that "it is important to examine the counter-possibility: that scientific anti-racism is a doctrine belonging to a historical phase which is now in its terminal stages." Scientific antiracism, he asserts, "must renew itself as society develops," but that will not be possible "if the scientific dimensions of race cannot be discussed frankly."[91] The almost tautological truth of this advice will not make it any more palatable to those of us who expected the comfortable old order to last forever. Kohn is right in asserting that a once "combative" antiracist science is now too often anodyne, predictable, and evasive. That many of the hostile responses to *The Bell Curve* have steered clear of human biology is more evidence of this disinclination to engage with the hard science wielded so clumsily by the racial right. Rushton's significance, Kohn points out, "lies in his ability to modernise nineteenth-century raciology, anthroporn and all, by weaving it into the discourse of contemporary evolutionary thinking." Rushton speaks in "the contemporary idiom — of sociobiology and economics entwined, of competition and hormones," and his ideas "may gradually percolate into the periphery of the public imagination by indirect routes."[92] If Kohn's prognosis is correct, and I believe it is, then the influence of the racial right will persist until evolutionary discourse about human development is superseded or changed in some fundamental way.

Antiracist science should respond in a more combative way by scrutinizing the claims of racialist science on the most detailed level, by forcing both lay and professional audiences to confront the ambiguous status of most laboratory-generated evidence about biomedical racial differences, and by focusing relentlessly on the social and historical factors that shape what we see as human biology, including the racial theater of sport. This strategy does not tolerate politically correct anti-racism that refuses on ethical grounds to examine peer-reviewed work on biomedical racial differences. Such evasiveness is self-defeating, because it only confers greater credibility on those who seize on biomedical evidence to advance racist agendas. Whenever the public "regime of truth" cannot tolerate findings reported in the refereed scientific literature, opportunistic pseudo-science will fill the vacuum.

So where, then, is the dangerous knowledge about racial biology that has made the body of the black athlete such an object of mystery? Having examined nerve fibers, muscle fibers, bone density, human growth hormone, the male sex hormone, and more, we have found that the data are only as dangerous as the evolutionary scenarios they can evoke, and that such scenarios originate less in our knowledge of human biology than in an imaginary realm that has been shaped by *National Geographic*, Tarzan films, and what we believe about the worst horrors of American slavery. This is not to say that bioracial differences of athletic significance do not exist. It is possible that there is a population of West African origin that is endowed with an unusual proportion of fast-twitch muscle fibers, and it is somewhat more likely that there are East Africans whose resistance to fatigue, for both genetic and cultural reasons, exceeds that of other racial groups.[93] But these hypotheses are not even close to scientific confirmation, and there is no scientifically justified reason to tie such plausible athletic traits to mental aptitudes, despite the promptings of the racist heritage that says we should. The fact that linking the physical and the mental in this way continues to inspire fear and anger simply demonstrates the unbroken power of the Law of Compensation at a time when it should have long since been repealed.

The persistence of this hierarchical model of human variation should prompt us to think about why we study the bodies of black people and how we imagine the physiological processes that occur inside them, since such investigations are always affected by ideas about race, whose influence can be difficult to detect. It is interesting, for example, to hear how white investigators discussed black African precocity after the initial excitement about superrobust Ugandan infants. "There seemed to be no doubt," the discoverers of these prodigies wrote in 1957, "that these African children had been born at a more advanced stage of development . . . than the normal European child," that "the distribution of muscle tone in the African child differed from that in the European."[94] Muscle tone implied athleticism, and it turned out that every one of these infants could run by the age of nineteen months.[95] Within a year, however, the aura of wonder around this physiological miracle was beginning to dissipate. An early worker in this field now suggested that observers of the Ugandan infants had misinterpreted their developmental level by exaggerating the significance of accelerated motor behavior, and he cautioned against "equating motor activity with intellectual potential." Another commentator agreed that "the method of presenting the data has exaggerated the extent of this so-called precocity of African children."[96] The possible athletic significance of this phenomenon appeared to be nullified by the fading of the reported precocity by the age of three.

What remained were questions about why Europeans had "read" these black babies as they did. Were they prompted by an unconscious wish to make amends for the traditional image of African retardation? Had racial myth prepared them to find physiological wonders in Africa? Here as elsewhere in the uncertain realm of racial biology, the attempt to produce reliable data became entangled in doubts about the reliability of the observers themselves. One result of this uncertainty was that yet another theory of black precocity and retardation was nipped in the bud.

The salt-retention theory of African-American hypertension offers a similar tale of belief in black hardiness. Many blacks and whites for whom the drama of natural selection exercises an irresistible appeal have been convinced by the idea that the terrible suffering of the Middle Passage somehow selected a physiological elite of salt-conserving slaves. Such dramatic reconstructions lead easily to seductive ideas about racial difference and the inflated vocabulary that can present them to good effect. Departing from the popular conception that "slavery represented a tragedy of unnatural selection on a gigantic scale," one physiologist has described a scenario involving "very recent selection for superefficient kidneys" as well as "superefficient sugar metabolism" among the "salt supersavers" who survived the ordeal.[97] Because this drama of "unnatural selection" was a good story, it found its way into many professional and popular publications. The seldom-noted problem with this theory was a willingness to believe that the black organism experienced what amounted to an improbably sudden transformation. "To attribute that magnitude of evolutionary change to a fairly brief period," one scientist argued, "is a kind of fantasy."[98] The

historian Philip D. Curtin agreed, noting that the salt-retention theory meant showing "that a physiologically traumatic experience lasting
less than a year could have genetic consequences more than two centuries later." "From the historical point of view," he concluded, "the
slavery hypothesis to explain African-American hypertension not only
lacks supporting evidence but also runs counter to the evidence we *do*
have."[99] Why, then, did this theory find such acceptance in the first
place?

One reason is that it is an evolutionary scenario that produces a black
elite, so that blacks can embrace racial biology rather than fear it. The
"superkidneys" of these black ancestors thus play a role in the survivalist myth that still captivates many African Americans. "Slavery," a
black physician told the African-American medical association in 1962,
"was the greatest biological experiment of all times. Slavery began with
the trip to America, during which all of the weak ones were killed or
thrown overboard or allowed to die. This was followed by the slave
block, further selection and sales as desirable animals. From this point
on, artificial mating occurred."[100] This fanciful recreation of the slaves'
ordeal offers their descendants a myth of eugenic progress rather than
the older myth of dysgenic inferiority, and the trials of black life can
make such eugenic fantasies an attractive option.

Today, however, black eugenics comes at a very high price, for it is the
black athlete, the product of another "unnatural selection" and the
most celebrated representative of black creativity, who carries the torch
of eugenic advancement for his people. His tragedy is that he can
neither advance nor lead his race in the modern world.

# Notes

*Introduction. Flying Air Jordan: The Power of Racial Images*

1. "The N.B.A. is visual. It is visceral. What happens to its players seems to deeply affect people. It triggers social debate." See Harvey Araton, "Stern Puts Out Fires and Keeps House in Order," *New York Times,* January 7, 1996.
2. The power of such images to shape the thinking of large numbers of people is impossible to calculate; for this reason alone, it is important to try not to overestimate or underestimate their influence. In his review of the Whitney Museum of American Art's exhibition titled "Black Male: Representations of Masculinity in Contemporary Art," the critic Adam Gopnik criticized what he regards as a fashionable inflation of the power of stereotypes: "The view that visual clichés shape beliefs is both too pessimistic, in that it supposed that people are helplessly imprisoned by received stereotypes, and too optimistic, in that it supposes that if you could change the images you could change the beliefs. In fact, visual clichés are probably the *weakest* link in the whole chain of racist thought." See Gopnik, "Black Studies," 139. While this is a useful observation, I am convinced that Gopnik's interest in deflating self-absorbed academic analyses of omnipotent "representations" leads him to underestimate the impact of some media images in an unrealistic way. Debunking the power of such images is particularly questionable when they are the aggressive male figures so common in violent television programming, action films, and certain sports, to which black youngsters become even more attached than their white counterparts. See, for example, Nightingale, *On the Edge,* 11, 29, 74, 138, 177.
3. Skip Myslenski, "Alaskan a Cool Court Pioneer," *Chicago Tribune,* December 3, 1994.
4. Gunnar Myrdal pointed out half a century ago that most people favor biological over environmental explanations for apparent differences in ability. "To conceive that apparent differences in capacities and aptitudes could be cultural in origin means a deferment of judgment that is foreign to popular thinking. It requires difficult and complicated thinking about a

multitude of mutually dependent variables, thinking which does not easily break into the lazy formalism of unintellectual people." See Myrdal, *An American Dilemma,* 98–99.

5. See, for example, White, "Of Mandingo," 70. A related fantasy of experimentation on black slaves appears in *Farewell Uncle Tom,* a film by Gualtiero Jacopetti and Franco Prosperi, the creators of *Mondo Cane* and *Women of the World,* a pair described by Pauline Kael as "perhaps the most devious and irresponsible filmmakers who have ever lived." *Farewell Uncle Tom* includes "a bizarrely fanciful sequence in which blacks in cages are used for mad scientific experiments." This is one spectacle among others (e.g., mass rape, blacks butchering whites) calculated to have a visceral appeal for modern audiences. See "Notes on Black Movies," *New Yorker,* December 2, 1972, 163, 164.

6. Ellison, "Twentieth-Century Fiction and the Black Mask of Humanity," in *Shadow and Act,* 28.

7. Quoted in Kane, "An Assessment of 'Black Is Best,'" 79. See also, "Slavery Was 'Great Biological Experiment,'" 58–59.

8. "The popular press and the television medium perpetuate these images with descriptions of African-American athletes as 'Aircraft Carriers' (Al McGuire), 'thoroughbreds' (Brent Musberger), 'superathletes' (Billy Packer) or kids 'who take off flying through the air à la Michael Jordan' (Dick Vitale)." See Harris, "The Image," 25. In 1983 the ABC-TV sports commentator Howard Cosell referred to a black football player as a "little monkey." In March 1996 the CBS-TV sports commentator Billy Packer called a black college basketball player a "tough monkey." See "Breaking the Cosell Rule," *Austin American-Statesman,* March 3, 1996.

9. Schoenfeld, "The Loneliness," 37.

10. "Out of Bounds," *Sports Illustrated,* July 25, 1994, 16. For a thoughtful commentary by a black sportswriter, see Bryan Burwell, "Blame Ignorance for Nicklaus' Comments," *USA Today,* August 11, 1994.

11. Nor is this syndrome confined to African Americans, since it affects the lives of black people in England and Canada as well. On blacks and athletics in England, see Cashmore, *Black Sportsmen;* on the black experience in Canada, see Solomon, *Black Resistance in High School,* 1–15, 63–77.

12. Loury, "The Impossible Dilemma," 22.

13. Writing in his memoir *Time Present, Time Past,* Senator Bill Bradley finds the prominence of black athletic stars to be a positive factor in American life.: "It introduces white people who may not know too many African-Americans to a range of individuals. It gets across pretty quickly that David Robinson and Dennis Rodman are very different. That projection forces us to go deeper." Quoted in Robert Lipsyte, "Bill Bradley: A Sense of Where He Is," *New York Times,* February 4, 1996.

14. Charles Barkley, a star player for the Phoenix Suns, is one of a tiny handful of American professional athletes who has an identifiable political identity. He is a doctrinaire conservative Republican who in December 1994 attended a birthday party for the formerly segregationist senator Strom Thurmond in the company of the ultraconservative Supreme Court justice

Clarence Thomas. See Tom Kertes, "Charles Barkley Talks about His Republicanism," *Village Voice,* December 27, 1994, 117–18. In 1995 there were some rumors that Barkley planned an eventual run for the governorship of Alabama or a seat in the U.S. House of Representatives. See "Paris Was Fine, Thanks, But It's Nice to Be Home," *New York Times,* June 4, 1995. Also in 1995 a white sportswriter offered a bitterly sarcastic portrait of Barkley, reporting that he had said he hated white people. "Defenders rush to Barkley, pointing out that he is married to a white woman. His best friend on the team, Danny Ainge, is white. Barkley plays golf with Dan Quayle, for crying out loud. How can he hate white people?" See Bernie Lincicome, "Barkley's Bark Shouldn't Pack So Much Bite," *Chicago Tribune,* February 15, 1995. J. C. Watts, another African-American athlete who is a Republican, was elected to the House from an Oklahoma district in November 1994. See "Two Former Football Players try to Master the Gingrich Game Plan," *New York Times,* January 28, 1995.

15. A headline describing Charles Barkley as "a frowning clown" appeared in the *Austin* [Texas] *American-Statesman* (no date); many articles about Dennis Rodman's eccentricities have appeared, only a few of which address his evident emotional problems, e.g., Bryan Burwell, "Rodman Not Talking Trash; He's Crying for Professional Help," *USA Today,* May 4, 1994; on Alonzo Mourning, see "Angry Hornet Kind and Caring Off Court," *Chicago Tribune,* November 4, 1994; the Shawn Kemp ad appeared in *Sports Illustrated,* October 16, 1995; the Greg Lloyd ad appeared in *Sports Illustrated,* January 8, 1996. On the "behavioral codes" that mandate "managing feelings" among inner-city males, see Nightingale, *On the Edge,* 43, 46, 49.

16. Michele Wallace, "When Black Feminism Faces the Music, and the Music Is Rap," *New York Times,* July 29, 1990.

17. Quoted in Nightingale, *On the Edge,* 182.

18. Amy Linden, "The Grand Old Men of Rap Strike Back," *New York Times,* June 23, 1993.

19. So testified Joe Stuessy, Ph.D., director of the division of music at the University of Texas at San Antonio. See "Expert Links Rap, Murder of Trooper," *Austin American-Statesman,* June 30, 1993.

20. "So Little Known to Be So Good," *New York Times,* October 23, 1994.

21. "Rap, R&B Stars Work to Look as Hot as They Sound," *USA Today,* January 6, 1994.

22. "Fresh Air," National Public Radio, February 8, 1996.

23. Lynn Hirschberg, "Does a Sugar Bear Bite?" *New York Times Magazine,* January 14, 1995.

24. The former coach (and later president) of the Utah Jazz of the NBA, Frank Layden, has ascribed the alleged misbehavior of NBA players to the promotion of the "bad boy" image of the Detroit Pistons during the early 1990s. See Ira Berkow, "New Barbarians Are Really Old Hat," *New York Times,* January 31, 1995.

25. See, for example, "Milwaukee Plan Would Ban Jail Weight Lifting," *Chicago Tribune,* March 24, 1994; "Building a Better Thug?" *Time,* April 11, 1994, 47.

26. "Image-Making Strategy in the Rodney King Case," *New York Times,* December 25, 1992.
27. "L.A. Officer Has Jurors on Edge of Seats," *USA Today,* March 24, 1993, 3A.
28. The phrase "an undertone of violence" was used by Charles Grantham, the black director of the NBA Players Association, who agreed that in the late 1970s the image of the NBA could be summed up in the phrase "blacks on drugs." See Harvey Araton, "Knicks Trade Talk Is Centering on Guns," *New York Times,* March 3, 1994. It has been reported that the commissioner of the NBA, David Stern, has expressed private concern about violence and "trash talking" among players in his overwhelmingly black league. See "Chuck and Coach K," *Sports Illustrated,* June 6, 1994, 15.
29. "It is this bogus, overly macho, preening, smackin' brand of basketball that has turned an original art form [trash talking] into a distorted counterfeit." See Burwell, "Rodman Not Talking Trash."

    A form of insanity is spreading through the NBA like a virus, threatening to infect every team in the league. Alarmingly, its carriers, pouting prima donnas who commit the most outrageous acts of rebellion, include some of the league's younger stars. There is a new outbreak nearly every week, with yet another player skipping practice, refusing his coach's orders to go into a game, demanding a trade or finding some new and creative way to act unprofessionally. Fines are levied, suspensions imposed, but such measures are nothing in the face of the epidemic. The lunacy is contagious. Madness reigns.

    See Phil Taylor, "Bad Actors," *Sports Illustrated,* January 30, 1995. A white sportswriter commented, "Root for [coach Don Nelson] not to fall to the monsters of greed, immaturity and selfishness supposedly threatening the tranquility we've known as the Fan-tastic game, the NBA." See Sam Smith, "Classy Nelson Feeling Threat of Brat Plague," *Chicago Tribune,* January 30, 1995.
30. One white sportswriter has commented on the predicament of the white NBA coach as follows:

    It's pretty obvious that coaching anywhere in the NBA these days is something akin to being asked to host the Academy Awards. There just aren't many people on the planet who can handle it. It's the kind of job in which you learn as you go and you get better if you can stick around long enough. In [P. J.] Carlesimo's case, he's been slow to grasp the rhythms of the pro game and even slower to understand the bewildering mentality of today's players.

    See Dwight Jaynes, "Firing Carlesimo Is Not the Solution to Blazers' Problems," *Oregonian,* March 1, 1996.
31. The fundamentalist Christian activist Pat Robertson uses the domesticated black athlete — in this case a professional basketball player — as a positive symbolic figure in his apocalyptic novel *The End of the Age.* The author's racial fears are embodied in the black counterpoint to the athlete, a militant black feminist U.S. attorney general. See Christopher Buckley, "Apocalypse Soon," *New York Times Book Review,* February 11, 1996, 8.

32. The negative stereotype of young African-American men has taken on the character of a universal belief that is so pervasive that it can provoke despair in those who would arrest its further development. The black conservative Glenn Loury, to take one of many commentators, has written that black elites "must counter the demonization of young black men in which the majority culture is now feverishly engaged . . . White Americans are, to put it bluntly, frightened by and disgusted with the violent criminal behavior that, with reason, they associate with inner-city black youths. Their fear and disgust have bred contempt; and that contempt in turn produced a truly remarkable publicly expressed disrespect and disdain for blacks." See Loury, "The Impossible Dilemma," 22.

33. "The National Opinion Research Center released a survey on 'Ethnic Images' in 1990, which revealed that over 56 percent of whites thought blacks to be 'violence-prone.'" See Nightingale, *On the Edge,* 24. According to another survey, 24 percent of white American college students, 33 percent at the larger univieristies, are "physically afraid of blacks." See *U.S. News & World Report,* April 19, 1993, 53. The black giant/white child juxtaposition can also be inverted. The cover of the February 1996 issue of *Sports Illustrated for Kids* shows a delighted black boy on a ladder measuring the height of the white giant Gheorghe Muresan, the seven-foot-seven center of the Washington Bullets.

34. For an example of the celebration of Mo Vaughn as a racial reconciler, see Gerry Callahan, "Sox Appeal," *Sports Illustrated,* October 2, 1995, 43–48. Vaughn appears on the cover of this issue.

35. Southern whites, Ellison wrote, "protect themselves from their guilt in the Negro's condition and from their fear that their cooks might poison them, or that their nursemaids might strangle their infant charges, or that their field hands might do them violence, by attributing to them a superhuman capacity for love, kindliness and forgiveness." See Ellison, "Richard Wright's Blues," in *Shadow and Act,* 92.

36. According to Harry Edwards, many whites "felt for years that the professional black athlete was actually genetically predisposed to be *nonviolent.*" See *The Revolt of the Black Athlete,* 26. This observation is related to the now striking fact that in 1918 the distinguished sociologist Robert E. Park referred to the African-American population as "the lady among the races." See Frederickson, *The Black Image in the White Mind,* 327.

37. See, for example, the color photograph that appears on the dust jacket of the book Jordan published in 1995. See also the color photograph of Herschel Walker, his bare chest only partly covered by a football, that appears in Allen Barra, "Football's Finest Failure," *New York Times Magazine,* September 24, 1995, 61.

38. See, for example, Michael Farber, "Blue Plate Special," *Sports Illustrated,* April 25, 1994; Steve Rushin, "Big," *Sports Illustrated,* September 4, 1995; "Big Daddy," *Sports Illustrated,* April 25, 1994; Leigh Montville, "The Way He Was," *Sports Illustrated,* June 20, 1994. The same interest in the overeating black athlete can be found in newspaper sports coverage; see, for exam-

ple, "Newton's Law: Eat and Grow to All-Pro," *New York Times,* January 28, 1993; "Keeping Score, One Pound at a Time," *New York Times,* November 17, 1994; "In Round 2 of Life-as-Champion," *New York Times,* May 24, 1995.

39. Montville, "The Way He Was."

40. The media images I speak of, remote from urban fact, have been teaching mass audiences everywhere that race differences belong to the past, that inequalities of power and status and means have disappeared, that at work and play blacks are as likely as whites to be found at the top as at the bottom, and that the agency responsible for the creation of the near-universal black-white sameness — the only agency capable of producing progress — is that of friendship.

See Benjamin DeMott, "Sure, We're All Just One Big Happy Family," *New York Times,* January 7, 1996.

41. Ibid.

42. Walter Goodman, "Missing Middle-Class Black in TV News," *New York Times,* May 22, 1990.

43. At the same time, it is not always clear who the black middle class will label as "criminals." Some black professionals identified profoundly with their "underclass" brethren who participated in the 1992 Los Angeles riots that followed the acquittal of four police officers who beat Rodney King. See "Middle Class But Not Feeling Equal, Blacks reflect on Los Angeles Strife," *New York Times,* May 4, 1993.

44. Cripps, "The Noble Black Savage," 687.

45. The continuing denial of black complexity may even affect critical assessments of black artists. When the African-American pianist Andre Watts performed Beethoven's Emperor Concerto at Avery Fisher Hall in 1995, one critic, in a review titled "A Beethoven Who's Mostly Muscular," called Watts's version "typically athletic," cautioning the artist that "athleticism merely begins to touch this work's possibilities." See James R. Oestreich, *New York Times,* August 5, 1995. This fusion of athleticism and art in the mind of a white critic shows once again how an omnipresent sense of black athleticism can subvert the African-American struggle for cultural as well as civic responsibility. Nor is reading blackness through the body confined to whites; Ralph Ellison integrated athleticism into black music when he described jazz as "an orgiastic art which demands great physical stamina of its practitioners." See Ellison, "The Charlie Christian Story," In *Shadow and Act,* 233.

46. I am indebted to Yevonne Smith of Michigan State University for bringing this parental resistance to the sports fixation to my attention.

47. Quoted in Grier and Cobbs, *Black Rage,* 71.

## 1. The African-American Sports Fixation

1. Murray and Herrnstein, "Race, Genes and I.Q.," 36, 37.

2. Ramos, "Base Data," 10.

3. See, for example, Fordham and Ogbu, "Black Students' School Success," and Kunjufu, *To Be Popular.* See also Solomon, *Black Resistance in High School:*

> Embracing the school curriculum and such attendant activities as speaking standard English, spending a lot of time in the library, working hard to get good grades, and being on time were perceived as "acting white." Here again, black students who engaged in academic pursuits were labeled "brainiacs" and were alienated, ostracized, or even physically assaulted by militant blacks. In their effort to develop, express, and maintain a black cultural identity, students engaged in a number of practices that were often in conflict with school norms. They were opposed to, and actively resisted, for themselves and their black peers, any behaviors they perceived as "acting white" (4).

See also Bissinger, "When Whites Flee": "These black [honors] students also talk about the way other black students often treat them, about how they are accused of being "nerds" and "sellouts" because they are on the honors track. "Why are you in a class with all the white kids?" they are asked. "Why are you using a white man's book?" (53).

4. Quoted in William Oscar Johnson, "How Far Have We Come?," 40.

5. Glenn Loury, "A Political Act," *New Republic,* October 31, 1994, 13.

6. Quoted in "A Lot of Things Seem to Be Better, But . . ," *Sports Illustrated,* August 5, 1991, 52.

7. Cashmore, *Making Sense of Sport,* 90.

8. See Tim King, "See the Dream, Face the Reality," *Chicago Tribune,* November 2, 1994.

9. Myrdal, *An American Dilemma,* 759, 758.

10. See Patrick B. Miller, "To 'Bring the Race Along," 114, 115.

11. The small number of African-American astronauts trained by NASA have been conspicuous by their absence from the public sphere, apart from occasional appearances in black magazines such as *Ebony* and *Jet,* and none has played the role of "race hero." "When the space program's token Negro astronaut was chosen," Nathan Hare wrote in 1965, "he hastened to protest that he had not been selected as a Negro but as an individual." See *Black Anglo-Saxons,* 84.

12. Walter Goodman, "Missing Middle-Class Black in TV News," *New York Times,* May 22, 1990.

13. Quoted in Judith Wilson, "Growing Up 'White'," 34.

14. See, for example, "Blacks vs. Shaft," *Newsweek,* August 28, 1972, 88; "Criticism Mounts Over 'Super Fly,'" *Jet,* September 28, 1972, 55; "How 'Super Fly' Film Is Changing Behavior of Blacks," *Jet,* December 28, 1972, 54–58; Poussaint, "Cheap Thrills," 22, 26, 27, 30, 31, 98; Hairston, "The Black Film," 218–22.

15. "Making the Grade — and More," *Chicago Tribune,* October 30, 1994.

16. Garibaldi, "Educating and Motivating African American Males," 7.

17. Fordham and Ogbu, "Black Students' School Success," 203.

18. Quoted in "Black Men Must Organize" [Interview with Dr. Alvin F. Poussaint], *The Black Scholar* (May/June 1987): 15, 13.

19. West, *Race Matters,* 129.
20. Lawson, "Physical Education and Sport," 194–95.
21. Staples, "Black Male Genocide," 7.
22. Quoted in Philip Hersh, "'Extraordinary Genius' Commands Our Love," *Chicago Tribune,* March 24, 1995.
23. Quoted in William R. Rhoden, "Recruiting Blacks for Administrations," *New York Times,* January 11, 1995.
24. Peoples, "Finishing the Course," 44.
25. Quoted in Ira Berkow, "Jesse Jackson Looking for the Light in a Sports World," *New York Times,* April 14, 1993.
26. See Patrick B. Miller, "To 'Bring the Race Along,'" 111–16.
27. Reed, "Airing Dirty Laundry," in *Airing Dirty Laundry*, 3.
28. Murray and Herrnstein, "Race, Genes and I.Q.," 36.
29. On the debilitated state of the Negro at the turn of the century, see Hoffman, *Race Traits and Tendencies;* for a critique of Hoffman, see Kelly Miller, "A Review," 3–36.
30. Du Bois, "The Problem of Amusement" [1897], in *On Sociology,* 236.
31. *Indianapolis Freeman,* March 2, 1901, 7.
32. G. F. Proctor, "Art and Intellect," *Chicago Defender,* April 3, 1915, 3.
33. *Chicago Defender,* November 15, 1915, 7.
34. Proctor, "Art and Intellect," 3.
35. *Indianapolis Freeman,* May 20, 1899, 3.
36. "In Pugilism the Black Man Is King," *Chicago Defender,* January 2, 1915, 7.
37. "Basketball," *Crusader Magazine* 1 (January 1919): 17.
38. This comment is taken from a letter William Pickens published in *Voice of the Negro* 2 (August 1905). See Patrick B. Miller, "To 'Bring the Race Along,'" 115, 116, 122, 123, 125, 128.
39. "Race Gleanings," *Indianapolis Freeman,* February 18, 1905.
40. "Says Jess Willard," *Chicago Defender,* June 19, 1915, 8.
41. "Can Willard Return the Pugilistic Scepter to the Caucasian Race?" *Chicago Defender,* April 3, 1915, 7.
42. Sammons, *Beyond the Ring,* 42.
43. Jenkins, "Salvation for the Fittest?," 50.
44. "Although competitive sport has met with upsets, yet athletic training has received an impetus that has placed it in the front rank of educational activities. Schools and colleges have been persuaded to give definite credit for such work towards promotion and the equipment, facilities, and time for gymnastic and athletic work have been greatly increased." See Johnston and Henderson, "Debating and Athletics," 130.
45. Du Bois, *The Souls of Black Folk,* 6, 63.
46. See Levine, *Black Culture and Black Consciousness,* 420–40.
47. "John Henryism" has been defined as "an individual's self-perception that he can meet the demands of his environment through hard work and determination," a resolve that has "been associated with sympathetic nervous system overactivity." See James, Hartnett, and Kalsbeek, "John Henryism and Blood Pressure Differences," 263. For the story of an extraordinary

black cotton picker that "has the tang of the John Henry legend," see Johnson, *Growing Up in the Black Belt,* 190–92.

48. "The World's Fastest Mail Sorter," *Opportunity* 1 (January 1923): 19.
49. See Crason, "Army Alpha," 278–309.
50. See, for example, "Race and Mental Tests," *Opportunity* (March 1923): 22–28.
51. Woodson, *The Mis-Education of the Negro,* 12.
52. Du Bois, *The Souls of Black Folk,* 32–33, 36.
53. Woodson, *The Mis-Education of the Negro,* 14–15, 41ff.
54. The single mention of athleticism in Du Bois's book appears at the beginning, when he recalls of his boyhood days, "That sky was bluest when I could beat my [white] mates at examination-time, or beat them at a footrace, or even beat their stringy heads" (2). Today, black boys routinely think about beating white boys in footraces but rarely at examination time.
55. Woodson, *The Mis-Education of the Negro,* 126, 75.
56. Locke, "The New Negro," in Locke, ed., *The New Negro,* 3, 4, 10, 9.
57. G. David Houston, "Weaknesses of the Negro College," *The Crisis* 20 (July 1920): 122.
58. "Race and Mental Tests," *Opportunity,* 28.
59. Arthur P. Davis, "The Negro College Student," *The Crisis* (August 1930): 270; "Students Answer the Professor," *The Crisis* (October 1930): 336–37; Arthur P. Davis, "The Menace of 'Education,'" *The Crisis* (August 1931): 270.
60. Langston Hughes, "Cowards from the Colleges," *The Crisis* (August 1934): 226, 227, 228. On the lack of social activism among black athletes, see Spivey, "Big-Time Intercollegiate Sports," 116–25.
61. Karl E. Downs, "Timid Negro Students!" *The Crisis* (June 1936): 171; Arthur P. Davis, "The Negro Professor," *The Crisis* (April 1936): 103.
62. George S. Schuyler, "The Rise of the Black Internationale," *The Crisis* (August 1938): 257; T. S. Jackson, "Racial Inferiority Among Negro Children," *The Crisis* (August 1940): 241.
63. Ellison, "Richard Wright's Blues" [1945], in *Shadow and Act,* 88–89.
64. Ibid.
65. Martin D. Jenkins, "Gifted Negro Children," *The Crisis* (November 1936): 331; "Students Answer the Professor," 337.
66. W. Forrest Cozart, "Industrial Education," *Indianapolis Freeman,* April 29, 1905.
67. Ellison, "Richard Wright's Blues," 91, 85.
68. Herskovits, *Myth of the Negro Past,* 195, 196–97. The interpretation Herskovits rejects is worth quoting at length:

> Formerly whipping served both Whites and Negroes as an accepted form of discipline and as a convenient outlet for sadism. The grandparents of the present young colored parents were themselves whipped by their white masters. The majority of old Negroes, in contrasting the present with the past, bring up the point of corporal punishment, saying: "They can't whip us now like they used to." The slaves adopted whipping as the

approved way of correcting and punishing faults. Moreover, they had no means of retaliating for their own beatings, unless on their own children . . . Although whipping was a pattern taken over from the masters, and still survives among their descendants, today the failure of Negro parents to whip their children may be criticized as "aping the Whites." A woman of sixty made that accusation against a young mother of the upper class, who always tries to explain things to her children and never beats them at all. It is of course true that reluctance to whip children is a newer white pattern which is gradually displacing the old (196).

Herskovits is quoting from Hortense Powdermaker, *After Freedom* (New York, 1939).

69. Brown, "The Mask of Obedience," 1248.
70. Shelby Steele has also adopted this theory of intellectual underdevelopment: "In oppression we were punished for having initiative and thereby conditioned away from it." See *The Content of Our Character*, 170.
71. Grier and Cobbs, *Black Rage*, 31, 138, 139.
72. Robert L. Hampton and Richard J. Gelles, "A Profile of Violence Toward Black Children," in Hampton, ed., *Black Family Violence*, 237.
73. Nightingale, *On the Edge*, 80; see also 81, 90–95, 104, 105.
74. Williams, "Perceptions of the No-Pledge Policy," 16.
75. John Williams (Tennessee State University), as interviewed in "Lawsuit Shatters Code of Silence Over Hazing at Black Fraternities," *New York Times*, December 21, 1994.
76. Williams confirms the practice of branding. See "Perceptions of the No-Pledge Policy," 2.
77. Lawson, "Physical Education and Sport," 188.
78. See, for example, Steele, *The Content of Our Character*, 28, 50–51.
79. J. Griffith, "The Negro and His Instinct," *The Crusader* 2 (September 1919): 20, 18.
80. T. S. Jackson, "Racial Inferiority," 241.
81. Frazier, *Black Bourgeoisie*, 181.
82. Edwin B. Henderson, "The Season's Football," *The Crisis* 9 (February 1915).
83. Edwin B. Henderson, "The Season's Basket Ball," *The Crisis* 12 (June 1916): 66.
84. William I. (Bill) Gibson, "The Old Football Rulers Pass," *The Crisis* (December 1934): 363.
85. Villard, "The Negro in the Regular Army," 727.
86. Howard University *Hilltop*, April 29, 1924; cited in Patrick B. Miller, "To 'Bring the Race Along,'" 111.
87. Elmer A. Carter, "The Negro in College Athletics," *Opportunity* (July 1933): 208.
88. Henderson, "The Negro Athlete and Race Prejudice," 77.
89. Joseph D. Bibb, November 3, 1945; quoted in Tygiel, *Baseball's Great Experiment*, 75.
90. Henderson, "The Negro Athlete and Race Prejudice," 78, 79.

91. Johnston and Henderson, "Debating and Athletics," 129.
92. Garibaldi, "Educating and Motivating African American Males," 9.
93. "Joe Louis and Jesse Owens," *The Crisis* (August 1935): 241.

## 2. Jackie Robinson's Sad Song: The Resegregation of American Sport

1. Tygiel, *Baseball's Great Experiment,* 9.
2. Ibid., 31, 39, 208.
3. Ibid., 239.
4. Olsen, "The Cruel Deception," 15; "Pride and Prejudice," 25.
5. Olsen, "The Cruel Deception," 17; Tygiel, *Baseball's Great Experiment,* 276.
6. One sociologist offered the following view to *Sports Illustrated* in 1991:

   But there has been another, more subtle, reason for white America's new and unprecedented trust in and adoration of black athletes. "I do think there's been a kind of general, abstract improvement in race relations in this country, more of a willingness to recognize merit," says Marvin Bressler, chairman of the sociology department at Princeton. "A white guy sitting in a bar in Detroit acknowledges that [Michael] Jordan should make more money than [his white teammate] John Paxson, and commercial endorsements are seen as part of the rewards for athletic merit. Some sense of fairness exists that now includes black people and formerly didn't. But does that white guy on the stool necessarily regard the black man on the street as any less threatening? I don't think so."

   See Swift, "Reach Out and Touch Someone," 56.
7. Bayles, "Post-Racism," 26.
8. Quoted in Swift, "Reach Out and Touch Someone," 58.
9. Spurr, *The Rhetoric of Empire,* 33.
10. Two African-American sportswriters who do offer thoughtful social commentary on a regular basis are William C. Rhoden of the *New York Times* and Bryan Burwell of *USA Today.*
11. The NBA, unlike major league baseball and the National Football League, cooperated with *Sports Illustrated* in its 1991 opinion survey of black professional athletes.

    Major league baseball and the NFL cited policies of not distributing material on behalf of news organizations, but a spokesperson for a National League baseball team said that the commissioner's office felt the survey was "racially biased." And a source in the NFL office said the league wanted to hinder *SI*'s efforts "for obvious reasons. They're concerned about looking bad." As a result of these reactions, many of the forms were thrown out or returned unanswered.

    See William Oscar Johnson, "A Matter of Black and White," 45.
12. I used this term while discussing the Michael Jordan phenomenon in Hersh,

"'Extraordinary Genius,'" 3. It later appeared in Ron Rosenbaum, "The Revolt of the Basketball Liberals," *Esquire,* June 1995, 104.

13. Quoted in Swift, "Reach Out and Touch Someone," 56.
14. de Jonge, "Talking Trash," 38.
15. Quoted in *Sports Illustrated,* June 3, 1991.
16. Quoted in de Jonge, "Talking Trash," 38.
17. Paul Attanasio, quoted in Bayles, "The Problem with Post-Racism," 26.
18. Schoenfeld, "The Loneliness of Being White," 34. Schoenfeld continues:
    While interviewing more than three dozen N.B.A. players for this article — slightly more than half of whom are white — I encountered several who had been cautioned by their team officials against speaking too freely on the subject of race relations within the N.B.A. One league official, a vice president with almost two decades' experience, called me at home to dissuade me from writing the article. "This is scurrilous — the N.B.A. is colorblind," he said. "I just don't see what you're getting at."
19. "Stereotypes Pit Ability vs. Intellect," *USA Today,* December 16, 1991, 2A.
20. "City-Suburban Tensions in Ohio Show It's Not Just a Game," *New York Times,* March 17, 1996.
21. "Chuck and Coach K," *Sports Illustrated,* June 6, 1994, 15.
22. Harvey Araton, "The 12-Step Coach," *New York Times Magazine,* April 14, 1993.
23. "Electronics Replacing Coaches' Clipboards," *New York Times,* May 5, 1993.
24. Adas, *Machines,* 153.
25. Tyack, *The One Best System,* 223.
26. "Does Integration Work in the Armed Forces?" *U.S. News & World Report,* May 11, 1956, 54–56; quoted in Rackleff, "The Black Soldier," 188.
27. "N.B.A. Dilemma: Boys Will Be Bad," *New York Times,* April 11, 1993.
28. "Players' Silence Not Golden to NBA Officials," *Chicago Tribune,* May 15, 1995; "Players Get Stern Reminder," *Chicago Tribune,* May 17, 1995.
29. See Spurr, *The Rhetoric of Empire,* 6.
30. Sam Smith, "Angry Hornet Kind and Caring Off the Court," *Chicago Tribune,* November 4, 1994.
31. "Pippen Goes on Attack," *Chicago Tribune,* December 29, 1994.
32. Bernie Lincicome, "Barkley's Bark Shouldn't Pack So Much Bite," *Chicago Tribune,* February 15, 1995.
33. Rosenbaum, "The Revolt of the Basketball Liberals," 104.
34. *Austin American-Statesman,* February 15, 1994, C2.
35. Bryan Burwell, "Rodman Not Talking Trash; He's Crying for Professional Help," *USA Today,* May 4, 1994.
36. Sam Smith, "NBA: Nurturing Bad Attitudes," *Chicago Tribune,* February 6, 1995.
37. "Pippen Goes on Attack."
38. Bob Verdi, "Fat Chance Krause Will Ever Change — Nor Should He," *Chicago Tribune,* February 14, 1995.
39. Ira Berkow, "'New Barbarians' Are Really Old Hat," *New York Times,* January 31, 1995. His sympathy with Johnson notwithstanding, Berkow

agreed with other sportwriters that what he called the "New Barbarians" were causing unwarranted trouble for the NBA:

> They are the handful-plus in the National Basketball Association who have created waves among management, made coaches nauseated, disgusted some old-timers — and even teammates — and given many fans a sour taste about the current state of the game. They whine about the coach, they throw tantrums as well as chairs, they are recalcitrant about practice. Among them are Derrick Coleman and Isaiah Rider and Scottie Pippen and Christian Laettner and Dennis Rodman and Chris Webber.

Laettner is the only white player mentioned. "The bad boys," said Phil Jackson, the head coach of the Chicago Bulls, "are [Charles] Barkley, Rodman, they're in the commercials. The marketplace likes them." See Sam Smith, "NBA: Nurturing Bad Attitudes."

40. Sam Smith, "Issel's Route: Depression to Decompression," *Chicago Tribune,* January 22, 1995.
41. Sam Smith, "Classy Nelson Feeling Threat of Brat Plague," *Chicago Tribune,* January 30, 1995.
42. Tom Friend, "Webber Rift Does in Warriors' Coach," *New York Times,* February 14, 1995.
43. See, for example, Terry Armour, "Foul Attitudes Becoming Mainstay of the NBA," *Chicago Tribune,* February 9, 1995; for earlier criticism of this kind, see Burwell, "Rodman Not Talking Trash."
44. Phil Taylor, "Bad Actors," *Sports Illustrated,* January 30, 1995, 19.
45. "Michael Delivers His Message," *Chicago Tribune,* March 21, 1995.
46. "Beauty of Basketball Lost in Flashiness, Says Wooden," *USA Today,* April 13, 1993, 12C.
47. "Black Men Must Organize," 13.
48. Glazer and Moynihan, *Beyond the Melting Pot,* 53; quoted in Kochman, *Black and White Styles,* 8.
49. Kochman, *Black and White Styles,* 19, 21; 24, 40; 108, 131, 125.
50. Myrdal, *An American Dilemma,* 960.
51. Grier and Cobbs, *Black Rage,* 126, 126–27.
52. Kochman, *Black and White Styles,* 130, 31, 143, 148, 150, 149.
53. "50 Years of Blacks in Baseball," *Ebony,* June 1995, 39. Jules Tygiel agrees that "black baseball became a more diverse and colorful game than the white variation." See *Baseball's Great Experiment,* 21.
54. Quoted in de Jonge, "Talking Trash," 38.
55. Layden is critical of the exhibitionistic black style and traces it back to the "Bad Boy" image of the Detroit Pistons of the late 1980s. If NBA teams dismissed or refused to sign the misbehaving players, he said in 1995, "I think the fans would understand." To this, Ira Berkow of the *New York Times* offered the following response: "I think Layden is right and he is wrong. He is right that such action is a way to root out basketball barbarians. He is wrong that fans would embrace it." See Berkow, "'New Barbarians.'"
56. See, for example, "Rutgers Chief Denies Intending to Link Heredity and Test Scores," *New York Times,* February 1, 1995; "Three Words Engulf

Rutgers's President," *New York Times,* February 6, 1995; Harvey Araton, "'They Wanted to Boycott,'" *New York Times,* February 9, 1995; "Protests Divide Rutgers Campus," *New York Times,* February 9, 1995; Bob Herbert, "Lawrence Must Go," *New York Times,* February 11, 1995; "A Campus Divided by Three Words," *Newsweek,* February 20, 1995, 51.

57. James Traub, "The Hearts and Minds of City College," *The New Yorker,* June 7, 1993, 43.

58. Quoted in *USA Today,* December 16, 1991.

59. Jason Whitlock, "Black People's Fear Derails Lick and MSU," *Ann Arbor News,* August 1, 1993, D1. The candidate in question was Dale Lick, president of Florida State University. On his controversial comments in 1989 while president of the University of Maine at Orono, see "Maine Official Is Criticized for Comment on Blacks in Sports," *New York Times,* April 1, 1989.

60. Ifetayo M. Lawson, "The Darkest Berries," *The Griot* [The Newspaper of African and African American Students at the University of Texas], 1 (Spring 1990): 3. For an extended explanation of the powers of melanin from a respectable publishing house, see Pasteur and Toldson, *Roots of Soul,* 30–37.

61. See Ortiz de Montellano, "Melanin, Afrocentricity, and Pseudoscience," 33–58. This essay is the definitive critique of melanin theory. The irony attending this pseudo-science is that melanin is a scientifically interesting compound. As one research team notes,

> the consistent appearance of melanin in living organisms at locations where energy conversion or charge transfer occurs (the skin, retina, midbrain, and inner ear) is of particular interest in view of the evidence for a role in such human disorders as parkinsonism, schizophrenia, and deafness. The role of melanin in these disorders may be in some way related to its ability to function as an electronic device.

See John McGinness, Peter Corry, and Peter Proctor, "Amorphous Semiconductor Switching in Melanins," *Science* 183 (March 1, 1974): 855. See also Peter Proctor, "The Role of Melanin in Neurological Disorders," *Pigment Cell* 3 (1976): 378–83. It is also possible that there is a relationship between melanin and race:

> Melanin binds calcium and releases magnesium. As an intracellular calcium buffering system melanin may control the intracellular and/or intercellular microenvironment. Furthermore, melanin/melanocytes are able to scavenge toxic free radicals. Therefore ethnic differences, as far as the amount of melanin is concerned, may play an important role in the etiology of diseases associated directly or indirectly with disturbance of calcium in the inner ear.

See Angela-Maria Meyer zum Gottesberge, "The Role of Melanocytes in the Pathophysiology of Experimental Hydrops," *Second International Symposium on Ménière's Disease* (1989): 348. It should be obvious that such hypotheses are wholly unsuited to arguments favoring racial superiority or inferiority. I wish to thank Dennis McFadden for bringing this literature to my attention.

62. McGurk, "Attitudes, Interests and IQ," 28–29.
63. "The idea that Negroes have natural rhythm was originally used by whites to depreciate any musical creativity observed among blacks. Today this stereotype is embraced by black people and elaborated in the creation of a singular music which the white cannot create and which he can neither play nor understand." See Grier and Cobbs, *Black Rage,* 126.
64. Bell, "The Sociological Contributions," 137.
65. Quoted in Kochman, *Black and White Styles,* 131.
66. Levin, "Race Differences," 203.
67. Murray and Herrnstein, "Race, Genes and I.Q.," 33, 36.
68. Ira Berkow, "The Coloring of Bird," *New York Times,* June 2, 1987.
69. Sam Smith, "NBA: Nurturing Bad Attitudes."
70. "It's a Dreary December for Cunningham," *New York Times,* December 15, 1994.
71. Skip Myslenski, "He's One Happy Camper," *Chicago Tribune,* April 21, 1995.
72. Rick Telander, "Headlong and Headstrong," *Sports Illustrated,* October 11, 1993, 44.
73. Olsen, "Pride and Prejudice," 27.
74. Wyatt-Brown, *Southern Honor,* 154.
75. Skip Myslenski, "Why Can't Johnny Shoot?" *Chicago Tribune,* March 6, 1995.
76. Sam Smith, "Fratello Puts Lid on Price — But May Pay One," *Chicago Tribune,* December 19, 1994.
77. Ira Berkow, "Stockton: Unrecognized, Unassuming, Unmatched," *New York Times,* January 23, 1995.
78. Schoenfeld, "The Loneliness of Being White," 37.
79. Bill Jauss, "Blue-Collar Blue Demon," *Chicago Tribune,* March 1, 1996.
80. George Willis, "Oklahoma Country Boy in National Spotlight," *New York Times,* March 22, 1995.
81. Skip Myslenski, "Kid from Gans Now the Man," *Chicago Tribune,* March 29, 1995.
82. Sam Smith, "Believe in Skiles — He Sure Does," *Chicago Tribune,* November 6, 1994.
83. de Jonge, "Talking Trash," 38.
84. "Dennis and the Five-Ring Circus," *Sports Illustrated,* March 18, 1996, 15.
85. "Stereotypes Pit Ability vs. Intellect," 2A.
86. Mark Fainaru, "Tower of Power," *Boston Globe,* July 27, 1994.
87. Jim Sleeper, *New Yorker,* January 25, 1993, 58.

### 3. Joe Louis Meets Albert Einstein: The Athleticizing of the Black Mind

1. "The Simpson Defense: Source of Black Pride," *New York Times,* March 6, 1995.
2. Henderson, "The Negro Athlete," 79.
3. Long, "Race and Mental Tests," 22.

4. Moses, *Black Messiahs*, 158.

5. "Joe Louis — Model," 113–14; reprinted in *The Crisis* 90 (April 1983): 22–23.

6. Goss, "Ali as Creative Black Man," 32.

7. A. R. Jensen, "Methodological and Statistical Techniques for the Chronometric Study of Mental Abilities," in C. R. Reynolds and V. L. Willson, eds., *Methodological and Statistical Advances in the Study of Individual Differences* (New York: Plenum, 1985), 55; cited in Kamin and Grant-Henry, "Reaction Time," 301.

8. Kamin and Grant-Henry, "Reaction Time," 301–2. For a more complete account of this episode and a detailed account of Jensen's affiliations with right-wing extremists, see Tucker, *Racial Research*, 239–64, 264–68. The racist psychologist Richard Lynn, cited as an authority by the authors of *The Bell Curve*, would later argue that while "Negroid children tend to have fast movement times," their "decision times" were slower than those of "Caucasoids and Mongoloids," thereby preserving the racist model that accentuates black physicality and white mental acuity. See Lynn, "Race Differences in Intelligence," 279.

9. Crouch, "The Electronic Guardian Angel," in *Notes of a Hanging Judge*, 36; "Jordan Once Again Looms in Chicago's Hoop Dreams," *New York Times*, March 11, 1995.

10. Moses, *Black Messiahs*, 159.

11. Miele, "For Whom the Bell Curves."

12. Madhere, "Models of Intelligence," 196–97, 198.

13. Mahiri, "Discourse in Sports," 310, 312.

14. Madhere, "Models of Intelligence," 197–98, 189, 199, 200; Mahiri, "Discourse in Sport," 309, 311.

15. Scales, "Alternatives to Standardized Tests," 100.

16. Berger, "'Black Learning Style.'"

17. Welsing, "The 'Conspiracy' to Make Blacks Inferior," 93.

18. Welsing, "Ball Games as Symbols," in *The Isis Papers*, 131–43.

19. In 1996 the International Narcotics Control Board, a United Nations agency based in Vienna, reported that between 3 and 5 percent of all schoolchildren in the United States were taking Ritalin (methylphenidate hydrochloride) for attention deficit disorder, and that 90 percent of the drug was being produced and consumed in the United States. See "Agency Sees Risk in Drug to Temper Child Behavior," *New York Times*, February 29, 1996. See also John Merrow, "Reading, Writing and Ritalin," *New York Times*, October 21, 1995. For critical African-American responses to the perceived targeting of black children for Ritalin therapy, see Lightfoot, "Hyperactivity in Children," 58–62; Banks, "Drugs, Hyperactivity, and Black Schoolchildren," 150–60; "Ritalin, Help or Harm?" *Destiny Magazine*, April 1995, 13. For noncritical African-American commentaries, see "Drugs for Learning?" *Essence*, March 1972, 18; "Your Child: Energetic or Hyperactive?" *Essence*, October 1978, 24.

20. See "Ritalin, Help or Harm?," 13. As William Banks comments, "Hyper-

kinesis is a specific biochemical condition which can be detected only through careful neurological and psychological examination." "To label children as medically hyperactive on the basis of culturally-biased criteria is unacceptable." See Banks, "Drugs, Hyperactivity, and Black Schoolchildren," 156, 157.

21. Levin, "Race Differences," 215n. Levin cites "The Culture Question," *New York Times Education Supplement* (1990): 22–25.

## 4. The Suppression of the Black Male Action Figure

1. Nerlich, *Ideology of Adventure,* xx, 5, 39.
2. Genovese, *Roll, Jordan, Roll,* 129.
3. Quoted in Bunch, "In Search of a Dream," 102.
4. John Wing, "The Negro Who Almost Conquered the World," *The Negro,* March 1945, 34.
5. "Black Pirates," 344.
6. "Negro Slavery at the South," 211.
7. Hooton, "Is the Negro Inferior?," 345.
8. Rogers, "The Negro Explorer," 7, 9, 8.
9. Carlisle, "Black Explorers of Africa," 210, 213.
10. Harmon, "Black Cowboys Are Real," 280.
11. White, "'It's Our Country, Too,'" 63, 61.
12. Peter Olsen, "Black Americans and the Sea," 220.
13. Kasbohm, "Tribute to Seafaring Blacks," 113.
14. McKay, "Once More the Germans," 324, 325.
15. Douglass, "Why Should a Colored Man Enlist?," 342.
16. Villard, "The Negro in the Regular Army," 721.
17. Motley, ed., *The Invisible Soldier,* 77.
18. Grant Reynolds, "What the Negro Soldier Thinks About This War," *The Crisis* (September 1944): 290.
19. Scott and Womack, *Double V,* 78.
20. Hunt, "The Negro as a Soldier," 40, 41, 54.
21. Ibid., 41, 43, 43.
22. Ibid., 43, 43.
23. Higginson, *Army Life,* 244–45, 250, 262.
24. Cartwright, "Caucasians and the Africans," 47, 51.
25. Reynolds, "What the Negro Soldier Thinks," 290.
26. Motley, *The Invisible Soldier,* 77.
27. Ottley, "Want Combat Duty," 10.
28. "Aviation," *Opportunity* 23 (January-March 1945): 35.
29. Fritzsche, *A Nation of Fliers,* 86, 89.
30. Scott and Womack, *Double V,* 152.
31. Connes, "Can a Black Man Fly?," 56.
32. Motley, *The Invisible Soldier,* 209.
33. Scott, "US Air Force Revises Policy," 835.

34. "No evidence was available to suggest that there was an increased elimination of cadets because of the sickling trait": see Findlay, Boulter, and MacGibbon, "A Note on Sickling and Flying." "There was no evidence that this trait interfered with their effectiveness as aviators"; see Sullivan, "Danger of Airplane Flight." "From these studies, we may conclude that, in general, the sickle cell trait is not a contraindication to high altitude flying": see Margolies, "Sickle Cell Anemia," 407. "Of the 154 veteran flying personnel from Tuskegee airmen (TA), 10 have been found to have the sickle cell trait (HbAS). They have flown in unpressurized aircraft without a threat to flying safety. One pilot flew 600 hours in combat": see Marchbanks, "Sickle Trait and the Black Airman," 1118.

35. Scott and Womack, *Double V,* 187.

36. T. S. Jackson, "Racial Inferiority Among Negro Children," *The Crisis* (August 1940): 241.

37. Scott and Womack, *Double V,* 69.

38. Motley, *The Invisible Soldier,* 246.

39. "First Black Airline Gets Off the Ground," *Ebony,* April 1976, 50.

40. Colonel Theodore Roosevelt, son of Teddy, said at the time that "Captain Lindbergh personifies the daring of youth. Daniel Boone, David Crocket [*sic*], and men of that type played a lone hand and made America. Lindbergh is their lineal descendant." See Ward, "Lindbergh's Flight," 9.

41. Bunch, "In Search of a Dream," 102.

42. Daniel, "Negro-White Differences," 413.

43. Scott and Womack, *Double V,* 71.

44. Vaughn, "Ronald Reagan," 5.

45. Bunch, "In Search of a Dream," 100.

46. "The Negro Pilot," *Opportunity* 18 (September 1940): 258.

47. Scott and Womack, *Double V,* 25–27, 61, 66; Locke, "Willa Brown-Chappell," 5–6.

48. Cripps and Culbert, "The Negro Soldier," 625, 627.

49. Michael Lind, "Brave New Right," *New Republic,* October 31, 1994, 24.

50. Myrdal, *An American Dilemma,* 106.

51. Sojka, "The Astronaut," 119, 121.


## 5. "Writin' Is Fightin'": Sport and the Black Intellectuals

1. The survey presented here focuses on African-American intellectuals who have established public profiles outside of academia. One scholar who has made notable contributions to the history of race and sport in the United States is Jeffrey T. Sammons, an American historian at New York University. See *Beyond the Ring* and "'Race' and Sport," 203–78. This extended review essay is an invaluable critical survey of both scholarly and more popular work in this area.

2. Edwards, "The Black Athletes," 45.

3. Quoted in Underwood, "On the Playground," 104.

4. Early, "The Black Intellectual and the Sport of Prizefighting," in *The Culture of Bruising*, 20.

5. This theme appears frequently in Frazier, *Black Bourgeoisie*, e.g., "The black bourgeoisie has lost much of its feeling of racial solidarity with the Negro masses" (108).

6. Ibid., 189.

7. George, *Elevating the Game*, 52, 240. For a review of George's book by Othello Harris, see *Sociology of Sport Journal* 12 (1995): 94–96.

8. Dyson, "Be Like Mike?," 64.

9. Early, "The Black Intellectual and the Sport of Prizefighting," 33, 13.

10. Wideman, *Fatheralong*, 106, 34, 15, 15. See also "My father's hands boxer quick" (57).

11. Quoted in "The Black Dominance," *Time*, May 9, 1977, 59.

12. Grier and Cobbs, *Black Rage*, 174.

13. Wideman, *Fatheralong*, 126.

14. Baraka, "LeRoi Jones Talking" [1964], in *Home*, 179–80.

15. Early, "The Case of LeRoi Jones/Amiri Baraka," in *Tuxedo Junction*, 200.

16. Baraka, "American Sexual Reference: Black Male" [1965], in *Home*, 216, 218.

17. Early, "The Case of LeRoi Jones," 202.

18. Baraka, "American Sexual Reference," 216; Baraka, "The Myth of a 'Negro Literature,'" in *Home*, 115.

19. Cleaver, *Soul on Ice*, 167, 169, 170, 175.

20. Ibid., 92, 93, 93.

21. Quoted in Early, "The Black Intellectual and the Sport of Prizefighting," 21.

22. "Indeed," wrote Gerald Early,

   Reed here sounds like a white writer of boxing, the very person he disdains, by expropriating the writer-as-boxer metaphor that white writers of boxing have found so attractive . . . This fantastic romanticizing of boxing, the strange metaphorical obsession expressed here, is the result of two common infantile imaginative impulses of bourgeois writers, especially some males. First, these writers feel inadequate about what they do for a living; it seems useless, indulgent, overly cerebral, elitist . . . Second, the writer thinks of boxing as conferring the gift of pure yet simplified competition upon the realization and function of his work. He is engaged and enraged in one fell swoop of undifferentiated passion.

   See "The Black Intellectual and the Sport of Prizefighting," 21–22.

23. Ibid., 24.

24. Baraka, "The Myth of a 'Negro Literature,'" 109–10.

25. Cleaver, *Soul on Ice*, 151.

26. Grier and Cobbs, *Black Rage*, 144, 148. These authors continue:

   Thus it would be a pity if black scholars were swept up in a tide of anti-intellectualism. It would be understandable, of course, since education has been yearned for by the masses and has proven a failure. We can understand their turning away as well as their mounting distrust of the complexities of modern affairs. Why shouldn't black masses look upon such complexities with a jaundiced eye? They have always meant exclusion. (152)

Indeed, "it is a greater source of wonder that black children choose to learn at all" (149).

27. Cleaver, *Soul on Ice,* 87, 89.

28. Ibid., 151, 152.

29. Reed, "Gwendolyn Brooks: Poet," and "The Fourth Ali: Boxer," in *Airing Dirty Laundry,* 106, 181.

30. Baker, *Blues, Ideology,* 4.

31. Reed, "Airing Dirty Laundry," "Beyond Los Angeles," "Bill Gunn: Director," "Reginald Lewis: Businessman," "Gwendolyn Brooks: Poet," in *Airing Dirty Laundry,* 7, 44, 116, 134, 106.

32. Reed, "Jess Mowry: Writer," in *Airing Dirty Laundry,* 164.

33. West, *Race Matters,* 121.

34. Ibid., 127, 26–27, 129.

35. Ibid., 119.

36. See Dyson, "Bum Rap," *New York Times,* February 3, 1994, and "Black or White? Labels Don't Always Fit," *New York Times,* February 13, 1994; see also "The Culture of Hip-Hop," in *Reflecting Black,* 3–15.

37. Dyson, "Be Like Mike?," 64, 64, 64, 69, 73.

38. Ibid., 64, 74, 67.

39. Ibid., 65, 73.

40. Early, "The Black Intellectual and the Sport of Prizefighting," 19.

41. Ibid., 12.

42. Ellison, "The Charlie Christian Story," in *Shadow and Act,* 233.

43. James Baldwin, "The Fight: Patterson vs. Liston," reprinted in Early, *Tuxedo Junction,* 327; Early, "The Black Intellectual and the Sport of Prizefighting," 13.

44. Crouch, "The Electronic Guardian Angel," in *Notes of a Hanging Judge,* 35.

45. Early, "The Grace of Slaughter: Joyce Carol Oates's *On Boxing,*" in *Tuxedo Junction,* 177.

46. Baker, *Blues, Ideology,* 5.

47. Crouch, *Notes of a Hanging Judge,* xv.

48. Steele, *The Content of Our Character,* 52, 62, 63. On black pride in athletic and dancing ability, see also Charles Johnson, "A Phenomenology," 609.

49. Patterson, "Rethinking Black History," 303.

50. Glenn Loury, "A Political Act," *New Republic,* October 31, 1994, 13.

51. Quoted in Spivey, "The Black Athlete," 125.

52. Lynda Richardson, "A Jazz Critic Stretches His Solos, Not Caring Who Winces in Pain," *New York Times,* August 29, 1993.

53. Calvin Sims, "Gangster Rappers: The Lives, The Lyrics," *New York Times,* November 28, 1993.

54. Paul Delaney, "Amos 'n Andy in Nikes," *New York Times,* October 11, 1993.

55. Arthur L. Cribbs Jr., "Gangsta Rappers Singing White Racists' Tune," *USA Today,* December 27, 1993, 9A.

56. It is worth noting that in another text Dyson does criticize rap's dependence on nitty-gritty realism: "While rappers like N.W.A. [Niggaz With Attitudes] perform an invaluable service by rapping in poignant and realistic terms about urban underclass existence, they must be challenged to expand their moral vocabulary and be more sophisticated in their understanding that description alone is insufficient to address the crises of black urban life." See "The Culture of Hip-Hop," 10–11.

57. Dyson, "Bum Rap."

58. Dyson, "The Culture of Hip-Hop," 15; "Sex, Race and Class," 171; "Rap Music and Black Culture," 17.

59. Dyson, "The Culture of Hip-Hop," 7, 10, 12.

60. The connection between music and the African-American search for respectability goes back at least as far as the turn of the century. "Coming to music," the *Negro Music Journal* editorialized in 1909, "we find in the Negro a being who has been formed in no less degree than other races. He is musical and has already proven his musical ability in the rich and original legacy of slave songs that he has given the world — I say the world because their messages have been carried to all parts of the earth." The editorialist proceeds to distinguish between these "noble slave songs" and "coon songs" as well as "ragtime," which is referred to as "this often low and degrading class of music." "I do not see," the writer continues, "why this music should be put upon the shoulders of the Negro solely, for it does not portray his nature, nor is its rhythm distinctly characteristic of our race." See *Negro Music Journal* 1 (March 1903): 137–38.

     Half a century later, the sociologist Nathan Hare pilloried this sort of self-consciousness in his mocking portrait of "the Black Anglo-Saxons": "Even in jazz, they soberly profess specialized tastes, claiming a disdain for 'that funky stuff' while professing a preference for [Dave] Brubeck or some other white jazzman." Or, "Working class Negroes developed America's primary contributions to music: jazz, blues and spirituals, which are loved and appreciated the world over. Until recently, both middle and lower class Black Anglo-Saxons looked with contempt on these musical forms." See *The Black Anglo-Saxons,* 45, 46.

61. Baraka, *Blues People,* 131.

62. Dyson, "The Culture of Hip-Hop," 9.

63. Cruse, *The Crisis of the Negro Intellectual,* 26.

64. Baraka, *Blues People,* 132.

65. Early, "American Prizefighter: Chris Mead's *Champion: Joe Louis, Black Hero in White America,*" in *Tuxedo Junction,* 179. In his review of Chris Mead's book, Ishmael Reed makes the following rather elliptical comment about Joe Louis and the black middle class: "Predictably, Mr. Mead dismisses criticism that Louis was not qualified to speak for 'Black America,' presumably because these criticisms were made by the black middle class, a class that comes in for considerable criticism from middle-class white and black writers." See "Champion," in *Writin' Is Fightin',* 109.

66. Early, "The Black Intellectual and the Sport of Prizefighting," 41, 42.

67. Bob Herbert, "Welcome Home, Convicted Molester," *New York Times,* June 10, 1995; Clarence Page, "What Kind of Hero?" *Chicago Tribune,* June 25, 1995; Jill Nelson, "Not Ready for Redemption," *New York Times,* June 17, 1995; Steve Rushin and Sonja Steptoe, "Second Chance," *Sports Illustrated,* July 3, 1995, 35.

68. Reed, "Mike Tyson and the White Hope Cult," in *Airing Dirty Laundry,* 71.

69. John Edgar Wideman, "Playing Dennis Rodman," *New Yorker,* April 29–May 6, 1996, 94, 95.

70. "Who Will Help the Black Man?" *New York Times Magazine,* December 4, 1994, 93.

71. Lee has adamantly denied that he bears any responsibility for the effects of promoting Air Jordan shoes to black youngsters as status symbols, which some children have killed to acquire: "The emphasis should not be on the sneakers or the Starter jackets. The emphasis should not be on the sheepskin coats or the gold chains. The emphasis should be on: What are the conditions among young black males that are making them put that much emphasis on material things?" See Breskin, "Spike Lee," 71. Lee's interest in deflating the myth of the black athlete apparently occurs in private and off-screen. At a visit to a Nike All-America basketball camp in 1994, he "tells the students a cold-blooded truth: they are being used and the one way to protect themselves is to know it. 'The only reason you are here is because you can make their schools win and they can make a lot of money,' Mr. Lee says of the coaches. 'This whole thing is about money.'" See Caryn James, "Athletes Who Dream the Dream but Face a Bleak Reality," *New York Times,* October 7, 1994. On Lee the Knicks fan, see Harvey Araton, "A Famously Unquiet Fan in the Knicks' Front Row," *New York Times,* January 19, 1995. On his five visits to Mike Tyson in prison, see Rushin and Steptoe, "Second Chance," 37.

72. Quoted in Michael Bérubé, "Public Academy," *New Yorker,* January 9, 1995, 73, 79.

73. "Lee cited a former Chicago Bull, Craig Hodges, outspoken on many race-related issues and who last spring was critical of his teammate (and Spike Lee pal) Michael Jordan for not being more socially involved. Hodges, a marginal player, was dropped by the Bulls after the playoffs and is mysteriously gone from the N.B.A., without so much as a tryout from another team." See Harvey Araton, "Planting the Seeds of Protest," *New York Times,* January 9, 1993. In December 1994 I interviewed Hodges, who was then the recently hired basketball coach at Chicago State University. On the bookshelf in his tiny office was a volume titled *The Logic of Social Control.*

74. Baker, "Spike Lee and the Commerce of Culture," 251.

75. Grier and Cobbs, *Black Rage,* 69.

76. Hooks, "Reconstructing Black Masculinity," in *Black Looks,* 102, 103, 112; Maya Angelou, "The Fight," in Harvey S. Wiener and Charles Bazerman, *Side by Side: A Multicultural Reader* (Boston: Houghton Mifflin, 1996), 112, 114.

### 6. Wonders Out of Africa

1. For a fine analysis of the new world order in cricket, see Marqusee, "For Love of the Game," 18–20.
2. "Beyond the Political Boundaries," *Guardian*, March 15, 1996.
3. "What's More, Cricketers Today Even Chew Gum!" *New York Times*, March 18, 1996.
4. Rice, *Captain Sir Richard Francis Burton*, 435, 436.
5. Hibbert, *Africa Explored*, 204.
6. Rice, *Captain Sir Richard Francis Burton*, 241.
7. Foa, *Résultats scientifiques*, 85.
8. See, for example, Pike, "Psychical Characteristics," 153–88; Jackson, "Racial Aspects," 30, 52; Mangan, *The Games Ethic*, 35, 56.
9. Edgerton, *Like Lions They Fought*, 37, 20, 183.
10. Edgerton, *Mau Mau*, 18.
11. Jeal, *The Boy-Man*, 104.
12. "Slur Slams into Heart of Compassionate Team," *Austin American-Statesman*, March 8, 1992.
13. Froberville, "Rapport sur les races nègres," 687.
14. Edgerton, *Like Lions They Fought*, 129.
15. Rice, *Captain Sir Richard Francis Burton*, 45; Hibbert, *Africa Explored*, 108, 98.
16. Vallois, "L'Exposition Coloniale," 59.
17. Basden, *Among the Ibos*, 132. See also Blacking, "Games and Sport," 6–8.
18. Basden, *Niger Ibos*, 347.
19. "A Manual of Ethnological Inquiry," *Journal of the Ethnological Society* 3 (1854): 202.
20. Nicolson, "Medicine and Racial Politics," 72. In a similar vein, Theodor Waitz writes, "The great vital energy of [the] savage, compared with civilized nations, is shown by the relatively greater healing power of nature (vis medicatrix naturæ) possessed by the former. The experiments made in this respect extend to all races." See *Introduction to Anthropology*, 126.
21. Stigler, *Rassenphysiologische Ergebnisse*, 37, 38.
22. I am referring here to the work of the amateur anthropologist François Péron, who joined an expedition to Australia at the end of the eighteenth century. See Degérando, *The Observations of Savage Peoples*, 78; Theodor Waitz, *Introduction to Anthropology*, 98.
23. See Hoberman, "Darwin's Athletes: The 'Savage' and 'Civilized' Body," in *Mortal Engines*, 33–61.
24. "Die Springflut der schwarzen Sieger," *Süddeutsche Zeitung*, September 16, 1988, 56.
25. The attempt to talk scientifically about black athletic aptitude goes back at least as far as R. Meade Bache's 1895 article "Reaction Time with Reference to Race." The achievements of black athletes such as Jesse Owens during the 1930s created enough interest in this subject to cause the African-American anatomist W. Montague Cobb to challenge the idea of ath-

letically significant racial differences. Cobb argued in 1942 that "the margins separating the performances of White and Negro stars have been insignificant from an anthropological standpoint." See "Physical Anthropology," 168. Five years later he wrote: "Science has not revealed a single trait peculiar to the Negro alone, to which his athletic achievements could be attributed." See "Does Science Favor Negro Athletes?," 77. Such caveats notwithstanding, a steady stream of speculative articles about racial athletic aptitude have appeared in the American popular press. See, for example, Smith, "Giving the Olympics an Anthropological Once-Over," 81–84B; Kane, "An Assessment of 'Black Is Best,'" 72–83; Burfoot, "White Men Can't Run," 89–95. For a useful survey of some of this material, see Wiggins, "'Great Speed But Little Stamina,'" 158–85.

26. In fact, such informal contests had already occurred at least a century earlier, and it is clear that they could provoke racial anxieties. "In Cooke's voyage, we are told of the marked inferiority of the English sailors, in wrestling or boxing, to the naked sun-burnt heroes of the South Sea Islands . . . An English bricklayer, blacksmith, or drayman, however, who liked the sport, and was practised in balancing and striking, might have challenged the whole of the tawny nation." Or, "With respect to the South Sea islanders, and the difference between them and the English sailors, I doubt whether there was any superiority in the training of the former, which gave them the advantage. An English sailor is, perhaps, the very perfection of agility in his own way. I do not know that the human powers can go beyond it." See Sinclair, *A Collection of Papers,* 10–11, 81–82.

27. Darwin, *The Descent of Man,* 170–71.

28. Waitz, *Introduction to Anthropology,* 109. It is interesting that Waitz appears to interpret this "energy of physical life" as a product of culture rather than as an innate biological capacity:

> This capacity for great physical efforts which we find in such a high degree among the [native] North Americans, is usually combined with great digestive powers, which, owing to continued fasting and frequent over-feeding, acquires among savage peoples an unexampled energy. That this is merely the result of habit and not a peculiarity of race, is proved by similar performances among the ancient Greek athletes and many Arabs. (115)

29. Reade, *Savage Africa,* 508, 509.

30. Davy, "On the Character of the Negro," clvii, clxv.

31. Quoted in Tatz, *Aborigines in Sports,* 26.

32. Edgerton, *Like Lions They Fought,* 133.

33. See, for example, Sinclair, *A Collection of Papers,* 82n; Flanagan, *The Aborigines of Australia,* 59; Foa, *Résultats scientifiques,* 117; Stigler, *Rassenphysiologische Ergebnisse,* 40.

34. Harley, "Comparison," 116.

35. See, for example, Phillips, *A Man's Country?*

36. Quoted in Mangan, *The Games Ethic,* 54.

37. Morris, *Pax Britannica,* 226, 485.

## 7. The World of Colonial Sport

1. See, for example, Mangan, *The Games Ethic.*
2. Adas, *Machines,* 256.
3. Wyatt-Brown, *Southern Honor,* 154.
4. Evans, *Exclusion, Exploitation,* 245.
5. Tatz, *Aborigines in Sport,* 17.
6. See Hoberman, *The Olympic Crisis,* 39.
7. Weatherly, "A World-Wide Color Line," 478.
8. See Tabili, "We Ask for British Justice," 22.
9. Evans, *Exclusion, Exploitation,* 142.
10. Stoddart, "Sport, Cultural Imperialism," 667.
11. Assigning ridiculous names to natives seems to have been common in the British Empire. Recounting a story from the Gold Coast, James Morris wrote: "The labourers were mostly indentured Kroomen imported from Liberia, who arrived filthy and virtually nude, were given names at random like Teapot, Big Nose or One Day Gentleman, and were locked into their compound at night." See *Pax Britannica,* 106.
12. Tatz, *Aborigines in Sport,* 23, 25, 25–26, 27.
13. Such strict segregation in cricket was not, apparently, universal. "In Ceylon they even had Natives playing cricket for the colony, and in 1894 Alan Raffel took 14 for 97 against the visiting M.C.C. Arrogance, indeed!" See Morris, *Pax Britannica,* 154.
14. "Gooch Points the Way Through Preparation and Desire," *Guardian,* January 15, 1994.
15. For a description of the racial diversity of the troops of the British Empire, see Morris, *Pax Britannica,* 27–34.
16. Killingray, "Race and Rank," 276, 277, 279, 285.
17. Kirk-Greene, "'Damnosa Hereditas,'" 395.
18. MacMunn, *The Armies of India,* 129, 130.
19. MacMunn, *The Martial Races of India,* 2; 1, 248, 252, 289; 239–240, 177.
20. Ibid., 195, 199, 252, 250.
21. Ibid., 160, 55.
22. The idea of modernity is crucial here. Manthia Diawara, for example, has defined *Englishness* as "a modernist phenomenon which ties the lives of colonized people to industrialization, literacy, Christianity, and individualism only for the ascendancy of England, and for the denial of the rights of these people to enjoy the fruits of modernism." See "Englishness and Blackness," 830.
23. "Wir kriegen euch schon noch, ihr Hunde," *Der Spiegel,* October 24, 1977, 194.
24. Edgerton, *Like Lions They Fought,* 67, 110.
25. Weatherly, "A World-Wide Color Line," 475.
26. Raymond Evans, *Race Relations in Colonial Queensland: A History of Exclusion, Exploitation, and Extermination* (Sydney: Australia and New Zealand Book Co., 1975), 78.
27. Edgerton, *Like Lions They Fought,* 110.

28. Edgerton, *Mau Mau,* 6, 196.
29. Morris, *Pax Britannica,* 183–84.
30. "Cricket's Hot Summer: Where Are the Gentlemen?" *New York Times,* September 13, 1992.


## 8. The New Multiracial World Order

1. Thomson, "Observations on New Zealand Men," 131.
2. Pike, "Psychical Characteristics of the English," 165.
3. See Rosselli, "The Self-Image of Effeteness," 127.
4. Sir Duncan Gibb, quoted in Hoffman, *Race Traits and Tendencies,* 172.
5. See Hoberman, "The Sportive-Dynamic Body."
6. O'Donnell, "Mapping the Mythical," 347–50.
7. Ibid.
8. Ibid., 350, 351, 351, 352, 353.
9. Ibid.
10. Ibid., 353.
11. See Adas, *Machines;* Mangan, *The Games Ethic,* 112.
12. The African failure to modernize has become a theme of the new scientific racism. Thus the racial psychologist J. Philippe Rushton predicts on the basis of a black African genetic deficiency that "the relentless peripheralization of Africa from the world economy will continue." See *Race, Evolution, and Behavior,* 161.
13. "Abuzz Over Africa's Week at, and in, the Movies," *New York Times,* March 4, 1995.
14. See Hoberman, "Toward a Theory"; Hoberman, "The International Olympic Committee"; Simson and Jennings, *The Lords of the Rings;* Jennings, *The New Lords of the Rings*.
15. "Blut an den Fingern," *Der Spiegel*, May 2, 1994, 192, 194. See also "Die Flut der erstklassigen Billigathleten," *Süddeutsche Zeitung*, March 8, 1995.
16. "Die Schüchternen halten sich für die Fittesten," *Süddeutsche Zeitung,* December 24–26, 1994.
17. "Gnadenlos ausgenommen," *Der Spiegel*, January 6, 1992, 143. Talent scouting by European soccer clubs is not limited to African youth. In February 1995, a fourteen-year-old soccer professional from Naples was killed when he collided with the goalie of his own team. See "Der Tod des Baby-Fußballers," *Süddeutsche Zeitung,* February 24, 1995.
18. "Die Mär von den schwarzen Wunderfußballern," *Süddeutsche Zeitung,* August 5, 1992.
19. "Schwarze Zukunft," *Der Spiegel*, June 20, 1994, 199–201.
20. "Heilige und Sündenböcke," *Der Spiegel,* April 17, 1995, 172, 169. As the German sports expert Gunter Gebauer put it, the black athlete in Germany is "half saint, half scapegoat" (169). It should be pointed out that the term "black gold" is a colloquialism and is not used by the German Soccer Federation (DFB). That racial integration of a kind can occur in the German context is confirmed by the fact that in February 1996 a young woman

of Ghanaian descent, the adopted child of German parents, was chosen as spokesperson for Germany's junior female track-and-field athletes. See "Einfach nur Basis-Demokratie," *Süddeutsche Zeitung,* February 22, 1996.

21. "Fußball gut, alles gut," *Der Spiegel,* October 26, 1992, 247, 249; "Frankfurt erteilt drei Rebellen die Freigabe," *Süddeutsche Zeitung,* December 5, 1994; "Der Feldwebel im Anzug zieht eine Roßkur durch," *Süddeutsche Zeitung,* December 10–11, 1994.

22. "Monster und Messias," *Der Spiegel,* March 3, 1994, 169–71. In April 1996 Germans were reading about the NBA's growing climate of incivility and violence. See "Gossenjargon und Faustrecht," *Süddeutsche Zeitung,* April 13–14, 1996.

23. "Schrempf? Was soll der denn dort?" *Süddeutsche Zeitung,* February 13, 1995.

24. "Interview der Woche: Henning Harnisch (25) Sprungwunder mit losen US-Kontakten," *Süddeutsche Zeitung,* October 23–24, 1993.

25. "Lottogewinn in Gefahr," *Süddeutsche Zeitung,* July 5, 1993; "Zwei leistungsorientierte Läufer, die zu leben verstehen," *Süddeutsche Zeitung,* February 7, 1995.

26. Searle, "Race Before Wicket," 43, 44.

27. "Eine Seuche zieht quer durch Europa: Wachsender Rassismus und Antisemitismus in den Fußballstadien," *Süddeutsche Zeitung,* January 27, 1993.

28. I wish to express my deep thanks to Lincoln Allison and Grant Jarvie for their invaluable assistance with this topic.

29. Gilroy, "Frank Bruno or Salman Rushdie?," 86, 88, 88.

30. Morris, *Pax Britannica,* 511.

31. Rob Hughes, "Blacks Who Beat the Poison of Prejudice," *Sunday Times,* December 16, 1990.

32. "Equal Opportunity? Sport, Race and Racism" (Birmingham: West Midlands Council for Sport and Recreation, 1990), 9.

33. James, *Beyond a Boundary,* 102.

34. Hughes, "Blacks Who Beat Prejudice."

35. Tessa Lovell, "Sport, Racism and Young Women," in Jarvie, *Sport, Racism and Ethnicity,* 64.

36. Cashmore, *Making Sense of Sport,* 89–90.

37. "Blacks Race to Catch Up," *Sunday Times,* October 1, 1989.

38. Ibid.

39. "Can Sport Ever Resolve Racism?" *Sunday Times,* May 6, 1990.

40. Horace Lashley, "Black Participation in British Sport: Opportunity or Control?" *Coaching Focus* [England] (Autumn 1989): 7.

41. See especially Phillips, *A Man's Country?*

42. Hyde, "White Men Can't Jump," 62–67.

43. Leilua, "Pacific Muscle," 26. This popular article describes the work of Philip Houghton, an associate professor of anatomy at the University of Otago.

44. Paul Wilson, "The Black Man's Burden," *Observer,* September 22, 1991, 41.

45. "Players Act on Race Slur," *Daily Mirror,* September 16, 1991.

46. Dave Hill, "The Race Game," *Guardian Guide,* August 31, 1991, viii.

47. "Charge Noades!" *Daily Mail,* September 16, 1991.

48. "Ron Is White Out of Order," *Daily Star,* September 13, 1991.

49. Hill, "The Race Game."

50. Hughes, "Blacks Who Beat Prejudice."

51. Hill, "The Race Game."

52. Stoddart, "Sport, Cultural Imperialism, " 664.

53. It is worth noting that as bowlers, nonwhite cricket stars have occupied a traditionally diminished role. "Those who toiled long and hard as bowlers," Richard Holt points out, "seldom received the kind of acclaim enjoyed by batsmen, especially the opening batsman, who strode majestically from the pavilion to the wicket in his whites with bat in hand . . . Batting required more courage and less strength than bowling and predictably batting came to be much more closely associated with the social elite than bowling." See "Cricket and Englishness," 48–49. In recent years, with the rise of nonwhite batting stars such as the Trinidadian Brian Lara, this stereotypical arrangement too has eroded.

54. Tatz, *Aborigines in Sport,* 30.

55. "Ambrose Sets the Standard for a Whole New Ball Game," *Guardian,* January 15, 1994.

56. See, for example, William K. Stevens, "Evolution of Humans May at Last Be Faltering," *New York Times,* March 14, 1995.

57. Robert Hartmann, "Die Springflut der schwarzen Sieger," *Süddeutsche Zeitung,* September 16, 1988.

58. Moore, "Sons of the Wind," 79.

59. Robert Hartmann, "Weiße als Exoten der Langstrecken," *Süddeutsche Zeitung,* April 19, 1988.

60. See Tunbridge, "Repression in Kenya," A39–A40.

61. "Das Laufen ist ihre zweite Natur," *Süddeutsche Zeitung,* September 3, 1991.

62. See, for example, Hoberman, *Mortal Engines,* 284–85.

63. "Fußball gut, alles gut," 249.

64. See especially Adas, *Machines.*

65. "Genial und kreativ," *Der Spiegel,* January 6, 1992, 144.

## 9. The Fastest White Man in the World

1. "Die Profis abkoppeln," *Der Spiegel,* August 23, 1993, 144.

2. See George, "The Virtual Disappearance," 70–78. It is worth noting that a white two-hundred-meter runner, Kevin Little, was a member of the American team that competed at the 1995 World Track and Field Championships in Göteborg, an anomaly that may have attracted more media attention in Germany than it did in the United States. "You feel intimidated when you're the only white in the field," Little told an interviewer. See "Außenseiter Little," *Süddeutsche Zeitung,* August 11, 1995.

3. Mennea's coach was Professor Carlo Vittori. See "Das ist erst der Anfang

gewesen: Dank westlichem Know-how kommt das überlegene Talent far-
biger Fußballer zum Tragen," *Süddeutsche Zeitung,* June 25, 1990. In 1995
an Australian sports magazine, quoting the American track coach Loren
Seagrave, invoked Mennea's still-extant world record as evidence that
black sprinters do not enjoy a natural physical advantage. See Hurst, "Running," 25.

4. "Ich werde die Schnellste Frau der Welt," *Süddeutsche Zeitung Magazin,*
   August 6, 1993, 13; "Laufend Gelt verdienen, mit allen Mitteln," *Süddeutsche Zeitung,* August 20, 1993.

5. "Klar for det søte liv," *Aftenposten,* September 14, 1994, 14.

6. "Wenn der Wengo zweimal kingelt," *Süddeutsche Zeitung,* October 26,
   1993.

7. "Eine Handvoll Großer und mitten drin der Flo," *Süddeutsche Zeitung,* July
   20, 1992; "Jetzt habe ich hier meine Arbeit getan," *Süddeutsche Zeitung,*
   August 16, 1993; "Erst beten, dann siegen," *Süddeutsche Zeitung,* August
   10, 1992; "Die Lungen Afrikas," *Zeitmagazin,* July 17, 1992, 15.

8. "Und das Nutellabrot kommt nicht mehr auf den Tisch," *Süddeutsche Zeitung,* September 6, 1993.

9. Post, "Prince of Times," 55.

10. See, for example, "Die Ehre des Abendlandes retten," *Der Spiegel,* March
    11, 1996, 198, 202, 203.

11. "Taking on Prize Guys," *The European,* November 12–15, 1992, 28.

12. "Blacks Race to Catch Up."

13. Gabriel, "China Strains for Olympic Glory," 40.

14. Smith, "Letter from Japan," 90.

15. "Avoiding Competition Against Blacks," *Atlanta Journal/Constitution,*
    April 17, 1994.

16. "Klein und wendig," *Der Spiegel,* November 21, 1994, 175.

17. "Knochen sinken," *Der Spiegel,* April 1, 1974, 131. This stereotype is also
    widespread among African Americans.

18. "Neste år skal Geir bli god," *Aftenposten,* August 12, 1995; "Sorte har
    styrken og farten," *Aftenposten,* March 10, 1996.

19. See "Von allein läuft nichts," *Der Spiegel,* August 14, 1995, 169; "Ein Di-
    lemma," *Süddeutsche Zeitung,* March 29, 1996. The same problem with
    reluctant sponsors has appeared in the only recently integrated world of
    Brazilian surfing. See "Die ganz große Welle," *Der Spiegel,* March 25, 1995,
    256.

20. "Die Ehre des Abendlandes retten," *Der Spiegel,* March 11, 1996, 202.

21. "Ein Dilemma."

## 10. Imagining the Black Organism

1. "Black Runners 'At an Advantage,'" *Guardian,* September 14, 1995, 3. On
   Jesse Owens's heel, see Cobb, "Race and Runners," 54.

2. "Bannister Says Black Athletes Have Edge," *Austin American-Statesman,*
   September 14, 1995; G. D. Williams et al., "Calf Muscles," 45–58. "The

proportionately longer tendon of the American negro and the proportionately shorter one of the American white will remain proportionately longer or shorter on the average, whether the individual is short, of medium stature, or tall" (52).

3. Kohn, *The Race Gallery,* 16. Kohn is paraphrasing Eike-Meinrad Winkler of the University of Vienna Institute of Human Biology.

4. "Bannister Says Black Athletes Have Edge."

5. Steven Goldberg, "Poverty Doesn't Make Blacks Better Athletes" [letter], *New York Times,* April 15, 1989.

6. "Duke Shows His True Colors," *Newsweek,* December 25, 1989, 53.

7. Quoted in Kohn, *The Race Gallery,* 78–79.

8. "Stereotypes Pit Ability vs. Intellect," *USA Today,* December 16, 1991, 2A.

9. Jokl and Cluver, "Physical Fitness," 2384–85.

10. Gibbs et al., "Nutrition in a Slave Population," 196.

11. Cartwright, "Diseases and Peculiarities," 65.

12. "Review of Cartwright on the Diseases of the Negro Race," *Charleston Medical Journal and Review* 6 (1851): 830; quoted in Haller, "The Negro and the Southern Physician," 251.

13. Haller, "The Physician Versus the Negro," 157.

14. Haller, "The Negro and the Southern Physician," 238, 252.

15. C. Jeff Miller, "Special Medical Problems," 733.

16. Lemann, "A Study of Disease," 34.

17. Hall, "Vegetative Dermatoses," 376.

18. McLendon, "A Comparative Study," 304.

19. Davenport, "Do the Races Differ," 89, 78–79.

20. See, for example, Nathanson, "The Musical Ability"; Seashore, "Three New Approaches"; Johnson, "A Summary of Negro Scores"; Sanderson, "Differences in Musical Ability"; Eagleson and Taylor, "The Preference for Chords."

21. Rosser, "Rectal Pathology," 93, 97.

22. "Impossibility of Race Identification by Blood Tests," *Journal of the American Medical Association* 76 (March 5, 1921): 674; "Telegony," *Journal of the American Medical Association* 105 (December 28, 1935): 2179; "Determination of Race," *Journal of the American Medical Association* 106 (January 11, 1936): 148; "No Blood Test for Race Identification," *Journal of the American Medical Association* 112 (1939): 465; "Sweat and Body Odor," *Journal of the American Medical Association* 114 (June 1, 1940): 2238; "Use of Antibiotics in Different Races," *Journal of the American Medical Association* 157 (January 29, 1955): 486.

## 11. The Negro as a Defective Type

1. Cartwright, "Diseases and Peculiarities," 66.

2. Cartwright, "Diseases and Physical Peculiarities," 508.

3. "Dr. Cartwright on the Caucasians and the Africans," 49.

4. "Negro Slavery at the South," 209.

5. Cartwright, "Diseases and Peculiarities," 65.

6. Ibid., 66; "Dr. Cartwright on the Caucasians and the Africans," 47. Cartwright addressed the relationship between the black's deficient willpower and his (naturally indolent) muscles again and again: "The Nigritian has such little command over his own muscles, from the weakness of his will, as almost to starve, when a little exertion and forethought would procure him an abundance" (p. 47). Or, "His muscles not being exercised, the respiration is imperfect, and the blood is imperfectly vitalized" (p. 47). Or, "They are obliged to move and exercise their muscles when the white man, acquainted with their character, *wills* that they should do so. They cannot resist their will, so far as labor of body is concerned" (p. 48).

7. Haller, "The Physician Versus the Negro," 155; Haller, "The Negro and the Southern Physician," 253. The quotation is from Dowler, "The Vital Statistics," 164.

8. Snyder, "The Problem of the Negro Child," 9, 10. This argument appears in the same journal in 1932, offered by a physician from New Orleans who reminds his readers that they cannot afford to ignore the health problems of the blacks who "cook our meals, serve us at table, clean our houses, make our beds, launder our clothes, care for our children, in short, live in intimate daily contact with us and our families, and handle the material things which are necessary for our very existence. For our own protection, therefore, if for no other motive, we must necessarily be our brother's keeper." See C. Jeff Miller, "Special Medical Problems," 733–34.

9. Murrell, "Syphilis," 848, 847, 849.

10. Hazen, "Syphilis," 463.

11. Du Bois, "The Problem of Amusement," in *On Sociology,* 236.

12. Appiah, "Illusions of Race," in *In My Father's House,* 29.

13. Du Bois, "The Conservation of Races," in *On Sociology,* 240, 241–42.

14. Pearl, "Biological Factors in Negro Mortality," 249.

15. Ibid. On Pearl's career, his relationship to the eugenics movement, and his anti-Semitism, see Barkan, *The Retreat of Scientific Racism,* 210–20.

16. Lemann, "Diabetes Mellitus," 522; Snyder, "The Problem of the Negro Child," 10; Rosser, "Rectal Pathology," 94.

17. Moehlig, "The Mesoderm of the Negro," 311.

18. From a commentary quoted in Davison and Thoroughman, "A Study of Heart Disease," 469.

19. "One Hundred Cases of Heart Disease," 2193. This phrase comes from Dr. Charles R. Grandy of Norfolk, Virginia.

20. Myrdal, *An American Dilemma,* 150.

21. Hingson, "Comparative Negro and White Mortality," 203, 203–4, 210, 211.

22. Reinhardt, "The Negro," 252.

23. Hoskins, "Hormones and Racial Characteristics," 335–36.

24. Cited in Hingson, "Comparative Negro and White Mortality," 211.

25. Smillie and Augustine, "Vital Capacity," 2058.

26. Klineberg, *Race Differences,* 126.

27. In an unpublished study, the writer found that 65 Negro soldiers averaged 664 cc. less in forced vital capacity than 335 white soldiers of very similar age, height, weight, and apparent motivation . . . If confirmed, this finding would pose the interesting question of which comes first, the Negroes' lowered pulmonary function or their susceptibility to pulmonary infection.

    See Damon, "Some Host Factors in Disease," 429. See also Abramowitz et al., "Vital Capacity," 287–92.

28. See Cartwright, "Diseases and Peculiarities," 66; Cartwright, "The Diseases of Negroes," 209–10.

29. Lewis, *The Biology of the Negro,* 18; Kiple and Kiple, "The African Connection," 214.

30. Smillie and Augustine, "Vital Capacity," 2056.

31. "Those who disagreed with the favorable opinions in regard to the negro's fitness for military service found fault largely with the lack of muscular development of the calf of the leg, and the extreme flat-footedness . . ." See Hoffman, *Race Traits and Tendencies,* 175. "Writers on the subject of physical anthropology have long agreed that the colored races in general, and the negroes in particular, show poorly developed calves." See Williams et al., "Calf Muscles," 45.

32. Douglas, "Difficulties and Superstitions," 737.


### *12. African-American Responses to Racial Biology*

1. Du Bois, *Health and Physique,* 16, 27, 63, 65, 90.

2. Frederickson, *The Black Image in the White Mind,* 249. *"Race Traits and Tendencies of the American Negro* became a prized source of information and conclusions for anti-Negro writers for many years to come and also had the practical effect of helping to convince most white insurance companies that they should deny coverage to all Negroes on the grounds that membership in the race by itself constituted an unacceptable actuarial risk" (249–50).

3. Hoffman, *Race Traits and Tendencies,* 176, 148.

4. Ibid., 173, 174, 175.

5. Ibid., 162, 167, 171, 164.

6. Murrell, "Syphilis," 848, 847.

7. Holmes, *Studies in Evolution and Eugenics,* 250.

8. Douglas, "Difficulties and Superstitions," 737.

9. C. Jeff Miller, "Special Medical Problems," 734.

10. Quoted in Haller, "The Physician Versus the Negro," 167.

11. In his "Notes on Virginia" (1784), Thomas Jefferson had written that "deep-rooted prejudices entertained by the whites; ten thousand recollections by the blacks of the injuries they have sustained; the real distinctions nature has made; and many other circumstances, will divide us into parties, and produce convulsions, which will probably never end but in the extermi-

nation of one or the other race." In *The Descent of Man* (1871), Charles Darwin had offered a more specific prediction: "At some future period, not very distant as measured by centuries, the civilized races of man will almost certainly exterminate and replace the savage races throughout the world." Quoted in Frederickson, *The Black Image in the White Mind,* 4, 230.

12. Hoffman, *Race Traits and Tendencies,* 148, 171.

13. Haller, "The Physician Versus the Negro," 167.

14. Frederickson, *The Black Image in the White Mind,* 276.

15. The acceptability of the black athlete as a role model for white children is exemplified by a "Top 10 List of Kids' Biggest Sports Heroes" that appeared in the September 1995 issue of *Parents' Playbook,* distributed by the publishers of *Sports Illustrated for Kids.* Of the ten professional athletes listed, eight are African American. The only white athletes named are quarterbacks who have won Super Bowl titles.

16. Stepan and Gilman, "Appropriating the Idioms of Science," 183. Miller was also a civil servant and teacher who would have been the first African American to earn a doctorate in mathematics if poverty and racism had not intervened to prevent it. This distinction went instead to Elbert Frank Cox, who received his doctorate in 1925 from the Imperial University of San Dei in Japan. See Patricia Clark Kenschaft, "Black Men and Women in Mathematical Research," *Journal of Black Studies* 18 (December 1987): 171–72.

17. Kelly Miller, "A Review of Hoffman's *Race Traits,*" 6, 7, 8.

18. Stepan and Gilman, "Appropriating the Idioms of Science," 187, 188.

> The Negro intellectuals' resistance to the white race dogma has been widely popularized among the Negro people through the Negro press, the Negro school and the Negro pulpit. As it corresponds closely to Negro interests, it will now be found to emerge as a popular belief in all Negro communities in America, except the backward ones. It may be assumed that formerly the Negroes more often took over white beliefs as a matter of accommodation.

See Myrdal, *An American Dilemma,* 96.

19. Quoted in Myrdal, *An American Dilemma,* 94.

20. Miller, "A Review of Hoffman's *Race Traits,*" 18.

21. Quoted in Degler, *In Search of Human Nature,* 16.

22. Du Bois, *Health and Physique,* 36. Du Bois did not, however, assume that blacks possessed a natural athletic superiority. He noted, for example, that "the fundamentals of physical education in order to develop the bodies of the children, is criminally neglected at least among Philadelphia's poorest Negroes" (90).

23. Rankin-Hill and Blakey, "W. Montague Cobb," 74.

24. W. Montague Cobb, "Race and Runners," 54, 56.

25. W. Montague Cobb, "Physical Anthropology," 169.

26. W. Montague Cobb, "The Negro as a Biological Element," 346, 340.

27. W. Montague Cobb, "Your Nose Won't Tell," *The Crisis* (October 1938): 332, 336.

28. W. Montague Cobb, "Physical Anthropology," 150, 155, 163, 155.
29. W. Montague Cobb, "The Negro as a Biological Element," 342; "Physical Anthropology," 168; "The Negro as a Biological Element," 336, 342.
30. "Negro Stock Is Praised," 102. Cobb's eugenic thinking was as speculative and naive as that of some of the white theorists he had criticized earlier in his career. "While modern genetics does not permit definite answers on the biological effects of this admixture," he told his audience, "it must be considered to have improved the stock, because the majority group so commonly used to allege that any brilliant Negro owed his superiority to his white blood. Perish the thought that any new form of racism is being promulgated here."
31. W. Montague Cobb, "An Anatomist's View," 192.
32. W. Montague Cobb, "The Negro as a Biological Element," 342; "Physical Anthropology," 170.
33. "Dr. William Montague Cobb," 30.
34. W. Montague Cobb, "Toward a Federation," 874.

## 13. Black "Hardiness" and the Origins of Medical Racism

1. Frederickson, *The Black Image in the White Mind*, 182, 181.
2. "Black History Month: So That We All Might Know," *Nokoa* [Austin, Texas], February 25–March 3, 1994.
3. Douglass, "The Claims of the Negro," 308.
4. "Blacks Take Strain of Army Life Better: Chaplain," *Jet* 51 (March 10, 1977): 20.
5. Early, "Waiting for Miss America," in *Tuxedo Junction*, 67.
6. Charles H. Garvin, "Negro Health," *Opportunity* (November 1924): 341.
7. Swados, "Negro Health on Plantations," 460, 472.
8. Quoted in Savitt, *Medicine and Slavery*, 9. While Stampp asserts that blacks and whites suffered from prevalent diseases in the same ways, Savitt points out that subsequent scholarship has confirmed "racial differences in the reactions of individuals to diseases. Modern medical scientists have in fact shown that such ethnic variations do exist" (9).
9. Quoted in Gibbs et al., "Nutrition in a Slave Population," 178. According to *A History of Georgia* (1811), rice farming there "could not be carried on successfully without the assistance of Africans, whose constitutions seemed formed by nature to bear the heat and exposure of a climate, most favorable for its production." See Van Deburg, *Slavery & Race*, 8–9.
10. Macdonald, "Colored Children," 1144; Macdonald, "Skin of Negro," 1400.
11. "One Hundred Cases of Heart Disease," 2193.
12. Myrdal, *An American Dilemma*, 964.
13. Quoted in Frederickson, *The Black Image in the White Mind*, 52.
14. Quoted in Evans, "Joe Louis as a Key Functionary," 106–7.
15. Murrell, "Syphilis," 847.
16. Lewis, *The Biology of the Negro*, 305.

17. Lutz and Collins, *Reading National Geographic,* 161, 174, 162.

18. "Physical Basis of Traditional Race Relations," in Edgar T. Thompson, ed., *Race Relations and the Race Problem: A Definition and an Analysis* (Durham: Duke University Press, 1939), 198.

19. Rosser, "Rectal Pathology," 94.

20. Terry, "The American Negro," 339.

21. Goldstein, "Theory of Survival," 223, 225.

22. This phrase appears in C. Jeff Miller, "Special Medical Problems," 734.

23. Lewis, *The Biology of the Negro,* 306.

24. Rosser, "Rectal Pathology," 94, 96.

25. Moehlig, "The Mesoderm of the Negro," 297.

26. Ibid., 304.

27. Savitt, "The Use of Blacks," 344.

28. Love and Davenport, "A Comparison of White and Colored Troops," 60.

29. Lewis, *The Biology of the Negro,* 305. See also Lemann, "A Study of Disease," 37.

30. Freemon, "The Health of the American Slave," 50.

31. Lewis, *The Biology of the Negro,* 382.

32. Rosser, "Rectal Pathology," 96.

33. George, "Glaucoma in the Negro," 202.

34. Veronica Chambers, "Old Smoothies," *New York Times Magazine,* August 13, 1995, 45.

35. Hingson, "Comparative Negro and White Mortality," 211.

36. Haller, "The Negro and the Southern Physician," 246.

37. Savitt, *Medicine and Slavery,* 113n.

38. Frederickson, *The Black Image in the White Mind,* 57.

39. Lewis, "Contribution of an Unknown Negro," 23–24.

40. Savitt, "The Use of Blacks," 345. For a critical appraisal of Sims's use of slave women, see Ojanuga, "The Medical Ethics of the 'Father of Gynaecology,'" 28–31.

41. W. Montague Cobb, "Surgery and the Negro Physician," 148, 148.

42. Douglas, "Difficulties and Superstitions," 735.

43. Lewis, *The Biology of the Negro,* 305.

44. Hunter, "Coronary Occlusion," 13. See also Davison and Thoroughman, "A Study of Heart Disease," 469.

45. Lemann, "A Study of Disease," 37.

46. Venable, "Glaucoma in the Negro," 7, 199.

47. Lemons, "Black Stereotypes," 111.

48. Murrell, "Syphilis," 847.

49. Douglas, "Difficulties and Superstitions," 737.

50. "There never was a syphiliphobiac in this race, for the knowledge that he is a syphilitic in nowise disturbs the negro. His idea of the medical world is that there is a remedy for every disease and that all the doctor does is to select the right medicine." See Murrell, "Syphilis," 847.

51. Comaroff, "The Diseased Heart of Africa," 318.

52. Haller, "The Physician Versus the Negro," 156.

53. Lewis, *The Biology of the Negro,* 362.
54. Miller, "Special Medical Problems," 738.
55. "South African Negro as a Parturient," 1037.
56. Bakwin, "The Negro Infant," 26.
57. Miller, "Special Medical Problems," 735.
58. "Rarity of Pelvic Endometriosis in Negro Women," 343.
59. Mengert, "Racial Contrasts," 414, 415.
60.   During the eighteenth century, climate was held responsible for the then unquestioned menarcheal precocity of tropical peoples. Montesquieu wrote "women in hot climates are marriageable at eight, nine or ten years of age . . ." This opinion was current among philosophers and physiologists, until Roberton in 1832 began a remarkable series of investigations in which he sought data from various parts of the world which, though strongly criticized, led him to the conclusion that climate had no influence on age at puberty; "if a difference exist it must be sought in race" (Roberton, 1845). The amount of progress that has been made since then in disentangling the role of race from that of climate, of nutrition, of social or other factors in causing variation in the age of menarche is disappointingly slight.
    See Roberts, "Race, Genetics and Growth," 44.
61. See, for example, Willoughby and Coogan, "Intelligence and Fertility," 114; Roberts, "The Negative Association," 410–12. It should be noted that the debate carried on by these papers does not refer to race.
62. Haller, "The Physician Versus the Negro," 161. Traditional commentary on black precocity sometimes concedes mental superiority to the black child prior to his decline, beginning in early adolescence, into permanent intellectual inferiority. The American eugenist Charles B. Davenport interprets one result of a mental imaging test thus: "The superiority of the black children over the white children thus suggests, what many of our results indicate, that the black children are more precocious than the whites." See "Do the Races Differ," 86.
63. Hunt, "On the Negro's Place in Nature," 11.
64. The comparative study of black and white motor development goes back at least as far as Davenport and Steggerda, *Race Crossing in Jamaica* (1929). For a critique of this book see Barkan, *The Retreat of Scientific Racism,* 166–67. See also Bakwin, "The Negro Infant," 10.
65. Williams and Scott, "Growth and Development of Negro Infants," 116.
66. Geber and Dean, "Gesell Tests," 1064, 1061.
67. Geber and Dean, "Development of Newborn African Children," 1219. Subsequent to the publication of this work, the American physician John C. Cobb offered a cautionary comment: "I think, however, that the method of presenting the data has exaggerated the extent of this so-called precocity of Negro children." See "Precocity of African Children," 867. A more critical commentary, by H. Knobloch, held that "the major difficulty is the question of the interpretation of the behavior exhibited by the infants." See "Precocity of African Children," 602.

68. Kilbride et al., "Comparative Motor Development," 1425. These authors write,

> Our findings clearly support Geber and Dean's finding that Ugandan infants (with our sample consisting entirely of Baganda) are advanced in motor performance when compared with American norms . . . Reasons for the advanced motor development of Baganda infants may be both genetic and environmental . . . Also of interest is the possibility that the precocity of Black infants may be related to "optimal intrauterine and perinatal" conditions. (1425–1426)

69. Knobloch, "Precocity of African Children," 603.
70. McGurk, "A Scientist's Report," 92–96. For a reply to McGurk's article, see Long, "The Relative Learning Capacities," 121–34. "Highly developed gross motor behavior and well developed language ability may be characteristics in which Negroes show precocious development when compared with whites, and, in infancy, could be called Negroid characteristics." See McGurk, "Attitudes, Interests and IQ," 28–29. McGurk eventually joined the editorial board of the racist *Mankind Quarterly.*
71. Hooton, "Is the Negro Inferior?," 346.
72. Bakwin, "The Negro Infant," 8.
73. "Negro's Ability to Stand," 380. See also Robinson et al., "Adaptations to Exercise," 156–58.
74. "Cateyes," *Time,* June 30, 1941, 50.
75. Diane D. Edwards, "Slave-Ship Hypothesis," 76; Salisbury, "Hypertension," 22–23. The principal proponent of the slave-ship hypothesis has been Dr. Clarence E. Grim of the Department of Medicine, Charles R. Drew School of Medicine, Los Angeles, California.
76. Fackelmann, "The African Gene?," 254.
77. Richard S. Cooper of Loyola University (Maywood, Illinois), quoted in Fackelmann, "The African Gene?," 255.
78. Klag et al., "The Association of Skin Color," 599–602.
79. The Negro patient could also be presented as a perversely mischievous, semicomic figure. Thus in May 1908 the major American medical journal summarized an article on "Handicaps in Negro Practice" that had appeared two months earlier in the *Mississippi Medical Monthly:*

> The principal ones are the negro's efforts to lead the physician to an erroneous diagnosis — he seems to have a delight in fooling the doctor if possible; an utter inability to understand and follow directions; the interposition of outsiders, who dissuade from obedience to instructions; the undying fondness for filling his belly; his morbid dread of water; his poverty and filth, and fondness for night prowling and sexual excesses. No reputation built on negro practice is secure.

See "Negro Practice," 1564.
80. Murrell, "Syphilis," 847.
81. Davison and Thoroughman, "A Study of Heart Disease," 467.
82. Miller, "Special Medical Problems," 735.
83. Venable, "Glaucoma," 7.

84. Ibid., 198, 200, 202.
85. Strogatz, "Use of Medical Care for Chest Pain," 290, 292, 293.
86. Davison and Thoroughman, "A Study of Heart Disease," 467.
87. Satcher, "Does Race Interfere," 1499.
88. "A large prospective study of [congenital] malformations showed that blacks had higher overall rates of malformations than whites . . ." See Chavez et al., "Leading Major Congenital Malformations," 205.
89. Shaler, "Our Negro Types," 45. "Recent studies have suggested that congenital deformities, which occur more frequently in white than in Negro people, may be the result of the universal presence of the Rh factor in the latter race." See Vinson, "Incidence of Esophageal Disease," 453.
90. *Indianapolis Freeman,* July 2, 1904.
91. Bond, "Two Views," 19.
92. Lewis, *The Biology of the Negro,* 313.
93. Cartwright, "The Diseases of Negroes," 212.
94. "Remarks by Reagan Doctor on Well-Fed Black Kids Criticized as Insensitive," *Jet* 65 (January 16, 1984): 6.
95. Silber, "Anorexia Nervosa," 29.
96. Lawlor et al., "Eating Disorders," 984.

## *14. Theories of Racial Athletic Aptitude*

1. For a survey of theories of black athletic superiority over the past hundred years, see Wiggins, "'Great Speed But Little Stamina,'" 158–85. See also Sailes, "The Myth of Black Sports Supremacy," 480–87; and Bayless, "Selected Research Studies." This doctoral dissertation is an uncritical and credulous recitation of all the sources the author could find. In addition, I have been unable to locate certain sources in her bibliography.
2. "[C]olored people are well known for the excellent quality of their teeth." See Lewis, *The Biology of the Negro,* 400. This myth of dental superiority had, however, been contradicted the year before: "The impression has prevailed that Negroes are blessed with unusually good teeth, but dental authorities state that this is another exploded tradition. Their teeth look white in comparison with their black skin." See Boland, "Morsus Humanus," 127. On the alleged rarity of appendicitis in the Negro, see Miller, "Special Problems," 739, and "Racial Trends in Certain Surgical Diseases," 997. On the alleged rarity of hemophilia in the Negro, see Lewis, *The Biology of the Negro,* 250.
3. "A Physician Discourses on the Race Problem," 89.
4. In 1995 an African-American woman who had played basketball for a major university program told me that her coach had rested white players with injuries while continuing to play black players with comparable injuries.
5. Jack Olsen, "Pride and Prejudice," 28.
6. "Alabama-Auburn and Racial Issues," *New York Times,* November 30, 1991.

7. Waitz, *Introduction to Anthropology*, 93; Vogt, *Lectures on Man*, 173.

8. Levine, *Black Culture and Black Consciousness*, 403.

9. *Indianapolis Freeman*, February 18, 1905.

10. Quoted in Todd, "Entrenched Negro Physical Features," 58. "This remarkable distinction," Todd comments, "was based upon the supposition, supported by wholly insufficient evidence, that closure of the coronal suture before the lambdoid occurs in the Negro but not in the White. Lyon and I have demonstrated that there is no distinction at all between Whites and Negroes in the order of the suture closure or in the age at which it occurs" (9).

11. Quoted in Myrdal, *An American Dilemma*, 95.

12. Stocking, *American Social Scientists*, 461.

13. Bache, "Reaction Time," 480, 481.

14. Allen, "Breaking World's Records," 308. As W. Montague Cobb pointed out at about this time,

    a number of recent comments in the press upon the current success of American Negro sprinters and broad jumpers have either directly ascribed this success to a longer heel bone or stronger tendon of Achilles than those of their white competitors, or implied that in some way it has been due to racial characteristics. The wide circulation which these suggestions have received warrants a careful appraisal of the facts.

    See Cobb, "Race and Runners," 3.

15. W. Montague Cobb, "Race and Runners," 6, 7. On the difficulties involved in analyzing elite athletic performance, see Hoberman, *Mortal Engines*.

16. Henderson, "The Negro Athlete and Race Prejudice," 79.

17. Abrahams, "Race and Athletics," 144.

18. Jokl and Cluver, "Physical Fitness," 2389; quoted in Rhoden, "Are Black Athletes Naturally Superior?," 140.

19. Murray and Herrnstein, "Race, Genes and I.Q.," 36.

20. Smith, "Giving the Olympics," 81–84B.

21. Kane, "An Assessment of 'Black Is Best,'" 72, 74.

22. Ibid., 74; Keith, "The Differentiation of Mankind," 301–5.

    Anthropologists have sought to account for the origin of the various human anatomic forms. Such factors as environment, natural selection, racial mixture and mutations, acting singly or together, have been advocated as the determinants of races. It has been pointed out that these theories do not suffice, and in recent years the idea has been advanced that the origin of racial characters is the action of hormones. This idea arose from the knowledge of the role of the glands of internal secretion in such pathological conditions as acromegaly, giantism, dystrophia adipogenitalis, dwarfism, infantilism, mongolism, and achondroplasia, where there are disturbances of body form and of growth. Keith has been the leader of this view.

    See Lewis, *The Biology of the Negro*, 25.

23. Kane, "An Assessment of 'Black Is Best,'" 75–76, 79.

24. Ibid., 80, 80, 81.

25. Herskovits, *The Myth of the Negro Past*, 294.

26. Kane, "An Assessment of 'Black Is Best,'" 79.
27. Edwards, "The Sources of Black Athletic Superiority," 33, 35, 38, 39, 40, 39.
28. On October 10, 1995, Amby Burfoot, the author of "White Men Can't Run," put a message onto the Internet that contained the following passage: "After 'White Men' appeared, I expected to be vilified by the liberal establishment. Instead, I heard almost exclusively from people yelling into my earpiece, 'Don't try to tell me I can't run no faster than some . . .'" I am indebted to David Black for bringing this document to my attention.
29. Edwards, "The Sources of Black Athletic Superiority," 39.
30. Rhoden, "Are Black Athletes Naturally Superior?," 136–46.
31. Johnson and Bond, "The Investigation of Racial Differences," 328–67. On Bond's career, see Urban, "The Black Scholar and Intelligence Testing," 323–34. On Cobb, see Rankin-Hill and Blakey, "W. Montague Cobb."
32. Waitz, *Introduction to Anthropology,* 93.
33. Carter, "Ethnic Variations in Human Performance"; Gerace et al., "Skeletal Differences," 260. A frequently cited study is Metheny, "Some Differences in Bodily Proportions," 41–53. For more recent thinking on racial bone density, see Heaney, "Editorial," 2289–90.
34. Davy, "On the Character of the Negro," clxii; Reade, *Savage Africa,* 508; Carter, "Skeletal Differences," 7.
35. Metheny, "Some Differences in Bodily Proportions," 51–52; Carter, "Skeletal Differences," 4–5; Gerace et al., "Skeletal Differences," 258–59.
36. "The Negro has narrower hips. This aids him in running by giving less angular reaction to the forward stride." The author sums up in the following words:

    On the whole, it would seem that there are two sides to the story. In some respects we find that the bodily proportions of the American Negro are such as to give him a slight kinesiological advantage (theoretically, at least) in certain types of athletic performance. In certain other types, such as distance running, he is somewhat handicapped . . . Furthermore, bodily proportions are only one aspect of the whole picture. Such physiological factors as reaction time and muscle viscosity, as well as various psychological factors, play a most important role in determining success in athletic activities, and these are not even touched upon in these data.

    See Metheny, "Some Differences in Bodily Proportions," 52.
37. Mengert, "Racial Contrasts," 413.
38. Garn et al., "Lifelong Differences in Hemoglobin Levels," 95–96.
39. Kraemer et al., "Race-Related Differences," 331.
40. Damon, "Negro-White Differences," 331.
41. Black athletic performance has also been used to challenge the results of intelligence tests employing responses to stimuli that determine "reaction time." See Kamin and Grant-Henry, "Reaction Time," 299–304.
42. "Moreover, the nervous system of the uninfected negroes shows fewer cases of instability than that of whites." See Love and Davenport, "A Comparison of White and Colored Troops," 60.
43. Terry, "The American Negro," 339.

44. Cobb, "Physical Anthropology," 155.

45. Lemann, "Diabetes Mellitus," 523–24.

46. Hunter, "Coronary Occlusion in Negroes," 13.

47. Cromwell, *Championship Technique,* 6.

48. For a comprehensive critique of Kane's article, including the relaxation theory, see Edwards, "The Sources of Black Athletic Superiority," 32–41.

49. Kane, "An Assessment of 'Black Is Best,'" 76.

50. On modern thinking about the primitive, see Torgovnick, "Defining the Primitive," in *Gone Primitive,* 3–41.

51. Lemann, "Diabetes Mellitus," 76, 75.

52. Myrdal, *An American Dilemma,* 90.

53. Stigler, *Rassenphysiologische Ergebnisse,* 25.

54. Lamplugh, "The Image of the Negro," 179.

55. This is Sommering's "Uber die korperlichen Verschiedenheiten des Negers vom Europäer," cited in Waitz, *Introduction to Anthropology,* 93. The issue of racial nerve size was debated by anthropologists throughout the nineteenth century. "Tiedemann also denied Sommering's assertion that the nerves of the Negro are larger, in proportion to the brain, than in the European; but Pruner Bey has confirmed Sommering's opinion." See James Hunt, "On the Negro's Place in Nature," 15.

56. Cartwright, "Diseases and Peculiarities," 65. It is worth noting that Cartwright repeatedly denigrates the muscular capacity of the black male.

57. Davis, "John Lamar," 416.

58. Bache segregated the realm of "higher thought" from that of (automatic) "secondary reflex action." See Bache, "Reaction Time," 479. The racial comparison of reflex times reappeared in 1935, when interest in black athletic aptitude was intensifying in the United States.

    Although the obtained differences between the patellar tendon reflex time of whites and negroes is small, yet it is significant. No explanation for the difference is at hand. In the light of what is known concerning the relation of reflex time to speed in sprinting, the faster patellar tendon reflex time of the negro group suggests that their spinal responses might have a bearing on the speed of negro athletes in the sprints. It should be added that until a more complete study of the neuro-muscular responses of the negro is made, the data presented here are only suggestive and by no means conclusive.

    See Browne, "A Comparison of Patellar Tendon Reflex Time," 124.

59. Kamin and Sharon-Henry, "Reaction Time," 301–2. The authors take issue here with Arthur Jensen's claim that even Muhammad Ali had demonstrated only average reaction time. For a brief history of the use of reaction time to test intelligence, see Jensen, *Bias in Mental Testing,* 686–88.

60. Ide, "Cross-Sections of Median and Sciatic Nerves," 484.

61. Klineberg, "An Experimental Study," 97.

62. T. R. Garth, *Race Psychology* (New York: Whittlesey House, 1931); quoted in Lambeth and Lanier, "Race Differences in Speed of Reaction," 257.

63. Lambeth and Lanier, "Race Differences in Speed of Reaction," 255, 285.

Lambeth and Lanier were cautious hereditarians: "It is probable that a rather high degree of its [Negro] deficit in performance on these tests can be attributed to heredity. This conclusion must, of course, be merely tentative in view of the many factors other than heredity which might condition such performances as those studied here, and which have received little experimental study" (283).

64. Klineberg, *Race Differences,* 128.

65. W. Montague Cobb, "Race and Runners," 54; Cobb, "The Negro as a Biological Element," 343.

66. See, for example, Dubowitz, "Cross-Innervated Mammalian Skeletal Muscle," 481–96; Morris, "Human Muscle Fiber Type Grouping," 440–44; Edstrom and Nystrom, "Histochemical Types and Sizes," 257–69; Ogata and Murata, "Cytological Features," 245; Guth and Yellin, "The Dynamic Nature," 277–300.

67. Gollnick et al., "Enzyme Activity and Fiber Composition," 312–19.

68. Ama et al., "Skeletal Muscle Characteristics," 1760.

69. Ama et al., "Anaerobic Performances," 510.

70. Underwood, "On the Playground," 107.

71. Sokolove, "Are Blacks Better Athletes," 33ff. Gaffney, says the author, "was taken aback to be contacted by a reporter about his unpublished research," and he made a point of characterizing this survey as an inconclusive study:

> It was a very small sample, nothing that I would publish in a medical journal. To do it right you would need two or three times that many subjects, and you might go to Nigeria or Kenya or somewhere for black subjects who would be more racially pure . . . I'm not sure I have a lot of faith in the fiber-type hypothesis as it relates to sports. It was not what you would expect if you go with the dogma, that sprinters have more fast-twitch fiber.

72. Browne, "Patellar Tendon Reflex Time," 124.

73. Burfoot, "White Men Can't Run," 89–95.

74. Saltin, "Kenyanska löpare," 20.

75. Saltin et al., "Morphology, Enzyme Activities and Buffer Capacity," 226.

76. Saltin et al., "Aerobic Exercise Capacity," 215, 219.

77. "There is some understandable skepticism regarding the representativeness of structural data obtained from tiny muscle biopsy samples containing only a few milligrams of muscle tissue and a few hundred muscle fibers." See Hoppeler, "Exercise-Induced Ultrastructural Changes," 187. "One explanation for the dearth of investigations [into changes in human skeletal muscle] is the technical constraints involved in the study of the fiber type distribution within the human muscle. Only biopsies, very small parts of the muscle, have been analysed, with consequent difficulties and limitations in the inferences of the results." See Lexell et al., "What Is the Cause," 276.

> Studying the age-related changes in microstructural characteristics of human muscle is difficult, because the available techniques are invasive and not completely free of discomfort. To obtain skeletal muscle tissue, a

biopsy needle is used to remove a small amount of muscle. However, because this process is invasive, the needle must be small and the number of samples from each muscle must be kept to a minimum. Consequently, studies of human muscle characteristics are plagued with sampling problems. The amount of tissue available is usually only a few milligrams and contains only a few hundred muscle fibers. Therefore, biopsies taken from different locations and depths within the muscle have produced different results, and . . . the variability of fiber-type composition between biopsy sites is larger than the variability within a single biopsy site.

See Spirduso, *Physical Dimensions of Aging,* 128–29.
78. Saltin, "Kenyanska löpare," 20; Saltin et al., "Aerobic Exercise Capacity," 215, 219, 220.

## 15. Athleticizing the Black Criminal

1. Frederickson, *The Black Image in the White Mind,* 275–81.
2. Du Bois, "The Conservation of Races," 247.
3. Quoted in Gutman, "Persistent Myths," 188.
4. Darwin, *The Descent of Man,* 156.
5. Quoted in Baker, "Black Images," 333–34.
6. See, for example, Cartwright, "Diseases and Peculiarities," 66.
7. Brown, "Negro Character," 191.
8. Davis, "John Lamar," 415.
9. Fredrickson, *The Black Image in the White Mind,* 276–77.
10. Shaler, "Our Negro Types," 44, 45.
11. Hrdlicka, "Anthropology of the American Negro," 208. Hrdlicka also reports that "in 1918, Pyle and Collins published a paper on the mental and physical development of all the children, white and colored, of a Missouri county, the measurements including those of height, height sitting, weight, lung capacity, strength in the hands, and muscular speed" (213). It is worth noting that Hrdlicka, curator of anthropology at the Smithsonian Institution, made his own small contribution to the idea of the muscular Negro: "Finally, in muscular strength the negro male is, relative to stature, slightly stronger than the white with whom he is here compared in all tests, though more in the left than in the right hand; he comes more closely in this respect to the white immigrant laborer." See "The Full-Blood American Negro," 27. On Hrdlicka and the race issue, see Barkan, *The Retreat of Scientific Racism,* 97–100.
12. Hrdlicka quotes
    my old, respected friend and one of the best of observers, Mr. R. L. Garner. The observation relates to the natives in the vicinity of Fernan Vaz, West Coast of Africa: *"Simian acts of African children.* One of the most simian-like acts that I have observed in African babies of the white race, while universal among the anthropoid apes, is the manner of learning to walk . . . In the early stages of walking the African baby more

frequently walks on hands and feet exactly the same as the young ape . . . In their early efforts to walk alone the negro baby also elevates the arms and waves them as the apes do, while the white babe holds the arms below the level of the shoulder."

See Hrdlicka, "Quadruped Progression," 353.

13. Moehlig, "The Mesoderm of the Negro," 297.

14. Oschinsky, *The Racial Affinities of the Baganda,* 4.

15. "His views on what constitute race represented the conventions prevailing in physical anthropology up to World War II. Since he trained most physical anthropologists in the United States, his impact was correspondingly wide." In addition, "Hooton would probably have used the name species for the larger [racial] groups, but preferred to avoid the controversy such a definition would entail." See Barkan, *The Retreat of Scientific Racism,* 101, 102.

16. As Hooton put it in *Up from the Ape* (1931), "The physical characteristics which determine race are associated, in the main, with specific intangible and non-measurable, but nevertheless real and important, temperamental and mental variations." Quoted in Barkan, *The Retreat from Scientific Racism,* 103. On the history of constitutional theory, see Hoberman, *Mortal Engines,* 160–72.

17. Hooton, *Crime and the Man,* 342–43.

18. In articles published in the *New Republic* around the same time (October 31, 1994), Alexander Star, for example, referred to "a compassion without consequences" ("Dumbskulls," 11); Glenn Loury condemned the authors' "condescending apologia" ("A Political Act," 13); and Ann Hulbert criticized "the 'would-that-it-weren't-so' tone of *The Bell Curve* as completely disingenuous" ("Freedom Is Slavery," 19).

19. Barkan, *The Retreat from Scientific Racism,* 102.

20. Hooton, *Why Men Behave Like Apes,* 108–9.

21. Hooton, *Crime and the Man,* 368, 344. As if to remove any doubt about what he meant in the second quotation, Hooton rephrased it as follows: "The criminals are decidedly the more Negroid, but not smaller and biologically inferior" (347).

22. Cartwright, "Diseases and Peculiarities," 68. "But observation proved that, so far from being the black color caused by disease, the blackest negroes were always the healthiest, and the thicker the lips, and the flatter the nose, the sounder the constitution." See "Diseases and Physical Peculiarities," 507.

23. "Negro Slavery at the South," 211.

24. Hooton, *Crime and the Man,* 362. Cesare Lombroso, the Italian founder of a pseudo-scientific school of criminal anthropology, was a highly influential figure during the late nineteenth century. He too saw Negroid traits in criminals, such as a flattened nose, fleshy lips, and flat feet. See Lombroso, *Criminal Man,* 15, 16, 21.

25. Sellin, "The Negro Criminal," 52.

26. Darwin, *The Descent of Man,* 131.

27. Shipman, *The Evolution of Racism,* 173, 175.

28. Smith, "Giving the Olympics," 81B, 84. A German medical visitor to East Africa had long since refuted the myth of the Negro's flat feet, arguing that it had resulted from an "optical illusion" deriving from the heavily muscled feet of blacks who had done a great deal of walking while barefoot. See Herz, "Der Bau des Negerfusses," 1416–17. Coon and Hunt also advanced (in 1963) the idea of black motor precocity: "Negro babies show earlier ossification than do Whites, and are also more precocious in motor development." Quoted in Swan, "Racial Differences and Physical Anthropology," 153.

29. Davy, "On the Character of the Negro," clxviii.

30. Lambeth and Lanier, "Race Differences," 294.

31. Myrdal, *An American Dilemma,* 957, 959, 763.

32. Kephart, "The Negro Offender," 47.

33. For a critical reaction to Kardiner in an African-American journal, see Black, "Race and Unreason," 75.

34. See, for example, Mischel, "Preference for Delayed Reinforcement," 57; Edwards, "Blacks Versus Whites," 39.

35. Worthy and Markle, "Racial Differences," 439–43; for a second paper confirming these results, see Dunn and Lupfer, "Black and White Boys' Performance," 24–35; for a dissenting view, see Jones and Hochner, "Racial Differences," 86–95.

36. This quotation is from 1980 and appears in Gaston, "The Destruction of the Young Black Male," 374.

37. Levin, "Race Differences," 215.

38. In addition to Rushton's many articles, see *Race, Evolution and Behavior.*

39. Levin, "Race Differences," 208, 209.

40. Wilson and Herrnstein, *Crime and Human Nature,* 81, 89, 469.

41. Wilson, "In Loco Parentis," 12, 13.

42. Wilson, "Crime, Race, and Values," 91.

43. Will, "Nature and the Male Sex," 70.

44. Quoted in Shipman, *The Evolution of Racism,* 237–38. For a brief but penetrating analysis of Goodwin's arguments, see p. 238.

45. Jones, "Educating Black Males," 13.

46. "Within the past year, 1970, there has been an upsurge of interest in the use of drugs to 'quiet,' 'control' and 'redirect the energies' of more than 200,000 grammar school children in the United States receiving amphetamine and stimulant therapy, plus 100,000 children receiving tranquilizers and antidepressants and approximately 30% of all ghetto children are future candidates." See Lightfoot, "Hyperactivity in Children," 61. See also Erenberg, "Psychotropic Drugs," 214–16; Banks, "Drugs, Hyperactivity," 150–60.

47. "Ritalin, Harm or Help," *Destiny Magazine,* April 1995, 13.

48. "Do Teachers Punish According to Race?" *Time,* April 4, 1994, 30.

49. Quoted in Burnham, "Jensenism," 154. This quotation is attributed to the *New York Times,* August 31, 1969.

50. Patrick Buchanan, "Crime and Race," *Conservative Digest,* 1989, 37.

51. Sleeper, "The Clash," 19.
52. Quoted in Shipman, *The Evolution of Racism,* 258.

### 16. The Fear of Racial Biology

1. Wendy Baldwin, "Half Empty, Half Full," 88, 87.
2. Osborne and Feit, "The Use of Race," 275, 278. "When scientists identify race as a marker for social deprivation, cultural attitudes, or any other determinants of disease, they should be required to follow their preliminary reports with more detailed analyses as a condition for publication" (279).
3. Pollitzer and Anderson, "Ethnic and Genetic Differences," 1245.
4. Finally, we would like to allude to the concern that may be raised about the propriety of probing into this sensitive area of research. We are aware that average racial/ethnic differences in testosterone levels may not only help to explain group variations in disease, but could also be relevant to group differences in behavior patterns, given that testosterone and its metabolites are neurologically very active. While cognizant of the possible misuse of information on race differences in sex steroids, we consider the prospects of beneficial effects to be much greater, particularly in the field of health. Nevertheless, especially in the short run, scientists should be on guard against even the hint of any misuse of research findings in this area.

   See Ellis and Nyborg, "Racial/Ethnic Variations in Testosterone Levels," 74. As I argue in this chapter, Nyborg's hormonal theory of human types points toward black intellectual inferiority.
5. Heaney, "Editorial," 2289.
6. Shreeve, "Terms of Estrangement," 63. This article offers a nontechnical introduction to competing views of the race concept within the field of anthropology. I am inclined to agree with Stephen P. Nawrocki's formulation: "There is a viable biological concept of race that is thoroughly grounded in the Modern Synthesis of evolutionary biology, and while sociocultural constructs and phenomena are surely interesting and important in the study of human biology, biological race can be studied quite apart from ethnicity." Quoted in Boaz, "The Re-Emergence of 'Race.'" A fine introduction for the lay reader is Marks, *Human Biodiversity*. For a well-informed and thoughtful argument against the biological concept of race, see Goodman, "The Problematics of 'Race,'" 215–39.
7. Krieger and Bassett, "The Health of Black Folk," 162, 164.
8. Osborne and Feit, "The Use of Race," 278; "Poor and Black Patients Slighted, Study Says," *New York Times,* April 20, 1994.
9. "Is There Still Too Much Extrapolation," 1049–50; "Examples Abound of Gaps," 1051–52; "Race Joins Host," 1065–66. On the politics of requiring and resisting racial, ethnic, and gender inclusiveness in clinical studies, see "NIH Reports Greater Diversity," A32.
10. "Examples Abound," 1051.
11. The debate over separate hemoglobin cutoffs is a fascinating case study in

the ambiguous status of clinical evidence that can be interpreted differently by more and less biologically inclined scientists. Some early studies on this topic are Garn et al., "Lifelong Differences," 91–96; Garn and Clark, "Problems in Nutritional Assessment," 262–67; Kraemer et al., "Race-Related Differences," 327–31. For a critical commentary on the policy of establishing separate cutoffs, see Goodman, "The Problematics of 'Race,'" 225–26.

12. M. Roy Wilson, "Glaucoma in Blacks," 281. See also Rich, "Race and Glaucoma," 410.

13. "A biologic basis probably underlies the greater risk of glaucomatous optic nerve damage among blacks." See Lotufo et al., "Juvenile Glaucoma," 251. "Available data strongly indicate an inherent predisposition for this disease among black persons." See Tielsch et al., "Racial Variations," 373–74.

14. See Gaston et al., "Racial Equity," 1353.

15. Krieger and Bassett, "The Health of Black Folk," 163.

16. Gina Kolata, "Deadliness of Breast Cancer in Blacks Defies Easy Answer," *New York Times,* August 3, 1994. All three studies cited in this article deal with racial difference at the level of hormone receptors. For example:
    One study, by Dr. Richard M. Elledge, Dr. C. Kent Osborne and colleagues at the University of Texas Health Sciences Center in San Antonio, examined more than 6,000 tumors sent to them from hospitals throughout the United States. They found that tumors from black women had more actively dividing cells than those from white women and had tumor cells that lacked hormone receptors, another indicator of a poor prognosis.

17. Kohn, *The Race Gallery,* 250.

18. Murray and Herrnstein, "Race, Genes and I.Q.," 36. This observation occurs among the "thoughts" that, according to the authors, are to be seen as "decidedly speculative, and hence did not become part of our book" (35).

19. Given the absence of this subject in *The Bell Curve* and the single glancing remark about racial athletic aptitude in their essay, it is reasonable to assume that what little Murray and Herrnstein know in this area derives from their appreciative reading of Philippe Rushton's *Race, Evolution, and Behavior.* Rushton in turn relied entirely on a single article in a popular running magazine, which I discussed in Chapter 14.

20. Quoted in Mead, *Champion: Joe Louis,* 105.

21. Cohen, "Jimmy 'the Greek,'" 44. The author of this essay is an attorney, an economist, and an associate professor of law at the George Mason University School of Law, Fairfax, Virginia.

22. Karsai et al., "Hearing in Ethnically Different Longshoremen," 500. These authors note "that histological studies also showed otosclerosis to be seven times less frequent among blacks than among whites in the United States" (501). Also, McFadden and Wightman note that "the direction of the effect is toward less hearing loss in the dark-skinned and/or dark-eyed population than in the fair-skinned, light-eyed population." These authors point out that there "appears to be converging evidence that some fundamental aspect(s) of the operation of the peripheral auditory system may involve the

melanin located in the inner ear. The mechanisms are not yet understood." See McFadden and Wightman, "Audition," 110, 11.

Also, Robinson and Allen noted in "Racial Differences in Tympanometric Results" that

Schubert, Lassman and LaBenz (1980) reported a significant difference in failure rate of pure-tone screening between Black and White 3-year-old children, with White children showing a greater failure rate. Although the researchers did not do tympanometry, they did conduct otoscopic examinations and found Black subjects had lower incidence of "anomalies associated with conductive loss problems" ... The results of this study confirm and extend the results of other investigations showing that Black children have significantly less middle ear dysfunction, as indicated by failure of tympanometric screening, than do White children of the same age and social class. (140, 143)

Do such tests indicate racial anatomical differences? "Reported differences between angle, width, and length of Eustachian tubes of Black and White Americans resulting in functional differences . . . are well-known influences on middle ear disease" (143). The authors also suggest "that Black children may have larger pneumatic mastoid cells on the average" (143). Otosclerosis is a hearing disorder involving the deposition of bone matter on the third bone in the middle ear system, leading to a loss of mobility and significant hearing loss. I wish to thank Dennis McFadden for this information.

23. R. H. Post, "Hearing Acuity Variation," 67. The same racial difference was reported in the same year by different authors: "Threshold comparisons suggested a trend toward better hearing in the negro men than in the white men at frequencies above 2000 cps [cycles per second]." See Shepherd and Goldstein, "Race Difference," 390.

24. R. H. Post, "Hearing Acuity Variation," 74, 71. It is only fair to point out that Post's essay begins with (and then tends to disregard) the caveat that applies to all work in the area of racial physiology: "Studies of contrasts between different populations or racial groups in the frequencies of diminished acuity of a sensory function are beset by many difficulties and dangers. Contrasts which may appear to reflect constitutional or hereditary differences between a pair of populations are almost always open to alternative interpretations, to mention but one difficulty" (65).

25. Ibid., 68.

26. In 1937 one author thus referred to "racial peculiarities in . . . response to endocrine products." See Moehlig, "The Mesoderm of the Negro," 311. "Biochemists," another author wrote in 1957, "have noticed that the endocrine 'make-up' of Africans differs from that of Europeans." See Hingson, "Comparative Negro and White Mortality," 210. "And there is a trifle of evidence — this aspect has been studied so little that it still is in the highly speculative state — that the black man's adrenal glands, a vital factor in many sports, are larger than the white man's." See Kane, "An Assessment of 'Black Is Best,'" 74.

27. Keith, "The Differentiation of Mankind," 303, 304, 305.
28. Quoted in Landau, *Narratives of Human Evolution,* 71.
29. "After simultaneous adjustment by analysis of covariance for time of sampling and age, weight, alcohol use, smoking, and use of prescription drugs, there remained a 15% difference in total testosterone levels and a 13% difference in free testosterone levels between blacks and whites." See Ross et al., "Serum Testosterone Levels," 47. Also, "Previous studies showed higher values for serum total and free testosterone in young adult black men. We did not find differences in the concentration of serum total testosterone, but did find that the testosterone/SHBG ratio, which theoretically reflects free testosterone, was higher in the black men." On the subject of human growth hormone (GH): "The 24-h[our] integrated GH concentration and GH secretory burst amplitude were significantly higher in the black than in the white men." See Wright et al., "Greater Secretion of Growth Hormone," 2295, 2292. For a brief commentary on the prostate as an androgen target at risk for disease, see Friedl, "Effects of Anabolic Steroids," 113.
30. C.G.D. Brook, "Editorial," 2841. See also Margolis et al., "Invited Review of a Workshop," 874–75.
31. "There were significant correlations between lean body mass and BMD [bone mineral density] of the trochanter and femoral neck in the two [black and white] groups of men. Lean body mass reflects muscle mass." See Wright et al., "Greater Secretion of Growth Hormone," 2295.
32. Heaney, "Editorial," 2289. For a review of work on race and bone density, see Pollitzer and Anderson, "Ethnic and Genetic Differences," 1244–59. For a critique of the claim that bone density is a racial trait, see Alan H. Goodman, "The Problematics of 'Race,'" 222–24.
33. An early paper on muscle and bone mass argues that "muscular contractions induce strains in the bones to which the muscles are attached. Can the forces which a muscle exerts on a bone influence bone mass?" These authors believe they can: "Electric currents developed in bone stimulate formation of new bone. Thus mechanical stresses induce electrical effects in bone. Electrical forces have been shown to produce growth of new bone." See Doyle et al., "Bone Mass and Muscle Weight," 392.
34. Ellis and Nyborg, "Racial/Ethnic Variations," 74. It is of some significance, as we shall see, that these authors thank J. Philippe Rushton for his "advice and help on this research project."
35. Ibid.; Nyborg, *Hormones, Sex, and Society,* 44.
36. Ibid., 24, 25.
37. Ibid., 115, 52, 83, 135.
38. Ibid., 115, 52, 83, 135, 138.
39. Quoted in Adam Miller, "Professors of Hate."
40. Nyborg, *Hormones, Sex, and Society*, 141. Nyborg also cites the work of the psychologist Hans Eysenck to argue that "very young blacks show more rapid sensorimotor development than whites" (143).
41. Hunt, "On the Negro's Place," 37.

42. Geber and Dean, "The State of Development," 1216. See also Geber and Dean, "Gesell Tests," 1055–65.

43. Kilbride et al., "The Comparative Motor Development," 1422–28.

44. Williams and Scott, "Growth and Development," 116. It is worth noting that one author who accepts the precocity model dissociates the observed behavior from any genetic basis: "The data given, however, would support the suggestion that African children are first slightly advanced and then slightly retarded in adaptivity, language, and personal-social behavior as compared with American children. This is consistent with the described cultural factors in their home life." See John C. Cobb, "Precocity of African Children," 868.

45. Rushton's travails have attracted wide media coverage in Canada. See, for example, "Anti-Rushton Protestors Face Dilemma," *Toronto Star,* January 4, 1991, A12; "Group Seeks Removal of Rushton," *Globe and Mail* [Toronto], May 24, 1991, A5; "Rushton's Findings Called 'Bad Science,'" *Montreal Gazette,* February 17, 1989, B1; "Rushton's Credibility Attacked by Professors," *Toronto Star,* February 20, 1989, A7; "Rushton's Research Should Be Stopped, Colleague Tells Group," *Toronto Star,* March 30, 1989, A20; "Race Theories Exponent Fails Performance Review," *Montreal Gazette,* May 19, 1990, A11; "Ontario Police Investigate Controversial Professor," *Winnepeg Free Press,* March 13, 1989, 11; "Rushton Reprimanded for Mall Poll," *Montreal Gazette,* May 3, 1989, B4; "Rushton's Theories on Race Are Loony but Don't Warrant Charges, Scott Says," *Toronto Star,* November 4, 1989, A3.

46. "Controversial Prof Cool on Talk Show," *Calgary Herald,* February 17, 1989, D7; "Where Biff-Baff-Boom TV Falls Down," *Globe and Mail* [Toronto], March 4, 1989, C5. Rushton's appearance on this sometimes brawl-marred program reenacted what must have been the primal scene of his intellectual development: "In 1973, when intelligence researcher Hans Eysenck was beaten up by angry Maoists at the London School of Economics, then 30-year-old Rushton sat horrified in the audience." See "Pursuit of 'Truth' leads to Threats, Personal Losses for Rushton," *Calgary Herald,* January 14, 1995, B4. He lived out the same primal encounter at a "debate" with the Canadian geneticist and television personality David Suzuki. Faced with "almost 2,000 chanting, shouting and jeering people who jammed a campus theatre" on the night of February 8, 1989, Rushton told this audience: "I am not a racist." See "Suzuki Calls Theory 'Monstrous' but Rushton Denies Being Racist," *Toronto Star,* February 9, 1989, A1.

47. Rushton, *Race, Evolution, and Behavior,* 1, 7.

48. Ibid., xiii, 216, 260, 163, 271. For critiques of this kind of thinking, see Lewontin et al., *Not in Our Genes;* Marks, *Human Biodiversity;* Nelkin and Lindee, *The DNA Mystique.*

49. Rushton, *Race, Evolution, and Behavior,* 8. Rushton's discussion of black athletic performance is based entirely on Amby Burfoot's "White Men Can't Run."

50. "Second Professor Financed by 'Racist' Fund," *Sunday Star* [Toronto],

February 19, 1989, A18; "'Racist' Journal Published Rushton Data, Group Says," *Toronto Star,* February 21, 1989, A7.

> Between 1984 and 1987 Rushton received almost $160,000 from the tax-exempt American foundation which was established in 1937 to finance research into "racial betterment" . . . The Fund also gives money to the World Anti-Communist League and the British journal *Mankind Quarterly.* The Washington publisher of the journal, Dr. Roger Pearson, founded the Northern League, a European white supremacist organization, and has been described as "one of the foremost Nazi apologists in America."

See Simmons, "The Rushton Controversy," 16.

51. Simmons, "The Rushton Controversy," 15.
52. "Race Theories Exponent Fails Performance Review," *Montreal Gazette,* May 19, 1990, A11.
53. "Professor Credits Genetics for Might of German Military," *Winnipeg Free Press,* February 14, 1989, 11.
54. "Academic Freedom: It May Protect Crackpots but It's Not Expendable," *Globe and Mail* [Toronto], February 13, 1990, A7. "Despite their criticism of his methods, few academics would like to have seen Rushton investigated or otherwise censured by extra-departmental bodies. Like the administration, they insist that no matter how shoddy his research or how objectionable his findings, Rushton's academic freedom must be protected." See Simmons, "The Rushton Controversy," 15. This attitude unfortunately puts the issues of "shoddy research" and "objectionable findings" in the same category.
55. "University Chief Defends Professor's Right to Voice Racial Theory," *Globe and Mail* [Toronto], February 4, 1989, A6.
56. Ziegler et al., "Philippe Rushton," 19, 20.
57. Rushton's abrupt rise to fame stimulated an early and substantial critical literature. See, for example, Fredric Weizmann et al., "Eggs, Eggplants and Eggheads: A Rejoinder to Rushton" (n.d.); Ziegler et al., "Philippe Rushton," 19–22; Weizmann et al., "Scientific Racism in Contemporary Psychology," 81–91; Cain and Vanderwolf, "A Critique of Rushton," 777–84; Weizmann et al., "Differential K Theory and Racial Hierarchies," 1–13; Leslie, "Scientific Racism," 891–912; Anderson, "Rushton's Racial Comparisons," 51–60; Vanderwolf and Cain, "The Neurobiology of Race," 97–98.
58. I wish to thank Dennis McFadden for his assistance on this point.
59. "Rushton's Findings Called 'Bad Science,'" B1; "Rivera Takes on Rushton for Size," *Vancouver Sun,* February 17, 1989, D4.
60. Browne, "What Is Intelligence," 3.
61. "Rushton's *Race, Evolution, and Behavior* offers little that can be considered [of] redeeming scientific value . . . Rushton provides an encyclopedia of the latest in racist thought coated with a veneer of science." See Armelagos, "Race, Reason, and Rationale," 106. "His argument is much weaker than it first appears, based on a great array of material resembling delicate needlework: superficially impressive, it boasts a discernible pattern,

but is revealed on closer inspection to be composed entirely of holes . . . I don't know which is worse, Rushton's scientific failings or his blatant racism." See Barash, review, 1132. "Realizing how much more we have to learn about our own biological and behavioral variability, I find the study of human variation compelling. I do not advocate retreating from such study for political or social reasons. But not every approach to the subject is useful, particularly one whose outdated racial taxonomy obscures the very variability we hope to understand. Overall, this book is a good example of bad science." See Relethford, review, 94. *"Race, Evolution, and Behavior* is an amalgamation of bad biology and inexcusable anthropology. It is not science but advocacy and advocacy for the promotion of 'racialism.'" See Brace, "Racialism and Racist Agendas," 176. The most favorable of these reviews contains the following passage:

> I could easily pick at Rushton's hypothesis and, much less easily, at his data for many pages. He has given us a lot of diverse material into which we can sink our teeth. It almost certainly fits together into a coherent pattern. I am not at all convinced that he has seen the right pattern, but I don't have anything better to offer . . . I believe that Rushton deserves congratulations for bringing together this very important pioneering work and, most of all, for trying to understand it within the framework of natural science. Perhaps there ultimately will be some serious contribution from the traditional smoke-and-mirrors social science treatment of IQ, but for now Rushton's framework is essentially the only game in town.

See Harpending, "Human Biological Diversity," 102. For a longer critical treatment of Rushton's work, see Weizmann et al., "Inventing Racial Psychologies," 187–205.

62. Herrnstein and Murray, *The Bell Curve,* 643.
63. Blinkhorn, "Willow, Titwillow," 418, 419; Sperling, "Beating a Dead Monkey," 665. Regarding the ideological use of Rushton's work, C. Loring Brace comments: "Perpetuating catastrophe is not the stated aim of Rushton's book, but current promoters of racist agendas will almost certainly regard it as a welcome weapon to apply for their noxious purposes." See "Racialism and Racist Agendas," 176.
64. Rushton, *Race, Evolution, and Behavior,* 271. See also Rushton and Bogaert, "Race Differences in Sexual Behavior," 546. Ellis and Nyborg report that "small but significant average racial differences in serum testosterone were found when comparing middle-aged black men and non-Hispanic white men." See "Racial/Ethnic Variations," 74.
65. See Young, "Implementation of SI Units," 138. See also Fuentes-Arderiu et al., "Errors in Interpreting Hormonal Assays," 798.
66. Kemper, *Social Structure and Testosterone,* 26.
67. I wish to thank David Hoberman and William Kraemer for their invaluable assistance with this material.
68. S. W. Douglas, "Difficulties and Superstitions," 738.
69. Quoted in Adam Miller, "Professors of Hate," 106.

70. The same caveat applies to the hypothesized role of human growth hormone in producing racial difference. Are systemic hormone differences
"sufficient to explain the bone mass difference between the races?" asks
Robert P. Heaney. "Possibly, but probably not. It is worth recalling that
despite a certain directional similarity of effect, high levels of GH make
acromegalic bones, not black bones." See "Editorial," 2290.

71. On the social status of androgens, see Hoberman and Yesalis, "The History
of Synthetic Testosterone," 60–65, and Hoberman, "Listening to Steroids,"
35–44.

72. "Mr. Rushton's work may be ignored by the fearful, damned by the liberals,
and misused by the racists. It is unlikely to be truly understood by anyone."
See Snyderman, "How to Think about Race," 80.

73. Quoted in Adam Miller, "Professors of Hate," 110.

74. D'Souza, *The End of Racism,* 437–41. On October 10, 1995, Burfoot went
on the Internet to respond to D'Souza's use of his article. Part of his
message reads as follows: "'White Men' didn't have a political content. I
made some obvious observations about track results and tried to find scientific reasons that might explain them. I found some; much is lacking." I wish
to thank David Black for bringing this message to my attention.

75. On Sarich's controversial status, see Selvin, "The Raging Bull of Berkeley,"
368–71.

76. Kohn, *The Race Gallery,* 79.

77. Rushton, "Race and Crime," 326.

78. Kohn, *The Race Gallery,* 86, 81, 86.

79. Nyborg, *Hormones, Sex, and Society,* 53.

80. Burfoot, "White Men Can't Run," 91.

81. See, for example, Marks, *Human Biodiversity,* 237–43; Hoberman, *Mortal
Engines.*

82. Quoted in Kohn, *The Race Gallery,* 79; Marks, *Human Biodiversity,* 237.

83. Sarich, "The Eternal Triangle," S173.

84. McGee, "Introduction," vii.

85. On Keith and the Neanderthals, see Landau, *Narratives of Human Evolution,* 91; Rushton, *Race, Evolution, and Behavior,* 223.

86. Burfoot, "White Men Can't Run," 92.

87. Heaney, "Editorial," 2290. "Acknowledging that organisms are not assembled by an all-wise creative hand of natural selection poses difficulties
for the explanation of biological forms." See Marks, *Human Biodiversity,*
190–91.

88. Kohn, *The Race Gallery,* 123.

89. Rushton, "The Eternal Triangle," S168.

90. "Cracking the 'Bell Curve,'" *Austin American-Statesman,* May 19, 1996.

91. Kohn, *The Race Gallery,* 25, 6.

92. Ibid., 138, 150.

93. It is, of course, significant that comparable speculations are not made about
white athletes' traditional domination of other quantifiable performances
in track and field, such as shotputting, discus throwing, and pole vaulting. I

regard the tiny number of black participants in these events as entirely
culturally determined; for instance, a world-class black discus thrower (Luis
Delis) has developed in Cuba rather than the United States, where this is by
custom a white event. It should be noted that an African-American colle-
gian, Lawrence Johnson, set an American record of nineteen feet seven and
a half inches in the pole vault in May 1996, and that an African American,
Michael Carter, still holds a phenomenal record of just over eighty-one feet
in the high school shotput. Carter won a silver medal in this event at the
1984 Los Angeles Olympic Games.

94. Geber and Dean, "The State of Development," 1219, 1217.
95. Kilbride et al., "Comparative Motor Development," 1425.
96. Knobloch, "Precocity of African Children," 602–3; John C. Cobb, "Precocity of African Children," 867.
97. Diamond, "The Saltshaker's Curse," 26, 27.
98. Richard S. Cooper, quoted in Fackelmann, "The African Gene?," 255.
99. Curtin, "The Slavery Hypothesis," 1683, 1686.
100. "Slavery Was 'Great Biological Experiment,'" 58.

# Bibliography

*Books*

Adas, Michael. *Machines as the Measure of Men: Science, Technology, and Ideologies of Western Dominance*. Ithaca, N.Y.: Cornell University Press, 1989.

Appiah, Kwame Anthony. *In My Father's House*. New York: Oxford University Press, 1992.

Baker, Houston A., Jr. *Blues, Ideology, and Afro-American Literature*. Chicago: University of Chicago Press, 1984.

Baraka, Amiri [Leroi Jones]. *Blues People*. New York: William Morrow, 1963.

———. *Home: Social Essays*. New York: William Morrow, 1966.

Barkan, Elazar. *The Retreat of Scientific Racism: Changing Concepts of Race in Britain and the United States Between the World Wars*. Cambridge, Eng.: Cambridge University Press, 1992.

Basden, G. T. *Among the Ibos of Nigeria*. Philadelphia: Lippincott, 1921.

———. *Niger Ibos*. London: Seeley, Service, n.d.

Bayless, Vaurice G. "Selected Research Studies and Professional Literature Dealing with Physiological, Socioeconomic, Psychological, and Cultural Differences Between Black and White Males with Reference to the Performance of Athletic Skills." Ann Arbor: University Microfilms, 1980.

Cashmore, Ernest. *Black Sportsmen*. London: Routledge & Kegan Paul, 1982.

———. *Making Sense of Sport*. London: Routledge, 1990.

Cleaver, Eldridge. *Soul on Ice*. New York: Dell, 1968.

Conrad, Joseph. *Heart of Darkness*. New York: Bantam, 1987.

Cromwell, Dean B. *Championship Technique in Track and Field*. New York: Whittlesey House/McGraw-Hill, 1941.

Crouch, Stanley. *Notes of a Hanging Judge*. New York: Oxford University Press, 1990.

Cruse, Harold. *The Crisis of the Negro Intellectual*. New York: Quill, 1984.

Darwin, Charles. *The Descent of Man, and Selection in Relation to Sex*. Princeton, N.J.: Princeton University Press, 1981.

Davenport, Charles B., and M. Steggerda. *Race Crossing in America*. Washington, D.C.: Carnegie Institution, 1929.

Degérando, Joseph-Marie. *The Observations of Savage Peoples*. Berkeley: University of California Press, 1969.

Degler, Carl N. *In Search of Human Nature: The Decline and Revival of Darwinism in American Social Thought*. New York: Oxford University Press, 1991.

D'Souza, Dinesh. *The End of Racism*. New York: Free Press, 1995.

Du Bois, W.E.B. *The Health and Physique of the Negro American*. Atlanta: Atlanta University Press, 1906.

———. *On Sociology and the Black Community*. Chicago: University of Chicago Press, 1987.

Dyson, Michael Eric. *Reflecting Black: African-American Cultural Criticism*. Minneapolis: University of Minnesota Press, 1993.

Early, Gerald. *The Culture of Bruising: Essays on Prizefighting, Literature, and Modern American Culture*. Hopewell, N.J.: Ecco Press, 1994.

———. *Tuxedo Junction: Essays on American Culture*. Hopewell, N.J.: Ecco Press, 1994.

Edgerton, Robert. *Like Lions They Fought: The Zulu War and the Last Black Empire in Africa*. New York: Free Press, 1988.

———. *Mau Mau: An African Crucible*. New York: Ballantine, 1989.

Edwards, Harry. *The Revolt of the Black Athlete*. New York: Free Press, 1969.

Ellison, Ralph. *Shadow and Act*. New York: Vintage, 1972.

Evans, Raymond. *Exclusion, Exploitation, and Extermination: Race Relations in Colonial Queensland*. Sydney: Australia and New Zealand Book, 1975.

Fanon, Franz. *Black Skin, White Masks*. New York: Grove Press, 1967.

Flanagan, Roderick J. *The Aborigines of Australia*. Sydney: Edward F. Flanagan and George Robertson, 1888.

Foa, Édouard. *Résultats scientifiques des voyages en Afrique*. Paris: Imprimerie Nationale, 1898.

Frazier, E. Franklin. *Black Bourgeoisie*. New York: Free Press, 1957.

Fredrickson, George M. *The Black Image in the White Mind: The Debate on Afro-American Character and Destiny, 1817–1914*. Middletown, Conn.: Wesleyan University Press, 1971.

Fritzsche, Peter. *A Nation of Fliers: German Aviation and the Popular Imagination*. Cambridge, Mass.: Harvard University Press, 1992.

Genovese, Eugene D. *Roll, Jordan, Roll: The World the Slaves Made*. New York: Vintage, 1976.

George, Nelson. *Elevating the Game: Black Men and Basketball*. New York: HarperCollins, 1992.

Gilroy, Paul. *Small Acts: Thoughts on the Politics of Black Cultures*. London: Serpent's Tail, 1993.

Glazer, Nathan, and Daniel P. Moynihan. *Beyond the Melting Pot*. Cambridge, Mass.: MIT Press, 1963.

Grier, William H., and Price M. Cobbs. *Black Rage*. New York: Basic Books, 1992.

Hampton, Robert L., ed. *Black Family Violence: Current Research and Theory.* Lexington, Mass.: Lexington Books, 1991.

Hare, Nathan. *The Black Anglo-Saxons.* Chicago: Third World Press, 1991.

Herrnstein, Richard J., and Charles Murray. *The Bell Curve: Intelligence and Class Structure in American Life.* New York: Free Press, 1994.

Herskovits, Melville J. *The Myth of the Negro Past.* New York: Harper & Brothers, 1941.

Hibbert, Christopher. *Africa Explored: Europeans in the Dark Continent 1769–1889.* Harmondsworth, Eng.: Penguin, 1982.

Higginson, Thomas Wentworth. *Army Life in a Black Regiment.* Boston: Fields, Osgood, 1870.

Hoberman, John. *Mortal Engines: The Science of Performance and the Dehumanization of Sport.* New York: Free Press, 1992.

———. *The Olympic Crisis: Sport, Politics, and the Moral Order.* New Rochelle, N.Y.: Aristide D. Caratzas, 1986.

Hoffman, Frederick L. *Race Traits and Tendencies of the American Negro.* New York: American Economic Association, 1896.

Holmes, S. J. *Studies in Evolution and Eugenics.* New York: Harcourt, Brace, 1923.

Hooton, Earnest Albert. *Crime and the Man.* Cambridge, Mass.: Harvard University Press, 1939.

———. *Why Men Behave Like Apes and Vice Versa, or Body and Behavior.* Princeton, N.J.: Princeton University Press, 1941.

James, C.L.R. *Beyond a Boundary.* New York: Pantheon, 1983.

Jarvie, Grant, ed. *Sport, Racism and Ethnicity.* London: Falmer Press, 1991.

Jeal, Tim. *The Boy-Man: The Life of Lord Baden-Powell.* New York: William Morrow, 1990.

Jennings, Andrew. *The New Lords of the Rings.* New York: Simon & Schuster, 1996.

Jensen, Arthur R. *Bias in Mental Testing.* New York: Free Press, 1980.

Johnson, Charles S. *Growing Up in the Black Belt: Negro Youth in the Rural South.* Washington, D.C.: American Council on Education, 1941.

Jordan, Winthrop D. *White Over Black: American Attitudes Toward the Negro, 1550–1812.* New York: Norton, 1977.

Kemper, Theodore D. *Social Structure and Testosterone.* New Brunswick, N.J.: Rutgers University Press, 1990.

Klineberg, Otto. *Race Differences.* New York: Harper & Brothers, 1935.

Kochman, Thomas. *Black and White Styles in Conflict.* Chicago: University of Chicago Press, 1981.

Kohn, Marek. *The Race Gallery: The Return of Racial Science.* London: Jonathan Cape, 1995.

Kunjufu, Jawanza. *To Be Popular or Smart: The Black Peer Group.* Chicago: African American Images, 1988.

Landau, Misia. *Narratives of Human Evolution.* New Haven, Conn.: Yale University Press, 1991.

Levine, Lawrence W. *Black Culture and Black Consciousness: Afro-American Folk Thought from Slavery to Freedom.* New York: Oxford University Press, 1977.

Lewis, Julian Herman. *The Biology of the Negro*. Chicago: University of Chicago Press, 1942.

Lewontin, R. C., Steven Rose, and Leon J. Kamin. *Not in Our Genes: Biology, Ideology, and Human Nature*. New York: Pantheon, 1984.

Locke, Alain, ed. *The New Negro: An Interpretation*. New York: Albert and Charles Boni, 1925.

Lombroso, Cesare. *Criminal Man*. Montclair, N.J.: Patterson Smith, 1972.

Lutz, Catherine A., and Jane L. Collins. *Reading National Geographic*. Chicago: University of Chicago Press, 1993.

MacMunn, G[eorge]. *The Armies of India*. Delhi: Gian Publications, 1911.

———. *The Martial Races of India*. London: Sampson Low, 1931.

Mangan, J. A. *The Games Ethic and Imperialism: Aspects of the Diffusion of an Ideal*. New York: Viking, 1985.

Marks, Jonathan. *Human Biodiversity: Genes, Race, and History*. New York: Aldine de Gruyter, 1995.

Mead, Chris. *Champion: Joe Louis, Black Hero in White America*. New York: Penguin Books, 1986.

Morris, James. *Pax Britannica: The Climax of an Empire*. New York: Harcourt Brace Jovanovich, 1968.

Moses, Wilson Jeremiah. *Black Messiahs and Uncle Toms: Social and Literary Manipulations of a Religious Myth*. University Park: Pennsylvania State University Press.

Motley, Mary Penick, ed. *The Invisible Soldier: The Experience of the Black Soldier, World War II*. Detroit: Wayne State University Press, 1987.

Myrdal, Gunnar. *An American Dilemma: The Negro Problem and Modern Democracy*. New York: Harper & Brothers, 1944.

Nelkin, Dorothy, and M. Susan Lindee. *The DNA Mystique: The Gene as a Cultural Icon*. New York: Freeman, 1995 .

Nerlich, Michael. *Ideology of Adventure: Studies in Modern Consciousness, 1100–1750*. Vol. 1. Minneapolis: University of Minnesota Press, 1987.

Nightingale, Carl Husemoller. *On the Edge*. New York: Basic Books, 1993.

Nyborg, Helmuth. *Hormones, Sex, and Society: The Science of Physicology*. Westport, Conn.: Praeger, 1994.

Oschinsky, Lawrence. *The Racial Affinities of the Baganda and Other Bantu Tribes of British East Africa*. Cambridge, Eng.: W. Heffer & Sons, 1954.

Pasteur, Alfred B. and Ivory L. Toldson. *Roots of Soul: The Psychology of Black Expressiveness*. Garden City, N.Y.: Anchor, 1982.

Phillips, Jock. *A Man's Country? The Image of the Pakeha Male — A History*. New York: Penguin Books, 1987.

Reade, W. Winwood. *Savage Africa*. London: Smith, Elder, 1864.

Reed, Ishmael. *Airing Dirty Laundry*. Reading, Mass.: Addison-Wesley, 1993.

———. *Writin' Is Fightin': Thirty-Seven Years of Boxing on Paper*. New York: Atheneum, 1988.

Rice, Edward. *Captain Sir Richard Francis Burton*. New York: Scribner's, 1990.

Rushton, J. Philippe. *Race, Evolution, and Behavior: A Life-History Perspective*. New Brunswick, N.J.: Transaction, 1995.

Sammons, Jeffrey T. *Beyond the Ring: The Role of Boxing in American Society*. Urbana: University of Illinois Press, 1988.

Savitt, Todd L. *Medicine and Slavery: The Diseases and Health Care of Blacks in Antebellum Virginia*. Urbana: University of Illinois Press, 1978.

Scott, Lawrence P., and William M. Womack, Sr. *Double V: The Civil Rights Struggle of the Tuskegee Airmen*. East Lansing: Michigan State University Press, 1994.

Shipman, Pat. *The Evolution of Racism: Human Differences and the Use and Abuse of Science*. New York: Simon & Schuster, 1994.

Simson, Vyv, and Andrew Jennings. *The Lords of the Rings: Power, Money and Drugs in the Modern Olympics*. London: Simon & Schuster, 1992.

Sinclair, John. *A Collection of Papers on the Subject of Athletic Exercises &c. &c.* London: E. Blackader, 1806.

Solomon, R. Patrick. *Black Resistance in High School: Forging a Separatist Culture*. Albany: State University of New York Press, 1992.

Spirduso, Waneen. *Physical Dimensions of Aging*. Champaign: Human Kinetics, 1995.

Spurr, David. *The Rhetoric of Empire: Colonial Discourse in Journalism, Travel Writing, and Imperial Administration*. Durham, N.C.: Duke University Press, 1993.

Steele, Shelby. *The Content of Our Character*. New York: HarperPerennial, 1991.

Stigler, Robert. *Rassenphysiologische Ergebnisse meiner Forschungsreise in Uganda 1911–12*. Vienna: Österreichische Staatsdruckerei, 1952.

Stocking, George, Jr. "American Social Scientists and Race Theory: 1890–1915." Ann Arbor: University Microfilms, 1960.

Tabili, Laura. *"We Ask for British Justice": Workers and Racial Difference in Late Imperial Britain*. Ithaca, N.Y.: Cornell University Press, 1994.

Tatz, Colin. *Aborigines in Sports*. Bedford Park: Australian Society for Sports History, 1987.

Torgovnick, Marianna. *Gone Primitive: Savage Intellects, Modern Lives*. Chicago: University of Chicago Press, 1990.

Tucker, William H. *The Science and Politics of Racial Research*. Urbana: University of Illinois Press, 1994.

Tyack, David B. *The One Best System: A History of American Urban Education*. Cambridge, Mass.: Harvard University Press, 1974.

Tygiel, Jules. *Baseball's Great Experiment: Jackie Robinson and His Legacy*. New York: Vintage, 1984.

Van Deburg, William L. *Slavery & Race in American Popular Culture*. Madison: University of Wisconsin Press, 1984.

Vogt, Carl. *Lectures on Man*. London: Longman, Green, Longman, and Roberts, 1863.

Waitz, Theodor. *Introduction to Anthropology*. [*Anthropologie der Naturvölker*. Vol. I.] London: 1863.

Welsing, Frances Cress. *The Isis Papers: The Keys to the Colors*. Chicago: Third World Press, 1991.

West, Cornel. *Race Matters*. New York: Vintage, 1994.

Wideman, John Edgar. *Fatheralong*. New York: Vintage, 1995.

Williams, John Anthony, Sr. "Perceptions of the No-Pledge Policy for New Member Intake by Undergraduate Members of Predominantly Black Fraternities and Sororities" (doctoral dissertation). Kansas State University, 1992.

Wilson, James Q., and Richard J. Herrnstein. *Crime & Human Nature*. New York: Touchstone, 1985.

Woodson, Carter G. *The Mis-Education of the Negro*. Trenton, N.J.: Africa World Press, 1990.

Wyatt-Brown, Bertram. *Southern Honor: Ethics and Behavior in the Old South*. New York: Oxford University Press, 1983.


*Articles*

Abrahams, Bertram. "Race and Athletics." *Eugenics Review* 44 (October 1952).

Abramowitz, S., et al. "Vital Capacity of the Negro." *American Review of Respiratory Disease* 92 (August 1965).

Allen, Bertram. "Breaking World's Records." *Harper's Monthly Magazine* (August 1936).

Ama, Pierre F. M., Pierre Lagasse, Claude Bouchard, and Jean-Aimé Simoneau. "Anaerobic Performances in Black and White Subjects." *Medicine and Science in Sports and Exercise* 22 (1990).

Ama, Pierre F. M., J. A. Simoneau, M. R. Boulay, O. Serasse, G. Thériault, and C. Bouchard. "Skeletal Muscle Characteristics in Sedentary Black and Caucasian Males." *Journal of Applied Physiology* 61 (1986).

Anderson, Judith L. "Rushton's Racial Comparisons: An Ecological Critique of Theory and Method." *Canadian Psychology/Psychologie canadienne* 32 (1991).

Armelagos, George. "Race, Reason, and Rationale." *Evolutionary Anthropology* 4 (1995).

"Avoiding Competition Against Blacks." *Atlanta Journal/Atlanta Constitution* (April 17, 1994).

Bache, R. Meade. "Reaction Time with Reference to Race." *Psychological Review* (1895).

Baker, Donald G. "Black Images: The Afro-American in Popular Novels, 1900–1945." *Journal of Popular Culture* 7 (Fall 1973).

Baker, Houston A., Jr. "Spike Lee and the Commerce of Culture." *Black American Literature Forum* 25 (Summer 1991).

Bakwin, Harry. "The Negro Infant." *Human Biology* 4 (February 1932).

Baldwin, Brooke. "On the Verso: Postcard Messages as a Key to Popular Prejudices." *Journal of Popular Culture* 22 (Winter 1988).

Baldwin, Wendy. "Half Empty, Half Full: What We Know About Low Birth Weight Among Blacks." *Journal of the American Medical Association* 255 (January 3, 1986).

Bale, John. "Idealized Olympians: European Ways of Seeing Tutsi Body Culture." Paper presented at the Sport, Philosophy and the Olympics Conference, Maryland College, Woburn, England, March 15–17, 1996.

Banks, Lacy J. "World's Leading Heart Transplant Sets Super Pace." *Ebony* 26 (April 1973).

Banks, William. "Drugs, Hyperactivity, and Black Schoolchildren." *Journal of Negro Education* 45 (Spring 1976).

Barash, David P. Review. *Animal Behaviour* 49 (April 1995).

Bayles, Martha. "The Problem with Post-Racism." *New Republic,* August 5, 1985.

"Beauty of Basketball Lost in Flashiness, Says Wooden." *USA Today,* April 13, 1993.

Bell, William M. "The Sociological Contributions of Physical Education to the Needs of the Negro." *Research Quarterly* 10 (1939).

Berger, Joseph. "What Do They Mean By 'Black Learning Style'?" *New York Times,* July 6, 1988.

Bissinger, H. G. "When Whites Flee." *New York Times Magazine,* May 29, 1994.

Black, Isabella. "Race and Unreason: Anti-Negro Opinion in Professional and Scientific Literature Since 1954." *Phylon* 26 (1964).

"Black Pirates on the Spanish Main." *The Crisis* (November 1940).

Blacking, John. "Games and Sport in Pre-Colonial African Societies." In William J. Baker and James A. Mangan, eds., *Sport in Africa: Essays in Social History.* New York: Africana, 1987.

Blinkhorn, Steve. "Willow, Titwillow, Titwillow." *Nature* 372 (December 1, 1994).

Boaz, Noel T. "The Re-Emergence of 'Race.'" *Physical Anthropology News* 12 (Fall 1993).

Boland, Frank K. "Morsus Humanus: Sixty Cases of Human Bites in Negroes." *Journal of the American Medical Association* 116 (January 11, 1941).

Bond, Jean Carey. "Two Views of Black Macho and the Myth of the Superwoman." *Freedomways* 19 (1979).

Brace, C. Loring. "Racialism and Racist Agendas." *American Anthropologist* 98 (March 1996).

Breskin, David. "The Rolling Stone Interview: Spike Lee." *Rolling Stone,* July 11–25, 1991.

Brook, C.G.D. "Editorial: Strong Bones Don't Break!" *Journal of Clinical Endocrinology and Metabolism* 80 (1995).

Brown, Bertram Wyatt. "The Mask of Obedience: Male Slave Psychology in the Old South." *American Historical Review* 93 (December 1988).

Brown, Sterling A. "Negro Character as Seen by White Authors." *Journal of Negro Education* 2 (1933).

Browne, Malcolm W. "What Is Intelligence, and Who Has It?" *New York Times Book Review,* October 16, 1994.

Browne, Robert L. "A Comparison of the Patellar Tendon Reflex Time of Whites and Negroes." *Research Quarterly* (1935).

Bunch, Lonnie G., III. "In Search of a Dream: The Flight of Herman Banning and Thomas Allen." *Journal of American Culture* 7 (Spring/Summer 1984).

Burfoot, Amby. "White Men Can't Run." *Runner's World,* August 1992.

Burnham, Dorothy. "Jensenism: The New Pseudoscience of Racism." *Freedomways* 11 (1971).

Cain, Donald P., and C. H. Vanderwolf. "A Critique of Rushton on Race, Brain Size and Intelligence." *Personality and Individual Differences* 11 (1990).

Carlisle, Rodney. "Black Explorers of Africa: Pioneers in Pan-African Identity," *Negro History Bulletin* 37 (January 1974).

Carter, Elmer A. "The Negro in College Athletics." *Opportunity* (July 1933).

Carter, James H. "Psychosocial Aspects of Aging: The Black Elderly." *Journal of the National Medical Association* (1984).

Carter, J. E. Lindsay. "Ethnic Variations in Human Performance: Morphological and Compositional Characteristics." Paper presented at the American College of Sports Medicine Symposium, Orlando, Florida, May 31, 1992.

Cartwright, Samuel A. "The Diseases of Negroes — Pulmonary Congestions, Pneumonia, &c." *De Bow's Review* 11 (1851).

———. "Diseases and Peculiarities of the Negro Race." *De Bow's Review* 11 (1851).

———. "Diseases and Physical Peculiarities of Negroes." *De Bow's Review* 11 (1851).

———. "Dr. Cartwright on the Caucasians and the Africans." *De Bow's Review* 25 (1858).

Chavez, Gilberto F., et al. "Leading Major Congenital Malformations Among Minority Groups in the United States, 1981–1986." *Journal of the American Medical Association* 261 (January 13, 1989).

Cobb, John C. "Precocity of African Children." *Pediatrics* 21 (1958).

Cobb, W. Montague. "An Anatomist's View of Human Relations." *Journal of the National Medical Association* 67 (May 1975).

———. "Does Science Favor Negro Athletes?" *Negro Digest* (May 1947).

———. "The Negro as a Biological Element in the American Population." *Journal of Negro Education* 8 (1939).

———. "Physical Anthropology of the American Negro." *American Journal of Physical Anthropology* 29 (June 1942).

———. "Race and Runners." *Journal of Health and Physical Education* (January 1936).

———. "Surgery and the Negro Physician: Some Parallels in Background." *Journal of the National Medical Association* 43 (May 1951).

———. "Toward a Federation of the World." *Journal of the National Medical Association* 78 (1986).

Cohen, Lloyd R. "The Puzzling Case of Jimmy 'the Greek.'" *Society* 31 (1994).

Comaroff, Jean. "The Diseased Heart of Africa: Medicine, Colonialism, and the Black Body." In Shirley Lindenbaum and Margaret Lock, eds., *Knowledge, Power, and Practice: The Anthropology of Medicine and Everyday Life.* Berkeley: University of California Press, 1993.

Connes, Keith. "Can a Black Man Fly?" *Flying* 85 (July 1969).

Crason, John. "Army Alpha, Army Brass, and the Search for Army Intelligence." *Isis* 84 (1993).

Cripps, Thomas. "The Noble Black Savage: A Problem in the Politics of Television Art." *Journal of Popular Culture* 8 (Spring 1975).

Cripps, Thomas, and David Culbert. "The Negro Soldier (1944): Film Propaganda in Black and White." *American Quarterly* 31 (Winter 1979).

Curtin, Philip D. "The Slavery Hypothesis for Hypertension Among African Americans: The Historical Evidence." *American Journal of Public Health* (December 1992).

Damon, Albert. "Negro-White Differences in Pulmonary Function (Vital Capacity, Timed Vital Capacity, and Expiratory Flow Rate)." *Human Biology* 38 (December 1966).

Daniel, Robert P. "Negro-White Differences in Non-Intellectual Traits, and in Special Abilities." *Journal of Negro Education* 3 (1934).

Davenport, C. B. "Do the Races Differ in Mental Capacity?" *Human Biology* 1 (January 1929).

Davis, Rebecca Harding. "John Lamar." *Atlantic Monthly,* April 1862.

Davison, Hal M., and J. C. Thoroughman. "A Study of Heart Disease in the Negro Race." *Southern Medical Journal* 21 (June 1928).

Davy, John. "On the Character of the Negro, — Chiefly in Relation to Industrial Habits." *Journal of the Anthropological Society* 7 (1869).

de Jonge, Peter. "Talking Trash." *New York Times Magazine,* June 6, 1993.

DeMott, Benjamin. "Sure, We're All Just One Big Happy Family." *New York Times,* January 7, 1996.

Diamond, Jared. "The Saltshaker's Curse." *Natural History,* October 1991.

Diawara, Manthia. "Englishness and Blackness: Cricket as Discourse on Colonialism." *Callaloo* 13 (1990).

Dickens, Dorothy, and Robert N. Ford. "Geophagy (Dirt Eating) Among Mississippi Negro School Children." *American Sociological Review* 7 (February 1942).

"Do Teachers Punish According to Race?" *Time,* April 4, 1994.

"Dr. William Montague Cobb (1904–1990): The Principal Historian of Afro-Americans in Medicine." *The Crisis* 98 (January 1991).

"Does Integration Work in the Armed Forces?" *U.S. News & World Report,* May 11, 1956.

Douglas, S. W. "Difficulties and Superstitions Encountered in Practice Among Negroes." *Southern Medical Journal* 19 (October 1926).

Douglass, Frederick. "The Claims of the Negro Ethnologically Considered." In Philip S. Foner, ed., *The Life and Writings of Frederick Douglass*. Vol. II. New York: International Publishers, 1950.

———. "Why Should a Colored Man Enlist?" [*Douglass' Monthly*, April 1863.] In Philip S. Foner, ed., *The Life and Writings of Frederick Douglass*. Vol. III. New York: International Publishers, 1950.

Dowler, B. "The Vital Statistics of the Negroes in the United States." *New Orleans Medical and Surgical Journal* 13 (1856).

Doyle, Frank, et al. "Relation Between Bone Mass and Muscle Weight." *The Lancet* (February 21, 1970).

Drake, Wilbur A. "The Gynecologist: Some of His Problems and His Obligations to the Present and the Future." *Journal of the National Medical Association* 12 (1920).

Dubowitz, V. "Cross-Innervated Mammalian Skeletal Muscle: Histochemical, Physiological and Biochemical Observations." *Journal of Physiology* [London] 193 (1967).

Dunn, Joe R., and Michael Lupfer. "A Comparison of Black and White Boys' Performance in Self-Paced and Reactive Sports Activities." *Journal of Applied Social Psychology* 4 (1974).

Eagleson, Oran W., and Lillian E. Taylor. "The Preference of Twenty-Five Negro College Women for Major and Minor Chords." *Journal of Experimental Psychology* 28 (May 1941).

Edstrom, L., and B. Nystrom. "Histochemical Types and Sizes of Fibres of Normal Human Muscles." *Acta Neurologica Scandinavica* 45 (1969).

Edwards, Daniel W. "Blacks Versus Whites: When Is Race a Relevant Variable?" *Journal of Personality and Social Psychology* 29 (1974).

Edwards, Diane D. "Slave-Ship Hypothesis of Hypertension." *Science News* 133 (January 30, 1988).

Edwards, Harry. "The Black Athletes: 20th Century Gladiators for White America." *Psychology Today* 7 (November 1973).

———. "The Sources of Black Athletic Superiority." *Black Scholar* (November 1971).

"Die Ehre des Abendlandes retten." *Der Spiegel,* March 11, 1996.

Ellis, Lee, and Helmuth Nyborg. "Racial/Ethnic Variations in Male Testosterone Levels: A Probable Contributor to Group Differences in Health." *Steroids* 57 (1992).

Erenberg, Gerald. "Psychotropic Drugs — Harm or Help." *Journal of the National Medical Association* 66 (May 1974).

Evans, Art. "Joe Louis as a Key Functionary: White Reactions Toward a Black Champion." *Journal of Black Studies* 16 (September 1985).

"Examples Abound of Gaps in Medical Knowledge Because of Groups Excluded from Scientific Study." *Journal of the American Medical Association* 263 (February 23, 1990).

Fackelmann, Kathy A. "The African Gene? Searching Through History for the Roots of Black Hypertension." *Science News* 140 (October 19, 1991).

Findlay, G. M., et al. "A Note on Sickling and Flying." *Journal of the Royal Army Medical Corps* 89 (July–December 1947).

Fordham, Signithia, and John U. Ogbu. "Black Students' School Success: Coping with the 'Burden of Acting White.'" *Urban Review* 18 (1986).

Foster, John. "Retroviruses, Genetic Lesioning and Mental Deficiency Among Blacks: A Causal Hypothesis." *Mankind Quarterly* 31 (Fall/Winter 1990).

Freeman, Frank R. "The Health of the American Slave Examined by Means of Union Army Medical Statistics." *Journal of the National Medical Association* 77 (1985).

Friedl, Karl E. "Effects of Anabolic Steroids on Physical Health." In Charles E. Yesalis, ed., *Anabolic Steroids in Sport and Exercise.* Champaign, Ill.: Human Kinetics, 1993.

Froberville, M. de. "Rapport sur les races nègres de l'Afrique orientale au sud de l'équateur." *Comptes Rendus de l'Académie des Sciences* (1850).

Fuentes-Arderiu, Javier, et al. "Errors in Interpreting Hormonal Assays." *Annals of Internal Medicine* 105 (November 1986).

"Fußball gut, alles gut." *Der Spiegel,* October 26, 1992.

Gabriel, Trip. "China Strains for Olympic Glory." *New York Times Magazine,* April 24, 1988.

Garibaldi, Antoine M. "Educating and Motivating African American Males to Succeed." *Journal of Negro Education* 61 (1992).

Garn, Stanley M., and Diane C. Clark. "Problems in the Nutritional Assessment of Black Individuals." *American Journal of Public Health* 66 (March 1976).

Garn, Stanley M., Nathan J. Smith, and Diane C. Clark. "Lifelong Differences in Hemoglobin Levels Between Blacks and Whites." *Journal of the National Medical Association* 67 (March 1975).

Gaston, John C. "The Destruction of the Black Male: The Impact of Popular Culture and Organized Sports." *Journal of Black Studies* 16 (June 1986).

Gaston, Robert S., et al. "Racial Equity in Renal Transplantation: The Disparate Impact of HLA-Based Allocation." *Journal of the American Medical Association* 270 (September 15, 1993).

Geber, Marcelle, and R.F.A. Dean. "Gesell Tests on African Children." *Pediatrics* 20 (1957).

———. "The State of Development of Newborn African Children." *The Lancet* (June 15, 1957).

"Genial und kreativ." *Der Spiegel,* January 6, 1992.

George, John. "The Virtual Disappearance of the White Male Sprinter in the United States: A Speculative Essay." *Sociology of Sport Journal* 11 (1994).

George, Theodore R. "Glaucoma in the Negro." *Journal of the National Medical Association* 44 (May 1952).

Gerace, Laura, et al. "Skeletal Differences Between Black and White Men and Their Relevance to Body Composition Estimates." *American Journal of Human Biology* 6 (1994).

Gibbs, Tyson, Kathleen Cargill, Leslie Sue Lieberman, and Elizabeth Reitz. "Nutrition in a Slave Population: An Anthropological Examination." *Medical Anthropology* 4 (Spring 1980).

Gibson, William I. (Bill). "The Old Football Rulers Pass." *The Crisis* (December 1934).

"Gnadenlos ausgenommen." *Der Spiegel,* January 6, 1992.

Goldstein, Marcus S. "Theory of Survival of the Unfit." *Journal of the National Medical Association* 47 (July 1955).

Gollnick, P. D., et al. "Enzyme Activity and Fiber Composition in Skeletal Muscle of Untrained and Trained Men." *Journal of Applied Physiology* 33 (1972).

Goodman, Alan F. "The Problematics of 'Race' in Contemporary Biological Anthropology." In Noel T. Boaz and Linda D. Wolfe, eds., *Biological*

*Anthropology: The State of the Science.* Bend, Ore.: International Institute for Human Evolutionary Research, 1995).

Goodman, Walter. "Missing Middle-Class Black in TV News." *New York Times,* May 22, 1990.

Goss, Clay. "Ali as Creative Black Man." *Black World,* January 1975.

Guth, L., and H. Yellin. "The Dynamic Nature of the So-Called 'Fiber Types' of Mammalian Skeletal Muscle." *Experimental Neurology* 31 (1971).

Gutman, Herbert G. "Persistent Myths About the Afro-American Family." *Journal of Interdisciplinary History* 6 (Autumn 1975).

Hairston, Loyle. "The Black Film — 'Supernigger' as Folk Hero." *Freedomways* 14 (1974).

Hall, Thomas B. "Vegetative Dermatoses in the Negro." *Southern Medical Journal* 32 (April 1939).

Haller, John S., Jr. "The Negro and the Southern Physician: A Study of Medical and Racial Attitudes 1800–1860." *Medical History* (1972).

———. "The Physician Versus the Negro: Medical and Anthropological Concepts of Race in the Late Nineteenth Century." *Bulletin of the History of Medicine* 44 (March–April 1970).

Harley, George. "Comparison Between the Recuperative Bodily Power of Man in a Rude and in a Highly Civilised State: Illustrative of the Probable Recuperative Capacity of Men of the Stone-Age in Europe." *Journal of the Anthropological Institute* (1888).

Harmon, John H. "Black Cowboys Are Real." *The Crisis* (September 1940).

Harpending, Henry. "Human Biological Diversity." *Evolutionary Anthropology* 4 (1995).

Harris, Othello. "The Image of the African American in Psychological Journals, 1825–1923." *Black Scholar* 21 (1990).

Hartmann, Robert. "Die Springflut der schwarzen Sieger." *Süddeutsche Zeitung,* September 16, 1988.

———. "Weiße als Exoten der Langstrecken." *Süddeutsche Zeitung,* April 19, 1988.

Hazen, H. H. "Syphilis in the American Negro." *Journal of the American Medical Association* 63 (August 8, 1914).

Heaney, Robert P. "Editorial: Bone Mass, the Mechanostat, and Ethnic Differences." *Journal of Clinical Endocrinology and Metabolism* 80 (1995).

"Heilige und Sündenböcke." *Der Spiegel,* April 17, 1995.

Henderson, Edwin Bancroft. "The Negro Athlete and Race Prejudice." *Opportunity* (March 1936).

Herz, Max. "Der Bau des Negerfusses." *Münchener Medizinische Wochenschrift,* August 26, 1902.

Hingson, Robert A. "Comparative Negro and White Mortality During Anesthesia, Obstetrics and Surgery." *Journal of the National Medical Association* 49 (July 1957).

Hoberman, John. "The International Olympic Committee as a Supranational Elite." Paper presented at the 110th meeting of the American Historical Association, Atlanta, Georgia, January 6, 1996.

————. "Listening to Steroids." *The Wilson Quarterly* (Winter 1995).

————. "The Sportive-Dynamic Body as a Symbol of Productivity." In Tobin Siebers, ed., *Heterotopia: Postmodern Utopia and the Body Politic.* Ann Arbor: University of Michigan Press, 1994.

————. "Toward a Theory of Olympic Internationalism." *Journal of Sport History* (Spring 1995).

Hoberman, John M., and Charles E. Yesalis. "The History of Synthetic Testosterone." *Scientific American,* February 1995.

Holt, Richard. "Cricket and Englishness: The Batsman as Hero." *International Journal of the History of Sport* 13 (March 1996).

Hooks, Bell. "Reconstructing Black Masculinity." In *Black Looks: Race and Representation.* Boston: South End Press, 1992.

Hooton, Earnest A. "Is the Negro Inferior?" *The Crisis* (November 1932).

Hoppeler, H. "Exercise-Induced Ultrastructural Changes in Skeletal Muscle." *International Journal of Sports Medicine* 7 (1986).

Hoskins, R. G. "Hormones and Racial Characteristics." In *The Tides of Life: The Endocrine Glands in Bodily Adjustment.* New York: Norton, 1933.

Hrdlicka, Ales. "Anthropology of the American Negro." *American Journal of Physical Anthropology* 10 (1927).

————. "The Full-Blood American Negro." *American Journal of Physical Anthropology* 12 (1928).

————. "Quadruped Progression in the Human Child." *American Journal of Physical Anthropology* 10 (1927).

Hughes, Langston. "Cowards from the Colleges." *The Crisis* (August 1934).

Hughes, Rob. "Blacks Who Beat the Poison of Prejudice." *Sunday Times,* December 16, 1990.

Hunt, James. "On the Negro's Place in Nature." *Memoirs of the Anthropological Society of London* (1865).

Hunt, Sanford B. "The Negro as a Soldier." *Anthropological Review* 7 (1869).

Hunter, William S. "Coronary Occlusion in Negroes." *Journal of the American Medical Association* 131 (May 4, 1946).

Hurst, Mike. "Running: Not a Black and White Issue." *Fun Runner* [Australia] 17:2 (1995).

Hyde, Tom. "White Men Can't Jump." *Metro: Essentially Auckland,* September 1993.

Ide, Hiro. "On Several Characters Shown by the Cross-Sections of the Median and Sciatic Nerves of Human Males According to Race." *Journal of Comparative Neurology* 51 (1930).

"Is There Still Too Much Extrapolation from Data on Middle-aged White Men?" *Journal of the American Medical Association* 263 (February 23, 1990).

Jackson, J. W. "On the Racial Aspects of the Franco-Prussian War." *Journal of the Anthropological Institute* 1 (1872).

James, Sherman A., Sue A. Hartnett, and William D. Kalsbeek. "John Henryism and Blood Pressure Differences Among Black Men." *Journal of Behavioral Medicine* 6 (1983).

Jenkins, Ray. "Salvation for the Fittest? A West African Sportsman in Britain in the Age of the New Imperialism." *International Journal of the History of Sport* 7 (May 1990).

"Joe Louis — Model for the Physician." *Journal of the National Medical Association* 54 (1962).

Johnson, Charles. "A Phenomenology of the Black Body." *Michigan Quarterly Review* 32 (Fall 1993).

Johnson, Charles S., and Horace M. Bond. "The Investigation of Racial Differences Prior to 1910." *Journal of Negro Education* 3 (1934).

Johnson, Guy B. "A Summary of Negro Scores on the Seashore Music Talent Tests." *Journal of Comparative Psychology* 11 (April 1931).

Johnson, William Oscar. "How Far Have We Come?" *Sports Illustrated,* August 5, 1991.

———. "A Matter of Black and White." *Sports Illustrated,* August 5, 1991.

Johnston, V. D., and E. B. Henderson. "Debating and Athletics in Colored Colleges." *The Crisis* 14 (July 1917).

Jokl, Ernst, and E. H. Cluver. "Physical Fitness." *Journal of the American Medical Association* 116 (May 24, 1941).

Jones, James M., and Adrian Ruth Hochner. "Racial Differences in Sports Activities: A Look at the Self-Paced Versus Reactive Hypothesis." *Journal of Personality and Social Psychology* 27 (1973).

Jones, Patricia A. "Educating Black Males — Several Solutions, But No Solution." *Crisis* 98 (October 1991).

Kamin, Leon J. "Behind the Curve." *Scientific American,* February 1995.

Kamin, Leon J., and Sharon Grant-Henry. "Reaction Time, Race, and Racism." *Intelligence* 11 (1987).

Kane, Martin. "An Assessment of 'Black Is Best.'" *Sports Illustrated,* January 18, 1971.

Karsai, Litty Klein, et al. "Hearing in Ethnically Different Longshoremen." *Archives of Otolaryngology* 96 (December 1972).

Kasbohm, Henry B. "Tribute to Seafaring Blacks." *Freedomways* 19 (Second Quarter 1979).

Keith, Arthur. "The Differentiation of Mankind into Racial Types." *Nature* 104 (November 13, 1919).

Kephart, William M. "The Negro Offender: An Urban Research Project." *American Journal of Sociology* 60 (July 1954).

Kilbride, Janet E., Michael C. Robbins, and Philip L. Kilbride. "The Comparative Motor Development of Baganda, American White, and American Black Infants." *American Anthropologist* 72 (1970).

Killingray, David. "Race and Rank in the British Army in the Twentieth Century." *Ethnic and Racial Studies* 10:3 (July 1987).

Kiple, Kenneth, and Virginia Kiple. "The African Connection: Slavery, Disease and Racism." *Phylon* 41 (Fall 1980).

Kirk-Greene, Anthony H. M. "'Damnosa Hereditas': Ethnic Ranking and the Martial Races Imperative in Africa." *Ethnic and Racial Studies* 3:4 (October 1980).

Klag, Michael J., et al. "The Association of Skin Color with Blood Pressure in U.S. Blacks with Low Economic Status." *Journal of the American Medical Association* 265 (February 6, 1991).

"Klar for det søte liv." *Aftenposten* [Oslo], September 14, 1994.

"Klein und wendig." *Der Spiegel,* November 21, 1994.

Klineberg, Otto. "An Experimental Study of Speed and Other Factors in 'Racial' Differences." *Archives of Psychology* 15 (1928).

Knobloch, H. "Precocity of African Children." *Pediatrics* 22 (1958).

"Knochen sinken." *Der Spiegel,* April 1, 1974.

Kraemer, Michael J., Robert Hunter, Cornelius Rosse, and Nathan J. Smith. "Race-Related Differences in Peripheral Blood and in Bone Marrow Cell Populations of American Black and American White Infants." *Journal of the National Medical Association* 69 (May 1977).

Krieger, Nancy, and Mary Bassett. "The Health of Black Folk: Disease, Class, and Ideology in Science." In Sandra Harding, ed., *The "Racial" Economy of Science: Toward a Democratic Future.* Bloomington: Indiana University Press, 1993.

Lambeth, Martha, and Lyle H. Lanier. "Race Differences in Speed of Reaction." *Journal of Genetic Psychology* 42 (1933).

Lamplugh, George R. "The Image of the Negro in Popular Magazine Fiction, 1875–1900." *Journal of Negro History* 57 (April 1972).

Lawlor, Brian A., Roger C. Burket, and Jon A. Hodgin. "Eating Disorders in American Black Men." *Journal of the National Medical Association* 79 (1987).

Lawson, Hal A. "Physical Education and Sport in the Black Community: The Hidden Perspective." *Journal of Negro Education* 48 (Spring 1979).

Leab, Daniel J. "The Gamut from A to B: The Image of the Black in Pre-1915 Movies." *Political Science Quarterly* 88 (March 1973).

Leilua, Iulia. "Pacific Muscle." *New Zealand Fitness,* February–March 1996.

Lemann, I. I. "Diabetes Mellitus in the Negro Race." *Southern Medical Journal* 14 (July 1921).

———. "A Study of Disease in the Negro." *Southern Medical Journal* 27 (January 1934).

Lemons, J. Stanley. "Black Stereotypes as Reflected in Popular Culture." *American Quarterly* 29 (Spring 1977).

Leslie, Charles. "Scientific Racism: Reflections on Peer Review, Science and Ideology." *Social Science and Medicine* 31 (1990).

Levin, Michael. "Race Differences: An Overview." *Journal of Social, Political and Economic Studies* 16 (Summer 1991).

Lewis, Julian H. "Contribution of an Unknown Negro to Anesthesia." *Journal of the National Medical Association* 23 (January–March 1931).

Lightfoot, Orlando B. "Hyperactivity in Children." *Journal of the National Medical Association* 65 (January 1973).

Long, Howard Hale. "Race and Mental Tests." *Opportunity* (March 1923).

———. "The Relative Learning Capacities of Negroes and Whites." *Journal of Negro Education* 26 (1957).

Lotufo, David, et al. "Juvenile Glaucoma, Race, and Refraction." *Journal of the American Medical Association* 261 (January 13, 1989).

Loury, Glenn. "The Impossible Dilemma." *New Republic,* January 1, 1996.

Love, Lieutenant-Colonel A. G., and Major C. B. Davenport. "A Comparison of White and Colored Troops in Respect to Incidence of Disease." *Proceedings of the National Academy of Sciences* 5 (1919).

Lynn, Richard. "Race Differences in Intelligence: A Global Perspective." *Mankind Quarterly* 31 (Spring 1991).

Macdonald, Arthur. "Colored Children: A Psychophysical Study." *Journal of the American Medical Association* 32 (May 27, 1899).

———. "Skin of Negro and Its Absorption of Heat." *Journal of the American Medical Association* 32 (June 17, 1899).

McFadden, Dennis, and Frederic L. Wightman. "Audition: Some Relations Between Normal and Pathological Hearing." *Annual Review of Psychology* 34 (1983).

McGee, W. J. "Introduction." In J. W. Buel, ed., *Louisiana and the Fair: An Exposition of the World, Its People and Their Achievements*. St. Louis: World Progress, 1904.

McGurk, Frank. "Attitudes, Interests and IQ — Hereditary?" *The Citizen* (November 1978).

———. "A Scientist's Report on Race Differences." *U.S. News & World Report,* September 21, 1956.

McKay, Claude. "Once More the Germans Face Black Troops." *Opportunity* 17 (November 1939).

McLendon, Sol B. "A Comparative Study of 'Dilantin Sodium' and Phenobarbitol in Negro Epileptics." *Southern Medical Journal* 36 (April 1943).

Madhere, Serge. "Models of Intelligence and the Black Intellect." *Journal of Negro Education* 58 (1989).

Mahiri, Jabari. "Discourse in Sports: Language and Literacy Features of Preadolescent African American Males in a Youth Basketball Program." *Journal of Negro Education* 60 (1991).

"A Manual of Ethnological Inquiry." *Journal of the Ethnological Society* 3 (1854): 202.

"Die Mär von den schwarzen Wunderfußballern." *Süddeutsche Zeitung,* August 5, 1992.

Marchbanks, Vance H., Jr. "Sickle Cell Trait and the Black Airman." *Journal of the National Medical Association* 73 (1981).

Margolies, M. Price. "Sickle Cell Anemia." *Medicine* 30 (1951).

Margolis, Ronald N., et al. "Invited Review of a Workshop: Anabolic Hormones in Bone: Basic Research and Therapeutic Potential." *Journal of Clinical Endocrinology and Metabolism* 81 (1996).

Marqusee, Mike. "For Love of the Game." *New Statesman & Society,* March 15, 1996.

Mengert, William F. "Racial Contrasts in Obstetrics and Gynecology." *Journal of the National Medical Association* 58 (November 1966).

Metheny, Eleanor. "Some Differences in Bodily Proportions Between American Negro and White Male College Students as Related to Athletic Performance." *Research Quarterly* 10 (December 1939).

Miele, Frank. "For Whom the Bell Curves." [Interview with Charles Murray.] *Skeptic* 3:2 (1995).

Miller, Adam. "Professors of Hate." *Rolling Stone,* October 20, 1994.

Miller, C. Jeff. "Special Medical Problems of the Colored Woman." *Southern Medical Journal* 25 (July 1932).

Miller, Kelly. "A Review of Hoffman's *Race Traits and Tendencies of the American Negro.*" Occasional Paper No. 1. Washington, D.C.: American Negro Academy, 1897.

Miller, Patrick B. "To 'Bring the Race Along Rapidly': Sport, Student Culture, and Educational Mission at Historically Black Colleges During the Interwar Years." *Harvard Educational Review* 35 (Summer 1995).

Mischel, Walter. "Preference for Delayed Reinforcement: An Experimental Study of a Cultural Observation." *Journal of Abnormal and Social Psychology* 56 (January 1958).

Moehlig, Robert C. "The Mesoderm of the Negro." *American Journal of Physical Anthropology* (1937).

"Monster und Messias." *Der Spiegel,* March 3, 1994.

Moore, Kenny. "Sons of the Wind." *Sports Illustrated,* February 26, 1990.

Morris, C. J. "Human Muscle Fiber Type Grouping and Collateral Reinnervation," *Journal of Neurological Surgery and Psychiatry* 32 (1968).

Murray, Charles, and Richard J. Herrnstein. "Race, Genes and I.Q. — An Apologia." *New Republic,* October 31, 1994.

Murrell, Thomas W. "Syphilis and the American Negro." *Journal of the American Medical Association* 54 (March 12, 1919).

Nathanson, Yale S. "The Musical Ability of the Negro." *Annals of the American Academy of Political and Social Science* 140 (November 1928).

"The Negro Pilot." *Opportunity* 18 (September 1940).

"Negro Practice." *Journal of the American Medical Association* (May 9, 1908).

"Negro Slavery at the South." *De Bow's Review* 7 (1850).

"Negro Stock Is Praised." *Science News Letter* 86 (August 15, 1964).

"Negro's Ability to Stand High Temperatures Important." *Science News Letter* 37 (June 15, 1940).

Nicolson, Malcolm. "Medicine and Racial Politics: Changing Images of the New Zealand Maori in the Nineteenth Century." In David Arnold, ed., *Imperial Medicine and Indigenous Societies.* Manchester, Eng.: Manchester University Press, 1984.

"NIH Reports Greater Diversity of Participants in Clinical Studies." *Chronicle of Higher Education* (March 15, 1996).

O'Donnell, Hugh. "Mapping the Mythical: A Geopolitics of National Sporting Stereotypes." *Discourse & Society* 5 (1994).

Ogata, T., and F. Murata. "Cytological Features of Three Fiber Types in Human Striated Muscle." *Tohoku Journal of Experimental Medicine* 99 (1969).

Ojanuga, Durrenda. "The Medical Ethics of the 'Father of Gynaecology,' Dr. J. Marion Sims." *Journal of Medical Ethics* 19 (1993).

Olsen, Jack. "The Cruel Deception." *Sports Illustrated,* July 1, 1968.
———. "Pride and Prejudice." *Sports Illustrated,* July 8, 1968.
Olsen, Peter. "Black Americans and the Sea." *Negro History Bulletin* 37 (February–March 1974).
"One Hundred Cases of Heart Disease in the Negro." *Journal of the American Medical Association* 65 (December 18, 1915).
"Opposition to Segregation of Bloods from White and Negro Donors in Blood Banks." *Journal of the American Medical Association* 119 (1942).
Ortiz de Montellano, Bernard R. "Melanin, Afrocentricity, and Pseudoscience." *Yearbook of Physical Anthropology* 36 (1993).
Osborne, Newton G., and Marvin D. Feit. "The Use of Race in Medical Research." *Journal of the American Medical Association* 267 (January 8, 1992).
Patterson, Orlando. "Rethinking Black History." *Harvard Educational Review* 41 (August 1971).
Peoples, Betsy. "Finishing the Course." *Emerge* (June 1995).
Pearl, Raymond. "Biological Factors in Negro Mortality." *Human Biology* (May 1929).
"A Physician Discourses on the Race Problem." *Opportunity* 2 (March 1924).
Pike, L. Owen. "On the Psychical Characteristics of the English People." *Memoirs of the Anthropological Society of London* 2 (1865–66).
Pollitzer, William S., and John J. B. Anderson. "Ethnic and Genetic Differences in Bone Mass: A Review with a Hereditary vs. Environmental Perspective." *American Journal of Clinical Nutrition* 50 (1989).
Post, Marty. "Prince of Times." *Runner's World,* December 1993.
Post, R. H. "Hearing Acuity Variation Among Negroes and Whites." *Eugenics Quarterly* 11 (1964).
Poussaint, Alvin. "Cheap Thrills That Degrade Blacks." *Psychology Today,* February 1974.
"Die Profis abkoppeln." *Der Spiegel,* August 23, 1993.
"Race Joins Host of Unanswered Questions on Early HIV Therapy." *Journal of the American Medical Association* 265 (March 6, 1991).
"Racial Trends in Certain Surgical Diseases." *Journal of the American Medical Association* 107 (September 9, 1936).
Rackleff, Robert B. "The Black Soldier in Popular American Magazines, 1900–1971." *Negro History Bulletin* (December 1971).
Ramos, Dante. "Base Data." *New Republic,* October 31, 1994.
Rankin-Hill, Lesley M., and Michael L. Blakey. "W. Montague Cobb (1904–1990): Physical Anthropologist, Anatomist, and Activist." *American Anthropologist* 96 (1994).
"Rarity of Pelvic Endometriosis in Negro Women." *Journal of the American Medical Association* 147 (September 22, 1951).
Reinhardt, James M. "The Negro: Is He a Biological Inferior?" *American Journal of Sociology* 33 (1927).
Relethford, John H. Review. *American Journal of Physical Anthropology* 98 (September 1995).

"Remarks by Reagan Doctor on Well-Fed Black Kids Criticized as Insensitive." *Jet* 65 (January 16, 1984).

Rhoden, Bill. "Are Black Athletes Naturally Superior?" *Ebony* 30 (December 1974).

Rich, Larry F. "Race and Glaucoma." *Journal of the American Medical Association* 266 (July 17, 1991).

Roberts, D. F. "Race, Genetics and Growth." In G. A. Harrison and John Peel, eds., *Biosocial Aspects of Race*. Oxford, Eng.: Blackwell, 1969.

Robinson, Dale O., and Doris V. Allen. "Racial Differences in Typanometric Results." *Journal of Speech and Hearing Disorders* 49 (May 1984).

Robinson, S., D. B. Dill, P. M. Harmon, F. G. Hall, and J. W. Wilson. "Adaptations to Exercise of Negro and White Sharecroppers in Comparison With Northern Whites." *Human Biology* 13 (May 1941).

Rogers, J. A. "The Negro Explorer." *The Crisis* (January 1940).

Ross, Ronald, et al. "Serum Testosterone Levels in Healthy Young Black and White Men." *Journal of the National Cancer Institute* 76 (January 1986).

Rosselli, John. "The Self-Image of Effeteness: Physical Education and Nationalism in Nineteenth-Century Bengal." *Past and Present* (1980).

Rosser, Curtis. "Rectal Pathology in the Negro." *Journal of the American Medical Association* 84 (January 10, 1925).

———. "Clinical Variations in Negro Proctology." *Journal of the American Medical Association* 87 (December 18, 1926).

Rushton, J. Philippe. "Race and Crime: A Reply to Roberts and Gabor." *Canadian Journal of Criminology* 32 (April 1990).

Rushton, J. Philippe, and Anthony F. Bogaert. "Race Differences in Sexual Behavior: Testing an Evolutionary Hypothesis." *Journal of Research in Personality* 21 (1987).

Sailes, Gary A. "The Myth of Black Sports Supremacy." *Journal of Black Studies* 21 (June 1990).

Salisbury, David. "Hypertension: A Discriminating Disease." *Technology Review* 93 (October 1990).

Saltin, Bengt. "Kenyanska löpare — kan fysiologiska tester visa att de är bäst i världen?" *Svensk Idrottsforskning* (December 1992).

Saltin, Bengt, et al. "Aerobic Exercise Capacity at Sea Level and at Altitude in Kenyan Boys, Junior and Senior Runners Compared with Scandinavian Runners." *Scandinavian Journal of Medicine and Science in Sports* 5 (1995).

———. "Morphology, Enzyme Activities and Buffer Capacity in Leg Muscles of Kenyan and Scandinavian Runners." *Scandinavian Journal of Medicine and Science in Sports* 5 (1995).

Sammons, Jeffrey. "'Race' and Sport: A Critical, Historical Examination." *Journal of Sport History* 21 (Fall 1994).

Sanderson, Helen Elizabeth. "Differences in Musical Ability in Children of Different National and Racial Origin." *Journal of Genetic Psychology* 42 (1933).

Sarich, Vincent M. "The Eternal Triangle: Race, Class, and IQ." *Current Anthropology* 37, Supplement (February 1996).

Satcher, David. "Does Race Interfere with the Doctor-Patient Relationship?" *Journal of the American Medical Association* 223 (March 26, 1973).

Savitt, Todd L. "The Use of Blacks for Medical Experimentation and Demonstration in the Old South." *Journal of Southern History* 48 (August 1982).

Scales, Alice M. "Alternatives to Standardized Tests in Reading Education: Cognitive Styles and Informal Measures." *Negro Educational Review* 38 (1987).

Schoenfeld, Bruce. "The Loneliness of Being White." *New York Times Magazine,* May 14, 1995.

"Schwarze Zukunft." *Der Spiegel,* June 20, 1994.

Scott, Roland B. "U.S. Air Force Revises Policy for Flying Personnel With Sickle Cell Trait." *Journal of the National Medical Association* 74 (1982).

Searle, Chris. "Race Before Wicket: Cricket, Empire and the White Rose." *Race & Class* 31 (1990).

Seashore, Carl E. "Three New Approaches to the Study of Negro Music." *Annals of the American Academy of Political and Social Science* 140 (November 1928).

Sellin, Thorsten. "The Negro Criminal." *Annals of the American Academy of Political and Social Science* 140 (November 1928).

Selvin, Paul. "The Raging Bull of Berkeley." *Science* 251 (January 25, 1991).

Shaler, N. S. "Our Negro Types." *Current Literature* 29 (July 1900).

Shepherd, David C., and Robert Goldstein. "Race Difference in Auditory Sensitivity." *Journal of Speech and Hearing Research* 7 (1964).

Sheridan, Richard B. "The Guinea Surgeons on the Middle Passage: The Provision of Medical Services in the British Slave Trade." *International Journal of African Historical Studies* 14 (1981).

"Should Blood be Labeled by Race of Donor?" *Journal of the American Medical Association* 223 (January 8, 1973).

Shreeve, James. "Terms of Estrangement." *Discover,* November 1994.

Silber, Tomas J. "Anorexia Nervosa in Black Adolescents." *Journal of the National Medical Association* 76 (1984).

Simmons, Erica. "The Rushton Controversy." *Canadian Dimension* (January–February 1989).

"Slavery Was 'Great Biological Experiment' Negro M.D. Claims." *Journal of the American Medical Association* 181 (September 1, 1962).

Sleeper, Jim. "The Clash." *New Republic,* September 19–26, 1994.

Smillie, W. G., and D. L. Augustine. "Vital Capacity of Negro Race." *Journal of the American Medical Association* 87 (December 18, 1926).

Smith, Marshall. "Giving the Olympics an Anthropological Once-Over." *Life,* October 23, 1964.

Smith, Patrick. "Letter from Japan." *New Yorker,* April 13, 1992.

Snyder, J. Ross. "The Problem of the Negro Child." *Southern Medical Journal* 16 (January 1923).

Snyderman, Mark. "How to Think About Race." *National Review,* September 12, 1994.

Sojka, Gregory S. "The Astronaut: An American Hero With the 'Right Stuff.'" *Journal of American Culture* 7 (Spring/Summer 1984).

Sokolove, Michael. "Are Blacks Better Athletes than Whites?" *Philadelphia Inquirer Magazine,* April 24, 1988.

"Sorte har styrken og farten." *Aftenposten* [Oslo], March 10, 1996.

"South African Negro or Bantu as a Parturient." *Journal of the American Medical Association* 133 (April 5, 1947).

Sperling, Susan. "Beating a Dead Monkey." *The Nation,* November 28, 1994.

Spivey, Donald. "The Black Athlete in Big-Time Intercollegiate Sports, 1941–1968." *Phylon* 44 (1983).

Staples, Robert. "Black Male Genocide: A Final Solution to the Race Problem in America." *Black Scholar* (May–June 1987).

Stepan, Nancy Leys, and Sander L. Gilman. "Appropriating the Idioms of Science: The Rejection of Scientific Racism." In Sandra Harding, ed., *The "Racial" Economy of Science: Toward a Democratic Future.* Bloomington: Indiana University Press, 1993.

Stoddart, Brian. "Sport, Cultural Imperialism, and Colonial Response in the British Empire." *Comparative Studies in Society and History* (1988).

Strogatz, David S. "Use of Medical Care for Chest Pain: Differences Between Blacks and Whites." *American Journal of Public Health* 80 (1990).

Sullivan, B. H. "Danger of Airplane Flight to Persons with Sicklemia." *Annals of Internal Medicine* 32 (January–June 1950).

Swados, Felice. "Negro Health on the Ante Bellum Plantations." *Bulletin of the History of Medicine* 10 (October 1941).

Swan, Donald A. "Racial Differences and Physical Anthropology." *Mankind Quarterly* 5 (January–March 1965).

"Sweat and Body Odor." *Journal of the American Medical Association* 114 (June 1, 1940).

Taylor, Phil. "Bad Actors." *Sports Illustrated,* January 30, 1995.

Terry, Robert J. "The American Negro." *Science* 69 (March 29, 1929).

Thomson, A. S. "Observations on the Stature, Bodily Weight, Magnitude of Chest, and Physical Strength of the New Zealand Race of Men." *Journal of the Ethnological Society* [London] 3 (1854).

Tielsch, James M., et al. "Racial Variations in the Prevalence of Primary Open-Angle Glaucoma." *Journal of the American Medical Association* 266 (July 17, 1991).

Todd, T. Wingate. "Entrenched Negro Physical Features." *Human Biology* 1 (January 1929).

Tunbridge, Louise. "Repression in Kenya." *Chronicle of Higher Education* (April 5, 1996).

Twyman, Robert W. "The Clay Eater: A New Look at an Old Southern Enigma." *Journal of Southern History* 37 (1971).

Underwood, John. "On the Playground." *Life,* spring 1988.

Urban, Wayne J. "The Black Scholar and Intelligence Testing: The Case of

Horace Mann Bond." *Journal of the History of the Behavioral Sciences* 25 (October 1989).

"Use of Antibiotics in Different Races." *Journal of the American Medical Association* 157 (January 29, 1955).

"Use of Negro Blood for Blood Banks." *Journal of the American Medical Association* 119 (May 16, 1942).

Vallois, H.-V. "L'Exposition Coloniale de Paris et les Congrès (1931)." In H. Vallois and R. Vaufrey, eds., *L'Anthropologie* 32 (1932).

Vanderwolf, C. H., and D. P. Cain. "The Neurobiology of Race and Kipling's Cat." *Personality and Individual Differences* 12 (1991).

Vaughn, Stephen. "Ronald Reagan and the Struggle for Black Dignity in Cinema, 1937–1953." *Journal of Negro History* (1992).

Venable, H. Phillip. "Glaucoma in the Negro." *Journal of the National Medical Association* 44 (January 1952).

Villard, Oswald Garrison. "The Negro in the Regular Army." *Atlantic Monthly,* June 1903.

Vinson, Porter P. "Incidence of Esophageal Disease in Negroes." *Southern Medical Journal* 38 (July 1945).

Wallace, Michele. "When Black Feminism Faces the Music, and the Music Is Rap." *New York Times,* July 29, 1990.

Ward, John W. "The Meaning of Lindbergh's Flight." *American Quarterly* 10 (Spring 1958).

Weatherly, U. G. "A World-Wide Color Line." *Popular Science Monthly,* November 1911.

Weizmann, Fredric, et al. "Differential K Theory and Racial Hierarchies." *Canadian Psychology/Psychologie canadienne* 31 (1990).

————. "Inventing Racial Psychologies: The (Mis)Uses of Evolutionary Theory." In Larry T. Reynolds and Leonard Lieberman, eds., *Race and Other Misadventures; Essays in Honor of Ashley Montagu in His Ninetieth Year.* Dix Hills, N.Y.: General Hall, 1996.

————. "Scientific Racism in Contemporary Psychology." *International Journal of Dynamic Assessment and Instruction* 1 (Fall 1989).

Welsing, Frances Cress. "The 'Conspiracy' to Make Blacks Inferior." *Ebony* 29 (September 1974).

White, Walter. "It's Our Country, Too." *Saturday Evening Post,* December 14, 1940.

Wiggins, David K. "'Great Speed but Little Stamina': The Historical Debate over Black Athletic Superiority." *Journal of Sports History* (1989).

Will, George. "Nature and the Male Sex." *Newsweek,* June 17, 1991.

"Willa Brown-Chappell: Mother of Black Aviation." *Negro History Bulletin* 50 (January–June 1987).

Williams, G. D., et al. "Calf Muscles in American Whites and Negroes." *American Journal of Physical Anthropology* 14 (1930).

Williams, Judith R., and Roland B. Scott. "Growth and Development of Negro Infants: IV. Motor Development and Its Relationship To Child Rearing Practices in Two Groups of Negro Infants." *Child Development* 24 (June 1953).

Willoughby, R. R., and M. Coogan. "The Correlation Between Intelligence and Fertility." *Human Biology* 12 (1940).

Wilson, James Q. "Crime, Race, and Values." *Society* 30 (December 1992).

———. "In Loco Parentis: Helping Children When Families Fail Them." *Brookings Review* (Fall 1993).

Wilson, Judith. "Growing Up 'White': The Crisis of the Black Middle-Class Child." *Black Enterprise* 9 (November 1978).

Wilson, M. Roy. "Glaucoma in Blacks: Where Do We Go from Here?" *Journal of the American Medical Association* 261 (January 13, 1989).

"Wir kriegen euch schon noch, ihr Hunde." *Der Spiegel,* October 24, 1977.

"The World's Fastest Mail Sorter." *Opportunity* 1 (January 1923).

Worthy, Morgan, and Allan Markle. "Racial Differences in Reactive Versus Self-Paced Sports Activities." *Journal of Personality and Social Psychology* 16 (1970).

Wright, Nancy M., et al. "Greater Secretion of Growth Hormone in Black than in White Men: Possible Factor in Greater Bone Mineral Density — A Clinical Research Center Study." *Journal of Clinical Endocrinology and Metabolism* 80 (1995).

Young, Donald S. "Implementation of SI Units for Clinical Laboratory Data." *Annals of Internal Medicine* 106 (1987).

Ziegler, Michael, Fredric Weitzman, Neil Wiener, and David Wiesenthal. "Philippe Rushton and the Growing Acceptance of 'Race-Science.'" *Canadian Forum* (September 1989).

# Index